IN THE ABSENCE
OF THE SACRED

IN THE ABSENCE OF THE SACRED

THE FAILURE OF TECHNOLOGY

AND THE SURVIVAL

OF THE INDIAN NATIONS

JERRY MANDER

Sierra Club Books ❖ San Francisco

The author gratefully acknowledges permission to reprint portions of the following copyrighted materials:
From *A Basic Call to Consciousness: The Hau De No Sau Address to the Western World,* published by Akwesasne Notes, reprinted by permission of Akwesasne Notes; from *Now That the Buffalo's Gone* by Alvin Josephy, Jr., copyright © 1982 by Alvin Josephy, Jr., reprinted by permission of Alfred A. Knopf, Inc.; from William N. Fenton, ed., *Parker on the Iroquois* (Syracuse: Syracuse University Press, 1984), excerpts from pp. 12, 32, 38, 39, 41, 55. By permission of the publisher; from *Stone Age Economics* by Marshall Sahlins, published by Aldine Publishing Company, Chicago. Reprinted by permission of Marshall Sahlins; excerpts from *Village Journey* by Thomas R. Berger. Copyright © 1985 by Inuit Circumpolar Conference. Reprinted by permission of Hill and Wang, a division of Farrar, Straus and Giroux, Inc.; from *Mind Children* by Hans Moravec. Reprinted by permission of the publisher, Cambridge, Mass.: Harvard University Press, copyright © 1988 by Hans Moravec.

Library of Congress Cataloging-in-Publication Data
Mander, Jerry.
In the absence of the sacred : the failure of technology and the survival of the Indian Nations / by Jerry Mander.
p.   cm.
Includes bibliographical references and index.
ISBN 0-87156-509-9
1. Indians—Social conditions.   2. Indians—Land tenure.   3. Indians—Civil rights.
4. Technology—Social aspects.   5. Technology—Moral and ethical aspects.   I. Title.
E98.S67M36   1991
970.004'97—dc20
91-13869
CIP

Jacket design by Paul Bacon
Book design by Seventeenth Street Studios
Composition by Wilsted & Taylor
Production by Amy Evans
Printed in the United States of America on acid-free paper containing a minimum of 50% recovered waste paper, of which at least 10% is post-consumer waste.
10   9   8   7

To the memory of Dan Bomberry

CONTENTS

In the Absence of the Sacred

INTRODUCTION
"INDIANS SHMINDIANS"

*T*ELEPHONE CALL FROM a New York editor: Mander, you've got two books out there now; they're both selling. Are you working on anything new?

Mander: Yes.

Editor: What's the subject?

Mander: Indians.

Editor: *Indians?* Oh God, not Indians. Nobody wants a book about Indians. Indians have been done in New York; they're finished. Indians shmindians.

Mander: That's the point. The Indian problem is not over. In some parts of the world it's worse than it was here.

Editor: Indians! Mander, you're some kind of goddamn romantic. Like Brando or somebody.

Mander: Don't worry, I'll deal with that "romantic" thing in the book.

Editor: How's your agent going to sell it? Indian books don't sell.

Mander: They said that about TV books. Anyway, Indian books do sell. Look at *Bury My Heart at Wounded Knee,* and look at Castaneda and Peter Matthiessen's books. Look at *Black Elk Speaks.* I don't think Indians are a passé subject at all. People do want to know about Indians. The trouble is that people are told mainly about dead Indians. They don't get to hear about what's going on now, or why.

Editor: What's the title?

Mander: Maybe I'll use your title.

Editor: What title is that?

Mander: *Indians Shmindians.* It's got a catchy paradoxical ring to it. It's memorable, it's sensational, and it does seem to summarize our cultural attitude.

• • •

Originally I planned to write two books. The first was to be a critique of technological society as we know it in the United States, a kind of sequel to *Four Arguments for the Elimination of Television.* Instead of concentrating on TV, though, it would have focused on the new technological age: "the information society," computerization, robotization, space travel, artificial intelligence, genetics, satellite communications. This seemed timely, since these technologies are changing our world at an astoundingly accelerating rate. Thus far, most people view these changes as good. But are they?

That our society would tend to view new technologies favorably is understandable. The first waves of news concerning any technical innovation are invariably positive and optimistic. That's because, in our society, the information is purveyed by those who stand to gain from our acceptance of it: corporations and their retainers in the government and scientific communities. None is motivated to report the negative sides of new technologies, so the public gets its first insights and expectations from sources that are clearly biased.

Over time, as successive generations of idealized technical innovations are introduced and presented at World's Fairs, in futurists' visions, and in hundreds of billions of dollars' worth of advertising, we develop expectations of a technological utopia here on Earth and in great domed cities in space. We begin to equate technological evolution with evolution itself, as though the two were equally inevitable, and virtually identical. The operating homilies become "Progress is good," "There's no turning back," and "Technology will free humans from disease, strife, and unremitting toil."

Debate on these subjects is inhibited by the fact that views of technology in our society are nearly identical across the political and social spectrum. The Left takes the same view of technology as do corporations, futurists, and the Right. Technology, they all say, is neutral. It has no inherent politics, no inevitable social or environmental consequences. What matters, according to this view, is who *controls* technology.

I have attended dozens of conferences in the last ten years on the future of technology. At every one, whether sponsored by government, industry, or environmentalists or other activists, someone will address the assembly with something like this: "There are many problems with technology and we need to acknowledge them, but the problems are not rooted to the technologies themselves. They are caused by the way we have chosen to use them. We can do better. We must do better. Machines don't cause problems, people do." This is always said as if it were an original and profound idea, when actually everyone else is saying exactly the same thing.

As we will see, the idea that technology is neutral is itself not neutral—it directly serves the interests of the people who benefit from our inability to see where the juggernaut is headed.

I only began to glimpse the problem during the 1960s when I saw how excited our society became about the presumed potentials of television. Activists, like everyone else, saw the technology opportunistically, and began to vie with other segments of society for their twenty seconds on the network news. A kind of war developed for access to this powerful new instrument that spoke pictures into the brains of the whole population, but the outcome was predetermined. We should have realized it was a foregone conclusion that TV technology would inevitably be controlled by corporations, the government, and the military. Because of the technology's geographic scale, its cost, the astounding power of its imagery, and its ability to homogenize thought, behavior, and culture, large corporations found television uniquely efficient for ingraining a way of life that served (and still serves) their interests. And in times of national crisis, the government and military find TV a perfect instrument for the centralized control of information and consciousness. Meanwhile, all other contenders for control of the medium have effectively fallen by the wayside.

Now we have the frenzy over computers, which, in theory, can empower individuals and small groups and produce a new information democracy. In fact, as we will see in Chapter 4, the issue of who benefits *most* from computers was already settled when they were invented. Computers, like television, are far more valuable and helpful to the military, to multinational corporations, to international banking, to governments, and to institutions of surveillance and control—all of whom use this technology on a scale and with a speed that are beyond our imaginings—than they ever will be to you and me.

Computers have made it possible to instantaneously move staggering amounts of capital, information, and equipment throughout the world, giving unprecedented power to the largest institutions on the earth. In fact, computers make these institutions possible. Meanwhile, we use our personal computers to edit our copy and hook into our information networks—and believe that makes us more powerful.

Even environmentalists have contributed to the problem by failing to effectively criticize technical evolution despite its obvious, growing, and inherent bias against nature. I fear that the ultimate direction of technology will become vividly clear to us only after we have popped out of the "information age"—which does have a kind of benevolent ring—and realize what is at stake in the last two big "wilderness intervention" battlegrounds: space and the genetic structures of living creatures. From there, it's on to the "postbiological age" of nanotechnology and robotics, whose advocates don't even pretend to care about the natural world. They think it's silly and out of date.

This first book was intended to raise questions about whether technological society has lived up to its advertising, and also to address some grave concerns about its future direction. Until now we have been impotent in the face of the juggernaut, partly because we are so unpracticed in technological criticism. We don't really know how to assess new or existing technologies. It is apparent that we need a new, more holistic language for examining technology, one that would ignore the advertised claims, best-case visions, and glamorous imagery that inundate us and systematically judge technology from alternative perspectives: social, political, economic, spiritual, ecological, biological, military. Who gains? Who loses? Do the new technologies serve planetary destruction or stability? What are their health effects? Psychological effects? How do they affect our interaction with and appreciation of nature? How do they interlock with existing technologies? What do they make possible that could not exist before? What is being lost? Where is it all going? Do we want that?

In the end, we can see that technological evolution is leading to something new: a worldwide, interlocked, monolithic, technical-political web of unprecedented negative implications.

• • •

The second book was to be a kind of continuation and update of Dee Brown's *Bury My Heart at Wounded Knee.* That book impressed me tremendously when I read it twenty years ago. In one sense it was a masterful work, detailing in excruciating fashion U.S. double-dealing and brutality against the Indians. But in another sense Brown did the Indian cause a disservice by seeming to suggest that they were all wiped out, and that now there is nothing to be done. The book put the reader through an emotional catharsis; having read it, it was as if one had already paid one's dues. Combined with the popular imagery from television and films, the book helped remand Indian issues to the past.

Even liberal-minded people, concerned about issues of justice, who acknowledge the atrocities committed on this land, tend to speak of Indian issues as tragedies of the distant past. So ingrained is this position that when, occasionally, non-Indians do come forward on behalf of present-day Indian causes—Marlon Brando, William Kunstler, Robert Redford, Kevin Costner, Jane Fonda—they are all put into that "romantic" category. People are a bit embarrassed for them, as if they'd stepped over some boundary of propriety. When environmentalists such as David Brower occasionally speak publicly about how we should heed the philosophies of the Inuit (Eskimos), they are thought impractical, uncool, not politic, not team players. (And when a specific issue pits native traditions against some current environmental concern, such as fur trapping, or subsistence sealing, or whaling, the native viewpoint is not given a fair hearing.) Literary luminaries like Peter Matthiessen have also been chastised for books on contemporary Indian issues *(In the Spirit of Crazy Horse* and *Indian Country),* with the implication that they should return to novels and Zen explorations.

I have had my own experiences with this. In *Four Arguments* I reported several encounters with Indians as a way of revealing bias in the media. I was surprised at the number of critics who cited those lines as foolish. Gene Youngblood, for example, a respected radical writer on media issues, said, "Mander is so naive. . . . My God, that old sixties chestnut, the Indians."

I thought that even Nelson Mandela got that treatment when he spoke about Indians at his 1990 Oakland rally. The news reports seemed to suggest that he didn't quite understand "our Indians."

The Indian issue is *not* part of the distant past. Many of the worst anti-Indian campaigns were undertaken scarcely 80 to 100 years ago. Your great-grandparents were already alive at the time. The Model-T Ford was on the road.

More to the point is that the assaults continue today. While the Custer period of direct military action against Indians may be over in the United States, more subtle though equally devastating "legalistic" manipulations continue to separate Indians from their land and their sovereignty, as we will see from the horrible events in Alaska, described in Chapter 16.

There are still over one and a half million Indians in the United States today. Significant numbers of them continue to live in wilderness and desert regions and in the far north of Alaska, often engaging in traditional subsistence practices on the same lands where their ancestors lived for millennia. Contrary to popular assumptions, most of these Indians are *not* eager to become Americans, despite the economic, cultural, and legal pressures to do so.

Elsewhere in the world, millions of native peoples also live in a traditional manner, while suffering varying degrees of impact from the expansion of Western technological society. In places such as Indonesia, Borneo,

New Guinea, the Amazon forests, Bolivia, Peru, Ecuador, Guatemala, parts of central Africa, the north of Canada, and even Scandinavia, the Soviet Union, China, and Tibet, tribal peoples are struggling to defend their ancestral lands. In other places, such as India, Iraq, Turkey, Mexico, Chile, the Pacific islands, New Zealand, and Australia, millions more native peoples live a kind of in-between existence, while they are under cultural, economic, or military siege.

According to Cultural Survival, the Boston-based human rights organization, there are at least 3,000 native nations in the world today that continue to function within the boundaries of the 200-odd countries that assert sovereignty over them. Many wars that our media describe as "civil wars" or "guerrilla insurgencies" are actually attempts by tribal nations to free themselves of the domination of larger nation-states. In Guatemala, it's the Mayans. In Burma, it's the Karens. In the Amazon, it's the Yanomamo and the Xingu, among others. In Micronesia, it's the Belauans. In Indonesia, it's the peoples of Irian Jaya.

Perhaps the most painful realization for Americans is that in many of these foreign locales—particularly South America, the Pacific islands, Indonesia, and the Philippines—the natives' struggles to maintain their lands and sovereignty is often directed against United States corporations, or technology, or military. More to the point, it is directed against a mentality, and an approach to the planet and to the human place on Earth, that native people find fatally flawed. For all the centuries they've been in contact with us, they've been saying that our outlook is missing *something*. But we have ignored what they say. To have heeded them would have meant stopping what we were doing and seeking another path. It is this very difference in world views that has made the assault on Indian people inevitable.

•   •   •

While planning to write these two books, however, it became apparent to me that their subjects were inseparable. They belonged together as one book. There is no way to understand the situation of Indians, Eskimos, Aborigines, island peoples, or other native societies without understanding the outside societies that act upon them. And there is no way to understand the outside societies without understanding their relationships to native peoples and to nature itself.

All things considered, it may be the central assumption of technological society that there is virtue in overpowering nature and native peoples. The Indian problem today, as it always has been, is directly related to the needs of technological societies to find and obtain remotely located resources, in order to fuel an incessant and intrinsic demand for growth and technological fulfillment. The process began in our country hundreds of years ago when we wanted land and gold. Today it continues because we want coal, oil, uranium, fish, and more land. As we survey the rest of the world—whether it is the Canadian Arctic, the Borneo jungle, or the Brazilian rainforest—the same interaction is taking place for the same reasons, often involving the same institutions.

All of these acts were and are made possible by one fundamental rationalization: that our society represents the ultimate expression of evolution, its final flowering. It is this attitude, and its corresponding belief that native societies represent an earlier, lower form on the evolutionary ladder, upon which we occupy the highest rung, that seem to unify all modern political perspectives: Right, Left, Capitalist, and Marxist.

Save for such nascent movements as bioregionalism and Green politics, which have at least questioned the assumptions underlying this attitude, most people in Western society are in agreement about our common superiority. So it becomes okay to humiliate—to find insignificant and thus subject to sacrifice—any way of life or way of thinking that stands in the way of a kind of "progress" we have invented, which is scarcely a century old. In fact, having assumed such superiority, it becomes more than acceptable for us to bulldoze nature and native societies. To do so actually becomes desirable, inevitable, and possibly "divine."

But the assertion that technological society is something higher than what came before, and that it is bound to bring us a better world, has lately fallen open to grave doubts. The Industrial Revolution is about a century old, and we have had ample time to draw a few conclusions about how it is going. It is not too soon to observe that this revolution may not be living up to its advertising, at least in terms of human contentment, fulfillment, health, sanity, and peace. And it is surely creating terrible and possibly catastrophic impacts on the earth. Technotopia seems already to have failed, but meanwhile it continues to lurch forward, expanding its reach and becoming more arrogant and dangerous.

The next questions become: Can we expect the situation to improve or worsen in the future? And what of the people who always told us that this way could not work, and continue to say so now? Finally, which is the more "romantic" viewpoint: that technology will fix itself and lead us to paradise, or that the answer is something simpler?

PART I

QUESTIONS WE SHOULD HAVE ASKED ABOUT TECHNOLOGY

*M*ODERN TECHNOLOGY ADVANCED *in such tiny increments for so long that we never realized how much our world was being altered, or the ultimate direction of the process. But now the speed of change is accelerating logarithmically. It is apparent that developing a language and set of standards by which to assess technological impact, and to block it where necessary, is a critical survival skill of our times.*

I

GROWING UP WITH TECHNOLOGY

I WAS BORN IN 1936. At that time there were no jet airplanes and commercial plane travel was effectively nonexistent. There were no computers, no space satellites, no microwave ovens, no electric typewriters, no Xerox machines, no tape recorders. There were no stereo music systems nor compact disks. There was no television in 1936. No space travel, no atomic bomb, no hydrogen bomb, no "guided missiles," as they were first called, no "smart" bombs. There were no fluorescent lights, no washing machines nor dryers, no Cuisinarts, no VCRs. There was no air conditioning. Nor were there freeways, shopping centers, or malls. There were no suburbs as we know them. There was no Express Mail, no fax, no telephone touch dialing, no birth-control pill. There were no credit cards, no synthetic fibers. There were no antibiotics, no artificial organs, no pesticides or herbicides. That was fifty-five years ago. During my lifetime all of this changed.

CITY, WOODS, SUBURBS

When I was four years old, our family moved from the Bronx to Yonkers, just three miles north of the New York City border. To me, it was like moving to the wilderness. I remember my first sight of our new house. Small, neat, brick with white trim, located at the end of a dirt road, surrounded by woods. I saw deer, pheasant, foxes, raccoons, and owls.

When I started school at age five, I walked there on a path through the woods. I still remember details of that path: a tangle of roots that I had to climb over; an old maple tree that I grew to like, much as one likes another person. Walking this path twice daily, I kept track of minor changes, like the ever-deepening channels the rain's runoff left in the mud. My mother told me, "That's how the Grand Canyon got started." I was dazzled by the thought.

Within two years, the dirt road in front of our house was converted to gravel, and four houses were built about fifty feet from each other. More were planned. I watched the trees fall to make way for the new construction. There was a big debate in our house: Should we buy the plot directly behind our property to keep it from being developed? We didn't buy it. My parents could not believe the hillside behind us would ever be developed. Within a few years it became the largest apartment development in that part of Yonkers. We planted fir trees along our back fence for privacy, but we were beginning to feel closed in. Soon after, we had our first parking problem.

Eventually our gravel street was converted to asphalt, and a few years later a yellow line was painted down the middle. My path through the woods became the New York Thruway. The unending noise of speeding cars and trucks blotted out the sounds of wind and birds. By 1955, the woods and the animals were gone, replaced by hundreds of little brick houses very much like our own, with lawns in front and back, and fences. Our neighborhood had become a middle-class suburb.

My parents took a friendly view of these changes. Although the nearly rural environment to which they had escaped was virtually destroyed, they and their friends found solace in the fact that this was progress, and that someone was making money from it all. Most of the neighbors were of Jewish and Italian immigrant backgrounds. To them, these developments confirmed the greatness of America.

SHOPPING

My mother's favorite activity was shopping, and I loved to go with her. My mother approached this task with the attitude of an Eastern European. She was born in Romania, where the town square was also its marketplace and social center.

Her favorite place to shop was back in the Bronx on Jerome Avenue, around the corner from where we used to live. Jerome Avenue might as well have been Eastern Europe. Shopkeepers put their wares out on the sidewalk: used clothing, knitting goods, leather, produce, kosher meats, baked goods, and fish. Interspersed with all this were delicatessens and tiny repair shops.

The food stores were the most exciting. Pickle barrels, hanging salamis, sawdust on the floor. The accepted manner of shopping for food was to yell and argue, often in Yiddish. People would gather around a pile of fish and have long debates about them, pointing, analyzing, picking, and turning them over. The street teemed with people and it seemed my mother knew at least half of them.

By the time I was ten, we stopped visiting Jerome Avenue. The Cross County Shopping Center in Yonkers was completed. Located a few miles from our house, Cross County was celebrated as the largest shopping center in the New York area, and some claimed it was the largest in the world. It was to become a prototype for the "malling" movement that has since swept the country. But in the mid-forties this kind of shopping environment was entirely new. Huge department stores were surrounded by small franchise operations (another marketing innovation of the forties). No "Mom-and-Pop" stores. No sawdust. No small food stores at all—one A&P supermarket dominated the scene. No discussions with proprietors about the nuances of codfish. In fact, no proprietors—these stores were owned by conglomerates, not people. Shopping stopped being fun. No longer a social event, no longer a community event, it was now a business transaction. No longer small-scale and intimate, shopping changed as the physical environment did: from woods to suburbs, from marketplace to mall.

FAMILY DOCTOR

The most admired and the most flamboyant person in Lincoln Park, our Yonkers neighborhood, was Morris Woodrow, the doctor. The immigrants who lived in this neighborhood were impressed by the simple fact that one of their own had become a doctor. But Woodrow was more than an ordinary doctor. He lived in the largest house in the neighborhood—a pillared, Georgian-style mansion. He kept two black Cadillacs parked conspicuously in front of his house, and he had a chauffeur—a daring act in Lincoln Park, where most people's goal was to seem as middle-class American as possible. If you had extra money, you didn't flaunt it. Woodrow did.

He was also interested in music and the arts, another daring stance in Lincoln Park. To express his interest, he would don his smoking jacket every Sunday morning and stroll slowly down Kneeland Avenue, holding two large Afghans on leashes, while singing arias in Italian. The neighbors thought this very eccentric, but they liked it.

As oddball as Woodrow was thought to be, if you became ill, you called him. He would come to your house any time, even in the middle of the night wearing a silk bathrobe, his long moustache freshly waxed, carrying his black satchel. Upon entering the house he would sing. If it was a child who was sick, he would also perform a few magic tricks. Much of the time Woodrow never actually examined his patients. He'd stare at you for a moment or two, then look at your tongue. Sometimes he'd yell at you to stop making believe you were sick; then he'd say that if you wanted to see *sick* you should come by his office sometime.

If you insisted that you really were sick, he might do some tapping on your bones or give you an unmarked concoction of his own invention. In rare cases he handed out sulfa drugs, and very rarely, penicillin. He spoke favorably of these new drugs, but strongly disapproved of doctors who ordered penicillin for colds.

Woodrow lived between the old medicine and the new, as did all of us in those days. He used modern techniques but only in emergencies. This applied even to such matters as eyeglasses. As a child I suffered from styes on my eyelids. An ophthalmologist blamed the styes on eye strain and prescribed glasses. When Woodrow saw me on the street one day and noticed the glasses, he took them away and said I didn't need them. He telephoned the ophthalmologist, yelled at him, called him a *shyster,* and hung up. Woodrow told me the styes were caused by dirt, or else they were inexplicable and anyway they would disappear when I got older, which they did. It wasn't until thirty-five years later that I started wearing glasses again.

Woodrow had a very special relationship with my father, who was a hypochondriac. My father would monitor every little muscle twitch and assume the worst. This took a toll on all of us, particularly me, but when Woodrow took charge, everything regained its proper perspective. As soon as Woodrow saw one of my father's worried looks, he would launch into a series of sex jokes. These embarrassed my father but he laughed if only to keep up his courage. Next came the examination, followed by a session of teasing. "Harry, would you stop worrying, for chrissakes, your constitution is so goddamned strong they couldn't kill you if they ran horses over you." Now and then Woodrow would give my father an aspirin, which he considered a bona fide wonder drug.

Years later, when my parents finally retired to Florida, they lost contact with Morris Woodrow. My father fell prey to that voracious breed of doctor that seems to be spawned by places where there are a lot of old people. One of the Miami doctors diagnosed my father as having high blood pressure. Pills were prescribed that, in turn, seemed to affect his heartbeat. When another doctor noted my father's irregular heartbeat he put him on other pills that caused water retention, requiring yet another round of pills to deal with that problem.

Through the Yonkers expatriate grapevine, Morris Woodrow, still living in Yonkers, heard what was going on. He telephoned one day to tell my father that "for chrissakes, you've always had an irregular heartbeat; the whole damned family has irregular heartbeats; stop taking those pills!" Woodrow said he'd never told my father about his heart condition because the news would have stimulated my father's hypochondria, causing him to worry so much that his blood pressure *would* have gone up. Woodrow assumed that he would be our family doctor forever, and that he'd be able to deal with problems as they arose.

Anyway, by the time of the phone call, my parents had accepted the high-tech medical solutions of the "big doctors" in Florida. The pill cycle continued: pills that made my father fuzzy-headed, which caused anxiety, which caused urine retention and release, which raised and lowered his blood pressure, and round and round. My father never did get off the pill wheel. About two years after Woodrow's call he was dead.

MILTON BERLE

I lived most of my childhood without television. It wasn't until 1949, when I was thirteen, that the first TV showed up on Kneeland Avenue. My family didn't have one until about a year later.

As a small child listening to radio I had clung to the idea that little people lived inside the radio box and were performing for me alone. Every other explanation of the technology was beyond my grasp. But by puberty, I'd accepted—without questioning, without understanding—that voices somehow were transmitted through wires as they were with the telephone (another mystery).

Television was only slightly more mysterious than the radio and the telephone. The idea that pictures could be transmitted through the air and through wires was befuddling to me then, and still befuddles me today, but I had learned a modern skill: acceptance.

One day my parents came home all excited and told me that the Edelsons down the street had bought a television set—"Like the movies but right in their house!"—and we were all invited to see it. The set was one of those original Philco projection systems. The cathode-ray tube was below the line of sight, inside a box; it projected its image onto a silverized angled screen. To see anything, you had to sit almost directly in front of the screen. If you sat off to the side, the image would fade. And the image was . . . Milton Berle! In addition were Sid Caesar, Imogene Coca, Mel Allen, Steve Allen, Edward R. Murrow, Omnibus, Hallmark Theater. Television programming in the early days was funkier and smaller scale than now: simple comedy, sports, and an up-close live theater format that was daring and spontaneous.

But probably the best thing about television in its early years was that there was not much of it. Programming began most days about 4 P.M. and continued only until 11 P.M. or midnight. And since few people owned sets, television viewing was a communal, neighborhood experience. Mrs. Edelson would invite everyone on the block and serve cake and cookies. On Milton Berle nights there might be a dozen people jammed in front of the screen, hooting and laughing. In those days TV had the quality of movie-going: viewing was a group event, with socializing before and after. Soon, however, each family had its own set, or sets. Programming extended to all hours, day and night. A community event was transformed into an isolated experience: at first, families watched alone; then soon each individual was left alone in his or her own room, silently watching.

FAMILY BUICK

Cars were a very important subject in Lincoln Park. There were constant discussions among males of all age groups concerning auto design, performance, and symbolic significance of a particular model: Was it "classy" or not? My friends and I had a game we would play to see who would be first to identify an oncoming car from blocks away by model, brand, and year. Howie Dugoff was the best. Within two blocks, he never missed.

The 1950s brought the concept of "planned obsolescence." The advertisements of the period emphasized newness and in Lincoln Park people took the idea seriously. Local mores required replacing your car at least every two years, and I knew only one person who defied this rule: my uncle and next door neighbor, Lou Oser. The Oser family owned two cars, one of which was an every-two-years new Oldsmobile. But Lou had a second car, a 1938 LaSalle coupe. He used that car for his daily ten-mile round trip from Yonkers to the northern end of the New York IRT subway line, which carried him the rest of the way to his office in lower Manhattan. What made this devotion to the LaSalle so surprising was that in every other dimension of his existence, Lou was an absolute conformist. But he saw no reason to trade in the LaSalle, which worked perfectly well. This stance caused enormous stress on his wife, his children, and the neighbors. People on Kneeland Avenue were embarrassed by this "old" car, and viewed Lou's commitment to it as an almost radical act in rare defiance of the virtually patriotic consumerist mood that was gaining speed in the 1950s.

My own family owned a Buick sedan, rotated every three years. My father believed strongly in *big* cars. Not only were they more prestigious, he felt, but in case of collision they would protect us better than some of those little European imports that everyone criticized.

I remember the car's wool-covered seats, good for sleeping on long drives from the grandparents' home in Brooklyn. When awake, I would fixate on the speedometer; I noticed that this Buick *apparently* could be driven at 120 miles per hour. I wondered, Why were cars built to go that fast when 60 miles per hour was the speed limit? I think that question signaled my first inkling of the role of imagination in technology.

In Yonkers, we used cars to go everywhere. If you needed to go three blocks to the grocery store, you drove. The only time of year that cars were not used was during the Jewish High Holy Days of Rosh Hashanah and Yom Kippur. On those days you walked, not drove, to the synagogue. What a sight! The usually empty sidewalks were filled with formally dressed people walking arm in arm to temple, as if it were a Sunday promenade in Vienna. The only cars that moved were operated by Italians. They drove slowly to respect the mood of the event.

I experienced another car-free moment when I was about eleven years old. A blizzard covered New York City with several feet of snow. The newspaper screamed CITY PARALYZED, and spoke of people panicking and cars stalled in drifts. The morning after the storm, at the height of the city's paralysis, my father absolutely had to get to his office in lower Manhattan. I went along. We walked through the snow about a half-mile to a streetcar line, which was still operating, and which took us to the New York subway, also operating. When we emerged at Eighteenth Street and Sixth Avenue, we encountered an amazing sight. The streets were quiet. Everything was white. Far from panicking, people were out playing in snow drifts, having a great time. The media had utterly distorted what was going on. Why? Panic makes better news than peacefulness and pleasure.

FLORIDA

At least once each year, my parents took us to Florida, their favorite place in the world. They had always dreamed of retiring there someday to what was still a tropical paradise: palm forests, great empty white beaches, flocks of storks and pelicans. But by the time my parents made their move, paradise had been paved, condo-ized, and submerged beneath high-rise buildings. Later, when I asked my parents if they were sorry about what had happened to Florida, they admitted they were, but that it was progress, and that was good.

Usually we took the train to Florida: two days, one night. It seemed unbearably long to me, though I loved sleeping in those neat little rooms and gazing out the window. The industrial soot-covered towns of the Northeast gave way to deep forests; further south, the landscape became green and sultry. In South Carolina and Georgia, the train passed within yards of shantytown villages. Black people, lounging in their yards or on porches, waved at us as the train sped by. My mind flew into those tiny houses, covered with tarpaper, but I could not imagine what life might be like for the people who lived there. At train stops, we would go out on the platform and drink at the fountains marked "Whites Only."

Now and then we traveled south by car. It was slower than the train and less comfortable, but it allowed us to stop at various roadside Wonders of the World: mystery houses, dinosaur bones, snake pits, petrified forests. Along the eastern edge of the Everglades in Florida, there was an "authentic Seminole Indian Village." I saw my first Indians. Though I had once read about Indians in school—what they wore, what they ate, and how they were all gone—I was surprised to find that any of them were still alive. I was told not to touch or go near any of them. The older Indians were making moccasins, beaded necklaces, and caps with "Seminole" stitched on them. One gigantic Indian man wrestled an alligator, successfully prying open its mouth and placing a stick in it to keep its jaws apart. Eventually my eyes wandered beyond the immediate scene; I saw that we were on the edge of a deep cypress swamp. There were Indian canoes at the edge of the water. Looking inside the cypress forest I could see houses that appeared to be built right into the trees. I couldn't imagine why anyone would live in a place like this. The swamp looked dangerous to me. I was glad when we finally left.

SUMMER CAMP

My summers were spent at camp in Massachusetts. It was a sports-oriented camp: baseball, basketball, swimming, and volleyball. Team sports. The emphasis was on winning. One period per week, however, we had what was called "nature." The nature counselor seemed weird to most of us since he *never* played sports. He was forever collecting ferns and working in his "nature shop." He would take us on walks through nearby meadows, pointing out flowers, telling us their Latin names, making us write notes. We hated these walks. They always seemed to come on the hottest day of the week; there were too many bugs, and we wanted to play baseball. Sometimes the nature counselor kept us indoors to dissect frogs and snakes, which was oddly fascinating. I learned that animals had virtually the same organs as human beings.

It was during summer camp in 1945—I was nine years old—that we all awoke from an obligatory afternoon nap to see the counselors huddled around a radio. Someone came running in with an afternoon newspaper: U.S. DROPS ATOMIC BOMB ON JAPS. There was excited discussion about how an entire city had been wiped out by just one bomb. I couldn't imagine such a thing, but I was impressed. Everyone was saying that it meant that the war—maybe *all* wars—would soon be over. For days I tried to understand exactly what an A-bomb was, but no one could explain it. President Truman spoke to the public on radio and said it was a grave responsibility to have invented this instrument, but it had been God's will that we produced it when we did. As a result we were able to save thousands of American lives. In the future, Truman promised, nuclear energy would be used only for peaceful, humane purposes.

Within a few years the Russians, without the help of God, also produced an A-bomb, and we were off to the races.

To me personally, the fact of nuclear weapons meant that throughout my teenage years I was always scared. I realized that in one instant my life could be over. We began doing regular air-raid drills in school. We memorized what to do if the bomb was dropped nearby: Don't look at the flash, get under your desk, don't drink the water, listen to the Civil Defense.

Of all the technological influences of my childhood, nuclear weapons clearly had the greatest impact on my mind. They made me doubt the future, and they were an iron-fisted message that fabulous technical forces were out there—forces that contained enough overwhelming power to shatter any lingering notion that I could control my existence.

By the time I was thirteen or fourteen I became obsessed with the possibility of nuclear war. I kept imagining nuclear explosions with my family being ripped apart. What a stupid situation. Here I was at the beginning of my life and already the thought of annihilation was foremost in my mind. A tremendous amount of my emotional and intellectual attention revolved around how to live my life, given the existence of this one piece of technology. Worst of all, no one seemed able to talk about it—not my school, not my family, not the media. It was a profound technological experience shared by everyone in the United States and in most other parts of the world, but each person went through it alone.

DEMOCRACITY

If nuclear technology created a terrifying vision of how life on Earth might turn out, it was virtually the only technology to so reveal itself. The dominant mood of the 1940s and 1950s was totally gung-ho for technology, with idealized romantic visions—fantasies, I'd say—of a technotopian future.

Foremost in the creation of this vision was the great New York World's Fair of 1939 and 1940. More than any previous event, it emblazoned into the public mind a new set of expectations for technology, which was coming just over the horizon. My parents took me there when I was four years old. I was awed by everything.

The most dramatic visions were within the corporate pavilions: dioramas of sparkling-clean, seven-tiered techno-cities. Monorails transporting people at 200 miles per hour. Sleek, long-finned cars moving at incredible speeds on elevated roadways. Private planes and helicopters whirling between 500-story buildings. Humans flying about with little rocket packs on their backs, while robots, at street level, walked the dogs.

The DuPont exhibit contained the "typical home of the future." Synthetic everything. A staff of robots could be summoned by the touch of a button. Another button encircled you with the "natural environment" of your choice: mountains, meadows, oceans. With the help of a computer–TV-looking thing you could order your groceries, get your newspaper, or speak to friends (with their images on-screen) anywhere in the world.

The diorama called "Democracity" predicted the urban and suburban lifestyles of the future. The cities of twenty years hence (1960) were de-picted as having eliminated all slums and blight. They were filled with parks. Energy sources were unlimited by then; the climate was perfectly controlled.

Outer-space exhibits showed smiling white Americans living happily inside domed environments on other planets. Another exhibit showed how, with modern air conditioning, we would soon be living under-ground. The "Frontiers of Medicine and Science" exhibit predicted the conquering of all disease, the extension of our lifespan to hundreds of years—or forever—the elimination of insect blight by pesticides, and the end of poverty.

More than 45 million people attended the New York World's Fair dur-ing its two-year run. All of them experienced what was essentially an ad-vertisement for a future lifestyle. Following a decade of depression, such a vision of techno-paradise looked wonderful. The DuPont dream could be everyone's dream. Wouldn't everyone want an automated household, with its own natural environments, and push-button shopping? Doesn't everyone love little robots? Wouldn't everyone want to live forever? It was a kick just thinking about it.

As a child of those times, I found the images thrilling and powerful. They became a kind of mental blueprint that I carried into the future, in common with most of my generation, I believe. These images affected the way we all envisioned our lives. That the vision was merely a corporate representation of the future never occurred to me. That there might be problems associated with that vision, or alternatives to it, was never indicated.

THE AMERICAN DREAM

During the two decades following the World's Fair, similar images be-came prevalent in the mass media, especially in advertising. A 1942 B. F. Goodrich advertisement proclaimed, "Following our victory in this war will come a new America. An America which will startle the world be-cause of the way people create . . . The men and machines are already on the job. The will and determination are already at work. But today the effort is devoted to winning the war. Tomorrow, they'll be devoted to the creation of a new America." It was the role of the advertising industry to be sure this new America was realized.

By the time the Second World War ended, advertising was extolling the virtues of appliances ("dinner without drudgery"), frozen foods, and clothes made of plastic ("plastics are new, plastics are smart, nothing is sewn"). American Cyanamid ads promised to move mountains, to build "thruways . . . pioneer triumphs of engineering and transportation, safety, speed, and convenience, without stoplights, crossings, sharp turns, or noticeable grades." Ads promoted throwaway living, disposable items to cut down household chores, and scientific food production, including feeding antibiotics to livestock and using pesticides on crops. DuPont was promising, "Better things for better living through chemistry." Westinghouse was saying, "There's a lift to living electronically."

These were the decades in which the American Dream was being created. Technology was going to make anything and everything possible. With the war over, not even the sky was the limit. Negative thinking was eschewed. A 1949 report by H. G. Moulton, president of the Brookings Institution, argued that the production capacity of the U.S. could support a population of 300 million people at eight times the (1949) standard of living. The report predicted a future abundance fueled by factories and mines that would produce five to ten times more, farms that would produce three times more, plus massive ocean cultivation and the reclamation of swamps and deserts for food production. "There is no known limit," said Moulton, "to the potential wealth of the world."

Ronald Reagan was the radio voice of the General Electric ad campaigns of that era. Years later, when he was president, Reagan employed the same kind of optimistic, expectant rhetoric. Hearing him speak of the wonderful things his Star Wars scheme would achieve, I heard the same style and many of the same words from the commercial imagery of the post–World War II period. In fact, Reagan's success may be explained in part by his connection to that optimistic time; everyone who is over thirty today grew up with that rhetoric ringing in his or her ears. It was cheerful, it created positive imagery, and it came at a time when amazing things really did seem possible.

The new value system that was sold in the forties and fifties was designed to fuel the most massive expansion of the U.S. industrial and marketing sectors in history. The "American way of life" became an advertising theme; it drew an explicit equation between how much you consumed and how American you were. During the Truman-Eisenhower years, the American ideal of consumerism was directly juxtaposed with Russia's emphatically nonconsumerist stance. In the 1950s, buying a washing machine was a blow against communism.

This value system incorporated certain key attitudes: Technological innovation is good. It is always good. It aids health. It saves labor. It is the engine that drives economic growth, which in turn drives the American standard of living upward, which benefits all people. Technical innovation promotes democracy, freedom, and leisure. Technical and scientific progress will spread around the world and relieve all people of the awful toil that has oppressed them since the dawn of time. Someday, every place will look like the World's Fair. It is inevitable. You can't turn back the clock.

For me, going through my teenage years in that period; for my family and neighbors; and I believe for most Americans, there was the disposition to go along with it all. Swept along by the rhetoric and hype, it was as though we found ourselves living within a gigantic environmental theatre. We sat and watched while they rolled away one diorama and replaced it with another and then another. While our world was being dramatically transformed, while places we loved were fast deteriorating, while lifestyles were sharply altered, while the forest receded, while open land was paved over and built upon, while pollution and smog became commonplace, while small towns began to look like New York City, and New York City began to resemble Fritz Lang's *Metropolis,* we watched as if it were a movie.

To say that we, the public, had no participation in these vast changes would be inaccurate. We lived in the world; we interacted with the changing environment. By our silence we gave our tacit approval. But no one ever inquired into what we thought about it all. No one ever indicated that there could be a question about the process. It all happened so fast, and with so much power, it was difficult to grasp what was changing, as it was changing. The process itself overpowered all doubt. We asked no questions. We never had time to think it through. Even if we'd had the time, we didn't have the thoughts or the words by which to articulate our concerns. There was no language of technological evaluation, nor is there one now. The parameters of the discussion, even the parameters of thought, were predefined by corporate, governmental, and scientific institutions. No formal means existed by which ordinary people could engage in discussions or debates, or could hear the pros and cons of what was happening. There were no national referenda, save for what apppeared in the media. And the media reports were mainly confined to advertising or government predictions. If there existed an alternative view, it remained within intellectual and cultural circles not visible to the average American.

In the absence of an alternative vision, the paradigm was confirmed that technological innovation was good, invariably good, and would be the principal means by which our society would solve its problems and produce a better world.

Fifty years later, however, as the world hurtles toward its greatest environmental crisis since the dawn of human life, a crisis driven by the insatiable need to feed resources to the technological machine, and to consume them as commodities, we are at an appropriate moment to question whether this path we have chosen and celebrated has lived up to its promise, and if not, if it ever will.

2

FANTASY AND REALITY

GIVEN THE CELEBRATORY claims of the 1940s and 1950s (and since) concerning the utopia that would result if our society vaulted itself into the new technological age, it's clear that we need some standards of measurement to compare the claims with the results. If even a small percent of the expectations had proven true, we'd be well on the way to becoming the first industrial-technological-scientific paradise on Earth. Over the last fifty years, new technologies have been advertised as enhancing happiness, freedom, empowerment, health, and physical comfort; or else as reducing toil, while also providing jobs, serving democracy, and making life more beautiful and pleasant. Over time the aggregate of such assertions created our technotopian fantasies of unlimited expectations. We believed them in the 1940s and 1950s, and we still believe them now. But have these promises been realized? And by what standards do we judge the success or the failure of the path we have followed?

I suppose that in order to be considered even minimally successful, a society must keep its population healthy, peaceful, and contented. All members should have sufficient food to eat, a place to live, and a sense of participation in a shared community purpose. Everyone should have access to the collective wisdom and knowledge of the society, and should expect that life will be spiritually and emotionally fulfilling for themselves and for future generations. This in turn implies awareness, care, and respect for the earth's life-support systems.

Obviously, anyone could quibble about certain points on this list, or wish to add others, but to me they seem to be a basic minimum. And since it's been for roughly half a century that this technological vision has been aggressively hyped, now is a good time to compare its promise with its performance.

• • •

People who celebrate technology say it has brought us an improved standard of living, which means greater speed (people can travel faster and obtain more objects and information sooner), greater choice (often equated with freedom of choice, which usually refers to the ability to choose among jobs and commodities), greater leisure (because technology has supposedly eased the burden and time involved in work), and greater luxury (more commodities and increased material comfort). None of these benefits informs us about human satisfaction, happiness, security, or the ability to sustain life on Earth. Perhaps getting places more quickly makes some people more contented or fulfilled, but I'm not so sure. Nor am I convinced that greater choice of commodities in the marketplace qualifies as satisfying compared with, say, love and friendship and meaningful work. Nor do I believe that choice equals "freedom," if one defines the latter as a sense that one has true control over one's own mind and experience.

As for leisure, I believe that what passes for leisure in our society is actually time-filling: watching television or buying things. Many writers have argued that given the consequences of automation and robotics, most free time may soon be spent searching for increasingly scarce jobs. And as Marshall Sahlins and others have pointed out (as we will see in Chapter 14), stone-age societies had more than twice the amount of leisure time we do today, which they used to pursue spiritual matters, personal relationships, and pleasure. Finally, people such as Ivan Illich have said that if you include the time needed to earn money to pay for and repair all the expensive "time-saving" gadgets in our lives, modern technology actually *deprives* us of time.

In addition to improved standard of living, another argument for the success of the technological path concerns the contributions of modern medicine. There is no disagreeing that modern medicine, though it has not produced eternal life as was predicted by the world's fairs of the 1940s (and now the 1990s), has contributed to longevity. Combined with antibiotic technology, sanitation, and improved diagnostics, modern medicine has improved life expectancy in the technologically advanced parts of the world.

On the other hand, critics such as Illich argue that modern medicine

may be a double-edged sword. By separating people from traditional holistic self-care practices, and by dubious medical interventions with drugs
and surgery, modern medicine may cause as much disease as it cures.
Other critics suggest that Western medicine cannot be separated from the
whole web of technologies that are its parents and children: computers,
certain reproductive interventions, biotechnology, and genetics, all of
which are problematic in some way. Still others say that length of life is
meaningless as compared with *quality* of life, which, due to increasing
pollution and devastation brought on by technological overdevelopment,
is now in sharp decline. The trend toward longer life may soon be reversed.

But conceding that technology, on the whole, aids longer life and that
this is good, what other measurements exist? How else can we assess the
impact of the technological path upon happiness, security, contentment,
well-being, and a sense of faith in the future? These are very difficult to
measure, but some statistics from U.S. agencies may tell us something, at
least about the level of personal contentment in this country. Though the
figures vary for other Western nations—crime statistics, for example, are
far lower in many countries—I think it is relevant to offer these numbers,
since the U.S. has been the mecca for technological expansion in this half-
century, and we have been its primary missionaries and salespeople, at least
until the recent emergence of the Japanese.

• According to figures from the San Francisco–based independent nonprofit National Council on Crime and Delinquency, the rate of criminal
activity in the U.S. sharply increased in the period following World War
II. By 1989, the national murder rate had reached more than 30,000 per
year. If you are a young black man in America, you are more likely to
die by homicide than in any other way. If you are a woman, you have
one chance in five of being raped in your lifetime, and one chance in
three that you suffered sexual molestation as a child.

• 1990 figures published by another independent research group, The Sen-
tencing Project, reported that the U.S. prison population has passed the
1 million mark. That represents a higher per capita rate of incarceration
than any country in the world. (South Africa is second; the Soviet Union
is third.) If you add to these figures the number of people in the U.S. in
juvenile detention or on parole, or in other controlled situations such as
halfway houses, the total figure is nearly 1.5 million.

• As has been widely reported, suicide and drug use in the U.S., especially
among young people, are at epidemic levels and growing. (This is also
true in most parts of the industrialized world.) In 1990, the National In-

stitute of Mental Health (NIMH) reported that suicide was the third leading cause of death among young people, ages 15 to 24.

• The U.S. Census Bureau's 1988 figures indicated that more than 13 percent of the U.S. population (about 32 million people) is officially classified as living in poverty. The Bureau also said that 17.5 percent lived "below 125 percent of the poverty level"; that is, at *nearly* the poverty level. The Harvard-based Physician Task Force on Hunger in America has estimated, based on National Academy of Science standards, that more than 20 million Americans "are chronically undernourished."

• The Census Bureau also reported that, as of 1989, 13 percent of the U.S. population (32 million people) had no health insurance.

• The National Coalition of Homeless People estimates that in late 1990 about 3 million Americans were homeless.

• According to the Barbara Bush Foundation for Family Literacy, approximately 27 percent of all Americans are "functionally illiterate."

• And the Public Citizen Health Research Group reports that about "25 percent of American hospital beds are filled by mental patients." The National Institute of Mental Health's Office of Scientific Information reported, in March 1990, that "28 million American adults, over 18 years old, suffer some mental disorder during a given six-month period." About 16 million suffer "anxiety disorders," 10 million suffer "depressive disorders," and about 2 million are classified as schizophrenics.

Whatever else can be said about these statistics, they are surely *not* indications of general contentment, or that human needs are being satisfied.

Of course, some people *are* doing well. According to the U.S. Federal Reserve, the top 10 percent of American families—whose incomes exceed $50,000 per year—own 78 percent of all private business, 86 percent of municipal bonds, 50 percent of real estate, and 72 percent of corporate stock. So much for the egalitarian aspects of rapid technological expansion.

I believe an objective observer—an anthropologist from Mars, perhaps—would conclude that our society is not functioning very well. Considering the violence, self-destruction, drug abuse, insanity, unequal distribution of wealth, and failure to provide freedom from fear, an observer would surely label the whole situation a failure. Can we blame technology for this? Only partly. But given that the promoters of technology claimed it would solve precisely these problems, it is worth noting how short of utopia the machines have left us—and, as we will see, how many problems technology has actually caused.

Perhaps more to the point are the considerations of environmental degradation (now a worldwide phenomenon) that are *unarguably* related to the growth of technology. Only within the last decade, just as technical expansion is reaching its zenith, has the world awakened to realize that toxic pollution is out of control, that the world's forest cover is being eliminated, and that the habitats of the remaining species of plants and animals are disappearing. We have seen the emergence of new technology-related caused diseases and a rapid growth in the cancer rate. We have seen major disasters in places such as Bhopal, India; Love Canal and Times Beach; Valdez, Alaska, and the Persian Gulf; Three Mile Island and Chernobyl. And now we are witnessing the first clear planetary breakdown of the earth's life-support systems: air and water contamination, holes in the ozone layer, and global warming, all effects predicted by environmentalists for many years, but ignored in the technological frenzy.

Considering all this, don't we have sufficient evidence to draw some humbling conclusions? Given that technology was supposed to make life better, and given its apparent failure in both the social and the environmental spheres, shouldn't reason dictate that we sharply question the wild claims we have accepted about technology? Lewis Mumford said that the "horn of plenty," i.e., the unlimited material goods that technological society promises, qualifies as a "magnificent bribe" meant to get us to overlook what has been lost in the bargain. Isn't it time for a society-wide debate on whether the costs—economic, social, health-related, and environmental—are justified, especially as the benefits (speed, leisure, length of life, commodities) are so marginal and perhaps superficial?

No such debate is taking place, and no such conclusions have been drawn. Bizarre claims as to the alleged benefits of new technologies continue to proliferate. We still hear that new generations of machines will solve the problems left by prior generations of machines. We still hear predictions that a new era of health, comfort, security, leisure, and happiness is just around the corner if only we deepen our commitment to technology.

The operating homilies remain the same: "You can't stop progress." "Once the genie is out of the bottle you cannot put it back." "Technology is here to stay, so we have to find ways to use it better." In reality, these are all rationalizations to cover up a culture-wide passivity; a failure to take a hard look at technology in all of its dimensions, or to draw the obvious conclusions from the evidence at hand.

INGREDIENTS OF THE PRO-TECHNOLOGY PARADIGM

In *The Whale and the Reactor,* Langdon Winner calls our current condition "technological somnambulism." He goes on:

> The most interesting puzzle in our times is that we so willingly sleepwalk through the process for reconstituting the conditions of human existence. . . . Why is it that the philosophy of technology has never really gotten under way? Why has a culture so firmly based upon countless sophisticated instruments, techniques, and systems remained so steadfast in its reluctance to examine its own foundations? . . . In the twentieth century it is usually taken for granted that the only reliable sources for improving the human condition stem from new machines, techniques and chemicals. Even the recurring environmental and social ills that have accompanied technological advancement have rarely dented this faith. . . . We are seldom inclined to examine, discuss or judge pending innovations. . . . In the technical realm we repeatedly enter into a series of social contracts, the terms of which are revealed only after the signing.

Our passivity to the technological juggernaut has been ongoing for millennia. Some find its roots in agriculture and husbandry. Others cite the emergence of patriarchy. And there is surely a case that the scientific revolution, which articulated a mechanistic view of nature and humanity, altered the prevailing views of life and encouraged fascination with and dependence upon the machine. Whatever the historical roots, we are now embedded in a system of perceptions that make us blind and passive when it comes to technology. I think the following factors are major contributors to the problem.

Dominance of Best-Case Scenarios

The most obvious problem is the manner in which technology is introduced to us. The first waves of description are invariably optimistic, even utopian. This is because in capitalist societies all early descriptions of new technologies come from their inventors and the people who stand to gain from their acceptance. Whether in advertisements, public-relations presentations, or at landmark events such as World's Fairs, the information we are given describes the technologies solely in terms of their best-case use. This is so even when the inventors have significant knowledge of terrible downside possibilities. It is logical that inventors and corporate and government marketers present only idealized, glamorized versions of technology, since they have no stake in the public being even dimly aware of negative potentials—the worst-case scenarios—though negative results are at least as likely to occur as positive results. Nuclear power is the single exception to this pattern. It has had a somewhat rougher road than other technologies because the public was aware of its worst-case potentials from the moment we first heard about it, at Hiroshima. If we had known the worst-case potentials of television, or automobiles, or computers, or pesticides, or robotics, or genetics, doubts might have emerged about those technologies as well, and thus slowed their progress.

Technology's Pervasiveness and Invisibility

Marshall McLuhan told us to think of all technology in environmental terms because of the way it envelops us and becomes difficult to perceive. From morning to night we walk through a world that is totally manufactured, a creation of human invention. We are surrounded by pavement, machinery, gigantic concrete structures. Automobiles, airplanes, computers, appliances, television, electric lights, artificial air have become the physical universe with which our senses interact. They are what we touch, observe, react to. They are themselves "information," in that they shape how we think and, in the absence of an alternate reality (i.e., nature), what we think about and know.

As we relate to these objects of our own creation, we begin to merge with them and assume some of their characteristics.

Workers on an assembly line, for example, must function at the speed of the line, submitting to its repetitive physical and mental demands. When we drive a car, we are forced to focus our minds and bodily reactions on being at one with the road and the machine: following the curves, moving through the landscape at appropriate speeds. The more we spend our lives in this manner, the more these interactions define the perimeters of our experience and vision. They become the framework of our awareness.

There is a paradox, however. Because technology is now everywhere apparent, pervasive, and obvious, we lose awareness of its presence. While we walk on pavement, or drive on a freeway, or sit in a shopping mall, we are unaware that we are enveloped by a technological and commercial reality, or that we are moving at technological speed. We live our lives in reconstructed, human-created environments; we are *inside* manufactured goods.

We do not easily grasp technology from the outside, or, in McLuhan's

terms, "extraenvironmentally." And once we accept life within a technically mediated reality, we become less aware of anything that preceded it.
We have a hard time imagining life before television or cars. We do not
remember a United States of mainly forests and quiet. The information
that nature offers to our minds and to our senses is nearly absent from our
lives. If we do seek out nature, we find it fenced off in a "park," a kind of
nature zoo. We need to make reservations and pay for entry, like at a
movie. It's little wonder that we find incomprehensible any societies that
choose to live within nature.

With each new generation of technology, and with each stage of technological expansion into pristine environments, human beings have fewer
alternatives and become more deeply immersed within technological consciousness. We have a harder time seeing our way out. Living constantly
inside an environment of our own invention, reacting solely to things we
ourselves have created, we are essentially living *inside our own minds*.
Where evolution was once an interactive process between human beings
and a natural, unmediated world, evolution is now an interaction between
human beings and our own artifacts. We are essentially coevolving with
ourselves in a weird kind of intraspecies incest. At each stage of the cycle
the changes come faster and are more profound. The web of interactions
among the machines becomes more complex and more invisible, while the
total effect is more powerful and pervasive. We become ever more enclosed
and ever less aware of that fact. Our environment is so much a product of
our invention that it becomes a single worldwide machine. We live inside
it, and are a piece of it.

Limitations of the Personal View

Technological change proceeds on so many fronts simultaneously, with
new technologies constantly interweaving to create new potentialities, that
there is no single focus, no center at which we can direct simple, piercing
questions to help us understand how it all works. The scale and complexity
of these technologies (such as the worldwide system of satellites and computers that enables banks and development agencies to instantaneously
reallocate financial resources anywhere on Earth) make it difficult for us
to grasp the big picture in assessing any individual technology. Failing to
see how machines connect, we are like the blind man seeking to describe
the elephant by feeling its ankle. Unable to see the whole creature, we tend
to define technology on a scale we can manage. We think of it in personal
terms, based on our own interactions with it.

We use machines in our lives and evaluate them in terms of their usefulness to us personally. The machine vacuums our carpets. The car drives easily and well. The television entertains us. The microwave cooks dinner in a flash. The computer helps us do our work. We make little attempt to fathom the multiplicity of effects that computers or television or microwave ovens or cars may have on society or on nature. Nor do we think about how the technological march is affecting the planet. As a result, we are left with a view of technology's impact that is much too personal and narrow.

It is perfectly natural to view machines this way. I too tend to think of my machinery in personal, visceral terms. I had a 1968 Volvo for fifteen years; it never had a serious breakdown. I wrote the television book on an old Underwood upright typewriter; it was a solid, perfectly performing machine. I now use an old IBM Selectric, also excellent.

When I work with these machines or speak on the telephone or use the copying machine or drive my car, I do not stop and recite the social, political, cultural, or health-related consequences of my actions. I use the machines as anyone does. That's the way the world is right now, though I would prefer it were not. It would be nearly impossible to function if one were constantly questioning a machine's effect in society at large: how it changes power arrangements, who gains and who loses because of its existence, how it affects the global environment.

When we use a computer we don't ask if computer technology makes nuclear annihilation more or less possible, or if corporate power is increased or decreased thereby. While watching television, we don't think about the impact upon the tens of millions of people around the world who are absorbing the same images at the same time, nor about how TV homogenizes minds and cultures. When we drive our car we don't think about how pavement suppresses the life beneath it. If we have criticisms of technology they are usually confined to details of personal dissatisfaction. Rarely do we consider the overall political, social, spiritual, or economic effects upon our country or the world.

There is an antidote for this problem: the creation of a truly holistic mode of analyzing technology, which would give greater importance to its multidimensional effects rather than its individual benefits.

The Inherent Appeal of the Machine

In *Four Arguments for the Elimination of Television* I discussed encounters between animals and certain technologies. The deer becomes fixated at oncoming headlights. The fish stares at the face mask of the diver who spears it. I used these examples because I felt they suggested something of our condition in Western society. We are hypnotized by the newness of the machine, dazzled by its flash and impressed with its promise. We do not have the instinct as yet to be fearful, or to doubt.

Partly, this is a problem with our genetic inclination. For thousands of generations our survival depended upon our keen attunement to the events in our environment. We gave particular attention to unusual or new developments: changes in animal behavior, unusual footprints, extraordinary weather. Perhaps these presented new dangers, perhaps opportunities.

In the relatively few years in which we have accelerated our separation from nature, our genetic and sensory evolution has not been able to keep pace with the evolution of the machine. In our new, techno-oriented habitat, we have not yet noticed that the information of our senses is no longer invariably accurate.

Three hundred years ago, if humans saw a flock of birds flying southward, they could count on the fact that the birds were actually doing that, and reliably draw conclusions. But since the introduction of moving-image media, the information of our senses (our eyes, in particular), which we have always believed is accurate ("seeing is believing"), may not be. The edited, re-created, re-enacted, sped-up, slowed-down, manufactured imagery we see on television or in film is *not* in the same category of imagery as birds we see in the sky. Failing to make that distinction, we believe what we see in the media is as true and reliable as the unmediated information from nature, which offers great opportunities to advertisers, program directors, and politicians. In giving such trust to media imagery, we are relying upon our genetic inclination to pay rapt attention to, and believe, whatever is new and unusual in our visual plain, just like the deer staring at the headlight.

Similarly, as suggested in the previous section, we assume that by observing a machine's performance *personally* we can understand its full implications. But the human species has not had sufficient experience, and absolutely no training, to enable us to understand from our own experience the effects the machine might have over time, or on a wider scale.

Compounding this problem is the fact that every technology *presents itself* in the best possible light. Each technology is invented for a purpose and it announces itself, as it were, in these terms. It arrives on the scene as a "friend," promising to solve a problem. *This* machine will move water from here to there. *This* one will bring down an animal at 400 yards. *This* will move a boat through water at high speed. *This* will kill insects that destroy our food. *This* one will light a city. All of these are attractive possibilities. There is an inherent appeal in the very *existence* of machines that have such promise.

What's more, the new machines actually do what they promise to do, which leaves us feeling pleased and impressed. It is not until much later, after a technology has been around for a while—bringing with it other compatible technologies, altering economic arrangements and family and community life, affecting culture, and having unpredictable impact on the land—that societies both familiar and unfamiliar with the machine begin to realize that a Faustian bargain has been made. But by then the situation is difficult to alter. What to do about this? How to counterbalance the apparent appeal of the machine? Practice skepticism!

The Assumption That Technology Is Neutral

No notion more completely confirms our technological somnambulism than the idea that technology contains no inherent political bias. From the political Right and Left, from the corporate world and the world of community activism, one hears the same homily: "The problem is not with technology itself, but with how we use it, and who controls it." This idea would be merely preposterous if it were not so widely accepted, and so dangerous. In believing this, however, we allow technology to develop without analyzing its actual bias. And then we are surprised when certain technologies turn out to be useful or beneficial only for certain segments of society.

A prime example is nuclear energy, which cannot possibly move society in a democratic direction, but *will* move society in an autocratic direction. Because it is so expensive and so dangerous, nuclear energy must be under the direct control of centralized financial, governmental, and military institutions. A nuclear power plant is not something that a few neighbors can get together and build. Community control is anathema. Even control by city or state governments is proving impossible, as is now obvious to those locales attempting to block the movement and disposal of radioactive wastes within their borders.

The existence of nuclear energy, and nuclear weaponry, in turn requires the existence of what Ralph Nader has called a new "priesthood"—a technical and military elite capable of guarding nuclear waste products for the approximately 250,000 years that they remain dangerous. So if some future society, tiring of the present path, should determine to move away from a centralized technological society and toward, say, an agrarian society, it would be impossible. The technical elite would need to remain, if only to deal with the various wastes left behind. So it is fair to say that nuclear technology *inherently* steers society toward greater political and financial centralization, and greater militarization.

Solar energy, on the other hand, is intrinsically biased *toward* democratic use. It is buildable and operable by small groups, even by families. It does not require centralized control. It is most cost effective at a small scale of operation, a reason why big power companies oppose it. And solar energy requires no thousand-year commitment from society.

So, where nuclear energy requires centralized control, solar energy functions best in a decentralized form. These attributes are inherent to the technologies and reflect the ideological bias of each.

What is true for energy systems is equally true for other technologies. Each new technology invariably steers society in *some* social and political direction, by its very nature. Each new technology is compatible with certain political outcomes, and most technology is invented by people who have some specific outcome in mind.

As stated earlier, the idea that technology is neutral is itself not neutral, since it blinds us to the ultimate direction in which we are heading and directly serves the promoters of the centralized technological pathway.

Combined with the best-case scenarios that dominate our information sources, and the way we are enveloped by technical reality, and the seductiveness and flash of the machine, and our tendency to think about technology only in personal terms, the idea of value-free technology confirms a formidable pro-technology mind-set. This, in turn, blinds us to the negative evidence at hand that technotopia has already failed and will only create more problems in the future.

3

THE IMPORTANCE OF THE
NEGATIVE VIEW

*I*N THE PRESENT climate of technological worship, arguing against
technology is not popular. Utter the most minor criticism of technology
and you run the risk of being labeled a "Luddite," an accusation meant to
equate opposition to technology with mindlessness. The reference is to an
important anti-technology movement in nineteenth-century England.
Huge numbers of workers in cottage industries went on a rampage against
the introduction of mass-production equipment, particularly within the
textile trades. They invaded factories and destroyed machines. The movement was deemed a sufficient enough threat that the death penalty was
established for the destruction of technology.

Given that history, it's little wonder people are not eager to be called
Luddites, but Langdon Winner has no such resistance. On a recent radio
interview he said, "I am delighted to be called a Luddite. The position of
the Luddites was in every way wise and perceptive. They opposed the imposition of a new economic order, which they predicted would destroy
their livelihood and traditions, and lead the world in a destructive direction. They were correct. Their resistance should be an inspiration."

Then Santa Fe psychologist and author Chellis Glendinning threw
down the gauntlet in a 1990 *Utne Reader* article titled "Notes toward a
Neo-Luddite Manifesto":

> Neo-Luddites are twentieth-century citizens who question the pre-
> dominant modern worldview, which preaches that unbridled tech-

nology represents progress. Neo-Luddites have the courage to gaze at the full catastrophe of our century. . . . Western societies are out of control and desecrating the fragile fabric of life on Earth. Like the early Luddites, we too are seeking to protect the livelihoods, communities, and families we love. . . . Stopping the destruction requires not just regulating or eliminating individual items like pesticides or military weapons. It requires new ways of thinking about humanity and new ways of relating to life. It requires a new worldview.

The roots of contemporary resistance to the direction of technology first took hold in the 1960s with the birth of the ecology movement. (The concept of ecology was an old one that was suddenly revived to describe an emerging vision of the interrelatedness of all life.) During those times I was coordinating national advertising campaigns for the Sierra Club, and later for Friends of the Earth. Though we were not really aware of it, the campaigns we undertook were a departure from traditional environmentalism, which had emphasized the protection of wilderness and wildlife, in that they began to focus on the dangers of specific technologies.

Included among these was the organized opposition to the Supersonic Transport (SST), to nuclear energy, and a bit later, to nuclear weapons. There was also opposition to constructing dams on wild rivers, including the Colorado in the Grand Canyon.

Rachel Carson's landmark book *Silent Spring* stimulated the fights against DDT and other pesticides. (By the early 1970s, the Vietnam experience had raised awareness of the dangers of herbicides and fungicides.) The movement also fought the use of nitrogen-fixed fertilizers and fumigants for fruits and vegetables. It opposed certain mining technologies (such as strip mining), certain fishing technologies (such as gill netting), and strongly promoted energy alternatives to fossil fuels and nuclear power.

During this era we questioned many assumptions about the desirability of the automobile. We opposed freeway construction. Proposals were developed, and some succeeded, to ban autos from certain areas of cities. Auto manufacturers were pressured to install smog-control systems and to build smaller, more fuel-efficient, longer-lasting cars.

Movements arose opposing disposable beverage containers, food additives, household sprays, non-biodegradable detergents, fluorescent lights, and fluoridated water. And as the first news of genetic engineering began to surface, pockets of resistance developed.

It remained unstated and perhaps unnoticed that these ecology actions were also anti-technology in character, and more radical than at first perceived. In resisting further evolution of technology into new areas of the environment, the ecology movement was beginning to draw a line against an 'entire mode of economic organization. It was to our discredit that we ourselves did not fully grasp this.

A small number of people, such as Leopold Kohr, F. F. Schumacher, and David Brower, were willing to seek principles by which to assess the whole direction of technology. "Smallness" rather than "bigness" was one such idea. The economics of continued technological growth, on a finite planet, came into question. And "appropriate technology" became the catch-term for new low-impact technology that operated on decentralized, small-scale principles: solar energy versus nuclear energy, diverse intensive farming versus agribusiness, steady-state economics versus economic growth.

But articulating these principles was slow, and meanwhile the juggernaut was growing out of control. With most environmentalists shy about asserting that each struggle was part of a larger, grander issue, each battle was fought as if isolated from the others. So careful were we not to be thought too radical that we rarely exposed the real problem: a system of logic, and a set of assumptions, that led to the problems of dams, pesticides, nukes, growth, and the rest of it. Meanwhile, industry, the media, and the government were all repeating the mantra that technology serves progress and that progress equals more technology. And at each stage of technical development, we fell more deeply into the techno-maelstrom.

"HOLISTIC" CRITICISM

I don't think I realized when I began working on *Four Arguments for the Elimination of Television* in 1973 that the project was really a stab at creating a new holistic language by which to discuss television and other technologies. It did not even occur to me at the beginning to advocate *no* television, but merely to broaden the terms used to discuss it, so that all possible dimensions of impact could be included: political, social, economic, biological, perceptual, informational, epistemological, spiritual; its effects upon kids, upon nature, upon power, upon health. A totality of effects, hence a "holistic" viewpoint.

I did place particular emphasis on the negative potentials of television—the worst-case possibilities—since those were absent from most

prior analyses. Whatever criticism of television existed at that time confined itself to the very narrow issues associated with the content of the
programs, and ignored the effects of television's existence on society.
McLuhan had already told us that "the medium is the message," but there
was little evidence that people understood what that meant.

McLuhan was saying that program content may not be the only problem, or even the principal problem, with television. The mere existence of
television, he said, causes society to be organized in new ways. As information is moved through different channels its character and its content
change; political relationships, concepts, and styles change as well. Even
the human spirit and human body change. Because of the way television
signals are processed in the brain, thought patterns are altered and a
unique, new relationship to information is developed: cerebral, out-of-
context, passive.

The point of my book was not to argue that there are no good programs
on television. It was to point out that the consequences of television's existence in our society are far more significant than its program content.
Ergo, the medium *is* the message. An analysis of television that does not
deal with the totality of these effects is not sufficient.

To try and make this difficult point, I originally titled the book *Sub-
urbanization of the Mind,* changing it later to *Freewayization of the Mind.*
Both titles were attempts to suggest what was happening to the way that
we think and understand information in the television age; our minds
were being channeled and simplified to match the channeled and simplified physical environment—suburbs, malls, freeways, high-rise buildings—that also characterized that period (and continues to do so today).
This effect would take place, I argued, even if the violence and sex shows
and the superficial comedies and the game shows were all removed from
the medium, because the process of moving edited images rapidly through
a passive human brain was so different from active information gathering,
whether from books or newspapers or walks in nature. As a result people
would become more passive, less able to deal with nuance and complexity,
less able to read or create. People would get "dumber," and have less understanding of world events even within an exploding information environment. The book predicted that a new kind of leader would emerge
from this process, one who fit the parameters of the medium, and who
understood its language: simple, assertive, without history or context, with
style superior to content. A few years later, Ronald Reagan became the
personification of that prediction.

After working on that book for several years, my concept of it evolved, and I considered naming it *Cloning of the Already Born,* in reference to the way television has homogenized culture throughout the world, a tendency not sufficiently noted by media pundits. Television was engaging all of humanity in similar thought patterns, similar experiences, similar imagery, and a similar context of reality, which was poisonous to diversity of culture. Soon, we would all be more alike, that is, more like Americans living in Holiday Inns.

But then when I'd finally finished the first draft, compiling hundreds of negative points about the medium, I felt television was an even more serious problem than I had first believed. I felt strongly that society would be better off without it. This realization did not particularly startle me. To believe that society would be better off without a certain technology didn't seem a very radical observation. Obviously some technologies are more harmful than they are beneficial, are they not? Yet many people were shocked, even angry, that I would advocate no television. Why were they so upset? What was the big deal?

I looked into the literature about television to find the names of other writers who had also taken a stance against it. I was startled to learn that nearly 10,000 books had been written about television since 1945, but not one of them argued that our society would be better off without it. Why had nobody ever made such a case?

Here was a technology that entered every home in the United States, brought imagery nightly into every brain for many long hours, reorganized family life, community life, political life, human understanding and experience and, through their advertising and their domination of program content, gave corporations an unprecedented degree of centralized power and control. Yet no one had thought to argue that we might be better off without it. Why? Did everyone really believe that TV was great? Definitely not. But everyone *was* caught up in the narrow idea that the programs were television's only problem; the solution was simply to produce better programs, to slip new ideas into the medium.

There was yet a deeper resistance. Saying no to a technology, *any* technology, was (and still is) beyond us. Virtually unthinkable. It does not even occur to most of us that we have the right or ability to turn back a whole technology. No precedent and no support exists for it in our culture.

In a truly democratic society, any new technology would be subject to exhaustive debate. That a society must retain the option of declining a technology—if it deems it harmful—is basic. As it is now, our spectrum of choice is limited to mere acceptance. The real decisions about technological introduction are made by only one segment of society: the corpo-

rate, based strictly on considerations of profit. This is clearly antithetical
to the democratic process.

Finally, I decided to put the idea of eliminating television into the title
of the book. My hope was that the existence of such a title—and a plausible argument to support it—would make the unthinkable thinkable, and
broaden the spectrum of possibilities. That the book has remained in wide
circulation after more than a decade suggests that there are more people
than one would expect who find such notions, if not acceptable, at least
enticing.

My only regret about the title is that it may encourage some people to
believe it's possible to separate TV from the rest of the technological system, as if it were some kind of modular unit. Television cannot be removed while everything else remains. To put it into computer terms, the
new technologies are "compatible" with each other, and combine to create
the monolith of technological society. Television has a critical role to play,
since it is the instrument that sends out the marching orders. It's the organizing tool for those who control society, the way the head communi-
cates with the body. It's a training instrument for new consciousness. To
speak of eliminating television without mentioning the other pieces of the
puzzle—computers, satellites, genetics, and corporations, among others—leaves the picture incomplete. Woven together, these technologies
comprise something beyond what any of them are individually. It is this
creature, the whole elephant, "megatech," that we must find a way of describing, making visible, and criticizing. To do this we must understand
each technology, in all of its dimensions, as well as how they all fit together.

GUILTY UNTIL PROVEN INNOCENT

In 1980 the San Francisco–based Foundation for National Progress,
which also publishes *Mother Jones* magazine, hosted a conference called
"Technology: Over the Invisible Line." Its goal was to seek a system of
standards by which to judge technologies before they envelop us and become exceedingly difficult to dislodge. The conference gave particular attention to the negative aspects of technology, since these were the least
apparent, and also the most dangerous, precisely because they were rarely
discussed. About 100 technology critics attended, and all struggled hard
to define a few categories and basic questions, such as Which segments of
society benefit from a new technology, and which segments do not? Who
gains and who loses? Does a new technology concentrate power or equal-

ize it? Does it serve democracy or not? How does a particular technology affect the human conceptual framework: what we think, how we think, and what we do know and can know? How does it affect the way we view ourselves and our relationships to each other, to the planet, and to other living creatures? What about effects on human and planetary health? Finally, all things considered, is it better or worse for the new technology to be introduced? And if we want it, at what scale of operation?

We knew this was only the barest beginning of a list, and that not every question would apply to all technologies. But our goal was to develop a holistic means of evaluation, in order to view technology from both negative and positive perspectives. We hoped this would help wrest control of the discussion from the corporations, who offer only best-case scenarios.

Of all the ideas generated at that meeting, the one that has stayed with me most powerfully was spoken by David Brower, then chairman of Friends of the Earth. "All technologies," he said, "should be assumed guilty until proven innocent." I love that idea because it emphasizes examining the hidden negative values of new technologies, in a society predisposed to see only the positive side of the story. It also assumes that a judgment could and should be made in time for a technology to be halted.

RETROSPECTIVE TECHNOLOGY ASSESSMENT: CARS AND TELEPHONES

I wonder: What if "guilty until proven innocent" had been society's rule when cars were invented? At the turn of the century the car was portrayed as a harbinger of personal freedom and democracy: private transportation that was fast, clean (no mud or manure), and independent. But what if the public had also known about the negative properties of the car? What would have been the outcome?

What if the public had been told that the car would bring with it the modern concrete city? Or that the car would contribute to cancer-causing air pollution, to noise, to solid waste problems, and to the rapid depletion of the world's resources? What if the public had been made aware that a nation of private car owners would require the virtual repaving of the entire landscape, *at public cost,* so that eventually automobile sounds would be heard even in wilderness areas? What if it had been realized that the private car would only be manufactured by a small number of giant corporations, leading to their acquiring tremendous economic and political power? That these corporations would create a new mode of mass pro-

duction—the assembly line—which in turn would cause worker alienation, injury, drug abuse, and alcoholism? That these corporations might
conspire to eliminate other means of popular transportation, including
trains? That the automobile would facilitate suburban growth, and its impact on landscapes? What if there had been an appreciation of the psychological results of the privatization of travel and the modern experience
of isolation? What if the public had been forewarned of the unprecedented need for oil that the private car would create? What if the world
had known that, because of cars, horrible wars would be fought over oil
supplies?

Would a public informed of these factors have decided to proceed with
developing the private automobile? Would the public have thought it a
good thing? If so, would there have been greater efforts to control the
overbuilding of roads, or to protect alternative transit forms? How might
the auto's impact on society have been modified as a result?

I really cannot guess whether a public so well informed, and given a
chance to vote, would have voted against cars. Perhaps not. But the public
was *not* so informed. There was never any vote, nor any real debate. And
now, only three generations later, we live in a world utterly made over to
accommodate the demands and domination of one technology.

• • •

Having raised the question as to whether our society would have chosen
the automobile if we had foreseen its consequences, a further question is
raised: Can we know a technology's effects ahead of time?

Many people argue that it's impossible to predict how a technology will
ultimately affect society. To plead this is yet another excuse for passivity.
For although the public is not informed in advance about the full impacts
of technology, there are people who know a great deal about its probable
outcomes: inventors and marketers, who go to great expense to ferret out
every nuance of implication before their products go to market.

Businesses do not like surprises. They are voracious in their appetite to
understand their products' full spectrum of commercial possibilities; large
numbers of highly paid people work full time to do just this. They also
want to know about any dire consequences, though they are certainly se-
lective about what they reveal to the public.

A marvelous series of studies financed by the National Science Foundation and managed by MIT documents the extent of private knowledge
of technology's consequences. The program, called "Retrospective Technology Assessment," investigated what the people most involved in devel-

opment predicted for various technical inventions. Sources for the studies were mostly private and corporate papers, but also included journals, public statements, and private correspondence. Among the technologies analyzed were the transoceanic cable system, the Erie Canal, the airport, water sewage technology, and (my favorite) the telephone.

Forecasting the Telephone, by Ithiel de Sola Pool, combines 300 predictions made about the telephone by business sources, scientists, and journalists. Many of the predictions were made around the time when the phone was invented in the nineteenth century; some were made as recently as the 1930s, when the phone was first becoming a popular communications instrument.

The predictions are most definitely holistic, in that they divide into such categories as effects upon the economy, learning and culture, concepts of self and the universe, and patterns of human settlement. It's tragic how few of these predictions were presented to the public.

To provide an idea of the breadth and depth of the early forecasts made about the telephone, I quote just a few examples:

- The telephone will become pervasive. . . . used by all economic classes.

- Telephone service will become a public utility.

- Telephone conversations will be recorded. [There were many references to business benefits of recording; there were also warnings about civil liberties implications.]

- The telephone will aid industrial and corporate centralization, since management at a distance will become more possible.

- The telephone will foster the growth of downtown areas. . . . create suburbs [and] advance the growth of skyscrapers. [The reasoning was that, without the telephone, businesses would not occupy skyscrapers readily because it would require too many messages to be carried by hand, overcrowding the elevators.]

- Telephone systems will require . . . directories.

- The telephone will be particularly attractive and valuable to farmers . . . will abolish loneliness, particularly for the farmer's wife. [Another prediction was that it would keep young people on the farm, which turned out not to be true.]

- The telephone will provide security despite isolation. [Note the possibilities for an advertising appeal.]

- Telephones will speed the conduct of finances.
- The telephone will increase job mobility . . . will reduce the use of hiring halls . . . will be used for shopping . . . will speed the movement of perishable goods . . . will broaden market areas . . . will reduce the travel of salesmen . . . will be used for advertising and canvassing.
- The telephone system will foster national integration . . . [and] will reduce regional dialect differences.
- The telephone will foster growth in the scale of government administration . . . will centralize the exercise of authority.
- The telephone system will speed news reporting . . . will link network radio broadcasting [creating larger networks] . . . will allow feedback for radio talk shows. [Talk shows began in the 1920s.]
- The telephone will be useful for [military] command and control . . . [and] encourage the centralization of command.
- Telephone crime will be a problem.
- Doctors will make diagnoses and give advice over the telephone.
- Overhead wires will be an eyesore . . . the increase of the telephone system will threaten the depletion of trees . . . and the depletion of copper.
- The availability of the telephone reduces the need for travel. [AT&T is running ads saying, "Paris, for only $1.29" by phone.]
- The use of women operators in manual exchanges will significantly increase economic opportunity for women.
- Young people will use the telephone more than their elders.
- The quality of letter writing will decline.
- The telephone ring will have an insistent demanding quality.
- The telephone will lower the emphasis on writing skills in schools.
- The telephone will change people's sense of distance.
- The telephone will foster impersonality.

The question raised again is this: What would the public have thought if there *had* been a systematic disclosure of all these predictions prior to the introduction of the telephone? It surely would have been useful to anticipate that telephones might stimulate the centralization of cities, the military, and corporate power. Or that they would stimulate the construction of skyscrapers. Each of these predictions, and others, represented potential major changes in the way our society operates: who is in charge, how power is distributed and accessed, how we live and work.

I don't know how a fully informed public might have voted in a referendum about the telephone. Perhaps the bias toward technological inventions created by previous decades of training would have resulted in a "yes" vote. Perhaps not. Perhaps there would have been demand to modify or control the telephone in some way. The point is that all of these predictions, and the hundreds more I have no room to list, remained privately held. There was scarcely any public discussion of these points, nor has there been since. But that the ingredients were present to fuel the debate, and that the possible implications for society were privately known, cannot be doubted. The same is true for every new technology.

VICTIMS OF TECHNOLOGY

In his book *Technology and Social Shock,* Edward W. Lawless collects 100 cases from the 1950s to the 1970s in which a new technology produced an environmental, genetic, or public health disaster. All were instances in which the most detrimental possibilities of a technology, previously unpublicized or unknown, became tragically apparent. Among his list Lawless cites thalidomide, which causes birth defects; hexachlorophene, the "wonder soap," which causes cancer; phosphate detergents, which kill fish; asbestos, which causes lung disease; polychlorinated biphenyls, which cause major health problems; herbicides, which cause malformations in newborn children; strontium 90 in mother's milk, which endangers babies; acid rain; x-radiation; oil spills; nuclear plant leaks.

Lawless reports these, then expresses his concern that American society is developing signs of ambivalence toward technological invention. He blames both government and the media for this. The agencies react only "after the Titanic has gone down," says Lawless, but he holds great hope that someday the federal Office of Technology Assessment will be given sufficient powers to intervene before disaster occurs, thereby assuring the public that technology can be controlled. As it is now, Lawless indicates, the technology assessment process is woefully inadequate: underfunded, reactive, and confining its analysis to technical problems, which sidesteps other dimensions of impact.

Lawless also criticizes the media for being reactive and for failing to provide the public with adequate information prior to the introduction of a new technology. Like government agencies, Lawless says, the media tend to get involved only when a disaster is imminent or in progress. In addition, he says, the media tends "to overdo the bizarre or the scare aspects at the beginning of a case and seldom follows through to summarize adequately the resolution of an issue."

According to Lawless, if there had been adequate assessment in advance of each new technology, and adequate media reporting, fully 60 percent of the 100 disasters cited in his book would have been averted or mitigated.

Perhaps so. But while blaming government and the media, Lawless does not mention the corporations that have the most knowledge of technology's impacts, and often act to suppress the information that will reveal negative possibilities. Such has been the case with the Dalkon Shield, Depo Provera, asbestos, PCBs, meat wrappings, pesticides and herbicides, nuclear energy, and hundreds of others, including many that Lawless himself discusses.

Author Chellis Glendinning adds many more items of technological disaster to Lawless's list. In her book *When Technology Wounds,* Glendinning interviews some fifty survivors of technology-induced health problems: soldiers ordered to witness above-ground nuclear blasts in the South Pacific and Nevada; women whose doctors gave them DES; anesthesiologists exposed to toxic chemicals; homeowners with contaminated water supplies; residents who live near toxic waste dumps; Vietnam vets exposed to Agent Orange; people caught in the flow of agricultural pesticides; and others.

Glendinning was interested in the mental and emotional effects of technology: a sense of helplessness, loss of social validation from those who do not question technology, and a loss of faith in social institutions, the government, and modern medicine. But she was surprised to find how many people are politicized by their experience. Rather than remaining victims, they become fully active, forming a new force against the excesses of technology and the blinders that have been placed on all of us. "At a time when the life-support systems of our biosphere are being wantonly destroyed by modern technologies," she says, "we find a precious and unexpected resource in the very people who have been technology's early victims. And their numbers are growing.

"When you add up the victims of birth-control systems, radiation, asbestos, smog, pesticides, toxics, and a thousand other technologies," Glendinning told me, "the numbers you get are in the millions. It reveals the scale of the deal that has been made by our society—without asking us—

trading off our health for the economic health of corporations." Glendinning proposes creating a new international organization, a kind of union of technology victims, or as she would rather think of it, "technology survivors, who will begin to look at technology for the scale of its impact and who organize to deal with the profound questions about technology's direction."

TEN RECOMMENDED ATTITUDES
ABOUT TECHNOLOGY

Now we are about to move into a new technological age, the brave new world of space colonies, laser weapons and communications, genetic engineering, robotics, and so on. We are already hearing familiar-sounding claims that this new generation of technologies will finally deliver that brighter, more glorious future. Part II of this book will present detailed analyses of some of these new technologies as well as some of the ones that are already upon us. Meanwhile, I offer here a little list of reminders that I keep pinned above my own desk. They help me maintain appropriate attitudes to protect against the one-sided information onslaught. Perhaps they'll be useful to you.

1. Since most of what we are told about new technology comes from its proponents, be deeply skeptical of all claims.

2. Assume all technology "guilty until proven innocent."

3. Eschew the idea that technology is neutral or "value free." Every technology has *inherent and identifiable* social, political, and environmental consequences.

4. The fact that technology has a natural flash and appeal is meaningless. Negative attributes are slow to emerge.

5. Never judge a technology by the way it benefits you personally. Seek a holistic view of its impacts. The operative question is not whether it benefits you, but who benefits most? And to what end?

6. Keep in mind that an individual technology is only one piece of a larger web of technologies, "megatechnology." The operative question here is how the individual technology fits the larger one.

7. Make distinctions between technologies that primarily serve the individual or the small community (e.g., solar energy) and those that op-

erate on a scale outside of community control (e.g., nuclear energy). The latter kind is the major problem of the day.

8. When it is argued that the benefits of the technological lifeway are worthwhile despite harmful outcomes, recall that Lewis Mumford referred to these alleged benefits as "bribery." Cite the figures about crime, suicide, alienation, drug abuse, as well as environmental and cultural degradation.

9. Do not accept the homily that "once the genie is out of the bottle you cannot put it back," or that rejecting a technology is impossible. Such attitudes induce passivity and confirm victimization.

10. In thinking about technology within the present climate of technological worship, emphasize the negative. This brings balance. Negativity is positive.

PART II

THE INEVITABLE
DIRECTION OF
MEGATECHNOLOGY

*O*UR ASSUMPTION OF *technology's beneficence, combined with our passivity to its advance, has permitted certain technological forms to expand their scale of impact, and to interlock and merge with one another. Together, they are forming something new, almost as if they were living cells; they are becoming a single technical-economic web encircling the planet,* megatechnology. *Among the key components of this invisible apparatus are computers, television, satellites, corporations and banks, space technology, genetics, and the alarming new "postbiological" machinery: nanotechnology and robotics. Holistic critiques reveal the role of each in the big picture, as well as the inevitable direction of the whole process.*

4

SEVEN NEGATIVE POINTS
ABOUT COMPUTERS

*W*ITHOUT COMPUTERS, THE megatechnological age simply would not happen. Computers are basic to every new technical innovation, whether in communications, the military, genetics, transportation, automation, or multinational corporate activity.

Because of this universality of applications and implications, computers have been celebrated more than any technology since electricity. Educators, corporate leaders, presidential candidates, futurists, and the media sing a unified chorus of praise.

The situation is ludicrous. Computer technology has sprung us headlong into an entirely new existence, one that will permanently affect our lives and the lives of our children and grandchildren. It will speed up profound changes on the planet, yet there is no meaningful debate about it, no ferment, no critical analysis of the consequences. As usual, the major beneficiaries are permitted to define the parameters of our understanding.

• • •

During 1988 alone, the microcomputer industry spent more than one billion dollars in advertising (most of it on television). You have only to watch your TV tonight to be repeatedly told that neither you, your business, nor your child can survive the future without computers. These messages from the microcomputer industry are in addition to those from other industries in praise of computers. Auto commercials promote their computerized features. Military recruitment ads trumpet the high-technology training the military offers: "High technology is taking over the world/Keep up with it or be left behind/Be all you can be/Join the Army." And if anyone failed to get the high-tech message from the ads, TV news images of the Iraq-U.S. war left no doubt about the glamor of computerized weaponry.

Watches, telephones, stereo equipment, and instruments of all kinds boast of their digital operation. I know one chief executive of a wilderness travel company who advertises the company's "data bank" of wilderness experiences.

Even environmentalists have failed to maintain the usual skepticism about corporate claims, accepting the apparent short-run benefits of computers without grasping that computers actually steer society in a direction that *contradicts* environmental goals.

And writers! I must have been asked two dozen times how I can say that computers are negative when they are so useful to writers. They save time and drudgery, they rearrange, they spell, they sort information, and you can play some fun video games with them, too. But are any of those features really the point?

Unfortunately, the major question about computers is not whether they serve you or your organization or your business well. I wish it were so simple to just take this personal view. We must look at the totality of how computers affect society, and life on Earth. We need to dredge each dimension of their impact and put it all together into one picture before we can judge their existence as beneficial or harmful.

This chapter, therefore, is an attempt at a holistic analysis of computers, divided into seven categories: 1) pollution and health, 2) employment, 3) quantification and conceptual change, 4) surveillance, 5) the rate of acceleration, 6) centralization, and 7) the worst-case scenario: automatic computer warfare.

I. POLLUTION AND HEALTH

Since its birth, the microelectronics industry has enjoyed a reputation as something apart from, better than, and cleaner than the old smokestack industries. Maybe this reputation goes with the neat design of the computers themselves, or maybe it's that the primary product is information rather than turbines or ball bearings. Perhaps it's the kind of people drawn to high-tech management, who reflect a New Age, "can-do," cutting-edge self-confidence; who exude the idea that "we are the future." Or maybe as my friend Ellen Weis of the Museum of Modern Mythology believes, it's the silence of the computers that sustains this squeaky-clean image. "Everything seems to happen by magic," says Ellen. "No moving parts."

Anyway, this reputation is not deserved. Computers are not the "free lunch" they were promised to be. Health and environmental problems are visible in the communities in which the machines are built, among the workers who build them, and among the people who use them on the job.

• • •

Computer manufacturing employs millions of gallons of acids and solvents that are eventually disposed of at toxic dumps. In communities where computers are manufactured, serious problems have arisen. In Silicon Valley, California, for example, high concentrations of trichloroethylene, (a solvent that the EPA has called carcinogenic) have seeped into the drinking water. At one point, computer manufacturers, while not admitting guilt, passed out truckloads of bottled water in the affected communities. The Environmental Protection Agency has identified eighty similar chemical spill sites associated with computer manufacturing, and expects the problem to escalate.

Suburban communities affected by toxic waste have been able to organize to mitigate the problems. But workers who manufacture computers and who have suffered health problems have been less effective. This is because most computer factory workers are nonunion and many are non-English-speaking and undocumented. So they have a hard time telling their story to management and/or the press. Lately, however, workers have succeeded in publicizing high rates of miscarriages and reproductive disorders, as well as hair loss, chronic asthma, and other conditions apparently resulting from exposure to toxic chemicals and gasses involved in manufacturing.

According to attorney Ted Smith of the Silicon Valley Toxics Coalition, "Workers and the general population are being exposed to the most deadly chemicals that have ever been synthesized." And Dr. Joseph La Don, chief of the Division of Occupational and Environmental Medicine at the University of California, San Francisco, has said, "The computer industry has an incidence of occupational illness more than three times that of the average manufacturing industry." Many companies have responded to such statements by moving manufacturing abroad to Korea and Southeast Asia, where workers are less informed and can be paid less, too.

Perhaps the most significant health problems associated with computers concern their use in the office or at home. If growing suspicions about the medical effects of personal computers are verified, tens of millions of people could be affected, and the orderly march of computers into every nook of American commercial and personal life will be slowed considerably.

There have been medical reports for many years about complaints such as fatigue, eye strain, migraines, cataracts, and, among pregnant women who use VDTs (video display terminals), miscarriages, birth defects, premature births, and infant deaths. At first it was not believed that computers could have such effects. Recent research, however, has concentrated on computer-related radiation. VDTs generate a range of electromagnetic radiation, from X-ray, ultraviolet, and infrared, to low-frequency (LF), very-low-frequency (VLF), and extra-low-frequency (ELF) wavelengths.

At one time it was believed that these low-frequency radiations were incapable of causing harm to human beings, but it has now been shown that people are far more sensitive to any radiation than previously believed, and that causal relationships are beginning to emerge. A large medical literature has now developed in the field to which, unfortunately, I cannot give justice in these pages. (For a very thorough overview, however, I refer you to Paul Brodeur's brilliant three-part series, "The Annals of Radiation," in the June 1989 *New Yorker* or his book, *Currents of Death*.)

Meanwhile, I will say this: The idea that computers are cleaner than other industrial products is wrong, and dangerous. Just as this book goes to press, the city of San Francisco has become the first to acknowledge this fact by creating some minimal standards for safer use of VDTs in the workplace. Hopefully, others will follow with more comprehensive rules. But, such new standards notwithstanding, if I were a woman contemplating having children, I would not work at a computer terminal.

2. EMPLOYMENT

At the 1940 World's Fair, American industry promised that computers and automation would eliminate toil, and thus free us to pursue higher goals. In the 1980s industry said computers would open new careers and new kinds of industry and would ease the burden of office workers. In reality, these claims are just advertising pitches attuned to the popular concerns of the moment. What automation and computerization actually do achieve is the elimination of jobs, which liberates human beings to stand in unemployment lines.

The utopian vision of a work-free society, in which machines do most of the work while all the humans relax, could only be realized if the economic benefits of automation and computerization were somehow shared by the workers. It would take a revolution to make this happen. For in capitalist society, the benefits are disproportionately allotted to the people who own the machines. Computers allow them to get the same job done with fewer pesky humans demanding increased wages, job safety, and health insurance. As my friend Jack Edelson, who runs a small manufacturing business in San Francisco, told me, "The worst thing about computers is that they are eliminating the middle class. Blue-collar workers are losing their jobs to robots; they can't afford to buy houses anymore. And we're soon going to be a country with more rich people and a lot more poor people. Big industry says automation is going to create jobs, but that's baloney. There are new jobs around, but they're at McDonald's at minimum wage."

As for easing the burden for office workers, that is hardly an open-and-shut case. Computers *have* eased the burden for managers, because the technology facilitates a level of on-the-job surveillance that makes personal observation virtually unnecessary.

A friend of my son Kai works as a 411-information operator for Pacific Bell. He told me about the experience: "The computer knows everything. It records the minute I punch in, it knows how long I take for each call, it knows how many calls I handle per hour, how long I take on my break, and exactly when I leave. I am supposed to average under eighteen seconds per call, and achieve a certain number of calls per day. Everything I do is reported to my supervisor on his computer, and if I've missed my numbers I get a written warning. I rarely see the guy. I am not allowed to be one minute late for work, ever, or to take longer than exactly fifteen minutes for coffee. It's intense. It's me and the computer all day. I'm telling you, at the end of the day I am wiped out. Working with computers is the coal mining of the nineties."

Diana Roose, who is research director of the National Association of Working Women (9 to 5), told me: "Since the introduction of the computer into office work, job design for secretaries has changed in negative ways. The typing part gets easier, but workers hate many aspects of these machines. . . . For the first time, secretaries have to deal with production quotas. Performance on the job is evaluated much more in strictly objective terms. It used to be that an office worker would also be evaluated for her personal, human contribution of energy and ideas. Now there is hardly any variety in office work. The jobs are dead-ended, and because the human connection is eliminated, jobs are less secure. Some people are calling office work the electronic assembly line."

3. QUANTIFICATION AND CONCEPTUAL CHANGE

The July 1984 issue of *New Age Journal* featured a story by R. H. Ring called "The Computerized Forest," which lamented the conceptual changes among U.S. Forest Service workers who are now asked to do their jobs mainly via computers. The entire forest system, says Ring, has been divided into "management units" containing "habitat capacity" models and "maximum sustainable yield" computations, all of which reduce the needs of species, and the workers' understanding of them, to quantified formulas.

Computers were introduced into forest management, like everywhere else, for the sake of "efficiency," the implication being that this would help preserve nature. In fact, the objective was to more efficiently account for forest *resources*—trees, animals, water, minerals—and to better develop them as part of commodity society. A former head of the Forest Service, John Crowell (who also formerly worked for Louisiana Pacific) said candidly that he favored "thinking of the natural world in terms of 'commodities' rather than 'amenities.'" So now the Flathead Forest in Montana has a planned "output" of 200 grizzly bears. And old-growth forest is called "accumulated capital."

As Ring wrote, "The ecosystem is not so easily reduced to computerized bytes. The needs of most wildlife species, their interrelationships and dependencies on their forest habitats, are not completely understood."

It ought to go without saying that certain elements of forests resist objectification: the unnameable feelings and moods, the subtle relationships. At one time, according to Ring, forest managers learned these more subtle dimensions of forest life by direct experience—by physically being out in the woods—and they integrated what they learned into their planning. But as management goals changed from preservation to development, the tools changed as well, and with those tools changed the concepts and the job. Ring reports that now Forest Service workers themselves are changing; the new breed does not come to the task with a basic loyalty to and personal involvement with the land. They are more concerned with production goals and budgets.

Of course, computers cannot be blamed for this change in direction for forest management. But they have made possible a new information system and an accelerated pace of development, which accommodates the desires of the prime movers in our society. Meanwhile, with nuances, moods, and personal observations subtracted from the information model—the very elements by which humans and nature have traditionally communicated with one another—the end result is passionlessness: a net loss in intimacy with, caring for, and love of nature. Workers who are not comfortable with this new mode of reckoning leave the Service, and are replaced with workers who don't mind the change.

The government of Canada has been as aggressive as the United States in introducing quantified, computerized resource management. At a recent conference of Circumpolar Peoples (Inuit and Indians) of the far north, the Canadian government announced a new initiative for bringing computers and computer training to native resource managers. The intention was ostensibly to be helpful, but the net result will be to destroy traditional resource management systems, and, perhaps along with that, native resistance to large-scale exploitation. The assumption is that objective data of the sort that computers emphasize will improve upon methods natives have employed for millennia.

Computers are actually antithetical to information sources that traditional societies have used: personal observation, sensory interaction, historical and geographic contexts, and teachings about the human-wildlife relationship that have been passed down from previous generations. These sources offer a broader spectrum than mere numerical data, and recent studies have shown them to be just as effective. The viability of native economic practices will be discussed at length in Chapter 14, but I want to suggest here what will be lost if computers take over the management of native peoples' resources.

• • •

Canadian anthropologist H. A. Feit, of McMaster University, Ontario, speaking at the 1986 Symposium of the Alberta Society of Professional Biologists, described the resource management methods of the Waswanipi Cree of northern Ontario. Their methods, used for thousands of years as they are today, are based on a philosophical premise of reciprocity among humans and animals. But they also lead to highly efficient management and accounting:

> In the culturally constructed world of the Waswanipi, the animals, the winds and many other phenomena are thought of as being "like persons," in that they act intelligently and have wills and idiosyncracies, and understand and are understood by people. Causality in the Waswanipi world is not mechanical or biological, it is personal. . . .

Waswanipi hunters say that they only catch an animal when the animal is given to them. They say that in winter it is the spirits, especially the north wind, and the animals' spirits themselves which *give* animals to the hunters and their families so that they will have what they need to live and survive. . . . The body of the animal a hunter receives nourishes him, but the soul returns to be reborn again, so that when men and animals are in balance, the animals are killed but not diminished, and both men and animals survive. . . . In return for the gifts, the hunter has obligations to the animals and the spirits to act responsibly, to use what is given completely, and to act respectfully towards the bodies and souls of the animals. . . . It is expected that men will kill animals swiftly, and avoid causing them undue suffering . . . not to kill more than he is given, not to kill animals for fun or self-aggrandizement.

Apparently, for thousands of years, the Waswanipi have divided their territory into hunting regions, ranging in size from 250 to 1,500 square kilometers. For each territory, an elder is appointed as steward, based on his personal "ties to spirits and the land, within a system of communal rights," says Feit. "The stewards, by repeatedly returning to the same tracts of land, have the opportunity to observe and assess the condition of the game populations . . . Stewards generally have the right and obligation to decide whether a hunting territory should be used for harvesting of big game and fur-bearers during any year, and they allocate [land] to hunters who do not have their own. They can thus decide how many hunters will use a territory, and they can indicate to those who do, how many of various kinds of game animals they may harvest. . . . their supervision is usually respected."

Feit reports that the stewards receive detailed reports from hunters returning from the fields on what has been caught and what has been seen:

Mature hunters can usually state whether there are more beaver colonies now than there were a year ago, or five years ago, or when the hunter's first child was born, possibly thirty years before. . . . They do not usually remember exact numbers but report relative quantities or trends. Hunters can often comment on whether the number of beavers per colony has been going up or down, on whether females are having more or fewer young per year; on trends in the frequency of different age/size categories, on changes in "shyness" to traps, on changes in the rates of wolves and other predation, and on changes in forest composition, regeneration, and the availability of food for beaver.

All of this is done without computers. The point is this: Given the detailed field-observation practices of native peoples, of whom the Waswanipi Cree are only one example, computer-based systems would probably not produce numbers much different from present estimates. (In fact, Dr. Feit gave examples of comparative research that proved this point.) What computers *would* achieve is a direct assault on an age-old system of human and animal relationships that is at the very heart of native cultures and that underlies the basic philosophical, social, and economic systems of Indian societies. Eventually, the Inuit, Indian, and other native groups who are given computers will begin to conceptualize nature in the objective terms used by Western development interests ("sustainable yield," "animal units"), while the more powerful mythical, sensory, and spiritual outlook that has informed and sustained native cultures for millennia is sacrificed. In the end, this destroys Indian culture and leads to overdevelopment.

• • •

What do you think about the computer takeover in schools? Computer fever is sweeping through the educational establishment. Computer manufacturers are successfully convincing school systems that they cannot get along without them. Many companies are supplying free computers to classrooms, with the eventual goal that each of fifty million high school and college kids will own a personal computer. The long-run potential for the computer industry of having every kid computer trained is obvious.

"Computer literacy" is already required in many colleges and high schools. Computers are replacing teachers and teaching functions. And they are changing the content of the information learned in schools, from the more subtle information that goes with the traditional teacher-student relationship, to the more hard-edged, data-based objective content that goes with the machine-user relationship. It has happened so quickly that there has been little systematic evaluation of what computers do that teachers don't, or vice versa. But it already has enabled school systems to get along with fewer teachers.

Ironically, one of the highly praised aspects of computers in schools has been its "personal" quality. The computer gives the assignment, the student responds; when all goes well, the computer gives "user-friendly" praise and encouragement. The student feels rewarded. Computer advocates say teachers are often too busy to be that "personal." Computers are also infinitely patient, never tiring of working with slow learners. And when completing, say, repetitive drills in math or science, the machine can advance students to new levels and keep the process going, even when there may not be a teacher on the same floor of the building.

The questions are these: What sort of person does this educational process produce? And what sort of knowledge is attained? Marian Kester, writing in the *Toronto Globe,* put it this way: "If children are separated from their parents by hours of TV, from their playmates by video games, and from their teachers by teaching machines, where are they supposed to learn to be human?"

The next question is: Do computers make kids smarter?

Seymour Papert of MIT has said that learning computer programming leads to "conceptually clear thinking," and that children who do so can better deal with complex problems elsewhere. But Joseph Menosky, writing in *Science* magazine, disagrees. He reports that Roy Pea of the Bank Street College of Education tested kids who had learned LOGO, the computer language from MIT, to see if those kids organized their work better or more clearly.

"According to Pea," said Menosky, "the children displayed 'production without comprehension.' In other words . . . children can seem to understand while only going through the motions. This is consistent with studies of college computer science majors with thousands of hours of programming who yet fail to understand the priciples that underlie even the brief programs. These studies raise serious doubts about the sweeping claims made for the cognitive benefits of learning to program."

I worry that the increased use of computers in education will produce three results:

First of all, as with the Inuit and the Forest Service workers, objective, linear knowledge will begin to dominate while other, more subtle forms will recede. Like the wilderness, which has disappeared from the landscape and from our minds, many ways of thinking will also disappear.

Second, as computers replace teachers, the certainty of computer programs will replace the subtlety of student-teacher interaction. I am not saying that all teachers are better than computers for all subjects at all times. It's just that something goes on among humans that is definitely not present in human-machine relationships.

Third, replacing teachers with computers will create an ominous uniformity of knowledge. Corporations already provide a vast amount of "educational materials" to schools; when they also provide the computer programs that kids interact with, especially in the absence of a mitigating human presence, they pave the way to an officially sanctioned, unified field of knowledge. That field will be narrower than at present (though perhaps deeper in a few areas, such as science), and it will be consistent with corporate values.

4. SURVEILLANCE

In terms of everyday life, the greatest danger of computers may be the level of surveillance they make possible. Computers have enabled the major institutions of our society—corporations, government agencies, the police, the military—to keep records well beyond what was previously possible. *New York Times* reporter David Burnham's splendid book *The Rise of the Computer State* covers this subject so thoroughly that I will devote only a few paragraphs here to summarizing it.

Burnham offers the example of TRW Corporation, which holds in its computers the credit records of 120 million Americans. These reveal where you bank, how much money you have, what your income is, how much you owe, what you own, where you shop, how much you spend, who your dependents are, whether or not you have a criminal record, how well you pay bills, where you work and live, your telephone number, your social security number, and names of the rest of your family.

The Medical Information Bureau has files on about 20 million people. Metromail, a direct-mail ad agency, has files on about 74 million Americans. AT&T has a comparable number.

Burnham acknowledges that the quantity of contemporary record keeping could have been managed before the invention of computers, but as a practical matter, it would have been absurd to attempt it. The collection process would have taken many times longer than it does now, and once collected, information retrieval would be extremely difficult, since it would involve an incredible amount of manual searching. "Computerization has now greatly reduced the economic disincentive to [gather and] inspect the files," says Burnham. So now the data *is* gathered.

The federal government is not to be outdone by the private sector. Every year government officials collect about four billion separate records about the people of the United States—an average of seventeen records per person. Most of these files are held by the FBI, CIA, and NSA, which share interlocking networks with local police and private security agencies. You and your organization are surely included.

What's more, only one or two remaining laws restrict these police and government agency networks from interlocking their data with your social security file, your phone number, your zip code, your IRS records, your employer, your bank accounts, your insurance, and all the private records that are now held by corporations. And soon, the interlock will be able to include your own dear home computer, the one that makes you "free."

Thus far, civil libertarians have held the line against meshing all these identification systems into one omniscient central computer file. But these are the years that people get elected president for trashing the ACLU.

5. THE RATE OF ACCELERATION

In recent years, there has been resistance to the idea that bigger is necessarily better. People like Leopold Kohr and E. F. Schumacher, as well as movements like the Greens and Bioregionalism, have argued that the sheer size and scale of the economies and technologies of modern countries create insurmountable organizational problems, and lead to alienation among people, hostilities among countries, and destruction of the environment. But if *small* is beautiful, as the cry goes, what about *slow*? Few people have noted that speed is an important dimension of scale.

Today's largest institutions—the military, corporations, governments, banks—can only be as large and as globally far-reaching as they are able to quickly communicate mind-boggling amounts of data among their diverse branches. Computers, combined with satellite telecommunications, have shattered the now-obsolete physical limits of size. An institution can now spread itself outward to encompass the entire planet. National boundaries are anomalies.

As computers have accelerated and geographically broadened the information cycle within large institutions, human beings have had to move quickly to keep up. And as institutions and people have sped up economic activity—satellite mapping of resources, entry into previously untouched areas, instantaneous movements of funds, development of infrastructures—the face of the planet has been changing more rapidly than ever before. Corporate activity accelerates, impact on the planet accelerates, and human activity does as well. Is this good?

• • •

In our society, speed is celebrated as if it were a virtue in itself. And yet as far as most human beings are concerned, the acceleration of the information cycle has only inundated us with an unprecedented amount of data, most of which is unusable in any practical sense. The true result has been an increase in human anxiety, as we try to keep up with the growing stream of information. Our nervous systems experience the acceleration more than our intellects do. It's as if we were all caught at a socially approved video game, where the information on the screen comes faster and faster as we try earnestly to keep up.

Video games are in fact a great example of this. They are often defended with such claims as "they speed up hand-eye coordination." Commercial video game parlors effectively claim this when defending against parents' groups that seek to ban them from a neighborhood. But *why* is it good to speed up hand-eye coordination? The only real benefit would be to improve one's basketball skills, or to prepare for the next sped-up video game. (Ronald Reagan praised video games as good training for the new generation of bomber pilots, like those who flew in Iraq, whose instruments resemble video games.)

For 400,000 generations human hand-eye coordination was attuned to an environment operating at what you might call natural speed. Everything that human beings had to deal with moved at speeds appropriate to our abilities. It had to be that way in order for our species to survive; species need to keep up with the tasks at hand.

With the Industrial Revolution, many things began moving at mechanical speeds. As the natural environment was paved over, and as human life moved into human-made environments, the natural rhythms of our reactions gave way to industrial rhythms. We learned to interact with mechanical speeds, as assembly-line workers and most auto drivers know. Now that machines move at electronic speeds, the wheel of activity turns even faster, with us on it.

Computer video games *are* good training for the faster world. When we play a video game, our goal is to merge with the computer program. The electronic symbols on the screen enter our brain, pass through our nervous system, and stimulate the fight-or-flight reaction that still lives within us and that expresses itself here through our hands. Very little thinking is needed or used. The object is to respond *without* thought, instantly.

A skillful video-game player stimulates the computer program to go faster, and as the cycle (computer program to nervous system to hands to machine to computer program) speeds up, the player and the machine become connected in one fluid cycle; aspects of each other. Over time, and with practice, the abilities of the human being develop to approximate the computer program. Evolution is furthered by this sort of interaction, but this is a notably new form of evolutionary process. Where evolution once described an interaction between humans and nature, evolution now takes place between humans and human artifacts. We coevolve with the environment *we* have created; we coevolve with our machines, with ourselves. It's a kind of in-breeding that confirms that nature is irrelevant to us.

Video games and computers accelerate a process that had already been stimulated by a generation of television viewing. Most people think of TV viewing as passive—which it is—while video games and computers are interactive. But the hyperactivity of TV imagery, while pacifying the brain, simultaneously speeds up the nervous system. TV makes us both dumb and speedy. In the end, television viewing just prepares us for the appropriate mental state for video games and computer fixation. And together, the technologies combine to produce a generation of people too sped up to attune themselves to slower, natural, primordial rhythms.

Video games. Television. Computers. Walkmans. Kids carrying those big radios down the street. And the *street*. And the assembly line. And the freeway. They are all part of an acceleration process that spins our lives faster and faster, making it seem more exciting when actually it is only hyperactive.

• • •

The prevailing paradigm that speed is inherently good benefits some elements of society more than it does others. Those who benefit most are the largest institutions, which can translate speed of transactions and travel directly into money and power. For most of the rest of the world, the emphasis on acceleration is harmful. It is surely harmful for workers. It is harmful for relationships among people. It creates anxiety. And it has very important ramifications for the survival of diverse non-Western cultures.

Indigenous peoples tend to operate in small-scale economic communities, by collective processes, with all decisions made by consensus. This presupposes a high degree of intimacy among the people of the community. Since time is one of several luxuries that indigenous peoples enjoy more readily than we do, communications are often characterized by deliberate slowness; people are not in a hurry. They don't believe in accomplishing more in less time, because there is sufficient time to accomplish what needs to be done. They revel in the personal engagement that *not* rushing allows. When things do have to get done, they get done by the group acting in concert.

In the past as in the present, the push of Western invading cultures has been to organize life along entirely different lines—clock time, schedules, goals—in order to increase surplus production. This, in itself, threatens the survival of non-Western cultures since it changes the people and their traditional institutions.

I thought of all this while reading an article in the October 1984 isssue of *Development Forum,* titled "Worshipping a False God," by Ken Darrow and Michael Saxenian. The authors have devoted much of their lives to bringing small-scale technology to villages in some of the world's poorest countries. The article reports on the computer craze —the same craze that has overtaken American school systems—that has taken hold among international development agencies and staffers who advocate computer-satellite linkups for rural communities where technical information is scarce. According to Saxenian and Darrow, the assumption goes that computers will offer "unprecedented low-cost instantaneous communications" for village development, thus solving their "technical information needs." The authors conclude that this assumption is "dangerous nonsense," and make the following points:

- "In a poor country, using a microcomputer linked by satellite to an information system half-way round the world . . . is absurd." It is technological overkill. Most poor countries need much simpler technologies, such as typewriters, reference books, hand tools, bikes, tape recorders.

- Finding skilled repairers of computers is nearly impossible, forcing "many local groups to purchase complete back-up computers, which can be cannibalized for parts."

- "The telephone system already offers instantaneous low-cost communication. . . . The unique advantages of computerized networks are few and expensive. Do you really want to call your mother on a computer?"

6. CENTRALIZATION

I recently attended a National Bioregional Congress; 250 people working toward the disintegration of central political power in favor of local control, economic self-sufficiency, and small-scale nature-based principles—Green principles. Several participants publicly advocated a role for computers in building networks among the bioregions, thereby facilitating rapid exchanges of information. Although it was acknowledged this might create some centralization, it was also argued that computers are a "neutral tool" that could help groups whose goals are anathema to the large institutions that invented them and that dominate their application. This is a *hot idea*: we take their invention and use a kind of jiujitsu to turn it against its creators. Tempting, but it fails to reckon with the intrinsic aspects of computers that will inevitably result in centralization.

The issue is confused at the outset by the fact that computers have the look of a small-scale democratic technology. People have them at home and find them empowering for themselves and their organizations. They are helpful in many ways and offer considerable personal control, unlike non-yielding technologies like television. Small social and political groups find computers valuable for information storage, networking, processing mailing lists, preparing clean copy, maintaining membership lists, keeping accounts, and so on. Yet all this begs the question. The real issue is not whether computers can benefit you or your group; the question is who benefits most from the existence of computers in society? The answer suggests that, for all of their small-scale benefits, the largest institutions have far more to gain, and they know it.

The computer invasion was not engineered by a group of high-minded technological do-gooders determined to further democracy. Though computers were invented in the 1920s, it was the American and British military that first put them to serious use, as guidance systems for missiles during World War II. Two decades later, IBM converted the technology to big-business uses. It wasn't until the 1970s that Atari and Apple launched the campaigns to put a computer in every home and schoolroom. Do-gooders didn't hit a plastic key until the mid-1970s, when the military and the large corporations had already integrated them deeply into their operations, with great benefit and greater geographical reach for centralized operations.

Computer technology is an intrinsic part of an advanced technical infrastructure; computers could only have emerged from a society already very far down a technical pathway. They are very costly to manufacture, they are intricately connected to centralized telephone systems, and some of their optimum uses, such as high-speed computation and satellite mapping of resources, are so costly that they are only available to the largest institutions.

Computers serve the economies of scale in the same way as other recently developed technologies, such as satellite communications, mechanical agriculture, robotics, pesticides. The larger an enterprise, the more computers it can afford. What's more, the computers will be more sophisticated, operated by better-trained staff, and have more interfacings among widely dispersed regions than in smaller institutions. As a result, larger businesses gain a comparative advantage. Though small businesses benefit from using computers, larger institutions benefit far more, since the scale and complexity and reach of operations that computers facilitate require much greater financial resources. Smaller businesses would actually be better off if computers had not been invented, since they are essentially one more tool that large businesses can use better.

Consider the role of computers for international banks and conglomerates. Moving money instantaneously from one market to another, feeding development here and then there, the multinational institutions of today could simply not operate as they do without computers in a satellite linkup. Computers have enabled these institutions to suddenly expand into a dimension never before possible. They are beyond multinational now; they are truly global. The accelerated pace at which forests are felled in Indonesia and Borneo, oceans are mined in the Pacific, and dams are built throughout the world, reflects the increased ability of corporations to operate from a central management and still influence daily activities in all corners of the planet.

It is profoundly naive for people who work to prevent planetary devastation to speak of the computer as if it were neutral; as if it were as useful for decentralization as it is to centralized development interests. Large institutions that seek the latter benefit far more than the do-gooders who plan to use computers for a high-tech jiujitsu. It is only misunderstanding the big picture, and a certain conceit, that allows us to think any other way. Environmentalists, bioregionalists, and other progressive activists would be better off realizing that for all the little benefits they offer us, computers set our movements back. We ought to begin dealing with them as an urgent environmental and political issue in themselves.

7. WORST-CASE SCENARIO: AUTOMATIC COMPUTER WARFARE

It was possible to annihilate the world before the invention of computers, but it was far more difficult and much less likely. The invention of the computer instantly changed the speed at which war could be waged, the scale of its impact, and the quantity of destruction.

Computer technology has already produced an unprecedented degree of military centralization. Generals sitting in an underground war room somewhere outside Washington can, in one moment, observe the position and readiness of all U.S. military hardware, and a high percentage of Soviet hardware, around the globe. Soviet generals outside Moscow can do likewise.

From military central it is also possible to fire missiles and track their progress via computerized displays not unlike those depicted in films like *War Games*. In fact, managing warfare now resembles playing a giant video game—following electronic blips on a massive screen—abstract, cerebral, removed from direct involvement. One could argue that this manner of waging war makes war more likely, since it separates humans from the consequences of their actions, unlike ground action, where you put bayonets through people's bodies and watched them bleed.

When enemy forces are reduced to blips on a video screen, impossible to verify by direct observation, there is a far greater chance of error. In one eighteen-month period ending June 30, 1980, U.S. strategic forces experienced 151 "false alarms," five of which were significant enough to put our forces on "alert" status. In several of these cases, the "alert" was in response to flights of birds. In one case, it was the rising moon.

This problem of computer error in a military context is one of the main concerns of Computer Professionals for Social Responsibility (CPSR), a group of Silicon Valley corporate executives, programmers, and engineers who are concerned about the military potentials of computers.

According to CPSR, "In all but the simplest computer programs, hidden design flaws can persist, sometimes for years, even though the system appears to work perfectly. . . . There exist no known methods for eliminating this uncertainty in complex computer programs. . . . No amount of testing under simulated conditions can replace the testing that comes from embedding the system in the actual environment for which it was designed [in this case, nuclear war]. . . . But all experience with complex computer systems indicates that it is the circumstances that we totally fail to anticipate that cause the serious problems."

CPSR argues that computer error can only be mitigated by human intervention. What makes the current military-computer collaboration so terrifying is that the computers have reduced the time available for decision-making to the point where it is now virtually automatic; humans are nearly out of the loop.

• • •

It will be informative to compare the situation in the 1940s with that of today. Even after the invention of atomic bombs, worldwide destruction was unlikely because of the amount of time and the degree of human participation that remained intrinsic to the process. Back then, bombers had to be physically loaded and then flown enormous distances at relatively slow speeds to their targets. The process took many hours, which allowed considerable time for circumstances to be altered. In addition, each bomb was carried by a group of human beings, rather than being fired automatically by a central button. Even if one bomb dropped, there might still be time to call things off before all the bombs dropped; the whole system did not hang on an irretrievable automatic "Go."

The invention of computers, which in turn made advanced rocketry possible, drastically shortened the time between the decision to act—to "push the button"—and the final outcome. Today, warheads do not fly in creaky bombers, but on computer-guided missiles, targeted and shot into space at astounding speed from military-computer-central. And now there's the incentive to fire *all* missiles at once, since an enemy can react so quickly. If war starts, total destruction is not only possible but likely.

U.S. and Soviet missiles are presently six minutes from each other's border. If U.S. computers suggest that an enemy attack is underway, six minutes are available to verify the accuracy of the data, locate and inform the president, and then, in the time remaining, for the president to make a decision. In reality, there would be no time to carefully consider options; the decision would be preplanned. In modern computerized warfare, human involvement becomes so proscribed at the most critical moments as to be effectively meaningless.

In recognizing the difficulty of human decision-making in modern warfare, we hear talk of "launch on warning" (launching missiles instantly at the first computer warning) as a viable policy. The technical capacity is already in place for people to be dropped out of the decision loop, leaving us with automatic warfare: our comptuer program versus theirs. So what is called nuclear war is not that at all; it is really microelectronic war, software war. And the arms race has become a battle of computer programmers seeking to gain an edge in a war that, when fought, will happen automatically with no people involved—until the hardware starts landing on them.

● ● ●

On October 28, 1983, the Defense Advance Research Projects Agency, a division of the U.S. Department of Defense, issued a document called the "Strategic Computing Plan." The SCP was a five-year, $600,000,000 program to develop a new generation of military applications for computers. The proposal included a thousand-fold increase in computing power and an emphasis on artificial intelligence. It envisioned "completely autonomous land, sea, and air vehicles capable of complex, far-ranging reconnaissance and attack missions." These vehicles would have human abilities, such as sight, speech, understanding natural language, and automated reasoning. The Strategic Computing Plan promoted the view that the human element in many critical decision-making instances could be largely or totally replaced by machines. In describing its "pilot's associate," for example, SCP argues that pilots are "regularly overwhelmed by the quantity of incoming data and communications on which they must base life-or-death decisions." Now the machine will do it. All that the pilot will do is take off and land.

The Computer Professionals for Social Responsibility has published an analysis of the Strategic Computing Plan. CPSR notes that the plan itself acknowledges certain problems, as expressed in this quote:

Improvements in the speed and range of weapons have increased the rate at which battles unfold, resulting in a proliferation of computers to aid in information flow and decision-making at all levels of military organization. A countervailing effect on this trend is the rapidly decreasing predictability of military situations. . . . Commanders remain particularly concerned about the role that autonomous systems would play during the transition from peace to hostilities when rules of engagement may be altered quickly. An extremely stressing example of such a case is the projected defense against strategic nuclear missiles where systems must react so rapidly that it is likely that almost complete reliance will have to be placed on automated systems. At the same time, the complexity and unpredictability of factors affecting the decisions will be very great.

Reliance on computers has already accelerated the rate of battle beyond the point at which human beings can be expected to react effectively. The military's answer to that problem is to create computers that can think and react better than humans. Even if such "smart' machines can be created, a uniquely human attribute is dropped out of the process: common-sense reasoning. The Computer Professionals for Social Responsibility have addressed this loss:

What distinguishes common-sense reasoning is the ability to draw on an enormous background of experience in the most unpredictable ways. In directing a friend to your house, for example, you don't have to give instructions about all the possible things that might happen along the way: fallen trees, accidents, flat tires, etc. . . . An extraordinary range of knowledge and experience [comes into play]; we never know what we'll need or when we'll need it. Nor do we usually even notice that we are using this background knowledge.

This is the kind of knowledge that leads us, when looking at a situation that seems perfectly clear-cut, to say, "Something doesn't make sense about this," to draw upon a subtle knowledge based upon years of experience in similar situations.

CPSR continues:

The rules on which all computer systems are based treat the world as if it were built from a stock of predefined building blocks, put together in carefully prescribed ways. Artificial intelligence systems are particularly good at dealing with very complex configurations of these building blocks, often better than more traditional computer programs. But they are ill equipped to respond appropriately to new kinds of blocks. . . . In more complex environments, unanticipated events are liable to trigger anomalous reactions. That is why radar reflections off the rising moon fooled the NORAD system: Moons are not among the building blocks in terms of what had been programmed into the computer. . . . It is the job of programmers to anticipate ahead of time the range of problems that a computer system will encounter. . . . The behavior of the system depends entirely on the structure of the programs—on the rules and the ways in which they are put together. . . . [But] as the Strategic Computing Plan itself points out, it is the unpredictability of war that poses the gravest threat.

CAN WE BLAME COMPUTERS?

The big question is this: Is it fair to blame computers for any or all of the above scenarios? Most people, even those who see the relationship between computers and increased destructive potential, consider the computers themselves to be harmless. Value free. Neutral. "People invent the machines," is the common wisdom. "People program them, people push the buttons."

And yet, it is a simple fact that if there were no computers, the process of engaging in war would be much more drawn out, with a lot more time for human beings to change their minds or seek alternatives. It is only because computers *do* exist that a virtually automatic, instant worldwide war, involving total annihilation, even enters the realm of possibility. So, can we say that computers are to blame?

It is also a fact that if computers somehow totally disappeared, the world would be instantly safer. Even if atom bombs continued to exist, they would no longer have effective delivery systems. Pakistan could still drop an atomic bomb on India, but the presently envisioned, all-out nuclear war, which quite possibly could extinguish the human species, would be impossible.

• • •

I know that this is a difficult position to accept. Critics call it throwing the baby out with the bath water. Just because computers are integral to modern systems of nuclear annihilation, does that mean we must rid ourselves of computers? I am not sure, but I think so.

This society upholds a fierce technological idealism. We believe we can get the best from a given technology without falling into worst-case scenarios of the sort described above. We maintain this idealism despite the fact that we have no evidence of technology ever being used at an optimal level, or even being sensibly controlled. This is certainly true of automobiles, which have virtually destroyed the natural world; and of television, which creates a common mental denominator; and of electrical energy generation, which is vastly overdeveloped to the detriment of the planet. Most technologies are actually deployed in the manner that is most useful to the institutions that gain from their use; this may have nothing to do with public or planetary good.

We are also influenced by the paradigm that technological evolution is a good thing, that no bounds should be put upon knowledge or possibility. Other societies have the concept of taboo to deal with destructive tendencies, but in our society the idea of taboo is itself taboo. And, as we have discussed, our society does not have mechanisms for evaluating the negative aspects of technology, so we bang ahead blindly, even in military development.

The military-computer matchup is irresistible; for them, it is a match made in heaven. It is intrinsic to military thinking to seek the ability to act in more centralized, more complex, faster, more far-reaching, and more destructive ways. If you are a general whose task is fighting and winning wars, you love computers. No single technology has ever offered so much aid in so many areas.

The U.S. military continues to be the largest single financial source for computer science research in the world. The attraction between the military and the computer sciences has an almost gravitational pull. In fact, one could argue that the recent *consumerization* of the computer is merely a glamorization, to help create public sympathy for its use as a panacea, when *military* use of computers is really the point.

Of all possible beneficiaries, the military benefits most from computers. Computers mean more to the military than they ever will to you and me, or to educators, or even to corporations and banks, though they run a close second. And of all the world-altering implications of computers, the military-computer collaboration is the most potentially devastating.

The possibility of computer-directed, instantaneous, worldwide holocaust is not theoretical. Every military in the world has attached itself to computers, and all military strategies are now computer based. The programs are written, the computers are ready to act. In the face of this reality, to speak of computers helping you edit your copy or run your little business seems a bit absurd.

5

TELEVISION (1):
AUDIOVISUAL TRAINING FOR
THE MODERN WORLD

*P*EOPLE WHO HAVE read *Four Arguments for the Elimination of Television* will recognize much of the information in this chapter. I am restating certain points in the present context because of the critical role television plays in the larger technological web.

For most human beings in the Western world, watching television has become the principal means of interaction with the new world now under construction, as well as a primary activity of everyday life. At the same time, the institutions at the fulcrum of the process use television to train human beings in what to think, what to feel, and how to be in the modern world.

In the chapter that follows this one, which deals with satellite television, we examine additional impacts of television in the less-developed countries, where it serves as an instrument of cultural cloning.

LIVING INSIDE MEDIA

Let's start with some 1990 statistics. They are of such monumental importance, and yet are so infrequently discussed, that I try to include them whenever I write about television.

• According to the U.S. Department of Commerce, 99.5 percent of the homes in the United States that have electricity have television sets. Electronically speaking, we are all wired together as a single entity. An electronic signal sent from a single source can now reach nearly every person in the country—250 million people across 3 million square miles—at exactly the same time. When such figures first appeared in the sixties, Marshall McLuhan hailed them as a portent of a new "global village," but he missed an important political point. The autocratic potential—the power of the one speaking into the brains of the many—is unprecedented. Its consequences are only discussed adequately in science fiction, by such people as Orwell and Huxley. The consequences are also keenly appreciated by those institutions large enough to attempt to control the medium: corporations, government, religion.

• According to the A. C. Nielsen Company, 95 percent of the U.S. population watches some TV every day. No day goes by without a "hit" of television, which indicates the level of engagement, or addiction, that people feel for the medium.

• Nielsen reports that the average American home has a television on for nearly eight hours per day. The average American adult watches TV nearly five hours per day. The average child between ages two and five watches about three and a half hours per day. The average adult over fifty-five watches nearly six hours.

Consider the situation of the average adult who watches for almost five hours daily. This person spends more time watching television than he or she spends doing anything else in life except sleeping or working or going to school. But if the *average* person is watching five hours per day, then roughly half of the U.S. population is watching *more* than five hours. (In practice, this means watching through most of each weekend, plus three or four hours each weeknight.)

It is hardly an exaggeration to say that the main activity of life for Americans, aside from work or sleep, has become watching television. Television has effectively replaced the diverse activities of previous generations, such as community events, cultural pursuits, and family life.

Ours is the first society in history of which it can be said that life has moved *inside* media. The average person, watching television for five hours per day, is physically engaged with—looking at and experiencing— a *machine*. To that extent, the person is not relating to anything else in the environment. But the environment of TV is not static, it is aggressive. It enters people's minds and leaves images within, which people then carry permanently. So television is an external environment that becomes an internal, mental environment.

The situation is really so odd that it lends itself well to science fiction descriptions. Imagine, for example, that a research team of anthropologists from Andromeda Galaxy is sent to Earth. Hovering above our country, the researchers might report back to their home base something like this:

"We are scanning the Americans now. Night after night they sit still in dark rooms, not talking to each other, barely moving except to eat. Many of them sit in separate rooms, but even those sitting in groups rarely speak to one another. They are staring at a light! The light flickers on and off many times per second [from the AC current]. The humans' eyes are not moving, and since we know that there is an association between eye movement and thought, we have measured their brain waves. Their brains are in 'alpha,' a noncognitive, passive-receptive mode. The humans are *receivers*.

"As for the light, it comes in the form of images, sent from only a few sources, thousands of miles from where the humans are gathering them in. The images are of places and events that are not, for the most part, related to the people's lives. Once placed into their heads, the images seem to take on permanence. We have noted that people use these images in their conversations with other people, and that they begin to dress and act in a manner that imitates the images. They also choose their national leaders from among the images.

"In summary, this place seems to be engaged in some kind of weird mental training akin to brainwashing."

If this is a fair description of the situation in the United States, it is also becoming a description of many other parts of the world. Right now, about 60 percent of the world population has access to television. In many places where television has recently arrived—remote villages in Africa, South America, Indonesia, northern Canada; places where there are not even roads—satellite communications have made it possible for people to ingest the dominant external society. In grass houses, on the frozen tundra, on tiny tropical islands, in the jungles of Brazil and Africa, people are sitting in their traditional homes of logs or mud or grass, and they are watching "Dallas" and "The Edge of Night" and "Bonanza."

More than 50 percent of the television watched outside the U.S. consists of reruns of popular American-made shows. Satellite communications, introduced as yet another democratic breakthrough for technology, are being used to place imagery of American-style commodity life, American values, American commercials, American-style experience in the heads of everyone, wherever they are. The end result will be worldwide monoculture.

FREEDOM OF SPEECH FOR THE WEALTHY

We think of television as a democratic medium, since we all get to watch it in our homes. But if it is "democratic" on the receiving end, it is surely not that on the sending end.

According to *Advertising Age*, about 75 percent of commercial network television time is paid for by the 100 largest corporations in the country. Many people do not react to this statistic as being important. But consider that there are presently 450,000 corporations in the United States, and some 250 million people, representing extremely diverse viewpoints about lifestyle, politics, and personal and national priorities. Only 100 corporations get to decide what will appear on television and what will not. These corporations do not overtly announce their refusal to finance programs that contain views disconsonant with their own; their control is far more subtle. It works in the minds of television producers who, when thinking about what programs to produce, have to mitigate their desires by their need to sell the programs to corporate backers. An effective censorship results.

While a small number of corporations pay for 75 percent of commercial broadcast time, and thereby dominate that medium, they now also pay for more than 50 percent of public television. During the Reagan years, federal support for noncommercial television was virtually eliminated, leaving a void that public television filled by appealing to corporations. As corporate influence has grown in public TV, so has the quality and length of the corporate commercial tags before and after the shows they sponsor. Whereas public television once featured such messages as "This program has been brought to you through a grant by Exxon," now we see the Exxon logo, followed by an added advertising phrase or two and an audio slogan.

The reason why only the largest corporations in the world dominate the broadcast signals is obvious: They are the only ones who can afford it. According to the present structure of network TV, a half-minute of prime time sells for about $200,000 to $300,000; during events such as the Super Bowl, the price is more like $700,000. Very few medium-sized corporations or businesses, and even fewer individuals, could pay $200,000 for a single message broadcast to the world.

If you and your friends decided that you had a very important statement to make about an issue—let's say the cutting down of old-growth redwoods in the Pacific Northwest—and if you were very fortunate (and rich), perhaps you could manage to raise sufficient money to actually place your message on the airwaves—*once*. Meanwhile, the multinational corporation doing the logging could buy the spot that appears before yours, and the one immediately after, and then three more later in the evening, and then five more tomorrow and the next day and the day after, and so on throughout the month. Some corporations have advertising budgets ranging from 100 million to over one billion dollars per year. Television is effectively a "private medium," for their use only.

That television is a private system in the hands of the largest corporations is difficult for most Americans to grasp. This is because we believe that freedom of speech is an inalienable right that we all enjoy equally. Nothing could be further from the truth. As A. J. Liebling said, "Freedom of the press is available only to those who own one." Similarly, freedom of speech is more available to some than to others, namely, to the people who can purchase it on national television. This leads to certain kinds of information dominating the airwaves.

The 100 largest corporations manufacture drugs, chemicals, cosmetics, packaged-processed foods, cars, and oil, and are involved in other extractive industries. But whether you are viewing a commercial for aspirin, cars, or cosmetics, the message is exactly the same. *All* advertising is saying this: Whether you buy this commodity or that one, satisfaction in life comes from commodities.

So we have the most pervasive and powerful communications medium in history, and it is totally financed by people with identical views of how life should be lived. They express this view unabashedly. Which brings us to the most shocking statistic: *The average American who watches five hours of television per day sees approximately 21,000 commercials per year.* That's 21,000 repetitions of essentially identical messages about life, aggressively placed into viewers' minds, all saying, *Buy something—do it now!*

So an entire nation of people is sitting night after night in their rooms, in a passive condition, receiving information from faraway places in the form of imagery placed in their brains, repeated 21,000 times per year, telling them how to live their lives. If the instrument responsible for this activity weren't TV, our familiar companion, then you, like the Andromeda scientists, would probably call it a system of mass brainwashing and political control, and would be damned worried about it.

THE TECHNOLOGY OF PASSIVITY

Economics is not the only reason why television is such a suitable medium for corporate control. Equally important is the nature of the television-viewing experience; how television affects human beings. From a corporate point of view, the effect is beneficial.

• • •

Even in the absence of chemical evidence of addiction, the amount of time people spend daily in front of their TV, and the way lives are scheduled around it, ought to be sufficient, *de facto* proof of TV's hypnotic and addictive abilities. In fact, when I interviewed people for *Four Arguments,* interviewees consistently used terms such as "hypnotic," "mesmerizing," or "addictive" to describe their experiences of television viewing. And many used the term "zombie" to describe how their kids looked while watching television.

Eventually, I sought scientific evidence about the validity of these anecdotal descriptions, and found some researchers ready to validate such characterizations.

For example, scientists who study brain-wave activity found that the longer one watches television, the more likely the brain will slip into "alpha" level: a slow, steady brain-wave pattern in which the mind is in its most receptive mode. It is a noncognitive mode; i.e., information can be placed into the mind *directly*, without viewer participation. When watching television, people are receiving images into their brains without thinking about them. Australian National University researchers call this a kind of "sleep-teaching." So if you look at your child in front of the TV and think of him or her as "zonked," that is apparently an apt description.

There are many reasons why the brain slips into this passive-receptive alpha condition. One reason is the lack of eye movement when watching TV, because of the small size of the screen. Sitting at a normal distance, the eye can gather most of the image without scanning the screen for it. The image comes in whole. This lack of *seeking* images disrupts the normal association between eye movement and thought stimulation, which is a genetically provided safety valve for human beings. Before modern times, any unusual event in the environment would attract instant attention; all the senses would immediately turn to it, including the vision sense and its "feeler," the eyes. But when an image doesn't have to be sought, an important form of mental stimulation is absent.

A second factor causing the brain to slip into alpha-wave activity is that, with the eyes not moving and the screen flickering on and off sixty times per second, an effective hypnosis is induced, at least in the view of psychologists who use hypnotism. Looking at the flickering light of a TV screen is akin to staring at the hypnotist's candle.

I think the third factor is the most important. The information on the TV screen—the images—come at their own speed, outside of the viewer's control; an image *stream*. One doesn't "pull out" and contemplate TV images, as if they were still photographs or images described in a written passage. If you attempted to do that you would fall behind the image stream. So there are two choices: surrender to the images, or withdraw from the experience. But if you are going to watch television (or film) at all, you *must* allow the images to enter you at their own speed. So, the nature of the experience makes you passive to its process, in body and mind. (More complete discussions of this process can be found in *The Plug-In Drug* by Marie Winn, and Australian National University's *Choice of Futures* by Fred and Merrylyn Emery, as well as in *Four Arguments for the Elimination of Television.*)

Does this problem also exist with other media? Not to the same degree. Take film, for example. The nature of the film-going experience is that one usually goes with a friend. That, in itself, stimulates the mind. And since film is shown in a public place, with other people present, there are many more stimuli and feelings accompanying the experience; a mood envelops the room.

Also, film imagery is much more refined and detailed than television imagery. The TV image, composed of tiny dots, is very coarse compared with film. A lot is lost in the television picture. Film, on the other hand, can bring out great background detail, much better images of nature, much greater subtlety. The richer the detail of the image, the more involving it is to the viewer. (This comparative advantage for film imagery over TV will only be partially mitigated when "high-definition TV" is introduced in a few years.)

Films are almost always shown on a much larger screen than are television programs, thus requiring considerably more eye movement. And when the film is over, the theater lights come up, people react, and finally rise to leave. They don't just sit there as the next stream of imagery invades them. The act of leaving, and then perhaps going to a café and talking it over, combined with the other elements of film-going, serve to bring the images up from the lower right brain (where images would otherwise reside, like dreams) into greater consciousness. The images come out of the unconscious, unusable realms into the conscious, where they can be examined to some extent.

Radio is a medium that does not impose images at all; in fact, radio stimulates the imagination in much the way books do. A situation is described and the listener actively visualizes. This very act suppresses alpha. When watching television, on the other hand, one's own image-making goes into dormancy.

Print media are by far the most engaging and participatory of any media. Since there is no inherent time limitation with books and newspapers, they can offer much more complex detail and background than any so-called visual medium. If I should now ask you to imagine a lush green field with a trickling stream, billowy clouds above, two great white dogs lying in the grass, lovers on a nearby hillside . . . you can certainly imagine that scene in great detail and color. You created these pictures in your own mind; they do not necessarily match the image I have in my mind of the same scene. If a similar image were shown on television, it would be flatter than the one you created. Meanwhile you would not be engaged in your own image-making; you would be passive to the process, relatively uninvolved.

No medium is as effective as print for providing information in detail. Since it does not have the limitations of time, it can deliver to the reader whatever it takes to achieve understanding, from one or two sentences to multiple volumes. But most importantly, gathering data from print is an active, not passive, process.

To read successfully, you must apply conscious mental effort. It is impossible to be in alpha level while reading, at least not if you want to understand what you read. We have all had the experience of reading a paragraph on a page, then realizing that we hadn't actually read it, then having to read the same material a second time. In doing this, we apply conscious effort to the process; we put our brain into a cognitive mode in order to grasp the information.

Also, when reading, one has the opportunity to review the material, underline it, write notes in the margin, tear out a page, Xerox it, send copies to friends, and reread at will, fast or slow. The reader controls most elements of the process and can create the conditions for accepting the information. All of this is impossible with TV-viewing. The information must be taken as it comes, without resistance. As a result, researchers at Australian National University described the TV-viewing experience as inherently pacifying. San Francisco brain researcher Erik Peper said, "The word 'zombie' is the best way to describe the experience." And Cornell University professor Rose Goldsen called television viewing "mnemonic learning"; that is, "learning without the conscious participation of the learner." It is sleep-teaching.

So television-viewing, if it can be compared to a drug experience, seems to have many of the characteristics of Valium and other tranquilizers. But that is only half of the story. Actually, if television is a drug, it is not really Valium; it is *speed*.

ACCELERATION OF THE NERVOUS SYSTEM

In their famous study of the effects of television, researchers at Australian National University predicted that as television became more popular in Australia, there would be a corresponding increase in hyperactivity among children. I found this prediction alarming because many parents of hyperactive children place their kids in front of the television set, where they seem to calm down. Apparently, the opposite effect is what finally results.

Here's how it works: While sitting quietly in front of the TV, the child sees people punching each other on the screen. There is the impulse to react—the fight-or-flight instinct is activated—but since it would be absurd to react to a television fight, the child suppresses the emotion. As the fighting continues, so does the cycle of impulse and suppression. Throughout the television-viewing experience, the child is drawn back and forth on this see-saw of action and suppression, all the while appearing zapped and inactive. When the set goes off, this stored-up energy bursts forth in the disorganized, frantic behavior that we associate with hyperactivity. Often, the only calming act is to again put the set on, which starts the cycle anew. But there are also more subtle ways that television speeds humans up.

•   •   •

I am a member of the pre-television generation. Until I was in my late teens, there wasn't any television. So as a child my after-school activities were different from those of the average child today.

I can recall how it felt coming home from school every day. First, I would look in the refrigerator to see if my mother had left me any snacks. I would quickly take care of those. Then, I might play with the dog. I would go up to my room. I would lie on the living room floor. I would become bored. Nothing to do.

Slowly I would slip into a state that I have lately begun to call "downtime" (not in the computer sense)—a kind of deadly boredom. A bottom of feeling, as it were. It was connected with a gnawing anxiety in the stomach. It was so unpleasant that I would eventually decide to *do something*. I would call a friend. I would go outdoors. I would play ball. I would read.

I think that the downtime I am describing was the norm for kids during the 1940s, when life was slower than it is today. Looking back, I view that time of nothingness as serving an important creative function. Out of this nothing-to-do condition some activity would eventually emerge. You got to the bottom of your feelings, you let things slide to their lowest state, and *then* you took charge. You experienced yourself in movement, with ideas. Taking all young people in the country as a group, this downtime could be considered a national genetic pool of creativity.

Today, however, after teenagers come home and begin to slip into downtime with its accompanying unpleasant feeling, they reach for the television knob. This stops the slide. Used this way, television is a mood-alteration system, like a drug. As the mood comes on, they reach for the drug, just as adults reach for the drink—or the TV—at the end of the day. So television for youngsters, in addition to *being* a drug, can be understood as early training for "harder" drugs.

Obviously, we all have ways of altering our moods. However, I don't think most of us see our TV-watching as a mood-altering device. Understanding it in such terms gives new meaning to the fact that the average young person watches for nearly four hours per day. By reaching for the TV drug, a generation of young people are short-circuiting their own downtime. They are not allowing themselves to live through the pits of their own experience, or to feel their own creative response to it. The net result, I think, will be a generation of young people who are less able to act on their own, or to be creative. Educators are already telling us that this is so. This habit may also be depriving young people of the fundamental self-knowledge that dealing with one's feelings produces. And it leaves this new drugged generation feeling that they can't experience life without technological and chemical props. So TV not only trains them for drug dependency, it also trains them for commodity dependency.

PERCEPTUAL SPEEDUP AND CONFUSION

When watching television, the viewer is moved into a perceptual universe that is much, much faster than ordinary life. To get an idea of how this works, I suggest that you turn on your television set now and switch to a commercial network. (This is an especially useful exercise to do during prime time, when more money is spent on production values.) Count the number of times something happens in the image that could not happen in ordinary life. One moment the camera puts you in front of the image, in another moment you are behind it or above it or rolling around it. Then you are out on the street; then it is tomorrow, or yesterday. A commercial appears on the screen with dancers, music, and cartoons. A couple walks on a hillside hundreds of yards away, but you can hear them speaking as though you were next to them. Words flash on and off the screen. There are suddenly two simultaneous images, or three. You are looking at a face, then suddenly at hands, then suddenly you are outdoors. Long periods of historical time are jammed together. You move from landscape, to sky, to humans in rapid succession. Young people are running toward you—*Cut*. Now they are on a beach—*Cut*. Now you are watching beer poured into a glass—*Cut*. Now music is playing—*Cut*. An announcer speaks from somewhere. Now you are in Europe. Now in Asia. There is a war, there is a commercial . . . All of this is jammed together in a steady stream of imagery, fracturing your attention while condensing time and mixing categories of reality, nonreality, and semireality.

These image fluctuations and technical changes, as well as hundreds of other kinds not mentioned, are what I have called technical events in television imagery. These alterations of the image could not happen in ordinary life; they are *technical* alterations only possible within moving-image media: films, video, or television.

If you actually counted these technical events as I suggested above, you would find that during commercials—especially during prime time—the image changes at an average of ten to fifteen times per thirty-second commercial. During a regular program on a commercial channel, camera movements or technical events occur about seven to ten times per minute. On public television programs, there are probably three to four camera movements or technical events per minute. (There are fewer on public television than commercial television simply because commercial television can afford more cameras, more edits, and more technology. Similarly, advertisers can spend more than any television program can afford. This is one reason why people pay attention to advertising despite the lack of real content. It is visually more engaging. When people say that "advertising is the most interesting thing on television" they are not aware they are speaking about the *technology* of advertising.)

This hyperactivated imagery continues for as long as a viewer is watching the screen. For heavy viewers of television it means five or six (or more) hours living within a perceptual universe that is constantly fractured, and in which time and events are both condensed and accelerated.

Finally, the set goes off. The viewers are back in their rooms. Nothing is moving. The room does not rise up or whirl around. People do not suddenly flash on and off in front of them. It doesn't become tomorrow or yesterday in a flash. Actually, nothing at all is happening. There is simply the same room as before: walls, windows, furniture. Ordinary life and ordinary feelings and thoughts. Very slow, by comparison. Too slow. Anxiety sets in.

Having lived in the amazingly rapid world of television imagery, ordinary life is dull by comparison, and far too slow. But consider how it affects one's ability to be in nature. The natural world is *really* slow. Save for the waving of trees in the wind, or the occasional animal movement, things barely happen at all. To experience nature, to feel its subtleties, requires human perceptual ability that is capable of slowness. It requires that human beings approach the experience with patience and calm. Life in the modern world does not encourage that; it encourages the opposite. Cars, planes, video games, faxes, Walkmans, television, computers, working and traveling on schedules dictated by assembly lines and offices—we in the Western world have attuned ourselves to rhythms that are outside of nature. We are trained to seek satisfaction in the packaging that technology provides. Big "hits." We live in a world of constant catharsis, constant change, constant unrest. While out in the *real* world, in nature, we become anxious and uncomfortable. We desire to get back indoors, to get that TV set back on, to get "up to speed."

For children, this change is very serious, and has been well noted by educators. Countless teachers have told me how young people are utterly unable to maintain attention. They become bored after only a few minutes of the same subject. They need constant change. And they need the teacher to "perform" rather then teach, to deliver material with snappy punch lines. As for reading, very few young people are now patient enough to get through a book such as *The Hunchback of Notre Dame,* where events move slowly and where detail, rather than constant explosive content, is what matters.

But not only children are affected by this replacement of our living environment with television. All human beings are changing. We are all being sped up. The natural world has retreated beyond our awareness. We hear people say that nature is boring, and it is clear why they say this. We don't know how to be with it. We are not slow enough. Caring about what happens to nature is not part of our emotional world, which helps pave the way for the exploitation of nature and native people. Simultaneously, it makes us think that our future is on some other planet out there in space.

Television synchronizes our internal processes with the new world of concrete, computers, space travel, and acceleration. It makes our insides— brain and nervous system—compatible with the world outside ourselves. For human beings, it is the worst possible combination of influences. It puts our brains into a passive alpha state, zapping our thinking processes and destroying our creative impulses. Simultaneously, it speeds up our nervous systems, making us too fast to feel calm, too fast to read, almost too fast to relate meaningfully to other human beings, and too fast for nature. From this alienation training, a new human emerges. Speed junkie. Videovoid. Technovoid.

THE POLITICS OF CONFUSED REALITY

When people spend the greatest part of their lives relating to television imagery, then television imagery becomes the greatest part of people's lives. It begins to seem like life itself. Television images define the terms of people's understanding, the boundaries of human awareness. Without an offsetting system of imagery in people's lives, television images take on a quality of reality that they do not deserve.

The political consequences of such a situation, where a population becomes isolated within an artificial information environment, has been a favorite subject of many science-fiction writers over the years.

George Orwell's *1984* describes an information environment so monolithic and aggressive that it became the total source and absolute limit of human knowledge. Every room had a two-way "telescreen" that could not be turned off; its nonstop programming consisted of official music, economic data, and constant reports of military victories.

In *1984,* television became the instrument of daily training sessions for human emotions via constant juxtapositions of the images of Good vs. Evil: the benevolent, beloved Big Brother versus the hated, loathsome enemy, Goldstein. "Two Minutes Hate" periods would be regularly scheduled each day; the "disgusting" image of Goldstein on the TV screen, amid streams of official invective, caused the entire populace to join frenzied mass rages, "a hideous ecstacy of fear and vindictiveness."

Print media—books, documents, diaries—were virtually eliminated. Without such written records, the past became a manufactured creation of the present. Anything that differed from the telescreen version of reality existed solely in the memories of a few individuals, who would eventually be found out. Earlier languages were destroyed, and it was forbidden to visit the wilderness, which was itself the past.

The effect of the total control of imagery was to unify mass consciousness within a single-media version of reality. With all information coming disembodied via the telescreen, and with the whole population receiving this monolithic information at the same time, and with no verifiable points of comparison, how was one to know what was true and real and what was not? Did Goldstein even exist? Did Big Brother? How could anyone know? Reality was up for grabs. Resistance to information was pointless. All minds merged with the official imagery. Eventually, people accepted even utterly contradictory "doublethink" statements: "WAR IS PEACE," "HATE IS LOVE," "IGNORANCE IS STRENGTH."

Obviously, there are big differences between the scenario depicted in *1984* and present-day America, but as television-viewing statistics indicate, the differences may be less significant than the similarities. Television has become the primary world we relate to. Like Orwell's nonstop broadcasts, TV enters and occupies our minds and causes similar results, as we will discuss.

In his science-fiction book *Fahrenheit 451,* Ray Bradbury tells of a society in which human relationships are less important than the relationships people have with characters in television shows. Every home has a wall-sized television screen. And the characters on the screen are programmed to address the viewers personally. The TV characters, therefore, become the primary characters in people's lives.

You have only to listen to conversations these days—on buses, in restaurants, or even at the office—to observe that many people discuss the characters in sitcoms and soaps as if they were neighbors or friends. People in our society often follow the lives of TV people with greater care and interest than they follow the lives of their own family members. For many people—especially heavy television viewers—life and television have already merged.

There are bizarre consequences to this. Years ago, 250,000 people wrote to Marcus Welby, M.D., asking for medical advice. Performers in soaps have often been assaulted and verbally abused by people on the street for their characters' behavior. Many researchers—most notably, Gerbner and Gross of the University of Pennsylvania—have established that Americans tend to take even fictional TV shows as true and believable. Recently, people such as Nancy Reagan, Henry Kissinger, and Michael Jordan have made guest appearances on sitcoms. Does this make the other characters, or the show itself, more real? Or does it make Kissinger less real? Fiction and reality have lost their boundaries.

People who immerse themselves in the surrogate reality of television life deal on a daily basis with a reality totally unlike any that has preceded it. For example, when watching television news, you are presumably taking in actual world events, happening before *you* as they happen in real-time. But actually, most of what you see happened earlier; you are viewing edited tapes of these events. Sometimes the events being described are not presented as images, but are verbal descriptions by the announcer. Then the news is interrupted by a commercial. The commercial is not happening in the same place as the event that just preceded it, nor is the announcer in that place. Yet they are all somehow within this image stream. Soon after this, you may be watching a fictional dramatic program, which uses real people performing scripted events, in an accelerated time frame, also interrupted by commercials that may feature well-known stars relating to unreal situations in a realistic manner. Then you watch a docudrama, which is a fictionalized re-creation of a real event, in which you are asked to grasp both the realistic elements and the re-created semifictional elements in the same plane of understanding. (In 1989, ABC News was discovered to have *simulated* a contact between an alleged U.S. spy and a Soviet agent; this was the first known case of "re-created actuality" within a format that claimed reality.)

In other instances, you may be watching the future, which looks real, but is actually a scripted drama. Or talk shows, in which real people, usually actors (who normally play fictional roles), talk about real events in their actual lives. Then again commercials appear, which have "real" actors who are playing roles, as well as real people like John Madden or Chuck Yeager (the test pilot) in acting roles, and so on.

I have not even scratched the surface of the numbers of categories of reality that come and go every few minutes on television. Meanwhile, however, *you* are actually sitting home in your room and all of this imagery enters your mind without vivid distinction. When you see Henry Kissinger in a drama you may say to yourself, "This is Henry Kissinger; he is not in the same category of reality as the other actors; there is another level of reality operating here," but probably you don't. You just accept the stream as it comes. For heavy viewers of television, practiced in this acceptance, distinctions become extremely blurred.

Whereas the fictional presentations of television take on a kind of reality, the real events of the political world, which are also fitted into the image flow, take on the characteristics of the fictional material on the screen. Wars, riots, international spying, and electoral contests all begin to be viewed as the latest exciting TV series or, in the case of presidential contests, as sporting events. They come and go as frequently as sitcoms or drama, and are just as dependent on the ratings. (The choice of subjects for TV news is often based upon what will attract and maintain viewers. See Edward J. Epstein's *News From Nowhere*.) And so each great tragedy or world crisis—even those as monumental as the Philippines revolution, or the democratic uprisings in China and Eastern Europe, or the Chernobyl disaster, or the Salman Rushdie death threat, or the war between the U.S. and Iraq—each news event dominates the tube for a short while, and then is put on the back burner or totally forgotten. Each of the productions fit nicely into evening-news formats; they run steadily for two to eight weeks, depending on the subject and the attention span of the viewers, and then are dropped.

They all deal with "real" world events, but they come to us in the steady, mixed-up stream of real, unreal, and semireal events that is everyday television. In our minds, these real news events merge with other material, becoming just another set of stored imagery that all have similar reality values. They enter and leave our lives with the accelerated rhythms of the rest of television events, eventually dissolving into the past. We become engaged, enraged, entertained, involved, and then they are over. We feel we have been experiencing our lives as we watch these world events, but really all that happened is that we sat home in our living rooms and watched television. This is true whether we are watching news, or Cousteau's whales, or our "friends" on the late-night talks shows or in the soaps. They are all part of the same pulsating stream of imagery and so they become equal in our minds. J. R. Ewing, John Madden, Johnny Carson, Imelda Marcos, Sylvester Stallone, Madonna, Roseanne, Moammar Khadafy, Bart Simpson, Michael Jordan, Michael Jackson, Laura Palmer, Saddam Hussein, Charlton Heston, Manuel Noriega, Clint Eastwood . . . (As you read each of these names, did you get a visual picture of each of them? You did! Did you realize that there were pictures of these people living in your mind? Or that you hold all these images, which represent wildly different categories of "real life," from politician to athlete to performer to fictional character, to cartoon, on more or less the same plane of reality?)

Though we can distinguish among the categories of reality that the television stream delivers to us, we rarely do. We let the images flow and lodge into our brains without distinction. That the resultant wipe-out of the lines between real and not real might lead us to some distortion in our political reality should have been obvious to us many years ago.

THE TELEVISION PRESIDENT

Comedians have often suggested that Ronald Reagan's immense popularity might have been helped by television-induced confusion. But I would like to make the case that this was concretely true, and that it's not so funny.

Ronald Reagan spent his adult life being an image, sometimes fictional—as when performing in films—and sometimes in that odd semi-reality that performers obtain in commercials. For his career combined film acting and, perhaps more important, spokesperson roles for General Electric Company advertising.

Because of his background, Reagan handled television as president with astonishing skill and power. He understood, as no one did before, that on television, style supersedes content: The way you behave and look is more important than what you say or do. He knew that complexity and historical perspective do not come across on TV as well as simplicity, bald assertion, the heavy use of symbolic content, and the appeal to formulaic values, deeply imbedded in Americans by previous decades of television and film: Good vs. Evil, America vs. The Enemy, Revere the Flag. (Reagan's protégé, George Bush, also learned these lessons; he was elected in 1988 because of his embrace of TV symbolism—the flag, the pledge of allegiance, black rapists—mixed with spots about Dukakis and pollution, which turned out to be lies.)

Reagan's most remarkable achievement was to incorporate in his own persona an amazing set of archetypes from the popular movies of the 1940s and 1950s. In the *real* role of president, Ronald Reagan re-created a set of images that had been reinforced by standard story lines since World War II; he was making real what was previously just imagery held in the minds of the population.

Ronald Reagan became the World War II hero, standing tall. He became the admiral on the bridge of the ship, taking on the hated Nazis and Japanese, though it became the Commies and the Iranians. He was the western hero, slow to anger, but push him too far and he became fierce in his response. He was not Rambo, a contemporary unfeeling slaughterer. He had morals. He was John Wayne. He was Gary Cooper in *High Noon.*

Reagan was also the family man of the 1950s: affable, homey, a little bit sexy, and in love with his adoring wife. He was kindly and grandfatherly, with a few personality quirks. He didn't remember things so good. He pronounced some of them fancy French names wrong. He meant Camus, but he said "Kaymus." But his fallabilities made us love him more; they gave him an unthreatening, comedic aspect, sort of like Jimmy Stewart.

Yet he was also the authoritative spokesperson—the same one he used to be for General Electric. He believed in the technological dream and was willing to sell it hard. He believed in the American vision of the good life. He knew technology could achieve anything. He loved the challenge of the future. "Progress is our most important product."

All of these characteristics were stereotypes from popular movies of the forties and fifties, and they remained in the minds of the millions of people who saw them. They conjured memories of a simpler time, when solutions were clear, when America was on top, and heroes and ordinary people could change things.

Ronald Reagan could reach into those memories of a generation, and incorporate them into himself. He appealed to the collective media unconscious to produce an almost alchemical result, making real what was previously fiction.

Reagan also grasped the antihistorical nature of TV reality, its *nowness.* He was very aggressive in his attempts to create historical truth. He understood that when a population is confined to a single information source, especially one that speaks imagery directly into the brain, that source has unprecedented power as a tool to control human minds. As in *1984*, real and unreal, truth and fiction, become equally arbitrary, for there is no way to clarify or check what TV asserts. And so Reagan could call his invasion of Grenada a "rescue" of students who were never in danger. He could assert that the Soviets knew that Korean Air flight 007 was a passenger plane before they shot it down, though subsequent stories suggested that Reagan *knew* that the Soviets did *not* know. (The initial image stuck, and the event is still understood in those terms today.) By asserting that Libya was behind the Berlin disco bombing, Reagan made *that* true for millions of Americans, and we supported his bloody retaliation, though later evidence showed that Syria had most likely created that event.

Ronald Reagan called MX missiles "peacekeepers." He said that lowering taxes on the wealthy benefited the poor, and he unabashedly claimed that massive rearming was the way to disarm. A few years later, George Bush said "the last best chance for peace" was to declare war against Iraq, and then said "the goal of the war is peace." All these statements qualify as advanced "doublespeak."

Reagan and Bush also understood the important Orwellian lesson in focusing public hatred on the repeated images of the enemy. Orwell had used the loathsome TV visage of Goldstein in "Two Minutes Hate" periods throughout the day. Reagan used Khomeni, then Khadafy, then Ortega. Bush continued the tendency, focusing American hatred on images of Willie Horton, then Manuel Noriega, then Saddam Hussein.

The degree to which the public has accepted such presidential behavior without rebellion, and has enthusiastically supported both Reagan and Bush, is the degree to which George Orwell's predictions have proven accurate, and that television's political importance has been realized.

LATE NEWS: VIDEO WAR

February 4, 1991. As I write these words we are three weeks into the Iraq-U.S. war. My friends tell me they are "glued" to their TV screens, and ask if I am too.

In fact, I have watched some TV, more in amazement and disgust than for any useful information. Radio news, notably from National Public Radio and the Pacifica Network, has been far more detailed, informative, historical, wide-ranging, multifaceted, and faster in covering important events.

As with other news in the past, television's ability to deliver has been highly overrated. From the first day of the war, when CNN's Baghdad correspondents reported bombing in the city, TV delivered very little in the way of actual war footage. This was partly due to Pentagon censorship, which prohibited reporters from going into the field except under controlled conditions, prohibited images of American dead or of body bags, permitted only scant contact with outside sources, and censored all military communiqués. Reporters were essentially confined to official versions of the story. Former *New York Times* political correspondent Richard Reeves characterized the TV industry, because of its submissive performance, as "PNN, the Pentagon News Network."

Also important were the technical limits of television. To get near the action, TV requires that relatively cumbersome, sometimes heavy video and sound equipment make its way across difficult terrain, and back. Radio and telephone transmission is far less difficult, more mobile, less expensive, and quicker under many circumstances. The net effect was that people who were at home glued to their TV screens were seeing mainly still photographs of CNN's or other correspondents, held on the screen for many minutes, while the story was actually reported by a telephone linkup. The only other images were occasional maps of the Middle East, or Pentagon stock footage of missiles or planes, or "talking head" shots of generals and commentators. Any usable, concrete information came almost exclusively in words, not images. So, while 100 million people believed themselves to be experiencing television, what they were really getting was radio, with a lit screen.

Throughout this massive barrage of military talking, there was scarcely one alternative viewpoint on television. Antiwar opinion was limited to an occasional twenty-second shot of a peace march, grossly underestimated rally counts, and no presentation of what marchers actually had to say. While there were many hours of interviews with military strategists, and loving details about weaponry, there were no serious interviews with antiwar leaders, or with people who could have provided a variety of viewpoints: leaders of women's organizations, artists, humanists, native people, environmentalists (except in reaction to the oil spill), pacifists, or, for that matter, people skilled in the arts of negotiation rather than war. Then, when poll results came in, everyone was surprised at the degree to which the public supported the war. How could the public do otherwise? What information were they given to perceive any alternative?

To their immense credit, noncommercial radio, and occasional news-paper reports, did provide some broader perspectives, but the monolithic power and domination of television made those voices, in those media, less significant than they should have been.

Television was essentially an instrument of official policy during the first weeks of the war. It adopted the role of cheerleader for the military-government viewpoint. The high point was probably the 1991 Super Bowl, which was indistinguishable from a multimedia pro-war extravaganza. The fans were shown waving American flags while sitting on red, white, and blue cushions. The players and coaches were interviewed about their hopes for our side in the larger game of war. The halftime show was a patriotic Disney display of the superiority of American values. And there were several intercuts to George and Barbara Bush, watching the game at home, and speaking to us about how their thoughts, like ours, were on the righteousness of our "just cause" in the Persian Gulf. And then, Peter Jennings showed us—oh no!—*those videos.*

Now it was time for television to really strut its stuff. The video images of the laser- and radar-guided missiles striking their targets with precision were made-in-heaven for television. It brought us, the viewers, into the cockpit of the plane; we could see the same screen the pilot saw. It demonstrated the unique artistic capability of the medium, equal to its delivery of multifaceted and multidimensional advertising imagery.

The laser-bomb images also revealed the natural symbiosis among video, computer, broadcast satellite, radar, and laser technologies, which stimulated 100 million people to glory in the miraculous technical superiority of our society. No other medium had ever been able to create such a brilliant advertisement, and instill such awe, for technology itself.

Of course, this so-called war footage that we were seeing—virtually the only war footage we saw during those first three weeks—had a familiar look to it. It was precisely the kind of imagery we had been trained to accept and to love, from a decade of playing video games. When Mr. Reagan said that video games were good training for bomber pilots, he failed to mention that it was also good training for *us;* it enabled us to truly identify with the bomber pilots, and brought us closer to them.

That the two sources of imagery—video games and war—became intertwined in our minds, and that the war itself became something of a giant video game, was so apparent that it was even noted by mass media pundits. What was not sufficiently noted was how amazingly odd this was.

I have described how Ronald Reagan had become a human presidential replay of previously implanted film and TV imagery. The images of high-tech war were also replays of previously implanted video imagery. They produced an instant hit of recognition, familiarity, and support for this utterly unprecedented technological merger. It was so neat, somehow, that all our favorite toys—computers, television, video games, and war games—had merged this way into something we could all experience right up there with our real pilots.

Nonetheless, there remained one area of confusion. For unlike the video-game wars in video parlors, the actual bombs had a final outcome that was not merely electronic: It was metal against flesh. This we did not experience.

Psychologist Robert Jay Lifton has written eloquently about the effects of high-technology warfare, which distances our society from the awareness of our acts. He calls it "psychic numbing." Our society remains appalled at the continuous acts of violence on our streets, where a killer so often acts impersonally, without feeling. And yet, says Lifton, through the collaboration and merging of the new technologies into TV imagery, we participate in the acts of violence performed by our military without actually experiencing them. And rather than being appalled by these acts, we like them. We are thrilled and excited by "the kill," as our military puts it, but are numb to the death that is involved. Rather than bringing us pain, it brings us pleasure. (The same is also true of the actual killers, the pilots.)

Finally what is revealed by television's performance in the war is its amazing efficiency when controlled by central authority. Of course we've already observed that efficiency over the last decades of television's control by corporations, which also train the population to view reality in a predetermined fashion, while minimizing alternative views. In times of war, the corporate role recedes temporarily. In fact, many advertisers withdrew their commercials for a time when war broke out, allowing the military issues to take center stage. Anyway, the celebration of high-tech war images ultimately supports corporate goals, which makes another neat symbiosis.

The main point to understand in all this is that the efficiency of television in influencing and controlling the populace does not result so much from any premeditated conspiracy by the military or corporations as it does from a *de facto* conspiracy of technical factors. As is the case with computers, TV technology is more efficient and more effective as an instrument of centralized control than it is for any other use.

The factors that conspire to create this inevitable condition include TV's incredible reach into every home in the country, and someday, every home in the world, combined with the power of the imagery it places in our brains. In addition, in more individual terms, it encourages passivity, isolation, confusion, addiction, and alienation; it homogenizes values and shuts out alternative visions.

Television is uniquely suited to implant and continuously reinforce dominant ideologies. And, while it hones our minds, it also accelerates our nervous systems into a form that matches the technological reality that is upon us. Television effectively produces a new form of human being— less creative, less able to make subtle distinctions, speedier, and more interested in *things*—albeit better able to handle, appreciate, and approve of the new technological world. High-speed computers, faxes, lasers, satellites, robotics, high-tech war, space travel, and the further suppression of nature are more palatable and desirable for us because of our involvement with TV. The ultimate result, in high-tech terms, is that television redesigns us to be compatible with the future.

6

TELEVISION (2):
SATELLITES AND THE
CLONING OF CULTURES

The Case of the Dene Indians

*I*F THERE IS a basic principle of environmentalism, it is that diversity
is good. Beyond good, it is a bottom-line necessity for natural systems
to survive. Writers such as Paul Ehrlich, Ray Dasmann, and Wes Jackson
have reported on the decline of the planet's plant and animal species,
which threatens to collapse the genetic pool by which the planet retains its
biological health. Technology can be blamed for many of these developments: for example, the role of pesticides in creating one-crop agribusiness, in lieu of diverse multicrop systems, or the role of dams in destroying
the unimaginably complex interactions among life forms in rainforests.
But the idea that communications technology, particularly television, can
have a role in destroying diversity within the *human* realm is rarely noted.

By its ability to implant identical images into the minds of millions of
people, TV can homogenize perspectives, knowledge, tastes, and desires,
to make them resemble the tastes and interests of the people who transmit
the imagery. In our world, the transmitters of the images are corporations
whose ideal of life is technologically oriented, commodity oriented, ma-
terialistic, and hostile to nature. And satellite communications is the mech-

anism by which television is delivered into parts of the planet that have, until recently, been spared this assault.

• • •

Like other technologies, satellite television was introduced amid praise for its democratic potential. The argument went that on the *sending* end, satellites would diversify television content since groups representing any viewpoint, even those excluded from the old broadcast system, could have equal access. Meanwhile, on the receiving end, satellite TV would be especially beneficial to the technologically deprived parts of the globe. People who live without roads or running water, in Borneo, Africa, and the far north, could now have direct access to the collective wisdom and science of the West. By now, because of satellite installations, more than 60 percent of the world population has access to television.

This best-case scenario for satellite TV left out three points: 1) the cost of sending programs and messages via satellite virtually precludes its use by anyone except the same corporations and governments who use broadcast signals; 2) the "primitive" peoples blessed with this new technology mainly get to *receive* our imagery, without being able to send much of their own; 3) the effect of this one-way communication into the brains and hearts of peoples living in the jungles and tundras is devastating. It paves the way for the technological juggernaut, while destroying native culture, economy, and political viability.

In 1984 I was invited to see firsthand how satellite television's arrival into a remote place can make sudden, serious impacts on the culture and economy of an area. The invitation came from the Native Women's Association of the Northwest Territories. The group asked that I go north to participate in some workshops concerning television, which was just then arriving in the region. The largest town in the NWT, Yellowknife (population now about 14,000), had been receiving TV signals by satellite for about ten years. But most of the smaller communities had refused to permit satellite dishes to be installed. Pressure from the Canadian government had been steady, however, and during the preceding few years some fifteen of the native communities had buckled. Others were considering doing likewise.

The Dene Indian and Inuit (Eskimo) women who are members of the Native Women's Association were worried. In communities where television had gained a foothold, they had noticed sudden and sometimes extreme changes in community and family life, in the behavior and values of young people, and in the interest in sustaining traditional survival skills in one of the world's harshest environments. The women thought I might help them develop an agenda of topics for their workshops.

"UNPOPULATED ICY WASTELAND"

If you have ever heard of the Mackenzie River Valley, it is probably because of the Russian nuclear satellite that began falling out of orbit to Earth in 1978. For weeks there was frightened speculation about where it would land, and spray its nuclear guts. What if it fell on New York, or London, or Moscow? To the relief of most people, the thing finally crashed to Earth in hundreds of bits along a 300-mile swath through what was termed an "unpopulated icy wasteland" near the Arctic Circle. Actually, the disintegrating satellite flew over a region containing some twenty-six communities of Dene and Inuit, whose people have lived there for 20,000 years. That the region could be called "unpopulated" reveals the degree to which indigenous people remain invisible to the main players in today's world. It was not as if the stuff had fallen on *real* Canadians.

Until recently it would have been fair to argue that the nearly one million square miles of land in the Northwest Territories was not really part of Canada at all. Though England granted Canada (including the vast north) its independence in 1867, there was no official presence in the NWT—save three tiny post offices and an occasional Mounted Policeman—until one government office was opened in 1967. For a century, the region had been governed, if you can call it that, from Ottawa. Mostly it was ignored. As a result, the Dene, Inuit, and a third small culturally distinct group, the Metis (mixed natives and whites) had maintained a way of life that was essentially unchanged for thousands of years.

In a climate where winter temperatures hover at 30 degrees below zero Fahrenheit, where the growing season is extremely short, and where total precipitation is so slight that the area nearly qualifies as desert, these people have survived. Their traditional economy has been based on hunting caribou and other animals, ice fishing in the thousands of tiny lakes, and, among the Inuit, hunting seals. In more recent times—since the seventeenth century—commercial trapping has become significant. The Hudson's Bay Company paid cash and/or guns for animal skins. They also bought the fabulous caribou and moose mukluks, decorated with beads and porcupine quills. So good was this business for the Hudson's Bay Company that in times of severe weather the company would send emergency food supplies to the Indians and actively urged the Canadian government to do likewise. But until the 1900s the Canadians had little interest in anything that went on in Indian country.

As recently as the turn of the twentieth century, there were only 137 non-native people in the entire Northwest Territories. For the most part, therefore, the native population remained as isolated as the Indian people of the Amazon or New Guinea; they were left alone on their land because there was no demand for its use.

Change began in the 1920s when oil was discovered in the northern Mackenzie Valley. For the first time the Canadian government felt it would be prudent to do something "legal" to gain a clear title to the north. The English grant of title the century before was barely known by the Indians and Inuit who were virtually the entire population; even if it was known, it was not recognized as valid. So the government decided to formalize matters with treaties.

Having observed the brutal treatment of the Indians by the United States, Canada set out upon a more "humanistic" Indian policy. Indeed, Canada never engaged in the sort of military massacres that characterized U.S.-Indian relations in the nineteenth century, and that are still common in many parts of the world. But the Canadians' choice of "nonviolence" is where the differences end.

The treaties of the 1920s were made with the same aggressive and misleading practices as they were in the United States, with similar disregard for human or legal rights. They are now the subject of bitter dispute.

The Indians, very few of whom spoke English, signed treaties that they believed said nothing about the cession of land. According to recent court testimony, the natives assumed the Mackenzie Valley was to remain *their* land and the treaties were only for "peace and friendship." The Canadians, however, produced pieces of paper written in English, purportedly signed by the Dene, which agreed to "cede, release, surrender, and yield up to the government" all rights, titles, and privileges to the land. In return, the natives were to be paid five dollars each per year, and were permitted to hunt, fish, and live in traditional places unless and until the government wanted to use the land in some other way.

Since little oil drilling, or any other kind of development, actually took place in the 1920s, the differing understandings went mostly unnoticed for a while. But during and after World War II Canada became more aggressive about getting the oil out of the ground and down to the cities, and made lease agreements with Exxon, Gulf, and British Petroleum for drilling rights in the Mackenzie Valley. A small pipeline was begun in the far north, and plans were developed to build a mammoth 1,500-mile gas pipeline south through the Mackenzie Valley to Alberta. But the Indians were not pleased. By the 1950s, the government started imposing restrictions on where the Indians could live, hunt, and fish. And then, like many other governments in the Western world, the Canadians began to encourage the original inhabitants to move off their traditional lands into new towns, promising them schools, jobs on the oil rigs, homes, money, and television.

Many native people, especially in the Norman Wells area, went into a kind of shock to see their land turned into oil fields, and the sudden influx of whites. The Indians did get some jobs on the northern oil rigs, but mostly as sweepers, waste-disposal workers, and security guards; they were first to be laid off when cutbacks were made. As with other tribal peoples in similar circumstances, the Dene and Inuit found themselves coping with growing alcoholism and family violence. Before long an active resistance began, led by the elders, including some who had been parties to the treaties decades before. They insisted that the Canadians did not own the land and could not make development leases for it, or control hunting or fishing. The Dene began to organize, although it meant making some painful changes in the traditional way they had organized their activities in the past.

Like their cousins the Navajo (Dineh), and the Apache, the Dene traditionally had not had any sort of centralized political structure. They lived in small, seminomadic bands comprised of a few families who did all things collectively. There were no chiefs or "head men." Authority within a band was fluid, moving among individuals according to the task at hand. When it was caribou-hunting time, those with the greatest skill at hunting would assume temporary authority. When there were community problems, someone skilled in relationships would rise to leadership. This process has kept them going for 20,000 years.

When the Canadians showed up wanting to make a treaty with somebody, they couldn't find any authoritative body to negotiate with. They literally had to solicit Dene from the various bands who were willing to discuss some sort of treaty, and eventually gathered a group together. An artificial Dene "government" was formed by this process, as was happening in the U.S. interaction with the Navajo 3,000 miles to the south at this very same time. (See Chapter 15.) Once the treaty was made, the Dene "government" disbanded and the Indians merged back into the land as before. But by the 1960s, with the Canadians asserting more authority in the region, the Dene understood that some sort of unified action was needed. The Canadians, operating with the mobility and communication tools of an advanced industrial society, were able to act simultaneously in many of the autonomous Indian communities. The traditional Dene structure, which maintained power in the family and the nomadic band, could not cope effectively with such a focused force.

After several years of heart-wrenching debate, the Dene finally decided to make a historic break with the past and create the first central Dene government in 1970. At first called the Indian Brotherhood of the Northwest Territories, it became the Dene Nation, with offices in Yellowknife, one block from the Canadian government building. Each of the twenty-six communities chose representatives to regularly convene in Yellowknife. The first act of the Dene was to hire attorneys to pursue aboriginal rights of ownership of the Mackenzie Valley region. Amazingly, they met with success.

In 1973, Justice William G. Morrow of the Supreme Court of the Northwest Territories ruled that sufficient evidence showed that the natives either were not told or did not understand what was in the English version of the treaties. Justice Morrow also cited evidence that many of the signatures on the treaties were forgeries. He ruled that since "there is sufficient doubt on the facts that aboriginal title was extinguished," the natives were well advised to put forward a legal claim to ownership of about 450,000 square miles of the Northwest Territories.

The Canadian government, meanwhile, for all its enlightened Indian policies, desperately sought loopholes in the court's decision. The problem was serious in that Canada had already made leases for oil exploration and drilling and preliminary work for the Mackenzie pipeline. The Indian opposition was profoundly inconvenient. Finally, however, the government recognized that it would be necessary to negotiate.

The Canadians attempted to limit the talks to one question: How much money is owed the Indians for the loss of their land? The Indians, meanwhile, said they had *not* lost their land and would not sell it; they only sought affirmation of their ownership. The ultimate outcome of the talks would determine who regulates and controls the oil, and whether or not the native political economy would be saved.

When the negotiations dragged on, the native people felt strongly enough to escalate the stakes, and sought a settlement that would divide the Northwest Territories into two autonomous provinces. One would be for the Dene and the Metis, called Denendeh; the other would be for the Inuit, called Nunavut. The line of demarcation between them would roughly be the tree line. Both provinces would remain part of Canada, governed by the native majority within each, using traditional political and economic principles, cultural values, and language. (I will discuss these negotiations further in Chapter 20.) Meanwhile, the Dene and the

Inuit have instituted new cultural and economic programs within their own communities, leading to the workshops concerning television.

INVASION FROM OUTER SPACE

I traveled to Yellowknife in October. It's a three-hour plane ride due north from Edmonton, Alberta, including stops at two native communities along the way, Fort Smith and Hay River. The plane flew low over the terrain, which seemed an endless expanse of tiny lakes, granite boulders, and forests. There was already snow on the ground.

Between sessions of staring out the window, I read the *Toronto Globe and Mail,* which had a front page report on the U.S. Environmental Protection Agency prediction that the "greenhouse effect" would soon be felt throughout the world. The newspaper included maps of the Canadian north, which would experience a significant warming. New vegetation, foreign to the region, would flourish.

I was met at the Yellowknife airport by Cindy Gilday, the Dene woman who had contacted me on behalf of the Native Women's Association. I had met Gilday once before, in Washington D.C., at a conference concerned with creating a pan-Indian network of western hemisphere tribal peoples, to resist multinational corporate activity on Indian lands. The conference had been sponsored by Ralph Nader's organization, the Multi-National Monitor, as well as the Anthropology Resource Center and the Indian Law Resource Center in D.C. Gilday had been one of about a dozen Dene and Inuit in attendance.

"Hey, you brought the California weather with you, the temperature's up over zero today," she said. She spotted my newspaper with the "greenhouse effect" headline and told me that everybody in the north was really having a good time with the story. "People are hoping we'll have palm trees and beaches. Some guys are planning to grow bananas, but what are we going to do with all the mukluks?"

We had a few hours before the first workshop began, so Gilday drove me around Yellowknife. The town rises on the northern shores of the Great Slave Lake, a gigantic expanse comparable to the Great Lakes. On this day, overcast and (to me) very cold, the lake had the color of slate. Yellowknife has some older buildings dating back to the gold-mining days of the 1930s, but at the time of this visit it was mostly a community of small, government-built wooden houses not unlike a middle-class suburban tract. Right in the center of town is the government office and courthouse building, with an exterior of a ribbed aluminum alloy that looked to me like a square washboard. "We call it the sardine can," said Gilday. Then she pointed to the roof. There, looking down on the town, was a row of gigantic ravens. When they flew off, their wing span was at least four feet. "Those aren't even big ones," Gilday said. I soon noticed that these huge ravens were perched on windowsills and roofs all over town.

Gilday checked me into the Yellowknife Inn, in the heart of downtown. It had the shabby look of many modern buildings, designed for more southern climates; after a few years they become very worn at the edges.

Gilday suggested we go to the hotel coffee shop. "It's the main hangout for Indians in town," she said. "If you sit here for half a day, you'll see just about everybody."

Gilday started telling me how she'd been enthusiastic at first about the arrival of television in the North. She explained that there was no effective, quick means of communication among Dene communities, which are often hundreds—and in a few cases more than a thousand—miles from each other. Except for the area directly surrounding Yellowknife, there aren't any roads into the bush; only airplanes, radio, and dog team. "Until recently," she said, "it didn't really matter. Most of those communities have been self-sufficient for centuries, but now that the government is out there changing everything so fast, people in the communities need to find out what's going on everywhere else."

Television seemed to be a logical way of easing the problem, but thus far it hasn't done so. In the communities that did accept television, 60 percent of the programs were from the United States, including "Dallas," "Edge of Night," "Happy Days," "The Six Million Dollar Man," and others, with the remainder coming from Ottawa and Toronto. "We're not getting any chance to deal with our own problems on TV," Gilday told me. "There's only one hour each week of locally produced programming in the Northwest Territories, and only occasionally does that include any Indians or Inuit, even though we are the majority population around here.

"Yellowknife, the capital and the most 'Canadian' of the cities in the north, was the first community to get TV. We can already see that it's had a devastating effect on the people here. Out in the Indian communities in the bush, where maybe it came only a year or two ago, it's even worse. People are sitting in their log houses, alongside frozen lakes with dog teams tied up outside, watching a bunch of white people in Dallas standing around their swimming pools, drinking martinis and plotting to destroy each other or steal from each other, or to get their friends' wives into bed. Then after that they see a show that is about a man turning into a machine.

"The effect has been to glamorize behaviors and values that are poisonous to life up here. Our traditions have a lot to do with survival. Cooperation, sharing, and nonmaterialism are the only ways that people can live here," she told me. "TV always seems to present values opposite to those.

"I used to be a schoolteacher and when TV came to the villages I saw an immediate change. People lost interest in the native stories, legends, and languages, which are really important because they teach people how to live. And it's hurting the relationships between men and women too, and between the young and old. We used to honor our old people and listen to them," Gilday said, "but that's changing fast. TV makes it seem like the young people are all that's important and the old have nothing to say.

"And, you know, TV has been confusing the Indian people who've never seen anything like it before. For example, I heard of one old woman who prays every night for the people in the soap operas. She thinks they're *real*. We are all getting pretty scared, especially the women who have traditionally kept the family life together and made sure the culture was intact. But what really put the women over the edge about TV was the news that soon the Playboy Channel would be available in the north. The Native Women's Association became really active after that. Violence has increased here since the oil companies showed up and a lot of the men gave up trapping and hunting and started working for wages. They move into those work camps and start spending their money on alcohol and then when they get home they continue drinking and beating up on people. That sort of thing seldom happened before. The women expect things to get a lot worse with that Playboy Channel.

"You have to realize," Gilday continued, "that most people still live in extended families here. Ten people might live in a one- or two-room house. The TV is going all the time and the little kids and the old people and everyone are all sitting there together watching it. Now they'll all be seeing men beating up naked women. It's so crazy and so awful. Nobody ever told us that all this would be coming in with television. It's like some kind of invasion from outer space or something. First it was the government, then those oil companies, and now it's TV."

Gilday told me that while I was in Yellowknife I was to speak with two groups of native people. First, the Native Women's Association, and then, the next day, I would give a workshop at the offices of the Dene Nation. That would be for about fifty people who were responsible for various community programs: language preservation, community education, training in traditional skills, communications, alcohol and suicide prevention, and so on. In the days following, I would also be going to two outlying communities, Rae and Edzo, where I would speak with school kids.

• • •

The Native Women's Association met in the local hall of the Veterans of Foreign Wars. There were about seventy-five women in the room, most of them from outlying communities as far away as Tuktoyaktuk, about 1,500 miles north. The age spread was very even; about an equal number of young and old, and quite a few very old women. I discovered after my talk was over that many of the old women did not speak English. Immediately after my speech, these women gathered in a circle while one of the younger women gave a lengthy account of what had been said.

My intention with the speech was to create an agenda that could provide the basis for the series of workshops the Dene planned in the next few days, and for later workshops out in the communities. I raised a series of questions divided into a few categories, roughly as follows:

• **Family Life:** Have Dene family and social relationships changed since the introduction of television? What sorts of traditional family and community activities are being sacrificed? Are people following the prior patterns of visiting, working together, gathering in groups, and talking? Are the changes good?

• **Political Power:** How has television affected the Dene effort to wrest political power back from the Canadians? What are the political consequences of a one-way information flow, from Ottawa, New York, and Los Angeles, into the Mackenzie Valley? What bearing will this have on regional autonomy, and resistance to oil development?

• **Dene and Inuit Culture:** Has television had an effect on native culture? If so, on which aspects? Respect for elders? Attitudes about property and land ownership? A sense of community? A sense of cultural worthiness? Does television leave the native people feeling better or worse about themselves?

• **Views of the Natural World:** How will television influence the native system of perception and values concerning animals, the land, and the human relationship to the environment? How will television affect attitudes that are crucial for survival in the North?

• **Commercialism:** How will the onslaught of commercials affect a culture that until very recently was not part of a money economy but was based on barter and sharing? Will the Indians be susceptible to the value systems in advertising?

• **Language:** How will television affect the desire to learn the native languages, as well as the stories and myths that have guided northern culture? Will English seem more glamorous? Will the mythic heroes for the Indians become those created in Los Angeles?

• **Images of the Indian:** How will Indians be shown on television? The urban drunk? The noble savage? Cowboys and Indians? How will the relative absence of Indians on television affect native viewers, and children in particular? How will this affect people's sense of self-worth?

• **Effects on Learning:** If TV is a useful educational instrument, what sort of education does it deliver? How does that mode of education affect Indian kids? What prior modes of learning are being lost? What is the trade-off?

I concluded with some comments about the manner in which television is usually introduced into cultures, and by whom. The people who introduce television, I said, are ordinarily the people who benefit: manufacturers, advertisers, and governments who understand that television is an opportunity to reach more minds much more efficiently. They don't say anything negative about it. They only praise its benefits. But once installed, TV is difficult to get rid of. In the United States, for example, television is barely one generation old and yet it is in virtually every home. Watching television has become the main thing Americans do with their lives. It has enveloped the culture, and yet it's only about forty years old. What is needed, I concluded, is the ability to understand the benefits and drawbacks of new technologies *before* they overtake us. In the North there is still time to engage in this discussion.

Before I had begun talking, Cindy Gilday had warned me not to expect much of an audience reaction. "Don't expect anyone to ask you questions or to make any comments today," she said. "They'll be too shy with a white speaker. But they'll think about it and tomorrow, in the workshop, they'll probably have a lot to say." That proved true. I had never given a speech met by such silence, though there was applause at the end.

The next day, things were different. The group was smaller and Cindy Gilday asked each person to give a brief report on their feelings and observations about television.

TESTIMONIES

Joanne Barnaby, communications department, Dene Nation:

Some of the questions you raise have been raised already in the communities. For example, in Fort Good Hope, television came in six months ago. Every year before that the CBC [Canadian Broadcast Company] would come around to the village and say, "Well, you people want TV now?" and every year the people would say, "No." Six months later, the CBC would come around again and ask the same question. The reason people were against TV was that they heard from other communities how people weren't visiting each other anymore, and that the children were being influenced by it. It was hard to get the kids to do anything. The women weren't sewing anymore, either, and the woodpiles were too low. But last summer CBC showed up again at a meeting where there were only two or three people. One person said, "Well, okay, let's have TV," and another one said, "Okay" and right away, very fast, CBC installed the satellite dishes. The people were in an uproar because they felt they weren't really consulted. But CBC told them if they took down the facilities now, then Good Hope could never again get them back. It was real pressure. The people finally voted to leave it there, but only by a one-vote majority. You can already see the difference.

Dene language instructor:

Nobody in Fort Franklin wanted TV either, but after a while people got in the habit of going over to the next village, Norman Wells, to watch the hockey games. That got it started. It's created a lot of problems. Franklin is a community where everyone speaks Slavey [one of twenty-two Dene languages] as a first language, and we were teaching English as a second language. But the English they're getting from TV is slang English, and they want to know why we don't teach them that. Another problem is that parents don't control the TV, so the kids stay up all night watching it and they're exhausted the next day. They keep falling asleep in school.

Barbara Smith, nutrition educator and writer:

I've got four kids and we used to live on the land. When we first came into town, the kids didn't like TV. They were scared of it. They wondered why that man on the TV was staring at them. But it didn't take them too long to get hooked on cartoons. I think if kids don't have TV in their childhood, then they're more creative later. But even my kids have been affected by it. A lot of the images they have in their heads now are TV images, like especially the people in "Fall Guy." I know a lot of kids who don't play at all anymore because they'd rather watch TV. It's easier than playing or reading. It's not enough to say that parents ought to turn the thing off because the

kids can then watch at the neighbors' or in school. TV has more influence than parents do.

Mary Wilson (sixty-five years old), Slavey translator:

> I was thinking how lucky I am that I brought up my children when
> there was no TV and no things to worry about, like sniffing glue and
> alcohol. I had a hard struggle to keep life together, but if I'd have
> had all these worries I don't know how I would have coped. At one
> time the women used to sit around all the time and talk about things
> and be sewing and competing to see whose husband was going to be
> the best dressed, but now they don't do that. The women are so in-
> volved in this soap opera thing. They even phone each other about
> what happened on the show.

Ethel Blondin, Department of Education, Government of the Northwest
Territories (now a Member of Parliament):

> I'm working with languages too, and I have mixed feelings about
> what you say. When we first got TV up at Tuktoyaktuk in the mid-
> 1970s, I felt suddenly I had to be an entertainer to compete with it.
> I really couldn't compete with that kind of sexual image they put on
> TV. But I have a certain zest for life, which those TV characters
> don't have. I think the kids understood that. But one time I got to
> use TV to teach native languages. When I had control of it, I think
> it worked out okay. But it does affect family life. I know I have to
> supervise the way my kids use it. They have to turn it off when I say
> so. It all depends on the strength of the family unit, I think.

Cindy Gilday:

> When TV first came to Rae, I was working there as a teacher. The
> social relationships of the people and the language and learning of
> the kids changed overnight. What they started learning best was all
> the stuff that's in those commercials from white society. But I would
> really like to know is what it is about TV that causes the addiction?
> I know something happens to me when I watch TV. I get glued to
> it, even if it's something like soap operas with those kinds of values.
> I wish I could figure out what keeps people watching because then
> maybe we could create a Dene soap opera. Could we ever get the
> kind of money they use on "Dallas" to put out our ideas of Dene
> life?

(The question of creating an Indian soap opera kept coming up. It was
observed that the behaviors that create interest in the soaps were problem

behaviors, such as adultery, emotional problems, lying, and scheming. To show Dene people engaged in those behaviors was not going to do the Dene any good. Also the rhythms of the soaps—a major crisis once or twice in every program—were different from the rhythms of life in the North, where events are very slow. "Would anyone want to watch a show about women sitting and sewing mukluks for hours, or hanging fish in the smokehouse?" one woman asked.)

Ernie Lennie, education coordinator, Dene Nation:

> The type of learning we get in school and also on TV is the type of learning where we just sit and absorb. But in family life it's a different kind of learning. Children learn directly from their parents. That is the native way of teaching. Learning has to come from doing, not intellectualizing. A long time ago they only taught people by doing things, but now they just sit and watch TV. Taking away TV is like taking away a bottle of alcohol.

Barbara Smith:

> There's an ancient native concept that words have power. So if you're putting a lot of energy into watching soaps, then you're concentrating your energy in a negative way. Pretty soon people who watch those shows start having problems like the people on the soaps. I know a lot of people who seem real negatively affected by TV.

Irene Bjornson, court reporter:

> When I was living in southern Alberta, I used to watch TV so much. And because my town was in a later time zone, my friends used to call me to find out what happened on the shows before they were shown. I would buy food that was very easy so it wouldn't get in the way of watching TV. I learned a lot from TV and I learned a lot from white society too, but all that time I didn't learn anything about myself. I didn't like being a Dene. When I went to school I learned English and French and they told me it was stupid to speak Dene. Now, my husband is white and my husband's family doesn't like Indians. All they saw about Indians was those drunks they saw on TV and that's how they judged me. But now I really speak my mind and believe in myself. I hardly watch TV anymore. But I've got a six-year-old daughter who's going on sixteen because she watches so much TV.

Ethel Lamsthe, community development worker:

> Those stereotypes on TV really twist people. The way they show
> what a terrific thing it is to have a drink. Their lifestyles are so dif-
> ferent. How does that make you feel about yourself? Every com-
> munity now has got those VCRs. I try to get people to talk, but they
> don't want to anymore. They just sit and watch.

EFFECTS ON STORYTELLING

One of the most intense discussions of the day concerned TV's impact
on traditional storytelling practices. For centuries it had been part of Dene
family life for the grandparents to tell tales to the kids for several hours
each night before bedtime. With television, storytelling has virtually
stopped. Meanwhile, many storytellers are dying off without passing along
their skills. One suggestion was that perhaps TV could now be used to
convey the stories.

Cindy Gilday:

> When I was a kid we were told the same stories over and over again,
> and then we'd ask for it to be told one more time. Every mother and
> grandmother would be into it. And everyone would tell the story
> slightly different. We wanted those stories so much we'd scheme so
> that maybe we could hear some story for the thousandth time.

Cindy's friend:

> Some of the old people were so good at storytelling. They had a
> breadth and level of language that my generation doesn't have any-
> more. When we talk about maintaining the legends we also have to
> talk about the level of language. If I was going to try to become a
> storyteller, I'd have to go back and live with the old people and eat
> and sleep with them and practice those stories over and over, because
> each time you hear those stories you hear something new in them.

Man from audience:

> It was such a refined art. They projected the stories in their bodies,
> not only in their words. There is both a conscious and a subconscious
> level in storytelling. Something will really be lost if we try to portray
> those stories on TV.

Barbara Smith:

> Legends are tools that help people grow in certain ways. A lot of
> what matters is the power and the feeling of the experience. It's like
> when you're tanning hides, it's not only important to learn how to
> do the scraping and the cutting. In the old way, the process was also
> a kind of meditation, a prayer to help put power into it. There used
> to be prayers for how to grind the corn. It wasn't just grinding corn,
> it was also the feeling in it. But when you put something in a mu-
> seum, or even on TV, you can see it all right, but you're really looking
> only at the shell.

• • •

I had been listening silently to most of the discussion up to this point, but
I could not contain my desire to discourage the use of video for re-creating
the legends and stories. It would not, I argued, be an adequate substitute.
In the old way, when elders told stories to the young, the subtle dimensions
were probably more important than the content of the stories. Sitting together on quiet, dark evenings, kids and grandparents huddled near a fire,
the old people themselves became a kind of window through which to see
thousands of years back into time, back to the sources of the Indian experience. Tremendous admiration, affection, respect, and love was mutually engendered by this tradition. Its continuation was critical to the
Indian sense of self-respect and identity.

The stories also embodied a teaching system. The old transmit to the
young their knowledge of how things are, in such a loving way that the
children absorb it whole and request more. The death of the storytelling
process will leave an absence of knowledge of Indian ways and thought,
and a sense of worth in Indian culture.

Another important factor is that the images woven by the storyteller are
actually realized in the listeners' minds. The children create pictures in
their heads, pictures that go far beyond the words of the storyteller, into
the more elaborate, more fabulous world of the imagination. So the child
is in some ways as creative as the teller of the tale, or put another way, the
storyteller is only a stimulus for the imagination of the child. If the stories
were conveyed by video, not only would the intimacy, love, and respect
between young and old be lost, but the child's creative contributions would
be lost as well. Finally, I said, video versions of the stories would be necessarily limited by the abilities and budget of the video makers. Even the
most talented video makers would find it impossible to equal what the
imagination does with a story told orally. So the net result of translating

stories to television would be to confine, and actually lessen, their power, meaning, and beauty. Audio tape or radio would be far better.

I recalled an experience I'd had many years earlier while interviewing John Mohawk, a Seneca Indian who was then editor of *Akwesasne Notes,* the largest Indian newspaper in North America. I had spent several days with John and used a tape recorder to record his views on various Indian political and social matters. I had asked him about the stories that influenced him as a child, and he resisted telling me. One time, however, on a five-hour drive from northern New York State to Syracuse, he agreed to tell me some stories, but only if I switched off the tape recorder. When I asked him why, he said, "First of all I'm not supposed to be telling you this story at all. Secondly, if you have the machine going, or if you're taking notes, you won't understand the story. It depends on your listening with your heart. That won't come out on a machine."

Similarly, putting the stories on TV would reduce their evocative power, narrow their content, and destroy the interchange between the young and old. Kids who heard their stories in that way would have a "cold" memory of Indian stories. The warmth of feeling for the stories described by the Dene at the workshop would be lost, and with it an important piece of the culture's vitality.

VISIT TO SCHOOL

The Dene villages of Rae and Edzo are located just above the northern finger of the Great Slave Lake, on opposite sides of another small lake, Lake Marion, which in October was already frozen solid. The highway to these towns runs northwest from Yellowknife along the shores of the Great Slave Lake. It is the only road out of the capital city of the Northwest Territories, but it is actually little more than a bulldozed dirt track with huge patches of ice and snow, and falloffs on either side. Making it still more hazardous are the occasional lumber trucks barreling along as if it were the New Jersey Turnpike.

The land is nearly flat, though the huge granite boulders sprinkled over the landscape and the countless small, bright blue lakes give the terrain a kind of harsh, brilliant appeal.

Soon after arriving in Rae, I was thrilled to get my first sight of dog teams. They were out on the lake lying alongside the ice holes, where the men had dropped their nets.

Most of the houses were built with stripped logs, in the traditional Dene manner, but tarpaper houses were not unusual. Every house had a small smokehouse adjoining it, where fish, caribou, and moose were smoked throughout the year. More dog teams were tied up nearby, and many of the houses had rifles outside, leaning against the front-door sash.

Our first official stop was at a new, modern school, typical of the sort found in American suburbs. Gilday told me that she taught at this school before she got married and moved down to Yellowknife. She was greeted warmly, and we were taken to a windowless amphitheatre. Four classes had been combined for our visit, about sixty kids in all, ages twelve (or so) to sixteen. There was a TV set in the room, which I had requested.

I began by asking the kids about their TV viewing habits. I learned that though TV had come to Rae only two years before, every home now had one. About 90 percent of the homes also had VCRs. There was unanimous agreement that the TV sets remained turned on in the homes virtually all of the time. Since most of the families lived in one- or two-room houses, all ages were watching TV until very late at night. I asked how many of the children had parents who attempted to control the viewing by setting times or selecting programs, or by turning it off altogether at a certain hour. Only two kids raised their hands. I asked how many of their families were still telling stories at night. There was no response. Television had apparently taken over in Rae, suddenly and totally.

My final question was whether or not they believed that what they saw in TV shows like "Dallas" or "Happy Days" was "real." About two-thirds of the children said they felt it was.

At this point we had been talking for about five minutes, but there were already signs of restlessness in the room. I decided to turn on the TV. My goal was to accomplish at least one thing: to instill in at least a few of the kids a way of viewing television images with less passive acceptance. I wanted to convey that the images are artificial constructs.

After turning on the television I explained what a "technical event" is and asked the children to count them in the images on the screen. They did so with enthusiasm. My hope was that these kids would find themselves continuing to count the technical events at home. Perhaps it would create a degree of resistance to unconscious immersion in the television world.

Within about half an hour the students were restless again. At that point Cindy Gilday stepped forward and passionately implored the kids to be aware of how the TV shows were affecting their attitudes and behavior. "Seeing those shows from the United States, with all that drinking in them, where all everybody wants is more money and more cars, has nothing to do with life here," she said. "You're being colonized by that, except that it's happening right in your heads. First it was the British, then it was the Canadians, then it was the oil companies, and now it's the TV." I had the feeling she got through to a few of the young people, especially some of the girls who seemed fixed to her every word. But mostly I came away impressed by the added power television has when introduced into a nearly "virgin" community.

After we had finished, several teachers said that the session had been useful, if only to have brought up the problem. The teachers felt that TV was a gigantic, though unobserved, problem in the school. They felt that they had to become performers, fast and sexy, in order to keep the kids' attention. The children had just about given up reading; their attention span seemed much shorter than only a few years ago; they were behaving in a much more aggressive manner; and their interest in speaking the local Dene tongue was fast disappearing. The teachers hoped that we would come back sometime, they said. Meanwhile they would try to find a way of discussing these questions with the students.

Next we went to Edzo, about ten miles around Lake Marion, to a special school for young people who, for one reason or another, had not previously been in school. Some of them were in their early twenties, but most were in their late teens. Some came from communities where there hadn't been schools; others just hadn't attended.

Whereas the younger kids in Rae had been restless and hyper, this group of about twenty young people were silent, passive, sullen. The TV set in this room was broken, so after asking them the same set of questions that I had asked the group in Rae, I had no technical crutch to help engage their attention. Gilday and I tried to start a discussion about what they liked and didn't like on TV, and how their ideas and desires were being changed by it. They said they liked *all* TV. I had the feeling Gilday and I both seemed absurd to them.

On the long drive back to Yellowknife, we were accompanied by a young non-Indian activist. When I mentioned that I was depressed at what I'd just seen in the two classrooms, he said that the situation among young people was even worse in the more northern communities where the oil companies have had their greatest impact. In some places there were outbreaks of suicide among young people, though further south the traditional fabric was still mostly holding together. "There is a lot of political activity here, and efforts to maintain the traditional ways," he said. "We've been trying to set up rap groups in the more impacted northern areas to get the young people talking to each other, letting off some of the steam— Indian males really keep it inside—and there's been some progress. We see these kids come and pour out their hearts to each other. It's inspirational. But things won't get really better until the Indians gain back some political power and control over what's going on up here."

When we arrived back at Yellowknife, I was given a collection of publications concerning Denendeh, the hoped-for new province of Canada with a mostly Dene leadership. "This is the answer for the Dene," I was told. "Regain political control of the region, or else the Indians will sink under the pressures from Canada and the U.S. The oil, the missiles, television; it's all part of the same assault."

The Dene envisioned that the Denendeh economic system would emphasize the traditional languages and lifestyle, based on self-sufficiency and renewable resources. Development projects would be judged by traditional criteria, such as impact on the environment and impact on the culture, rather than on short-term economic benefits. The Dene would be in charge of all wildlife and wilderness management. In areas such as health, education, social services, the arts, media, and recreation, the Dene would establish their own institutions, though with the same level of support that Canada provides for other less culturally autonomous provinces.

The Canadian government, meanwhile, was worried that too much Dene economic and political control might lead to severe restrictions on oil development.

The Dene had already created a cultural awareness program, hoping to psychologically arm the people against the Canadian culture. Aside from the communications project, of which the television workshop was part, each community had created programs in the following areas: Dene as a first language; oral histories with elders describing traditional values; programs on how to live off the land in summer and winter; and training in traditional music and storytelling. Summer camps had been set up, run by the elders to give training in wilderness survival, snare setting, catching, cleaning, drying, and cutting fish; skinning animals, and animal behavior, as well as hand games, songs, and chants. The Dene were also promoting interest in new economic ventures that would not threaten Dene community life, such as outfitting and guiding hunters, boat building, aquaculture, domestication of wild game, and small-scale tourism.

THE RAVENS

During my last few days in Yellowknife I had time to visit with an old colleague from decades earlier, Marie-Helene Laraque. While living in Berkeley, California, she had been the editor of the first bilingual pan-

Indian newspaper, *Indigena,* which concerned itself with the problems of native people throughout the Americas and the need to establish contacts between them.

Laraque was born in Haiti of mixed racial ancestry, but she identifies most strongly with her Arawak Indian heritage. (Few people are aware that Haiti had an Indian population before the arrival of Westerners.) Through her work, she met and later married one of the Dene chiefs from the community of Fort Smith. There, Laraque gave birth to two children and became active in the movement to block a dam on the Slave River, which would have.destroyed a vast Dene hunting and fishing ground. (The power from the dam was to be shipped to the cities of the South.) When the marriage ended in 1980, Laraque took her children north to Yellowknife, and recently remarried. For a while she was the editor of the Dene Nation Newsletter, which recently ceased publication. "I was really sorry that publication stopped," she told me. "It was a way of keeping the Dene communities informed without them having to buy TV sets, which don't carry Dene news anyway. Also, we sent the paper to all of the other Indian tribes in North America, and I still feel that communication among the tribes is very important."

I asked Marie-Helene how she, a Haitian by birth and for most of her life an urban dweller, could survive in the harsh environment of the far north. "I stay here," she said, "because this is where my children were born, and they are Dene. I want them to grow up as Indians, and there's no way that could happen in New York or San Francisco, and there's no way I can go back to Haiti. Here they're close to their grandparents and cousins. It's the kind of family life that I couldn't reproduce for them in the South. They'd drift away. And it's a good place for interracial getting along. Much better than anywhere I've ever known or lived. Anyway, I'm devoted to helping the Dene get through these times in a good way. They are really getting organized and they've got a chance to make it. If I can continue to help, I want to do that."

That evening Marie-Helene had a party at her house, for about thirty people. For hours beforehand, the invited guests dropped off food: two wild ducks that Marie-Helene made into soup, fresh caribou and moose meat, two platters of bannock (a hard bread made of flour and, in this region, fish eggs), and, from the Great Slave Lake, fresh whitefish and trout much larger and oilier than any I'd ever had in the South.

As I helped her put the food on the buffet table, I noticed that Marie-Helene cut a small piece from each item and placed it into a separate dish that was *not* put on the table. I asked what she was doing, but she only said, "I'll tell you later."

At the party I found myself talking to a Catholic priest, Rene Fumo-leau, who told me that he had come to the Canadian North in 1953 from France and had never left. Fumoleau was the author of a definitive work about the treaty negotiations, *As Long as This Land Shall Last,* which was used as evidence in the Justice Morrow hearings concerning fraud in the treaties. "When I came here in 1953 it was really free," he said. "That's what I loved about it. Not much police presence. No foreign laws. The government left people alone. The communities were very happy with life in those days, much happier than now."

Barbara Smith was there with three of her kids, and I thanked her for her wonderful participation in the TV workshop. Smith, who wears very thick glasses, had more to say: "My own relationship to TV is different from most people's because I am, legally speaking, a blind person. My vision is so poor that my memory comes in sound, accompanied by blurred colors and shapes. I can't close my eyes and imagine my sons' faces. I've been trying to understand how other people are affected by images. TV is not really a threat to me but I realize that it's a danger to the Dene culture in general. The images people used to get from the old stories are just being blotted out. And it also affects how they live, and what they eat. I have been working to explain proper nutrition to people who have bought into the junk food from the TV. Most Dene who have moved in from the land to fixed communities don't eat the sort of fresh fish and meat we're eating tonight. Unless somebody goes out and shoots a moose or a rabbit, people will just go over to the grocery and buy junk. Candy, canned food. It's really harming people's lives and the TV is encouraging that. The kids used to go out on the ice and bring home fish for dinner. But now they're all indoors watching TV, which is telling them to eat the junk food. They use their welfare checks for the groceries."

The conversation got around to the "greenhouse effect" again, which usually produces laughter when it's discussed. The people in Yellowknife are amazed at the prospect that their world could be unalterably changed because of pollution in the South. And then there's talk of the cruise missile test-flights that the U.S. is now doing. Despite Dene opposition, the Canadian government granted permission to the United States to fly missiles at low altitude all the way down the Mackenzie Valley, some 1,500 miles to Alberta. "Seems like you people are always wanting to drop things on somebody," someone jokingly said to me.

At the end of the evening I helped Marie-Helene clean up the dishes. She had already divided the edible leftovers among the guests. The bannock went home with this one, the caribou meat with that one. I asked her again about the little dish in which she had placed small cuttings from each course. She told me that many native people traditionally make offerings of part of their meal. "What I do at the end of the evening," she said, "is add those cuttings to a bowl of table scraps and put them all outside for the ravens." I watched her as she went out into the night and climbed a small, snowy hill behind the house, put the dish down, and then stood there for a few moments. When she came back into the house, she said, "In five minutes the bowl will be empty."

7

CORPORATIONS AS MACHINES

*T*HE GREAT FRENCH philosopher and technology critic Jacques Ellul makes it one of his central points that evaluations of technology must not be confined to the machines themselves. Equally important, he says, is to grasp that in technological society, the structure of all of human life and its systems of organization reflect the logic of the machine. All are encompassed by Ellul within the single term *technique,* which suggests that in contemporary society, human behavior, human thought, and human political and economic structures are part of a seamless fabric inseparable from machines. *Technique* is machine logic extended to all human endeavors.

This point is most easily understood when we think about our relationship to the assembly line, or to the automobile or the clock; how we tune in to and reflect the characteristics of those machines. Those examples suggest a human-machine symbiosis that alters both sides of the connection, as part of a long, back-and-forth process of merging, or coevolution.

But *technique* is also apparent in the modes of organization that tend to gain favor in technological society. This will be dealt with more thoroughly in Part III, when we compare technological and native societies. This chapter, however, will focus on one particular organizational mode, a very dominant mode in our society—the corporation. The corporation is not as subject to human control as most people believe it is; rather, it is an autonomous technical structure that behaves by a system of logic uniquely well suited to its primary function: to give birth and impetus to profitable new technological forms, and to spread techno-logic around the globe.

• • •

Given the extent to which corporations affect both technical change and the forces of nature, it is surprising how little attention we give them. It's not that we are entirely unaware of them; we hear their names trumpeted and flashed at us whichever way we turn. But most of us accept their existence unquestioningly, unconsciously, like background noise. We don't focus on them as the primary players they are, and we have very little understanding of *why* they behave as they do.

We usually become aware of corporate behavior only when a flagrant transgression is reported in the news: the dumping of toxic wastes, the releasing of pollutants, the suppression of research regarding health effects of various products, the tragic mechanical breakdowns such as at Three Mile Island, in Bhopal, or in Prince William Sound, Alaska. Sometimes we become concerned about a large corporation closing a factory, putting 5,000 people out of work, and moving to another country.

Even when we hear such news, our tendency is to respond as if the behaviors described stem from the *people* within the corporate structure—people who are irresponsible, dishonest, greedy, or overly ambitious. Or else we attribute the problem to the moral decline of the times we live in, or to the failure of the regulatory process.

Seeing corporate behavior as rooted in the people who work within them is like believing that the problems of television are attributable solely to its program content. With corporations, as with television, the basic problems are actually structural. They are problems inherent in the forms and rules by which these entities are compelled to operate. If the problems could be traced to the personnel involved, they could be solved by changing the personnel. Unfortunately, however, *all* employees are obliged to act in concert, to behave in accordance with corporate form and corporate law. If someone attempted to revolt against these tenets, it would only result in the corporation throwing the person out, and replacing that person with another who would act according to the rules. Form determines content. Corporations are machines.

• • •

The failure to grasp the nature and inevitabilities of corporate structure has left our society far too unconscious and passive to corporate desires, and has helped corporations increase their influence, power, and freedom from accountability. Corporations already influence our conceptions of how life should be lived more than any other institution, including government. Corporate ideology, corporate priorities, corporate styles of behavior, corporate value systems, and corporate modes of organization have become synonymous with "our way of life." Corporate "culture" has become the virtual definition of American life, to be defended at all costs, even militarily. When Secretary of State George Schultz said in 1985 that in Nicaragua and El Salvador "we are fighting for our way of life," it was the threat of collectivism to free enterprise and commodity culture that motivated his remarks. Conversely, when our leaders celebrate the new "freedom" of Eastern Europe, they are really celebrating free enterprise and the market economy.

Living in the United States today, there is scarcely a moment when you are not in contact with a corporation, or its manifestation.

It is very likely that you work for a corporation. If so, your daily schedule is determined by corporate needs. You dress and behave according to corporate concepts, you interact with the machines by which corporations accomplish their tasks—computers, typewriters, telephones, fax machines, copiers. You spend your day living within corporate rhythms.

The building you live in was probably created by a corporation, as were your furniture, appliances, the clothes in your closet, your perfume—all the result of corporate concepts and action.

Taken as a group, corporations are the largest landowners in the United States, with the exception of the federal government. Corporations are also the major financial backers of electoral campaigns, and the major lobbyists for laws that benefit corporate goals.

If you switch on your radio or television, or open your newspaper, corporations speak to you. They do it through public relations and through advertising. American corporations spend more than $100 billion yearly on advertising, which is far more than is spent on all secondary education in this country. In some ways corporate advertising is the dominant education institution in our country, surely in the realm of lifestyle.

As I mentioned in Chapter 5, the average American now views 21,000 commercials every year. Twenty-one thousand times, corporations place images in your brain to suggest something great about commodities. Some commercials advertise cars, others advertise drugs—but all commercials agree that you should buy *something,* and that human life is most satisfying when inundated with commodities. Between commercials there are programs, also created by corporations, that espouse values consistent with the ads.

Corporations are also the major providers of educational materials for American schools. Some of the largest corporations are now providing books, tapes, films, and computer programs free of charge to public and private schools, as a "public service" in these budget-conscious times. They get a lot of praise for these contributions. Oil and chemical companies have been particularly generous in providing materials to help explain nature to young people—materials that portray nature as a valuable resource for human use and that celebrate concepts such as "managing nature" through chemicals, pesticides, and large-scale agribusiness. Thus, a generation of youngsters is trained to regard nature in a way that coincides with corporate objectives. They are also trained to accept corporate interpretations and perspectives from a very early age, and are thereby prepared for what is to come.

CORPORATE SHAME

I keep awaiting the day when a corporate president expresses shame for a corporate transgression against the public or the environment. The statement would go something like this:

"On behalf of my company, its management, and its shareholders, I wish to express our grief concerning injuries suffered by people living downstream from our factory, along the Green River. We are ashamed to admit that over the years, our poisonous wastes have found their way into the river, putting the community in peril. We will do anything to relieve the suffering we have caused. We are also concerned that safe storage for such potent chemicals now seems impossible, and so henceforth we will only use our facilities for safer forms of manufacturing. Under no circumstances will we give thought to abandoning this community or its workers."

No such statement has ever been made, nor will ever be made, by a publicly held corporation in America, for several reasons.

No corporate manager could ever place community welfare above corporate interest. An individual executive might personally wish to do so, but to make this sort of admission would subject the company, and the individual, to legal action by local, state, and federal authorities, as well as to damage suits by victims.

It could also open management to lawsuits from its own shareholders. U.S. corporate law holds that management of publicly held companies must act primarily in the economic interests of shareholders. If not, management can be sued by shareholders and firings would surely occur. So managers are legally obliged to ignore community welfare (e.g., worker health and satisfaction, environmental concerns) if those needs interfere with profitability. And corporate managers must also deny that corporate acts have a negative impact of any kind, if that impact might translate into costly damage suits that hinder profits.

As a result, we have witnessed countless cases in which corporate acts caused death or injury or illness, while the company denied any responsibility. We have heard cigarette companies deny that cigarettes are harmful. We have heard the same from manufacturers of pesticides, chemicals, asbestos, and birth-control technologies.

Often, corporations are privately aware of the dangers of their products or processes, but withhold that information. Even as I write these words, a National Public Radio news program is reporting on the efforts of certain plastic-wrapping manufacturers to conceal from the government and the public what their own research had told them twenty years before the government or public found out: The plastic wrapping on our supermarket meats, fish, and other items can leave carcinogenic residues in our food.

In instances such as these, withholding information means that people—perhaps tens of thousands of people—become sick. Some people die. In other contexts, murder charges would be in order.

CORPORATE SCHIZOPHRENIA

That murder charges are not levied against corporations, and that corporations do not express shame at their own actions, is a direct result of the peculiar nature of corporate form, its split personality. Though human beings work inside corporations, a corporation is not a person, and does not have feelings. In most senses a corporation is not even a "thing." It may have offices, and/or a factory or products, but a corporation does not have any physical existence or form—no corporality. So when conditions in a community or country become unfavorable—safety standards become too rigid, or workers are not submissive—a corporation can dematerialize and then rematerialize in another town or country.

If a corporation is not a person or a thing, what is it? It is basically a *concept* that is given a name, and a legal existence, on paper. Though there is no such actual creature, our laws recognize the corporation as an entity. So does the population. We think of corporations as having concrete form, but their true existence is only on paper and in our minds.

Even more curious than a corporation's ephemeral quality is that our laws give this nonexistent entity a great many rights similar to those given to human beings. The law calls corporations "fictitious persons," with the right to buy and sell property, or to sue in court for injuries or for slander and libel. And "corporate speech"—advertising, public relations—is protected under the First Amendment to the Constitution, governing freedom of speech. This latter right has been extended to corporations despite the fact that when the Bill of Rights was written in 1792, corporations as we now know them did not exist. (The First Amendment was originally intended to protect *personal* speech, in a century when the only media consisted of single news-sheets, handbills, and books. The net result of expanding First Amendment protection to *corporate* speech is that $100 billion worth of advertising from a relative handful of sources gets to dominate public perception, free from nearly all government attempts at regulation. Democracy is effectively thwarted, rather than aided.)

Though corporations enjoy many "human" rights, they have not been required to abide by human responsibilities. Even in cases of negligence causing death or injury, the state cannot jail or execute the corporation. In rare instances, individuals within a corporation can be prosecuted, if they perpetrate acts that they know can cause injury. And a corporation may be fined or ordered to alter practices, but its structure is never altered, its "life" is never threatened.

In fact, unlike human beings, corporations do not die a natural death. A corporation usually outlives the human beings who have been part of it, even those who "own" it. A corporation actually has the possibility of immortality. Of course, the owners of a corporation can put it to death under certain conditions, but society cannot exercise that kind of control.

Lacking the sort of physical, organic reality that characterizes human existence, this entity, this concept, this collection of paperwork called a "corporation" is not capable of feelings such as shame or remorse. Instead, corporations behave according to their own unique systems of standards, rules, forms, and objectives.

The most basic rule of corporate operation is that it must produce income, and (except for that special category of "nonprofit corporations") must show a profit over time. Among publicly held companies there is another basic rule: It must expand and grow, since growth is the standard by which the stock market judges a company. All other values are secondary: the welfare of the community, the happiness of workers, the health of the planet, and even the general prosperity.

So human beings within the corporate structure, whatever their personal morals and feelings, are prevented from operating on their own standards. Like the assembly-line workers who must operate at the speed of the machine, corporate employees are strapped onto the apparatus of the corporation, and operate by its rules.

In this sense a corporation is essentially a machine, a technological structure, an organization that follows its own principles and its own morality, and in which human morality is anomalous. Because of this double standard—one for human beings and another for "fictitious persons" like corporations—we sometimes see bizarre behavior from executives who, though knowing what is right and moral, behave in a contrary fashion.

THE CORPORATE/HUMAN DILEMMA:
THREE CASES

In 1986, Union Carbide Corporation's chemical plant in Bhopal, India, accidentally released methyl isocynate into the air, injuring some 200,000 people and killing more than 2,000. Soon after the accident the chairman of the board of Union Carbide, Warren M. Anderson, was so upset at what happened that he informed the media that he would spend the rest of his life attempting to correct the problems his company had caused and to make amends. Only one year later, however, Mr. Anderson was quoted in *Business Week* as saying that he had "overreacted," and was now prepared to lead the company in its legal fight *against* paying damages and reparations. What happened? Very simply, Mr. Anderson at first reacted as a human being. Later, he realized (and perhaps was pressed to realize) that this reaction was inappropriate for a chairman of the board of a company whose primary obligations are not to the poor victims of Bhopal, but to shareholders; that is, to its profit picture. If Mr. Anderson had persisted in expressing his personal feelings or acknowledging the company's culpability, he certainly would have been fired.

When the *Exxon Valdez* crashed onto a reef in 1989, and spilled its oil into the sea and onto the beaches of Alaska—in part because of the intoxication of the ship's captain—the corporation at first reacted with apologies, and promised to make amends: clean the water, clean the beaches, save the animals, pay for damages. I was surprised at the company's stance. It ran counter to the normal manner in which corporations react. Perhaps in this case the cause and effect were simply indisputable, unlike cases of birth malformations from herbicide spraying or injury to workers in computer manufacturing, where causes and effects are separated by many years. On the other hand, maybe certain top executives at Exxon *were* truly horrified and felt moved to make things right. If so, like Union Carbide's Anderson, they soon came to their senses. The cleanup turned out to be very expensive. Within six months the company ceased all of its efforts to allay the effects of the spill. In a typical corporate cost-benefit approach, it was reasoned that fighting the lawsuits and making settlements that courts or negotiators might require would certainly be cheaper than cleaning the mess.

For me, the most disturbing example of corporate schizophrenia occurred in the personal context of a family event during the late 1960s. At the time, I was involved in efforts to retard the Manhattanization of San Francisco. I authored a series of ads attempting to halt the construction of high-rise office buildings that were increasing traffic and pollution, and destroying the vistas that are a big part of life in that city. Among our arguments was that high-rise development cost the city—in services such as police, fire, sewage, expanded electrical power generation, and road maintenance—far more than could be redeemed in property taxes. We had studies to prove this.

While working on these campaigns a friend of my family's—I will call her Genevieve—telephoned to say that her father was in town from Chicago for a few days. She wanted to drop by with him and the kids. At that moment we realized that Genevieve's father was president of one of the largest corporate developers of skyscrapers. Several of his buildings were ones we were opposing.

On a bright Sunday morning, Genevieve and her family came for brunch in our garden. Mr. Butterfield turned out to be most charming: friendly, personable, affectionate with his grandchildren and with our children.

Out of friendship for Genevieve, I did not raise any environmental issues on this occasion. But when Mr. Butterfield remarked on how wonderful it was that we enjoyed such a lush garden in the midst of the crowded city, and asked about the vacant lot adjoining our house, things changed. We informed him that only three days ago a bulldozer had been in the adjoining lot to level a lovely Victorian house and a wonderful formal Italian garden with tomatoes, beans, squash, roses, geraniums, and two small redwood trees. The garden had been tended by an elderly Italian couple who had lived in the house for forty years. When the couple died—the husband within three weeks of the wife—the bank sold the property to developers, who planned to build a twenty-six-unit apartment building. Soon, our views would be blocked and shadows would fall on our garden.

Mr. Butterfield was aghast. "How horrible," he said. "It is amazing they would permit huge apartments on such a lovely quiet street."

I could no longer restrain myself. Assuming that Mr. Butterfield would easily see the parallels between the destruction of our views and the far larger problems caused by his own thirty-story buildings less than a mile away, I told him of the campaigns to stop such development. He was altentive and concerned. He said he had no idea there was resistance in San Francisco to high-rise development.

This statement, in turn, shocked me. The movement against these new buildings had been going on for several years and included public protests and considerable media attention. I wondered if he was being truthful with me. I knew that among top corporate executives, who live in a world of spreadsheets and financial manipulations, there is sometimes little awareness of how their actions affect real people. Maybe the protests in San Francisco were not sufficiently threatening that the president of a Chicago corporation would even know about them. If so, it was a humbling reality for anyone seeking to influence corporate actions. I decided to take Mr. Butterfield at his word. In any event, it was the polite way of handling the situation.

The conversation went on. He asked me why people were opposed, and I told him about the studies showing the effects of this kind of development. He was fascinated. He handed me his business card and asked me to write to him directly, and to forward the studies and any other relevant information. He said he would personally assess the situation and get back to me. He thanked me warmly for the news I brought.

I came away from the exchange convinced the man was in earnest. And probably, while sitting in my garden, he was.

I gathered the material, wrote him a long explanatory letter, and sent it in a package marked "Personal," as he had suggested. I soon received a reply saying he would study the reports and be in touch very soon. He never wrote back. A subsequent letter that I sent to him was not acknowledged. Finally, I decided that his polite behavior at brunch was, like my own, out of concern for his daughter. Back at corporate headquarters, a different set of rules superseded all feelings.

ELEVEN INHERENT RULES
OF CORPORATE BEHAVIOR

It is clear that human beings within a corporation are seriously constrained in their ability to influence corporate behavior. And yet, I have mentioned only two of the rules that serve to constrain this influence: the profit imperative and the need for growth. The following list is an attempt to articulate more of the obligatory rules by which corporations operate. Some of the rules overlap, but taken together they help reveal why corporations behave as they do, and how they have come to dominate their environment and the human beings within it.

1. The Profit Imperative

As noted earlier, profit is the ultimate measure of all corporate decisions. It takes precedence over community well-being, worker health, public health, peace, environmental preservation, or national security. Corporations will even find ways of trading with national "enemies"—Libya, Iran, the Soviet Union, Cuba—when public policy abhors it. The profit imperative and the growth imperative are the most fundamental corporate drives; together they represent the corporation's instinct to "live."

2. The Growth Imperative

Corporations live or die by whether they can sustain growth. On this depends relationships to investors, to the stock market, to banks, and to public perception. The growth imperative also fuels the corporate desire to find and develop scarce resources in obscure parts of the world.

This effect is now clearly visible, as the world's few remaining pristine places are sacrificed to corporate production. The peoples who inhabit these resource-rich regions are similarly pressured to give up their traditional ways and climb on the wheel of production-consumption. Corporate planners consciously attempt to bring "less developed societies into the modern world," in order to create infrastructures for development, as well as new workers and new consumers. Corporations claim they do this for altruistic reasons—to raise the living standard—but corporations have no altruism.

Theoretically, privately held corporations—those owned by individuals or families—do not have the imperative to expand. In practice, however, the behavior is the same. There are economies of scale, and usually increased profits from size. Such privately held giants as Bechtel Corporation have shown no propensity to moderate growth; their behavior, in fact, shows quite the opposite.

3. Competition and Aggression

On the one hand, corporations require a high degree of cooperation within management. On the other hand, they place every person in management in fierce competition with each other. Anyone interested in a corporate career must hone his or her abilities to seize the moment. This applies to gaining an edge over another company, or over a colleague within the company. As an employee, you are expected to be part of the "team"—you must aggressively push to win over the other corporations—but you also must be ready to climb over your own colleagues.

The comparison with sports is clear. All members of a professional football team (itself a corporation) compete with each other, yet all players must cooperate to defeat an opposing team.

Corporate (or athletic) ideology holds that competition improves worker incentive and corporate performance, and therefore benefits society. Our society has accepted this premise utterly. Unfortunately, however, it also surfaces in personal relationships. Living by standards of competition and aggression on the job, human beings have few avenues to express softer, more personal feelings. We all know what happens to anyone who cries under stress in business or in politics. (In politics, nonaggressive behavior is interpreted as weakness.) And yet, in the intimacy of the home, such true expressions of real feelings are what tend to matter the most. Such contrary standards on the job and at home can lead to a kind of schizophrenia that often plays itself out in busted relationships.

4. Amorality

Not being human, not having feelings, corporations do not have morals or altruistic goals. So decisions that may be antithetical to community goals or environmental health are made without suffering misgivings. In fact, corporate executives praise "nonemotionality" as a basis for "objective" decisions.

Corporations, however, seek to hide their amorality, and attempt to act as if they were altruistic. Lately there has been a concerted effort by American industry to seem concerned with contemporary social issues, such as environmental cleanups, community arts, or drug programs. The effort to exhibit social responsibility by corporations comes precisely because they are innately *not* responsible to the public; they have no interest in community goals except the ones that serve their purposes. This false altruism should not be confused with the genuine altruism human beings exhibit for one another when, for example, one goes for help on behalf of a sick neighbor, or takes care of the kids, or loans money. Corporate efforts that seem altruistic are really public relations ploys, or else are directly self-serving projects, such as providing schools with educational materials about nature. In other cases, apparent altruism is only "damage control," to offset public criticism.

For example, there has recently been a spurt of corporate advertising about how corporations work to clean the environment. A company that installs offshore oil rigs will run ads about how fish are thriving under the rigs. Logging companies known for their clear-cutting practices will run millions of dollars' worth of ads about their "tree farms," as if they were interested in renewable resources, when they are not.

Other corporations will show ads of happy employees; usually these are companies with serious labor problems. Or companies will run ads about how they are assisting in community programs—day care, the arts, drug education, historic preservation—in communities where citizens have been outraged by corporate irresponsibility. In fact, it is a fair rule of thumb that corporations will tend to advertise the very qualities they do not have, in order to allay a negative public perception. When corporations say "we care," it is almost always in response to the widespread perception that they do not care. And they don't. How could they? Corporations do not have feelings or morals. All acts are in service to profit. All apparent altruism is measured against possible public relations benefit. If the benefits do not accrue, the altruistic pose is dropped. When Exxon realized that its cleanup of the Alaskan shores was not easing the public rage about the oil spill, it simply dropped all pretense of altruism and ceased working.

5. Hierarchy

Corporate law requires that corporations be structured into classes of superiors and subordinates within a centralized pyramidal structure: chairman, directors, CEO, vice presidents, division managers, and so on. The efficiency of this hierarchical form, which also characterizes the military, the government, and most institutions in our society, is rarely questioned.

The effect on society from all organizations adopting hierarchical form is to make it seem natural that we have all been placed within a national pecking order. Some jobs are better than others, some lifestyles are better than others, some neighborhoods, some races, some kinds of knowledge. Men over women. Westerners over non-Westerners. Humans over nature.

That effective, nonhierarchical modes of organization exist on the planet, and have been successful for millennia, is barely known by most Americans.

6. Quantification, Linearity, and Segmentation

Corporations require that subjective information be translated into objective form, i.e., numbers. This excludes from the decision-making process all values that do not so translate. The subjective or spiritual aspects of forests, for example, cannot be translated, and so do not enter corporate equations. Forests are evaluated only as "board feet." Production elements that pose danger to public health or welfare—pollution, toxic waste, carcinogens—are translated to value-free objective concepts, such as "cost-benefit ratio" or "trade-off." Auto manufacturers evaluating the safety level of certain production standards calculate the number of probable accidents and deaths at each level of the standard. This number is then compared with the cost of insurance payments and lawsuits from dead drivers' families. A number is also assigned to the public relations problem, and a balance is sought.

When corporations are asked to clean up their smokestack emissions, they lobby to relax the new standard, to contain costs. The result is that a predictable number of people are expected to become sick and die.

The operative corporate standard is not "as safe as humanly possible," but rather, "as safe as possible commensurate with maintaining acceptable profit."

The drive toward objectification enters every aspect of corporate activity. For example, on the production end, great effort is made, through time-and-motion studies, to measure each fragment of every process performed by a worker. The eventual goal is to sufficiently segment tasks so that they may be automated, eliminating workers altogether. Where the task is not eliminated, it is reduced to its simplest repetitive form. As a result, workers become subject to intense comparisons with other workers. If they survive on the jobs, doing the repetitive tasks leaves them horribly bored and without a sense of participating in corporate goals. They feel like they are part of a machine, and they are.

7. Dehumanization

If the environment and the community are objectified by corporations, with all decisions measured against public relations or profit standards, so is the employee objectified and dehumanized.

Corporations make a conscious effort to depersonalize. The recent introduction of computer surveillance technology into business operations, especially in measuring and supervising the performance of office workers, has made this dehumanization task simpler and more thorough. Now, every keystroke and every word of every worker can be counted by a central computer that compares each individual's performance against others and against corporate standards. Those people found to be too slow, or inconsistent, or who take too many breaks, are simpler to find and to discipline or dismiss.

In very small businesses, the tendency toward dehumanization is obviously mitigated, since some employer-employee personal contact can scarcely be avoided. But in the great majority of corporations, employees are viewed as ciphers, as cogs in the wheel, replaceable by others or by machines.

As for management employees, not subject to quite the same indignities, they nonetheless must practice a style of decision-making that "does not let feelings get in the way." This applies as much to firing employees as it does to dealing with the consequences of corporate behavior in the environment or the community. But, as has been described, the manager's behavior, objectifying all decisions and all people, also acts to objectify and dehumanize himself or herself.

8. Exploitation

All corporate profit is obtained by a simple formula: Profit equals the difference between the amount paid to an employee and the economic value of the employee's output, and/or the difference between the amount paid for raw materials used in production (including costs of processing) and the ultimate sales price of the processed raw materials. Karl Marx was right: A worker is not compensated for the full value of his or her labor; neither is the raw material supplier. The owners of capital skim off part of the value as profit. Profit is based on underpayment.

Capitalists argue that this is a fair deal, since both workers and the people who mine or farm the resources (usually in Third World environments) get paid. But this arrangement is inherently imbalanced. The owner of the capital—the corporation or the bank—always obtains additional benefit. While the worker makes a wage, the owner of the capital gets the benefit of the worker's labor, plus the surplus profit the worker produces, which is then reinvested to produce yet more surplus. This even applies to the rare cases where workers are very highly paid, as with professional athletes and entertainers. In those cases, the corporations pay high wages because the workers will produce more income for the corporation than they are paid. So the formula remains intact: Profit is based on paying less than actual value for workers and resources. This is called exploitation.

9. Ephemerality

Corporations exist beyond time and space. As we have seen, they are legal creations that only exist on paper. They do not die a natural death; they outlive their own creators. And they have no commitment to locale, employees, or neighbors. This makes the modern corporation entirely different from the baker or grocer of previous years who survived by cultivating intimacy with the neighbors. Having no morality, no commitment to place, and no physical nature (a factory someplace, while being a physical entity, is not the corporation), a corporation can relocate all of its operations to another place at the first sign of inconvenience: demanding employees, too high taxes, restrictive environmental laws. The traditional ideal of community engagement is antithetical to corporate behavior.

10. Opposition to Nature

Though individuals who work for corporations may personally love nature, corporations themselves, and corporate societies, are intrinsically committed to intervening in, altering, and transforming nature. For corporations engaged in commodity manufacturing, profit comes from transmogrifying raw materials into saleable forms. Metals from the ground are converted into cars. Trees are converted into boards and then into houses, furniture, and paper products. Oil is converted into energy. In all such activity, a piece of nature is taken from where it belongs and processed into a new form. In rare instances, elements of nature can be renewed, or trees can be replanted, but even in such cases they do not return to their original forms. So all manufacturing activity depends upon intervention and reorganization of nature. After natural resources are used up in one part of the globe, the corporation moves on to another part. With the transformation process well under way in Southeast Asia and the Pacific, Antarctica is the new target. Soon it will be the moon.

This transformation of nature occurs in all societies where community manufacturing takes place. But in capitalist, corporate societies, the process is accelerated because capitalist societies and corporations *must* grow. Extracting resources from nature and reprocessing them at an ever-quickening pace is intrinsic to their existence. Meanwhile, the consumption end of the cycle is also accelerated—corporations have an intrinsic interest in convincing people that commodities bring satisfaction. Modes of fulfillment that are based on self-sufficiency—inner satisfaction, contentment in nature or in relationships, a lack of desire to acquire wealth—are subversive to corporate goals. For production to be hyped, i.e., for natural materials to be transformed into commodities and then into profit, the consumption end of the cycle must similarly be hyped. The net effect is the ravaging of nature.

Corporate entities that do not directly engage in processing raw materials, such as banks or insurance companies, are nevertheless engaged in ravaging nature. Banks finance the conversion of nature; insurance companies help reduce the financial risks involved. The more nature is exploited the greater the profit for all corporations. Of course, on a finite planet, the process cannot continue indefinitely.

11. Homogenization

American rhetoric claims that commodity society delivers greater choice and diversity than other societies. "Choice" in this context means *product* choice, choice in the marketplace: many brands to choose from, and diverse features on otherwise identical products. Actually, however, corporations have a stake in all of us living our lives in a similar manner, achieving our pleasures from things that we buy. While it is true that different corporations seek different segments of the market—elderly people, let's say, or organic food buyers—*all* corporations share an identical economic, cultural, and social vision, and seek to accelerate society's (and individual) acceptance of that vision.

Lifestyles and economic systems that emphasize sharing commodities and work, that do not encourage commodity accumulation, or that celebrate nonmaterial values, are not good for business. People living collectively, for example, sharing such hard goods as washing machines, cars, and appliances—or worse, getting along without them—are outrageous to corporate commodity society. The nuclear family is a far better idea for maintaining corporate commodity society: Each family lives alone in a single-family home and has all the same machines as every other family on the block. Recently, the singles phenomenon has proved even more productive than the nuclear family, since each *person* duplicates the consumption patterns of every other person.

As for native societies, which celebrate an utterly nonmaterial relationship to life, the planet, and the spirit, and which are at opposite poles to corporate ideology, they are regarded as inferior and unenlightened. Backward. We are told they envy the choices we have. To the degree these societies continue to exist, they represent a threat to the homogenization of worldwide markets and culture. Corporate society works hard to retrain such people in attitudes and values appropriate to corporate goals. But in the undeveloped parts of the world, where corporations are just arriving, the ideological retraining process is just getting under way. Satellite communications technology, which brings Western television and advertising, is combined with a technical infrastructure to speed up the pace of development. Most of this activity is funded by the World Bank and the International Monetary Fund, as well as agencies such as U.S. AID, the Inter-American Bank, and the Asian-American Bank, all of which serve multinational corporate enterprise.

As for the ultimate goal? In *Trilateralism,* editor Holly Sklar quotes the president of Nabisco Corporation: "One world of homogeneous consumption . . . [I am] looking forward to the day when Arabs and Americans, Latins and Scandinavians will be munching Ritz crackers as enthusiastically as they already drink Coke or brush their teeth with Colgate."

Sklar goes on: "Corporations not only advertise products, they promote lifestyles rooted in consumption, patterned largely after the United States. . . . [They] look forward to a postnational age in which [Western] social, economic, and political values are transformed into universal values . . . a world economy in which all national economies beat to the rhythm of transnational corporate capitalism. . . . The Western way is the good way, national culture is inferior."

FORM IS CONTENT

The most important aspect of these eleven rules is the degree to which they are inherent in corporate structure. Corporations are *inherently* bold, aggressive, and competitive. Though they exist in a society that claims to operate by moral principles, they are structurally amoral. It is inevitable that they will dehumanize people who work for them, and dehumanize the overall society as well. They are disloyal to workers, including their own managers. If community goals conflict with corporate goals, then corporations are similarly disloyal to the communities they may have been part of for many years. It is *inherent* in corporate activity that they seek to drive all consciousness into one-dimensional channels. They must attempt to dominate alternative cultures and to effectively clone the world population into a form more to their liking. Corporations do not care about nations; they live beyond boundaries. They are intrinsically committed to destroying nature. And they have an inexorable, unabatable, voracious need to grow and to expand. In dominating other cultures, in digging up the earth, corporations blindly follow the codes that have been built into them as if they were genes.

Would our society have been better off if we had been told, from the beginning, that corporations would behave as they do? As with every other new piece of machinery, large or small, we were only presented with the pros, never the cons, of this creature called the corporation. There was never a vote as to whether, on balance, corporations destroy more than they contribute. Nor was there ever any effort to articulate the principles by which they operate and the manner in which they would inevitably behave. Articulating these principles now gives us a picture we should have been given a long time ago.

Now that we see the inherent direction of corporate activity, we must abandon the idea that corporations can reform themselves, or that a new generation of executive managers can be re-educated. We must also abandon the assumption that the form of the structure is "neutral." To ask corporate executives to behave in a morally defensible manner is absurd. Corporations, and the people within them, are not subject to moral behavior. They are following a system of logic that leads inexorably toward dominant behaviors. To ask corporations to behave otherwise is like asking an army to adopt pacifism. Form is content.

8

LEAVING THE EARTH: SPACE COLONIES, DISNEY, AND EPCOT

Y OU KNOW, JERRY, I feel like things are really closing in. There doesn't seem to be any escape now; nowhere that's not being made over."

Speaking to me was the artist Elizabeth Garsonnin. She continued:

"I can really identify with the young people today; how trapped they must feel. The natural world is almost gone, and it's being replaced by this awful hard-edged, commercial creation, with techno-humans running it. They're already in Antarctica. They're in all the jungles. They're tagging all the animals. Their satellites are photographing everything. They know what's in the ground and what's on the land. Soon they'll be on Venus and Mars. And they're inside human cells. Where is there left for the mind to flee? They've even invaded the subjective spaces, the fantasy world. As an artist I feel as if the sources of creation are being wiped out and paved over. It makes the only viable art protest art, but I hate that. It means they already have us confined; we can only react to *them*. I am so sad."

• • •

The exploration of the earth's uncharted wilderness is now nearly complete. The drive of Westerners to convert wild, uncontrolled, and unexplored terrain into productive commodity forms is seeking new frontiers. Lately it has found two: explorations *off* the earth, into the vast wilderness of space; and exploration into the infinitely small, the genetic structure of life (which will be discussed in the next chapter).

In both cases, as with all technical procedures of the past several centuries, the public is told that the purpose of the explorations is to benefit human beings—and truly it could not possibly benefit any species other than human beings—but this is not the purpose. It is only the selling point. In reality, the purpose of the explorations is economic gain, military advantage, the satisfaction of ego, and satisfaction of technological society's intrinsic drive to expand.

• • •

In a recent issue of *Earth Island Journal,* Gar Smith wrote:

> Only thirty years ago, a child of Earth could look up on dark, chilly nights and marvel at the mystery of the stars. But today, the night sky is no longer an inaccessible mystery of the stars. It is now "the last frontier" complete with "challenges to overcome," with "new worlds to conquer," with places to be "colonized." Significantly, this is the same vocabulary that in the past justified the desecration of mountains, rivers, forests, and indigenous peoples: It is the rhetoric of economic growth. Clearly, the same philosophy that propelled our exploitation of the planet now fuels our ambition to explore the stars.

When I first read Gar Smith's lines, my mind went back to when I was a child at summer camp in Massachusetts. I was lying on a cot late at night, looking out the open screen at the sky ablaze with stars. Even now I can feel in my body what I felt then. It was a kind of bursting; a reaching outward into infinity. The sight of the night sky filled me with warmth and satisfaction, even though it was also frightening. I had no words to articulate the feeling, but I could definitely feel my connection to something infinite, timeless, constant, and beyond all imaginings and comprehension. It stimulated my spirit, my heart, and my mind.

Forty years later, I am sitting in an office at Public Media Center in San Francisco. A group of us are meeting with a disarmament organization working to block funding for Star Wars and the militarization of space. The client wants an ad campaign that will emphasize the expense, the unworkability, and the military ineffectiveness of Star Wars and a new arms race in space. We agree to that approach, but I am left feeling that perhaps the most important aspect of the issue has been left out. For me, the very fact of launching human beings into space, together with our satellites and technical apparatuses, will forever alter, if it hasn't already, a vital territory of the human imagination and experience. For now, when we look at the stars we are as likely to imagine machines flying around as we are to make a spiritual and emotional connection, as all our human ancestors did before us. The human exploration of space, as with all wilderness, shifts our concepts away from the subjective, poetic, emotional, and spiritual realms, into a realm that is bounded by technical perspectives.

• • •

However worrisome the militarization of space, I worry more about the corporate invasions of space, now in full swing. The militarization movement has at least been met with well-organized resistance, but corporate activities, which will ultimately have greater impact, are going mostly unopposed, and are accelerating.

In February 1988, the Reagan White House announced an initiative to encourage the private sector to explore space. The progam provided for advance purchasing of commercial space products and services, thereby limiting risk for entrepreneurs, and offered an effective subsidy to business pioneers in space. A similar crash program decades earlier had made feasible nuclear research and development by private industry.

The rationalizations for government-supported private development of space had already been provided by decades of utopian visions, as far back as the World's Fair of 1940 up to today's visionary environments, such as EPCOT Center. Following the rule that new technical endeavors are introduced in idealized terms by the people who stand most to gain, corporations have been advertising the economic gains that space development will offer humanity. New space resources will lead to both Earth and space jobs, international cooperation, new horizons, and loftier visions, all of it somehow trickling down to benefit Earth's teeming billions.

Of course the real driving motives for space exploration and development have nothing to do with what will benefit the majority of people on Earth, or the planet itself. It has only to do with the intrinsic drives of corporate and technological society to expand and to grow whether or not there is any benefit, and whether more harm is done than good.

Technological society *is* running out of resources to fuel its growth, having run directly into the inherent limits of a finite planet. Once every inch has been explored, and photographed from space with infrared cameras; once the resources are mapped, the people driven off the land, and the last resources converted to commodities, what next? Just as economic managers in earlier centuries saw the need to explore and colonize new continents, to expand their sources of supply, we have turned today to space colonization.

It was not out of altruism that the Europeans ravaged the New World; it was out of greed. Nor was it altruism in the 1800s when the process was called Manifest Destiny—when "God's will" mandated that we spread our form of life over the continent and its peoples. Nor is it altruism today on Earth or in space. As Ronald Reagan's secretary of commerce put it, when announcing the new private initiatives for space development: "The real business of space exploration is business." Indeed it is. And as with every other wilderness on Earth—being reshaped, cut down, dug up, and moved around—space wilderness is already being transformed, from *source* of our imaginings, our spirit, and our psyche, to *resource* for industrial growth.

BUSINESS OPPORTUNITIES IN SPACE

The kinds of businesses proposed for space thus far are mainly mining oriented, and will begin on the moon. Gar Smith reports that "oxygen may be the first major commodity that scientists try to extract. Sixty percent of the lunar soils are composed of silicon-based oxides, and researchers are toying with the idea of using nuclear reactors or solar furnaces to turn moon dust into oxygen." Each 10,000 tons of lunar soil would also release a ton of hydrogen, useful in rocket fuel and in many manufacturing processes. The moon could also be mined for anorthosite (which has a higher aluminum content than rocks here on Earth) as well as titanium.

NASA scientists have predicted a population of 1,000 on the moon by the third decade of the twenty-first century. Active tourism should begin before then, with shuttle service from Earth, moon hotels, and guided tours of the moon's surface. After the moon, according to Smith, "the next target for exploitation will be the asteroid belt," where science would like to "harvest" the little rocks for hydrogen, oxygen, water, platinum, and nickel-iron alloys to fuel space industries. Under one plan, "massdrivers" installed on smaller asteroids could eject the waste material from mining into space, providing enough thrust to propel the asteroid into Earth orbit. The downside of these delicate procedures, adds Gar Smith, is that should there be a miscalculation, one of the asteroids could apparently fall into the earth's atmosphere, causing what one researcher warns would be a "Hiroshima-class explosion."

Plans for Mars include "terraforming," which is the creation of an artificial Earthlike environment. The idea goes well beyond the primitive visions of people like Gerard O'Neill, who advocates that cities on planets be enclosed by domes in which a mini-Earth environment could be re-created. These O'Neill space-cities would have everything necessary to live a normal life off the planet. Within the dome there would be air. Farms would grow food; water would be recycled and circulated. There would be stores and baseball and movies. People could basically live the same kind of life they live now in California.

"Terraforming" goes the fantasy one better, converting the entire atmosphere of Mars into one that human beings could inhabit without domes. The idea is explained in James Oberg's book *New Earths: Restructuring Earth and Other Planets.* The restructuring process begins with giant mirrors aimed at the Martian ice caps, vaporizing the frozen water and altering the content of the atmosphere. Some steps down the line algae and lichens would be provided to create oxygen, and then, *voila!* Here come the Best Western hotels, with "outdoor" swimming pools and shopping malls.

Hundreds of corporations are already heavily invested in such space activities. According to Gar Smith, before the 1988 initiative NASA had already spent $200 million to "make space safe for American business." Among the businesses that NASA has effectively subsidized—specifically by deferring some $75 million in shuttle-launch costs—is Space Services, Inc. of Houston, which "plans to orbit a $250 to $500 million, forty-five-foot-long space factory powered by a 200-foot array of solar panels." This company, working with a consortium of Florida morticians and retired Kennedy Space Center engineers, will soon be billing customers $3,000 each to rocket-launch human remains for a permanent, orbiting "burial" in space. (Why anyone would want to be "buried" in space is a question that stumps me; my only guess is that it brings the deceased nearer to heaven, making it a shorter flight for the spirit.)

Regardless of the motive, with more and more bodies flying around in space there will be an increased risk of collisions with other junk that human beings have already placed into orbit. This is not a joke. In the single generation since space exploration began, some 15,000 objects from Earth have accumulated in planetary orbit. These include spent payloads, rockets, clamps, human excrement, shrapnel from exploded satellites, and discarded tools. And collisions have occurred. One Soviet space probe was shattered after colliding with space junk, and an American shuttle flight was endangered by flecks of paint hurtling through orbit.

•   •   •

Physical crowding in space is one problem, but a more serious problem is the crowding caused by communications satellite signals. There are 139 satellites already in orbit, many of them jamming each other's signals. Most of these satellites are operated by corporations engaged in mapping the earth's resources. Using photographic equipment that is now so precise it can capture, from outer space, the expression on a human face, orbiting satellites are making records of every plant, animal, body of water, and, via infrared and other spectroscopic techniques, the subsurface minerals that are hidden from view all over the planet. In this way, satellite communications technology greatly accelerates the final stages of the worldwide process by which corporate interests convert all of nature into commodity form.

Looking at the bright side, however, Gar Smith points out that this satellite overview capability might benefit organizations that oppose military or corporate domination. For example, he argues that the French SPOT satellite "makes it possible for ordinary citizens and nongovernmental agencies to monitor nuclear test sites, naval concentrations, and troop movements," thereby decreasing the probability of surprise invasions. According to this logic, ordinary people could map the earth's resources in the same way that large corporations do, thereby anticipating where the bulldozers might show up next.

I am afraid that Smith is revealing here some best-case scenario fantasies. In fact, he may be falling into the same best-case fantasy trap that has historically misled and muted progressive-thinking people when trying to criticize technology. The inevitable fact is that satellite technology and space exploration are far more accessible to large institutions, military and corporate, and are hundreds of times more likely to benefit their goals than yours or mine or the Sierra Club's. These space communications technologies were invented to provide a competitive edge to the institutions that invented them, and to assist their intended exploitation of nature. People who wish to live within the confines of the planet's organic limits, and who are not committed to a constantly expanding economy, or to seeking control of resources or land, do not need satellites to map resources. The people who live near what we call "resources" already know they are there, and are happy to leave them in place.

FUTURISTS LOVE SPACE TRAVEL

In creating public support for the massive financial expenditures involved in space exploration, futurists are playing a critically important role. Against the background of two generations of psychological preparation (from World's Fairs to Buck Rogers to "Star Trek" to *Star Wars*) the futurists' role is to provide the intellectual and/or the spiritual sales points of space development. They have a stake in doing so, because the profession needs places and subjects to ponder anew, just as corporations need new raw materials. If all that was left to futurize about was, say, the evolution of agrarian communities, or the renewal of resources, there wouldn't be much economic future in futurism. So futurists love space travel. They are devoted to urging it along, with appropriate images and arguments.

Particular leadership in space futurism has been demonstrated by the late Gerard O'Neill and Herman Kahn. Both have written important books (Kahn wrote *The Next 200 Years,* and O'Neill wrote *The High Frontier*), which created the visions most prized by corporate-technological society: a future based on expanding resources for a growing industrial and corporate system.

For Kahn, space exploration is the inevitable next step in the evolution of technology and the advancement of human society toward affluence. He believes we are at the threshold of realizing the magnificent promise that has motivated technological society. In *The Next 200 Years,* Kahn writes:

> Two hundred years ago almost everywhere human beings were comparatively few, poor, and at the mercy of the forces of nature, and 200 years from now, we expect, almost everywhere they will be numerous, rich, and in control of the forces of nature. The 400-year period will thus have been as dramatic and important in the history of mankind as was the 10,000-year period that preceded it, a span of time that saw the agricultural revolution spread around the world, giving way finally to the birth of the Industrial Revolution. At the midway mark in the 400-year period, we have just seen in the most advanced countries the initial emergence of superindustrial economies where enterprises are extraordinarily large, pervasive forces . . . to be followed soon by postindustrial economies where the task of producing the necessities of life has become trivially easy because of technological advancement and economic development.

I am still astonished when intelligent people describe life in preindustrial times as dirty, miserable, poor, and subject to the awful expressions of nature. Surely they must be aware that indigenous peoples of the temperate zones of the planet—long before the harshness of sixteenth- and seventeenth-century Europe—lived very pleasant and relatively easy lives. (See Chapter 14.) But if Kahn acknowledged that, then how could he justify advancing the industrial-technological age?

Kahn is also overstating matters when he says that industrial production has made it "trivially easy" to provide the necessities of life. If that were true, then why are so many people starving and why is the planet being devastated? Kahn says that technology will fix these problems. He predicts a future where everyone on the planet will live as Americans do. Space exploration, says Kahn, provides the resources to grow, and will move some of the uglier, more polluting industries off the planet to space.

In Herman Kahn's view, space colonization has yet another role. It serves as a hedge, just in case things actually do totally break down on the planet— if we have a nuclear war, or an Armageddon brought on by toxic waste or pollution or climatic change. If that happens, says Kahn, the space colonists can just cloister themselves in their domes for a while and return later when Earth can be cleaned up. For Kahn, space represents simply another "continent" to be exploited; a place where people can get more resources, try out some new lifestyles, create some new trends, do some industrial things that are difficult to do on Earth, ship home some neat new technologies, and keep the economy growing. Corporations love this vision.

Like Kahn, Gerard O'Neill understands that we cannot keep expanding economically if we are confined to Earth. Resources get used up, markets get dried up, population has to stabilize, and there's a limit to spaces for parked cars. Space is the answer. Use up this planet; go find another.

O'Neill rationalizes the need for this continued growth with fantasies of preindustrial life that are even grimmer than Kahn's:

Through many tens of thousands of years human beings were few in numbers and insignificant in power over the physical environment. Not only war but famine and plague decimated populations whenever they grew large. Centuries passed without great increase in the total human population. The quality of life, for most people in those preindustrial years, seems to have been low even in times of peace. Although there were, nearly everywhere, small privileged classes enjoying comparative wealth, most people lived out their lives in heavy labor, many as slaves.

Is O'Neill suggesting there is something good about expanding population? As for his descriptions of the miserable "quality of life" for preindustrial peoples, what societies could he possibly have been describing? His vision might apply to a few Middle Eastern societies during the time Christ was alive, or to a later period in Europe, or for a time in China and Japan. But this description reveals how uneducated O'Neill is about the indigenous societies that lived all over the planet for tens of thousands of years *without* privileged classes, *without* slavery, and in relative comfort, especially as compared with many parts of the industrialized world.

The familiar assumption that everything before industrialism was pain, poverty, slavery, and victimization by nature is the assumption that works best for the technological-capitalist agenda and its massive invasion of these "afflicted" societies. It makes it seem as if capitalism and industrialization were altruistically motivated; do-gooder activities. This makes moving into space seem like a continuation of these do-gooder impulses, when actually space development is an attempt to flee the mess created here on Earth by these same corporate drives.

(For a more complete discussion and analysis of Kahn's, O'Neill's, and other futurists' work, I recommend Gary Coates' brilliant essay "Future Images, Present Possibilities: Revisioning Nature, Self and Society" in *Resettling America* [see bibliography].)

STAR SEEDING: SENDING THE "BEST HUMANS" TO SPACE

A third "visionary" who I feel needs mention is the acid guru of the 1960s, Dr. Timothy Leary. He is still around, still held in high esteem by a fair number of middle-aged people, and his message is important. He provides something that few other futurists do: a New Age techno-religious rationale for space colonization. It could be described as "Space-Colonization-as-Evolution." It goes like this:

The planet is some kind of living creature, and all of its elements are connected as part of a single living entity. This is called "Gaia" in some quarters. (So far, so good. It matches the view of native people who have been making a similar argument for millennia. I like that part. But not the rest.)

As part of nature's evolutionary design, the role of human beings is to be the consciousness of the entire planetary creature. *We* are the creature's brain. We may even be the reason for evolution, its goal. We are like the seed of the flower, existing to propagate more flowers in distant meadows.

As Leary sees it, and this part is very popular with certain elements of the New Age movement, all events until now were in preparation for this moment, when our species would hold the position of leader, thinker, and, well, president of all creatures, and the whole planet. It is our responsibility to rule wisely and to further evolution.

My own exposure to Leary's ideas about space travel came during the late 1960s while he was still in jail. It was then that I met Tim's wife, Joanna, who was traveling widely to propagate Leary's vision; it was called "Star Seeding." Its premise was that since human beings are the consciousness not only of this planet, but of the whole universe, we must prepare to leap off the planet to "seed" the universe with our higher consciousness and purpose.

What I liked least about Star Seeding was the notion that we should quickly find and train the "5,000 people with the greatest minds," in order to launch them into space as soon as a suitable space base was established. From that base, these 5,000 "best people" would use their higher consciousness to form utopian communities and undertake further explorations. We on Earth would continue to provide these higher beings with every technological tool our meager selves could create.

I remember asking one of Leary's followers exactly how the 5,000 highest-consciousness people would be chosen. By whom? By what standards? Do they have to be technically fluent? (Of course—this is a high-tech dream.) How many would be artists? ("The greatest artists.") Any Indians? (There are "some incredibly high Indians.") Men? Women? Gays? Communists? The only thing that became clear to me from asking these questions was that asking them meant I was clearly not qualified for the top 5,000. It's okay, though—I wasn't eager to go.

What attracts people to Leary's vision, and similar ones floating around in New Age circles, is that it seems like a utopian dream *not* rooted in capitalist economic gain. It *seems* to be about something far loftier—furthering evolution. Herman Kahn's utopia is just, well, sort of like an industrial Phoenix, Arizona. The Gerard O'Neill vision upgrades the image to, say, a domed Palo Alto with a great recycling program and good gardeners. But Leary's vision has an almost naturalist cast to it. And it works well for the New Agers, who already think of themselves as pioneers of a future based on "higher consciousness." A lot of New Age people *love* the idea of leaving the planet, being chosen by evolution to be its personal astronauts escaping into space. The prospect of personally fulfilling nature's evolutionary design is so thrilling an idea that its advocates don't see, or don't care, that it is only a modern-day continuation of Manifest Destiny, with the same outcome.

The assertion that our species is the ultimate expression of evolution, the consciousness of the planet, and that some people—technologically oriented Westerners in particular—are on the evolutionary frontier, merely provides a rationalization that makes space travel seem lofty when it is really business as usual. We continue to impose ourselves onto formerly pristine environments; we continue to regard ourselves as better and more important; we continue to rationalize our purposes as being higher than the meager visions of 10,000-year-old societies who may see things in other ways; we continue to seek and exploit new resources to fuel our voracious appetites; we continue to lay waste to what we touch and leave

messes behind us; and we continue to call this superiority, destiny, and vision. These attitudes, if unchanged, will assure that what has been done
to this planet will eventually be done to others.

BANISHMENT FROM EDEN

Over the years, I have wondered about the apparently strong appeal of
space travel and development to the public mind. I can understand why
corporations, militaries, and governments want to promote departing
from the planet, and I have mentioned its appeal to the New Age collective
ego. But it hasn't been easy for me to grasp why the idea is so attractive to
others. I finally realized that space travel is not new; it is only the final stage
of a departure process that actually began long ago. Our society really "left
home" when we placed boundaries between ourselves and the earth, when
we moved en masse inside totally artificial, reconstructed, "mediated"
worlds—huge concrete cities and suburbs—and we aggressively ripped
up and redesigned the natural world. By now, nature has literally receded
from our view and diminished in size. We have lost contact with our roots.
As a culture, we don't know where we came from; we're not aware we are
part of something larger than ourselves. Nor can we easily find places that
reveal natural processes still at work.

This is exacerbated for Americans in particular, since our country is
made up almost entirely of immigrants whose original connections with
a homeland were severed, and who have no special attachments to the soil
we live on. The Native Americans, who do have roots here, are not nearly
as enthusiastic about leaving the earth as the rest of us are, as we will see.

Corporate culture has also contributed mightily to the process, since it
asks its retainers to care more about an abstract corporation than about the
communities where they live and work. Corporations regularly abandon
communities, sometimes impoverishing them when they depart, and they
ask some employees to also pack up and leave for the next locale.

Such disconnection from the places where we live and work obviously
diminishes any sense of stewardship, which is a very important break with
the past. As a corporate culture, we have begun to feel that one place is as
good as the next; that it's okay to sacrifice this place for that one, even when
the new place is not even on Earth. In the end, this leaves us all in a position
similar to the millions of homeless people on our streets. In truth, we are
all homeless, though we long to return.

My friend Gary Coates, an architecture professor at Kansas State University, whom I previously mentioned as author of *Resettling America,* has

argued provocatively that our quest for space is actually a distorted expression of a desire to return *home* to Eden, the place we abandoned. He sees our whole culture as caught in a replay of the Adam-and-Eve story.

In a recent conversation, Coates put it to me this way:

"Like all creation myths, the story of the Garden of Eden is not something that never happened or only happened long ago; it is something that is happening in every moment. . . . It was the murder of Abel, who represented a state of oneness with the earth, that set Cain off wandering in a never-satisfied quest for the return to, or re-creation of, paradise. Within the confines of our totally artificial environments on Earth, as they will soon also be in heaven, we also seek to re-enter Eden. In particular, the creation of the Leisureworlds, Disney Worlds, megamalls, Air Stream mobile home cities, lifestyle-segregated condominium communities, and especially genetic engineering, space colonization, and terraforming of planets, are all updated forms of Cain's desire to return home by remaking the original creation. The tragedy is that in attempting to recover paradise we accelerate the murder of nature. It's yet another repeat of the story of Cain and Abel, another acting out of the founding myth of Western history."

Coates is especially passionate about the role played today by theme-park environments; megamalls like Canada's West Edmonton Mall, and places like Disney World, Seaworld, and EPCOT Center. He argues that it is in these megamalls and theme parks that we are all being psychologically trained for our future in space. In those places, he adds, "we can see the emerging mindscape and landscape . . . we can actually experience our existence as preprogrammed participants in someone else's pre-engineered fantasies."

If not everyone can get to live in the utopian future world within plastic bubbles on Mars, everyone *can* experience more or less what it would be like right here on this planet in these self-contained bubbles of artificial life on Earth.

"Like the initiatory temples of Egypt and Greece," says Coates, "Disney World and the other worlds are the actual places where it is possible to understand fully the new mysteries. Space and time are collapsed and reality is re-created and fragmented just like on television. Things are only held together by the collage of stories that constitute the mythology of Progress. . . . When we are in Disney World or Seaworld or Leisureworld, as with television-world, we are inside someone else's story; we cannot tell what is reality and what is not. In the preplanned lifestyle communities, we construct our places of dwelling into stage sets for the re-creation of TV fantasies. We are finally figuring out how to live forever, disembodied inside our television sets, so that we shall never have to go outside again. This situation trains us well for the disconnected world of space colonies, robotics, genetic engineering, and Star Wars that are our "real" tomorrowland. Combined, the theme parks reveal the logic and architecture of hyper-reality; the world Umberto Eco calls 'the absolutely fake.'"

Coates persuaded me that I should visit some of these places, and to view them as training grounds for a future disconnection from Earth. "They are every bit as powerful as the World's Fair of 1940," he said, "and with similar implications." So in 1988 I visited the West Edmonton Mall and EPCOT Center. Of the two, EPCOT is the more explicit in its goals. It *intends* to train people to live in and to like a certain kind of future. The West Edmonton Mall, on the other hand, is only a commercial shopping mall and amusement park, albeit the largest in the world. I doubt it was conceived as a preview of life in a Martian self-contained bubble environment. But it is such a preview nonetheless.

THE WEST EDMONTON MALL, EDMONTON, CANADA

Edmonton is emphatically un-Martian. The city is the center of a spectacular natural landscape of sensuous grassy plains, wild rivers, great Rocky Mountains; it serves as the gateway to the untamed northern wilderness of Canada. But on the edge of the city is the West Edmonton Mall, and the point of that place is to re-create artificial versions of environments that are not in the vicinity. In that sense it is an otherworldly container of artificial reality planted into an alien landscape. In one visit you can get a fair sense of what would be considered crucial to a future life off the earth, where all human needs and pleasures are preplanned. Or, as the mall's brochure puts it, "The very best and most exciting natural wonders of the earth," within an environment of 889 stores. The brochure calls the mall "The Eighth Wonder of the World." And it is.

When I visited the mall, my favorite "natural environment" was the World Waterpark. Contained within a glass dome sixteen stories high, the Waterpark is the size of five football fields. It includes a giant concrete beach with a raging surf and real waves up to eight feet high, controlled by a computerized wave machine. Unfortunately, surfboarding was not permitted, although I saw dozens of people bodysurfing.

The air outside the mall was 20 degrees Fahrenheit on the day I visited, but inside the World Waterpark it was maintained at a constant 86 degrees. There were sunlamps for tanning and twenty-two water slides, including the Raging River, which simulates river rapids. You can rent rubber tubes and ride the "rapids" any day of the year.

If you prefer the open ocean to beaches, the West Edmonton Mall offers a "Deep Sea Adventure." You can take an underwater cruise in a thirty-three-foot submarine, which submerges and cruises in fifteen feet of water. Or you can pet the four Atlantic bottlenose dolphins swimming in the same miniocean in which the submarine cruises.

There are more than thirty aquariums throughout the mall, containing "more than 1,000 hand-picked specimens from the waters of Hawaii, Mexico, the Philippines, Australia, the Caribbean, South America, Japan, Canada, and the U.S.," according to the mall's brochure.

If your taste in natural wonders runs to birds and animals, the West Edmonton Mall has plenty. Glass-enclosed environments amidst the stores contain more than 250 exotic birds, including great flamingos from South America, several varieties of "intelligent and talented parrots," giant elands from South America, and many others. "All birds are housed in large aviaries," according to the developers, "which are representative of their natural habitats."

As for animals, there are mountain lions, tigers, spider monkeys, squirrel monkeys, black bears, French lopears, and jaguars, and your child can pet a "wide range of domestic animals throughout the complex." There are also 28,000 plants living nicely inside the mall, "many of which are rare and exotic species."

In addition to "natural wonders," the West Edmonton Mall offers some of the most romantic travel destinations on Earth. Want to be in Rome? The mall's Fantasyland Hotel features Roman rooms you can rent, with white marble, Roman statues and pillars, and an authentic Roman bath with mirrored walls. How about Arabia? Beds are surrounded with imitation sand dunes. The Polynesian rooms feature beds within a "warrior catamaran under full sail," as well as simulated volcanic eruptions. The West Edmonton Mall world traveler can also visit a re-creation of Bourbon Street, New Orleans, or a replica of a Parisian neighborhood on Europe Boulevard.

Elsewhere, the mall offers a full-sized ice-skating rink, an amusement park featuring a sixteen-story roller coaster, a 1.5-mile jogging track, a miniature golf course called Pebble Beach, a scaled replica of Christopher Columbus's ship *Santa Maria,* and, oh yes, 210 women's fashion stores, 35 menswear stores, 55 shoe stores, 35 jewelry stores, 11 major department stores, 19 movie theatres, 110 restaurants, 2 car dealerships, and 351 other miscellaneous shops, services, and natural wonders. Hey, if you can re-create such a complete world within a dome in Edmonton, Canada, why not do it on Mars?

EPCOT CENTER, ORLANDO, FLORIDA

May 1988. My sister, Anita Rosenstock, telephones from New York. She tells me that her son, Rob Waring, a prominent classical and jazz musician in Norway, is going to be performing soon in Florida at EPCOT Center, part of Disney World. Rob will be part of a musical ensemble presenting traditional Norwegian folk songs at the opening of a Norway pavilion. Since our mother lives in Florida, my sister and I agree to gather as many of the family as possible and turn Rob's visit into a family reunion.

Never having been to Disney World, I try to educate myself about the place. From the book *Walt Disney World,* published by the Disney Company, I learn the goal is "to make dreams come true." I also learn the place is ten times the size of Southern California's Disneyland, covering 27,000 acres—it is a self-contained total universe divided into four areas: the Vacation Kingdom, which contains all the hotels, golf courses, artificial lakes, water paradises, and artificial beaches; the Magic Kingdom, EPCOT Center, and within EPCOT, the World Showcase.

The largest and main attraction is the Magic Kingdom, itself divided into six "theme parks": Main Street, U.S.A.; Fantasyland; Adventureland; Frontierland; Liberty Square; and Tomorrowland. Each of these "theme parks" is an unabashed attempt to concretize our popular fantasies about American life and American adventure and travel. Each park reaches into our minds to pull out and re-create the movie and schoolroom images from our childhoods, and to put us in them as if they *were* real.

Main Street, U.S.A. is a prime example. According to the brochures, Main Street, U.S.A. "gives us a tantalizing look at the best of the 'good old days.' It is America between 1890 and 1910." It's a world of gingerbread houses, charming horse carts sharing the road with "old" cars, barbershop quartets, choo-choo trains, and penny arcades. No unions in this vision. No blacks-only and whites-only water fountains. No Indians. No poverty. It's a series of Hollywood images of America that might have emerged from the brain of Ronald Reagan.

Where Main Street, U.S.A. fictionalizes reality, Fantasyland makes "real" what has been imaginary: the Disney film characters. Cinderella is there with all the other cartoon people, including Peter Pan, Pinocchio, Snow White, the dwarfs, and all their cartoon environments of castles, drawbridges, forests, and fairylands.

As for Adventureland, the official Disney book says, "Disney Imagineers strove to make it 'a wonderland of nature's own design.' It is obvious to anyone who journeys through this exotic land that this direction was followed, leaf, stalk, and petal. A veritable United Nations of plants was assembled to represent the tropical regions of the world.

The word EPCOT is actually an acronym for Experimental Prototype Community of Tomorrow. "The dominions of Future World literally know no bounds," says the official Disney document, speaking the infinite-growth wisdom of corporate society. EPCOT Center was invented to make us comfortable with these nonboundaries of tomorrow. One exhibit puts EPCOT's goals very explicitly: to "help people who are unsure about these changes, or feel intimidated by futuristic [environments and] seemingly complex systems, the . . . exhibits are aimed at making us feel comfortable with computers and other implements of high technology."

• • •

By the time we arrived in Florida, Rob was already there, part of an official Norwegian delegation of 400, headed by the crown prince.

"We had our first rehearsal this morning at 6:45," Rob told us, "because the rehearsing has to be completed before 9 A.M., when the park opens. They have a rule that the public must not see rehearsals or have any glimpse backstage. They don't want to break the illusion. The goal is for people to remain in a kind of fantasy state. For the same reason none of the musicians or performers are ever named, and none of the filmmakers get credit for the films shown in the exhibits. EPCOT wants it all to be an unconscious gestalt of some kind, experienced whole, without anyone realizing that humans worked on things. It might bring people out of their fantasies."

Rob and his colleagues were not scheduled to play until the following evening, which gave the family some time to visit the EPCOT pavilions. First, we dropped into Exxon Corporation's Universe of Energy. We entered a room that was set up as a huge theatre. We were startled to realize that the rows of the theatre were moving and rearranging themselves into a gigantic moving vehicle. A disembodied voice told us we were embarking on a "journey through time," to experience the history of the creation of energy. A diorama of the "world of dinosaurs" showed the creatures moving and threatening each other and us; strong scents were somehow emitted. The presentation effectively evoked a terrifying prehuman time. When our gigantic vehicle passed beyond the time travel, the loudspeaker said, "Welcome back, folks, to the twentieth century." Sighs of relief all around. Then the music suddenly alluded to *Star Wars* themes—with no credits to composers or performers—and we were launched into visions of tomorrow, a time "of unlimited electric energy" to fuel our dreams of a better world.

Next was the Horizons pavilion, created by General Electric Corporation. There, we were immediately put on a space shuttle to tomorrow, where they played almost exactly the same music as Exxon played (do these composers all know each other?), and where we could see dioramas of vast undersea cities and cities that float on top of the sea. We saw high-tech colonies in space. And in the section about the earth, we saw the most impressive display of all: a huge farm stretching to the horizon amidst what was once a desert. Now, we were told, the farm grows computer-controlled, worker-free, genetically engineered crops. The General Electric announcer kept repeating the slogan, "If we can dream it, we can do it."

Third, we visited "the land created by Kraft Foods Corporation." We were placed into little boats that floated downstream on a "journey to a place most of us have forgotten about: the place where food is grown." They showed the family farm—amidst appropriate odors of hay and dung—a wonderful relic from a bygone era. "Each year," came the voice over the loudspeaker, "the family farm is being replaced by business as farming becomes a science. With better seeds, better pesticides, and better techniques, we're moving into a new era." Soon after, our boat floated into a modern laboratory within a kind of greenhouse. Here was obviously where food is *now* grown. "This is what's called Controlled Environment Agriculture. . . . Nature by itself is not always productive," says the scientific voice of Kraft. We then floated past exhibits of totally mechanized farming. We saw new plant species now being developed that discard such wasteful elements as branches or trunks; we saw fruit growing directly out of plastic tubes. Many new species need no soil to grow in; they are hung in the lab and fed by an automatic, computer-controlled spray.

Throughout, we hear a chorus of children's voices singing a Woody Guthrie–type melody, "Let's listen to the land we all love . . ."

And so it went throughout EPCOT. The corporations and the new technologies are there to make our lives better. The future will be a lot better than the present. We don't need to maintain our charming but hindering bonds to such anomalies as land, family farms (or any farms), or community, or the natural world. All we need do now is relax, float in our little cars, and be awed with the skill, thoughtfulness, imagination, and devotion of these can-do visionary corporations and their astounding new tools. We can all look forward to a future of very little work, total comfort, and complete technological control of the environment, the weather, nature, and *us*. Our role? To trust their leadership and vision. To enjoy it, to live in it, and to watch it like a movie.

• • •

The technological visions of EPCOT Center didn't bother me much. I had seen such things before, all the way back to the 1940 World's Fair. What *really* got to me was walking around the grounds in the world of EPCOT. Like everywhere in Disney World, the grounds were perfectly groomed; so manicured that they seemed unreal, part of a stage set, which of course is what they were. The idea was to show the perfect control over the environment that technical experts can achieve. I never saw a loose piece of paper or a patch of brown grass. The rivers that meandered through the place were encased in concrete culverts, totally dead save for the movement of the waters—except for one little lake that had been stocked with minnows and other small fish. I was surprised at that until I realized these real life forms were there on behalf of a small flock of pink flamingos, who ate them. Pink flamingos! Dreambirds.

Just as the "natural environment" at EPCOT had been perfected and packaged so as to eliminate any of nature's troubling variabilities, so had the people who worked there. Everyone wore green and white costumes, similar to the crew of "Star Trek." Everyone was clean and perfectly groomed. (The EPCOT representative who ushered around the Norwegian musicians told them that she had recently been criticized for allowing her fingernails to grow longer than one-sixteenth of an inch.)

Everyone at EPCOT smiled. Every question was answered in perfect sentences as if prerecorded. Everyone followed the rules to the letter. And it was clear that *we* had better follow the rules as well.

On one occasion during a very hot day, we went for a beer at a taco stand near the Mexican pavilion. As we were about to step back onto the walkway, a young woman appeared from nowhere and firmly (though sweetly) told us that we were not permitted to leave the enclosure with our beers.

Soon after that experience my twenty-one-year-old son, Yari, and I stepped a few feet over a white line that had been painted along an exit pathway in one of the exhibits, to ease ourselves around the crush of a large crowd. This rule violation was spotted within a split second by an attendant, who firmly (though sweetly) told us, "Kindly get back behind the white lines and next time do not step out of them." Yari barked back, "There won't be a next time."

Soon we all started to feel paranoid, as if we were being followed, and possibly photographed. We had the feeling that "security" was every-where. It was definitely clear to us that we were walking through an alien world, hostile to human beings. It would have been naive to think that the aliens who ran EPCOT might not notice how weird *we* were. For if there is a single word to describe EPCOT Center, I would say it's *control*.

The whole place is a visionary, futuristic projection of a utopian, com-puterized, technologized police state, where human behavior is as prede-fined as the perfect grass lawns. It is a logical extension of the corporate vision that has been steadily evolving for decades. We were shown a future where every blade of grass was in place, and the bird population is ideal-ized to pink flamingos, all as part of an ideal future that includes every human being's emotions, genes, and experience. Brave New World. You either follow the lines or you are shipped out. The purpose? Efficiency, production, expansion, and a kind, measured, commodity-oriented, mes-merized, programmed, fictional, Disneyesque "happiness."

• • •

The day finally came when Rob and the Norwegian musicians were to perform, but by then my mother, seventy-six years old at the time, was tired. She dreaded having to make the long walk in 100-degree heat from the parking lot to the Norwegian pavilion, a distance of about a half-mile. Rob inquired with the EPCOT people if his grandmother couldn't go with the musicians directly from the hotel to the performance site. The answer was no.

Rob explained that his elderly grandmother could barely walk, and was definitely not a security threat, but to no avail. Apparently a week's notice would have been required to approve such an extraordinary request.

So we would have to get my mother there by the usual means. I decided to take the probably futile step of asking the parking lot attendant if there was some rule that would permit us to drive right up to the front gate of EPCOT, rather than having to park a half-mile away across a steaming asphalt parking area. I expected a prepackaged answer. But to my amaze-ment this parking attendant, wearing his perfect little "Star Trek" uni-form, looked inside the car, saw my mother, and said, "Okay, just go on down." I was so surprised that I forgot to say thanks. I just stared at him. But *he* said, "You're welcome." In the car, we discussed whether or not the attendant's "you're welcome" was his way of being rude to us because I hadn't thanked him. Or was he simply exhaling more automated behav-ior—you're welcome, no matter what we say or do. If it was the former, a moment of rule-breaking by an irritated attendant on a hot day, we had witnessed the very first crack in the facade of EPCOT. It gave me hope.

Finally, we made it to the Norway pavilion for the performance, and it was magnificent. The group sang ancient songs about love and rural life, about farms, animals, loneliness. Unfortunately, however, the performance took place on an outdoor stage while various quaint Disney vehicles—double-decker buses, old cars, various go-carts—drove by, and while thousands of tourists walked by noisily, stopping only long enough to pick up a phrase or two of a song, satisfied with the "colorful" Norwegians, but not actually interested in the music. I could see that the performance itself was totally irrelevant to the EPCOT plan; it was just part of the fantasy dream-park theme, where the world of tomorrow also retains "the best of an earlier time," like a kind of psychic wallpaper. In the world of tomorrow that EPCOT truly envisions, there wouldn't actually be a Norway that would be distinguishable from any other place.

Meanwhile, as all the tourists and buses and cute cars were inching by, Rob was trying to signal the sound engineers who were located across the yard in one of the papier-mâché castle towers. Apparently the EPCOT engineers couldn't get the mikes to work properly; the amplifiers were out of balance, and there was an irritating audio feedback throughout the show. They never did get it all working properly. Here we were in this celebration of the perfect technotopian tomorrow, and the engineers of the place couldn't get some sound equipment to function acceptably.

So it would be, I thought, when they try to build those space utopias. After all the money has been spent on the space program, and all the peoples of the world have been sold on it, and all the idealized controlled environments created, and all the corporate visions realized, the whole damn thing will end up functioning with the efficiency of, say, the subway or the phone company. It will work sometimes, but not always. To me this was cause for optimism: The grass always will grow up through the cracks. Nature probably will survive even if people do not. Total control never works.

SAN FRANCISCO, THE THEME PARK

If places like the West Edmonton Mall and EPCOT Center are expressions of, and training grounds for, a culture preparing itself to depart from the planet, everyday life is becoming that way as well. The city of San Francisco, for example, where I live, has begun a process similar to many American cities, assessing its unique features and packaging them for a world of travel consumers hungry for a taste of unrooted, artificial-authentic experience. Whatever authenticity the city once had is quickly disappearing as its authentic features are converted into commodity form. This is the same logic as the West Edmonton Mall, which re-creates Bourbon Street and Polynesia in a domed environment in the freezing north of Canada. Uprooted as we all are, not attached to any place in particular, anyplace can now be anywhere, and authentic places can become "theme parks" of themselves.

When I first moved to San Francisco in 1960, the cable cars were transportation. My kids paid a quarter and rode them to school every day. Now, the cable cars have been reassessed. Most of the lines have been ripped out, save the ones that run from downtown hotels to Fisherman's Wharf. Now, a cable car costs $2.50 per ride, and you rarely see a San Franciscan on one. Similarly, Fisherman's Wharf, which used to be for working fishermen, now has only a facade fishing fleet, to lure tourists. In fact, the entire city is rapidly becoming a replica of itself, and life within the city approaches what it would surely be like if lived inside Disney World. San Francisco is becoming "San Francisco, the theme park." Soon, we will find a way to re-create the 1989 earthquake.

Gary Coates put the trend this way: "I fully expect that before too long, some entire nation with a depressed economy, perhaps England, will change its name to Olde England, charge visitors a fee at the border, and hand them a book of tickets for the various attractions: Double-decker buses! Charming Shakespearean Stratford! Real soccer riots for your entertainment! The actual battlefield of the 300 Years' War between Olde England and Olde Ireland!"

Remaking authentic communities into packaged forms of themselves, re-creating environments in one place that actually belong somewhere else, creating theme parks and lifestyle-segregated communities, and space travel and colonization—all are symptomatic of the same modern malaise: a disconnection from a place on Earth that we can call Home. With the natural world—our true home—removed from our lives, we have built on top of the pavement a new world, a new Eden, perhaps; a mental world of creative dreams. We then live within these fantasies of our own creation; we live within our own minds. Though we are still on the planet Earth, we are disconnected from it, afloat on pavement, in the same way the astronauts float in space.

That our culture has taken this step into artificial worlds on and off the planet is a huge risk, for the logical result is disorientation and madness and, as Coates argues, the obsessive need to attempt to re-create nature and life.

ANTIDOTE: REINHABITATION
OF THE EARTH

In 1967 David Brower, then executive director of the Sierra Club, asked our ad agency to prepare an advertisement entitled "EARTH NATIONAL PARK." The ad pointed out that, as the technologically advanced countries prepare to launch themselves into space, where presumably they would behave as they do here, we Earthlings should recognize that we have only one home.

Our species, *Homo sapiens,* emerged from the chemical soup and soil that is this earth. We are part of an intricate web of life that exists only here. Nowhere else in the universe could possibly be "home," however ingenious we become in re-creating Earthlike environments in space. Given this reality, Brower argued that we should have second thoughts about stepping into space. If we did do so, he warned, we should at least simultaneously think of our home environment, all of it, as irreplaceable and nonreplicable, requiring as much preservation as was still possible. Brower argued we should think of our planet as a kind of conservation district within the universe: a park, a nature preserve. So that once we had spent some time in outer galaxies, in hyper-reality, and mined all the minerals, and built some space stations, and given birth to non-Earthling children, there would be a place these kids could come back to, to experience their roots in nature.

The advertisement was ahead of its time. Few people considered the idea of an Earth National Park seriously. Conflict brewed even within the Sierra Club about whether Brower should have been running ads about space travel. (Finally he departed to form Friends of the Earth and then founded Earth Island Institute. Later, Brower returned to the Sierra Club Board of Directors, and perhaps these few paragraphs—being published by Sierra Club Books—can serve to reintroduce the idea of Earth National Park to the membership. The ad should be rerun *now*.)

While Brower was arguing that the whole Earth needed to be conceived of as home (now that there was the possibility of departing from it), similar movements began to appear. In the 1960s many groups spoke in terms of human beings "reinhabiting" this planet, particularly taking stewardship over the places where they live. Included in these were the new urban environmental movements that seemed to blossom simultaneously all over the country, as if they were conspiratorial. They fought similar battles against overdevelopment, crowding, pollution, and the control of cities and neighborhoods by absentee owners. Some of these movements—such as the present Green City program in San Francisco, organized by Peter Berg's Planet Drum Foundation—added yet another dimension: making urban inhabitants aware of the native plant and animal species and environmental features of the places they inhabit, the goal being a natural renewal within the cities.

Similarly, the bioregional movement appeared in the 1970s, seeking to empower humans within a naturally cohesive region—such as a watershed or a delta region or a valley region—to seize stewardship of that place and protect it from the larger forces acting to change, or to dominate and cause ecological harm. More radical than traditional environmental groups, the bioregionalists resist the authority of nation-states, which make no sense in ecological terms, and also value non-human life forms and their inherent right to exist. (By now there are 300 bioregional organizations in the United States, though they remain little known since, by their nature, they are locally oriented.)

In that same period of awakening, the Greens movement emerged in Europe. Less *place*-oriented than bioregionalists or the urban ecology movements, the Greens advocate firm limits to economic growth and the need to alter activity on the planet according to the limits imposed by nature.

All of these movements express certain aspects of the larger, global movement among the world's tribal peoples. The native populations have been speaking to us of their relationship to the earth for centuries, but we have ignored them. Native movements are diametrically opposed to the high-tech, corporate, expansionist philosophies that have disconnected humans from our roots.

Any movement that seeks to re-invigorate the relationships between human beings and the places on the globe where we actually live becomes an antidote to the space craze.

9

DEVELOPING THE GENETIC
WILDERNESS

OUR SOCIETY IS characterized by an inability to leave anything in nature alone. Every piece of land, every creature, every mineral in the oceans, every growing plant, every mountain, every inch of desert is examined for its potential contribution to commercial development and exploitation, and to the expansion of technological society.

Even the essential building blocks of nature—the atom, the proton, the electron—are subject to commercial scrutiny. Where science can intervene science does so; corporations then package the process and sell it.

In the previous chapter I suggested that the last two frontiers of this expansionist process, the last two relatively undeveloped wildernesses, are space and the genetic structure of life. That they have existed this long in their pristine state is not due to any recognition that some places in nature should be allowed to exist in an untrammeled and unrevised form; it's just that until now technological evolution had not provided machinery capable of seriously intervening in these wilderness regions. That is all changing now, at a rapid rate. Meanwhile, organized resistance groups are slow to realize that space and genetics are wilderness issues at all.

It is somewhat simpler to understand space as a wilderness issue. All human beings have a conscious (or unconscious) relationship to space. We look to the heavens and we can actually see that vast wilderness, one that is still in virtually the same condition (save for the presence of satellites and space junk) as when the first humans appeared on Earth. The constellations and planets continue to move according to their own rules. Humans have had nothing to do with them thus far. So the heavens still reveal

natural form. Space exploration also raises traditional environmental issues, such as pollution, ozone depletion, space war, nuclear danger, and the
like.

The genetics issue, however, is more subtle. Environmentalists have not
seen genetics as a wilderness issue because most of us cannot physically *see*
this wilderness, in the way we can see space. This wilderness exists deep
inside our cells, where ordinary folks, lacking microscopes, cannot see or
grasp what is going on. But the people who do see it—scientists and the
corporations they work for—are excited. They have granted themselves
sanction to alter, redesign, and profit from this hidden world, just as if it
were a valley to be dammed or land to be turned to one-crop production.

The premise of genetic technology and intervention is that life is not
really different from any other undeveloped virgin wilderness. Since biotechnology and computers have now made intervention possible, techno-
moguls are gung ho to exploit that wilderness, as they have done with the
others. In the absence of public outcry, the technical elite gives itself permission to proceed. *I* have not given them permission. Neither have you.
Permission has been surmised by the absence of opposition, and by the fact
that the inventors of the technologies, the governments that supervise the
explorations, and the corporations that expand the process all agree that
it's good for them. They then rationalize why it is also good for us. These
rationalizations become advertisements and World's Fairs and EPCOT
Center visions of how life shall be lived.

● ● ●

February 17, 1988. The *New York Times* carries an astounding image on
its front page: a photo of three genetically identical Brangus bulls produced by the Granada Corporation of Houston. They are so alike in every
detail that, at first, I believe I am looking at a single photo repeated three
times. The article accompanying the photo reports that livestock breeders
can now clone identical animals from a single embryo, and that the technique is nearing wide-scale application in the U.S. and Canada. From the
Times:

> The cloning technique is the latest in breeding technologies that
> have allowed animal scientists to steadily separate reproduction in
> livestock from natural mating and thereby gain tighter control over
> the hereditary traits of cattle, pigs and sheep. What breeders lacked,
> though, was a reliable technique for precisely duplicating superior
> animals so as to create the kind of uniform quality and production

in farm animals that were once thought to be confined only to manufactured goods.

The article goes on to say that such a development creates the imminent possibility of applying such techniques to humans. Prior animal experiments, such as in-vitro fertilization and surrogate motherhood, have been successful with humans, so why not this? "This possibility that a woman's embryo could be manipulated in a laboratory to produce numerous genetically identical babies carried to term in the wombs of surrogate mothers would likely add to the controversy that often surrounds advances in genetic engineering," said the *Times,* raising the image of mass-produced, identical "designer babies."

Unfortunately, however, this recent biotechnological breakthrough has *not* added to the controversy. Except for a few early legal challenges by a handful of dedicated opponents (notably Jeremy Rifkin of the Washington D.C.–based Foundation on Economic Trends, author of several excellent, critical books on the subject), biotechnological research and development has met with little resistance and is growing at maximum speed. It has been limited only by the researchers' abilities to make their inevitable breakthroughs and by the exigencies of the profit standard.

SCIENTIST AS BUSINESSMAN

The absence of options available to the public to limit the onrush of biotechnology, or even to undertake meaningful public debate on the subject, is not unusual. As I spelled out earlier, all new technologies are introduced in terms of their utopian possibilities. The downside of the story is left for a later generation to discern and experience, when the technology is much more difficult to dismantle. As usual the parameters of the debate are set by the people who benefit from a positive outcome, the corporations who will profit from the rapid advance of biotechnology. But there is a difference this time. Biotechnology gained its foothold during the Reagan years. Perhaps because of that, the usual distance between university scientists, engaged in the invention process, and the corporations who undertake the exploitation, did not exist. Following Reagan's Law, the scientists, like everyone else, were "looking out for number one." This time the scientists *themselves* are the founders of the corporations, and they're making millions. At least two Nobel Laureates have converted their discoveries into marketplace payoffs, and they were only the first of the breed. So the tradition of academic objectivity and criticism, already seriously threatened by government-military contracts for various technologies, has now collapsed altogether, as now the university scientists *are* the corporations. Now the scientists behave just as the CEOs of, say, tobacco companies. They present the positive, omit the negative, and call their few critics, such as Rifkin, "troglodytes."

The corruption of scientific criticism and objectivity—and thereby the suppression of debate—has reached beyond individual scientists. Whole universities are becoming dependent upon biotech corporate funding, in one of the neatest financial symbioses between corporations, academia, and science ever to take place. And not just any old college is selling out: MIT, Stanford, Harvard, and UC Berkeley have become "suppliers" to the genetics industry in exchange for corporate grants.

According to an unusually extensive five-part *San Francisco Chronicle* report on genetics (from September 28–October 2, 1987), the pharmaceutical giant Smith, Kline, Beckman contributed $7.8 million to the Stanford University Center for Molecular and Genetic Medicine and "in exchange, gets licensing rights to future products." And Harvard University's medical school accepted some $70 million from Hoechst AG, a West German drug manufacturer, "to set up a new department of molecular biology. Hoechst scientists are trained at the [Harvard] hospital and the company gets any patents arising from the research it finances."

Harvard University Nobel Prize winner Dr. Walter Gilbert sees no problem with this symbiosis, by which scholars become entrepreneurs: "At a university you want a happy millionaire faculty who are going to endow you when they go," he told the *Chronicle*. He might have added that biotechnology is more efficiently developed when the university and the corporate world both have stakes in muting criticism.

As of 1990, 500 companies were deeply engaged in research and development of new genetically engineered products, spending more than four billion dollars. That amount may double by the time this book is published. Two-thirds of these research dollars come from the U.S. government, which is the fourth part of the corporation-university-science network. (The government view is that biotechnology, one of the few fields in which the United States now has an advantage over other nations, will enhance U.S. competitiveness in world markets.)

Meanwhile, the general public receives its news almost entirely from these huge institutions—government, universities, corporations—all of which are deeply invested in a predetermined outcome. We get to hear the predictions about how genetics will benefit humanity and then, like a ride at EPCOT Center (where the message is identical), we watch it pass us by like some kind of diorama, or the latest hit television series, no more or less important than "Twin Peaks" or Lithuanian independence or Supreme Court nominees or the World Series or presidential races. But genetic engineering is not merely of passing importance. It represents the culmination of all scientific efforts to intervene in and alter life on Earth. This time the scientists are not satisfied to merely rearrange or kill off certain life forms. This time scientists will be perfecting life, re-creating it according to their own ideas, selecting characteristics that will work best in the marketplace, and putting the processes of life creation in the hands of private corporate interests.

BEST-CASE SCENARIOS

Of course, very few scientists ever believe themselves to be engaged in something harmful. The opposite is true. They believe they are doing a good thing. In the genetics field, typical enthusiasm is shown by Dr. Martin Eglitis of the National Institute of Health, who was quoted in the *Chronicle* series as saying, "This is without question the most exciting time I've had in my life. . . . I feel like if I work an extra two hours this week I'm saving the life of someone who, within two hours, might have died. The practicality of what I'm doing is very vivid. It's clear. It's beyond good science. It's knowing that what I was doing this afternoon is going to lead directly, acutely, to benefit mankind. That's pretty mind-bending."

I have read similar statements from scientists in many other fields: scientists at Lawrence Livermore Nuclear Laboratory, who develop weapons to save the "free world"; computer scientists, who think advanced computation can rid the world of toil and disease; satellite mappers, who seek to discover all the world's resources, and thereby end hunger. No one wants to believe he or she is engaged in something horrendous, so they seek to justify its imagined benefits. This is natural. The problem is that the media often presents these self-serving observations without offering equal time to alternative arguments. On the rare occasion when the media *does* present opposing views, there is then no public mechanism to act on the issues.

The language of the new genetic sciences is brimming with optimism and hope. The projects in the works are a litany of do-gooder ventures, including drugs for fighting heart attack, cancers, and blood clots; cures for dwarfism, anemia, hemophilia, hypertension, heart failure, burns, skin wounds, even AIDs. New, genetically designed plant species would resist disease and insects, thereby increasing world food productivity; plants resistant to herbicides would allow herbicides to be sprayed onto *other* plants that may attack *our* food supply. Scientists are working to develop plants that can produce their own fertilizers and their own natural pesticides, thereby eliminating chemical pesticides. (We haven't heard from the chemical industry yet on that one.) New plants and microbes are being invented that might possibly replace oil. We can expect plants that operate at a much higher rate of photosynthesis, thereby growing larger and faster. We can look forward—and this is imminent—to larger identical animals, with more meat and less fat, as well as new animal species that resist certain diseases and that use fewer resources to sustain themselves.

Finally, there are the wonderful possibilities for eliminating genetic diseases among humans. As many as 3,000 diseases that we presently suffer might theoretically be eliminated by reorganizing genetic codes.

How can anyone be against these things? How can any harm come from any of this? It sounds so great that even I might be for it if I had not, for the past two decades, learned the awful consequences of accepting best-case scenarios for new technologies. Breaking that habit—as I strongly advise you to do—enables you to seek the hidden, negative aspects. You begin to ask about the perspectives that are not presented: What do the environmentalists say? What do the farmers say? How will these technologies affect wealth and power in our system? How will they affect the biological balance on Earth? Is there any catastrophic danger? Have we thought it all through? Do we know who benefits and who loses? What are the spiritual aspects? The psychological aspects? The economic and political aspects? In sum, do we know what we are doing?

SIX NEGATIVE POINTS ABOUT GENETICS

By listing the following six major issues concerning genetics, I hope to point out how serious it is that biotechnology has *not* caused extensive debate in the public press, nor been hotly contested within the halls of science, nor been the subject of important new bills in Congress, nor been a major issue in electoral politics. Our society is standing silently on the platform, being herded onto a very dangerous train going we don't know where. Perhaps, when all of the issues are presented at one time, the big picture will start to become clearer.

1. The "Andromeda Strain"

The term refers to Michael Crichton's popular science-fiction book in which genetic research produces a new bug capable of resisting all efforts to kill it: when inadvertently released from a laboratory, the bug ravages all life on Earth. Of all the possible dangers of genetic engineering, this is the only one that has achieved significant publicity, partly due to the book, partly because of its inherent sensationalism, and partly because of a series of lawsuits by Jeremy Rifkin.

According to Rifkin, the problem is not so much that bugs might escape the labs, but that many genetically engineered products are being deliberately released, such as the viruses sprayed on potato patches and strawberry fields to protect against frost. The fear is that such viruses might have survival ability far beyond what is anticipated, might be transported via wind or vehicle to another ecosystem where they might indeed cause havoc, perhaps even on a worldwide scale, as the fictional book proposed.

For a few years, major concerns about biotechnology focused around such apocalyptic dangers. So far, however, the first few viruses to have been deliberately placed into the environment have not produced any catastrophic result, so the industry has been able to say, "I told you so," and issue the familiar charge of "Luddite" against Rifkin and others. And since we Americans have such short attention spans, if a cataclysm doesn't occur soon after a warning, we just go back to watching television. Hindsight indicates it may have been counterproductive for critics of biotechnology to emphasize this potentiality above others, as we will see.

But just because the catastrophe has not yet happened doesn't mean it won't. Remember that when critics of nuclear energy predicted catastrophe they were called "Luddites"; twenty years later came Chernobyl. The same was true of releasing toxic wastes and chlorofluorocarbons into the environment, which eventually produced Love Canal and ozone depletion, respectively. Both of these disasters are only the early warnings of staggering global catastrophe.

The problem for critics is that a specific experiment is unlikely to produce a catastrophic result, because with each experiment the risk is small. But as the experiments increase in number, so does the risk. Now with the genetics debate having virtually stopped, scientific labs, government agencies, and corporate producers of these bugs are exercising few if any effective controls. Scientists and corporations assert that their labs are designed with safety in mind. For example, some bugs are being designed so that if one should somehow escape the various fail-safe lab systems, it would instantly die. Should we be reassured by this?

In the absence of specific, strong, enforced safety standards—and one could argue that there are no standards safe enough to preclude all possible events—economics are what determine the level of safeguarding that a corporation exercises. That a corporation would sacrifice profitability for safety is preposterous, given the rules of corporate behavior. If I were a betting man, I would take the long odds and put my money down that within the next few decades a bug *will* get loose, will survive, and will cause one hell of a lot of unexpected, possibly catastrophic problems.

2. Mandatory Genetic Screening

There is growing opinion that all children should be tested at birth to identify their genetic characteristics. The motives, as usual, are supposedly altruistic: to identify the genetic characteristics that predetermine disease later in life, in order to reduce the risks for the gene carriers and others. For example, people with certain sets of genes might be well advised to avoid workplace environments in which chemicals known to stimulate the disease are used. In other cases, gene screening might help people avoid marriages between two carriers of a dangerous hereditary trait. There are also racial implications: black people, for example, are far more likely to carry the genes that may later produce an outbreak of sickle-cell anemia.

Population-wide genetic screening seems like a positive idea to many people because of the potential to reduce or eliminate certain diseases and protect future generations. But again, this is the best-case vision. The other side of the story is that such testing could be used by insurance companies to refuse coverage, or by employers to deny work, or by the government to intervene in people's life decisions.

Whether or not to quarantine some elements of the population, such as people with AIDS, is actually being seriously debated, as of this writing. One can easily imagine new levels of discrimination, based on race as connected to gene structure, or based on gene structure regardless of race. I believe a significant percentage of the population would find this a morally appropriate thing to do.

3. Creation of New, Patentable Animal Species

Experimentation with the genetic structure of animals is advancing rapidly, despite opposition from animal-rights groups and humane societies who deplore the practice for two reasons: first, because of the pain inflicted upon animals used in experiments; second, because of the invasion and breakdown of "the sanctity of species." There is also opposition among small farmers who, already battling the overwhelming economic power of agribusiness, now find that invented animal breeds are another weapon in the corporate arsenal. The new animals, controlled and patented by these huge corporations, will be doled out only to farmers who can pay a monopoly price, thus endangering the viability of family farming even more.

(The Supreme Court has ruled that new life forms, and new animal breeds, may be legally patented, just like any other piece of technology. The first such decision concerned a new mouse, invented by Harvard University, genetically altered to be especially susceptible to breast cancer; not good for the mouse, but helpful for cancer researchers. The U.S. Patent Office granted the patent and the Supreme Court approved. Now similar patents for new genetically engineered pigs, cattle, and sheep—if those words still apply to describe these animals—as well as new aquatic species, are expected to stand up in court. The Patent Office policy was undertaken without congressional debate on the ethical, moral, or environmental issues, although twenty members of Congress had protested.)

In addition to creating new breeds within an animal species, the genetics industry contemplates intermixing genes from different species to create entirely new animals with greater commercial potential. Creating new kinds of animals is not so new—horses and donkeys were bred to produce mules, for example—but what is new is the goal of creating new animals that can reproduce themselves, as mules cannot.

According to some genetics visionaries, someday we may be able to intermix the genes of animals and humans. (We are, alas, also animals and may be subject to similar indignities.) This may seem far-fetched right now, but I imagine that if scientists could create a humanoid combining the strength and size of a gorilla with the ability to speak English, some genetics company would figure out the creature's market potential. And if there were a market, do you think some moral argument would keep them from producing it? It would depend on the level of public debate at that time. Present trends are not promising.

There are a few vocal opponents of altering animals' genetic structures. Dr. Michael Fox, scientific director of the United States Humane Society, was quoted in the 1987 *San Francisco Chronicle* series:

> It is very frightening to treat animals as simply assemblies of genes that can be manipulated at will by humans. It is our feeling that the inherent nature of an animal needs to be respected. . . . Exchanging genes from totally different species . . . is fundamentally and morally wrong . . . a violation of the sanctity of being. The patenting of life is another ethical issue. We are opposed to this commoditization of creation. Animals not only have extrinsic value to us, they have inherent value in and of themselves.

Jeremy Rifkin put it more succinctly: "We're talking about reducing life to the status of a manufactured commodity, indistinguishable from other commercial products. . . . It is the ultimate desecration of life."

4. Gene-Line Therapy and "Designer Babies"

If we can preselect desirable genes for the "lower" life forms—plants and animals—we can do the same for human animals. The question of where to draw the line has created some dis-ease among scientists. Most see no problem with genetic manipulation of plant life, but a few are ambivalent about the alteration of animal gene codes. Others think that fooling with plants and animals is fine, but not humans. Others say that genetic engineering is okay even among humans, though some draw the line at "gene-line therapy," which they consider raises too many moral and ethical issues.

"Gene-line therapy" is work now under way to map and then manipulate the basic human genetic code. Sperm and/or egg cells will be changed in order to permanently alter the reproductive line for all generations to come. Particular targets will be certain gene structures known to produce genetic diseases, such as Down's syndrome, Tay-Sachs disease, and sickle-cell anemia. Experimenting with the genetic structures of future generations, who by definition have no say in the matter, is at the heart of the argument, since the kind, quality, and degree of experimentation are difficult to control once the process begins. Who, for example, decides when it is ethically permissible to alter the gene structures of future generations? Few people object to eliminating a specific disease, but what about gene-line experimentation for permanent cosmetic, racial, or sexual alterations?

A significant number of genetic scientists don't object to gene-line therapy for treating genetic characteristics leading to disease, but are very worried about the potential to produce new races (which is called eugenics), or about genetic "enhancement," i.e., making people taller, blonder, blue-eyed, stronger. Some scientists see no problem even with cosmetic enhancement: Why shouldn't society produce taller, blonder people if that's what the public wants? They say the marketplace should decide. (There is obviously a role for advertising in this: "THIS WEEK ONLY, GET TWO OF OUR *ALPHA-PLUS* NEW IMPROVED EMBRYOS FOR THE PRICE OF ONE— BLONDER, TALLER, BETTER-LOOKING THAN EVER BEFORE.")

The ethical, philosophical, and political issues involved are so subtle and complex that even scientists who call themselves "medical ethicists" are at odds about where to draw the line. One leading "ethicist," Professor

LeRoy Walters of Georgetown University, told the *San Francisco Chronicle* that genetic enhancements are perfectly appropriate. He, for one, would love to see geneticists design children with better memories, which would be useful for academic life. "As long as this would be a familial decision," says Dr. Walters, "as long as every couple were free to decide, 'Do we want this kind of intervention for our children?' which they presumably pass on to their children, then I think that decision would be perfectly compatible with a democratic society."

What about those families who could not afford or did not want to buy better-designed children with longer memories? Would they not constitute a new class facing a new category of discrimination? Dr. Walters has an answer for this: Gene-line alteration should be available to all families, democratically. He compares it to public education; every family should have equal access to the technology. (Equal access to technology has never yet been achieved with any technology in any modern society. Why would genetic engineering be any different?)

Dr. Sheldon Krimsky, who heads the Committee for Responsible Genetics, finds all gene-line therapy intervention deeply troublesome:

> Gene therapy on germ-line cells would take us precipitously close to reshaping human evolution and toward some kind of prototype human being. . . . You might start with height or with skin color or even with gene sequences associated with intelligence or longevity. . . . These are very troubling decisions that tremendously partition society and create a kind of genetic aristocracy. Sure, we want to better our children's lives and improve their possibilities for surviving in the world . . . but to do this by gaining control over genetics will give some people greater control over other people than we have today.

Dr. George Annas, a professor of health law at Boston University, adds this (also from the *San Francisco Chronicle*): "We already have artificial insemination clinics that use students from specific medical schools on the theory that they produce superior sperm. . . . Surrogate motherhood is similar. People want good-looking surrogate mothers . . . surrogate agencies have [picture] catalogs of surrogate mothers." This kind of entrepreneurship, says Annas, will lead to some astounding scenarios:

> In the future one will be able to pick out both the mother and the father, combine the sperm and egg, and then take the embryo that results from that and split it or clone it. Let's say you clone it one hundred times. You freeze ninety-nine of them and grow one

up. . . . You grow it up a year or two, then test it, [and] photograph it. [Then you put it up for sale] saying your kid will be exactly like this. . . . we're talking designer babies in the extreme.

Does this sound like some third-rate 1950s sci-fi or Nazi scientist flick? The analogy is not far-fetched to Dr. Edwin Chargoff, a professor of biochemistry at Columbia University Medical School. He recently wrote in *Nature* magazine: "A new era has begun. . . . Science is now the craft of the manipulation, modification, substitution and deflection of the forces of nature . . . human husbandry." Envisioning a time when human embryos will be mass-produced for experimental purposes, he issues this warning: "What I see coming is a gigantic slaughterhouse, a molecular Auschwitz in which valuable enzymes, hormones and so on will be extracted instead of gold teeth."

Thus far, efforts to influence the National Institute of Health to ban gene-line therapy, or to at least place meaningful restrictions on it, have failed. At this time there are few controls other than the dubious systems that corporate and university labs themselves create. That safety will someday be compromised as genetics researchers chase an elusive but highly profitable goal is, to me, obvious. Similarly, if we allow geneticists to intervene in future generations, especially without strict controls, then only marketability will determine the new colors, sizes, attitudes, and abilities of humans.

5. Monoculture in the Genetic Wilderness

As human beings become subject to preplanning and redesign, and our less popular or less commercially salient characteristics drop out of the gene pool, the human world will experience a reduction of genetic diversity. This is akin to the reduction of plant and animal species that has come with one-crop agriculture, seed selection and monopolization, and the conversion of varied ecosystems into monolithic suburban or urban forms. Of course, long before genetic engineering the gene pool has been altered by natural forces; but the human, commercial forces are ones we can theoretically control. We have seen how commercial interests regard the relative importance of marshlands, deserts, and forests. They are given low priority as compared with their redevelopment possibilities. The net result is that life on Earth is far less varied. Animal species have declined precipitously as habitats—wetlands, wildlands, forests—have disappeared. The same can be said of plants and millions of kinds of microorganisms and insects. As environmentalists know well, the net reduction of the planet's biotic diversity produces a net reduction in the worldwide gene pool, which is the source of new life. Too much reduction in the gene pool causes an insufficiency of the billions and trillions of interactions required for a healthy ecosystem—whether we are speaking of one river delta or the whole earth.

6. Gene Wars

In their book *Gene Wars,* Charles Pillar and Dr. Keith R. Yamamoto reverse the usual assumptions about the dangers of genetic research. Normally, the worst-case scenario for the consequences of genetic research contemplates one of two catastrophes: either an accidental release of a lethal new organism, or an intentional release of a presumably benign organism, which then goes out of control. In *Gene Wars* the authors contemplate an entirely different worst-case scenario, in which horrible new bugs and/or chemicals, known to be terrible killers, are *deliberately* released into the environment.

Unlike the accidental scenarios that most people discuss, this one is not theoretical. Pillar and Yamamoto call the 1980s "the decade of military biology," a description that may apply as well to the 1990s. They point out that the growth rate for U.S. chemical and biological warfare (CBW) expenditures outstripped all other growth rates within military classifications. They also point out that the rate was actually higher than indicated, since the official rate doesn't include other life sciences research by the military, which, according to the authors, has "clear applications to biological warfare."

The U.S. Department of Defense has argued that, unlike the Soviet Union, U.S. research is defensive. But according to Pillar and Yamamoto, "the secrecy inherent in military operations makes it impossible to evaluate the claim." As for the difference between offensive and defensive CBW research, the authors make a chilling point: Whether they are researching offensive or defensive uses, they create exactly the same bugs, exactly the same deployment scenarios, and design everything with the maximum degree of kill potential. "Even the DOD acknowledges that in BW research the difference between offense and defense is purely a matter of intent," say Pillar and Yamamoto. "This largely holds true for development, testing, production and training . . . to develop an acceptable biological warfare defense—though virtually impossible against a potentially infinite array of genetically altered BW agents—the same features are essential. The U.S. 'defensive' program involves nearly all aspects of the BW process. It is not that offense and defense merely appear similar. They, in fact, share identical components."

So protecting humans and other life forms on the planet is less dependent upon lab procedures to keep the bugs contained (as in civilian research safety systems) than it is on the intent and the interpretation of events by military hierarchies. It is also important to note that chemical and biological weapons production is not nearly as complex and costly as some of the other weapons of Armageddon, such as Star Wars systems and ICBMs. Small nations therefore can easily develop such weapons. At least two such nations, Iraq and Libya, have already used such weapons, with quite deadly effect. And Iraq continues to threaten to use them against its various enemies. Chemical and biological warfare has become "the poor man's atomic bomb," causing both the U.S. and Soviet Union to protest its development beyond *our* boundaries.

Here is a partial listing of the principal military applications of the new biotechnologies that Pillar and Yamamoto warn about:

- *Bacteria that can resist all antibiotics.* The offensive application is obvious. But the defense needs to develop these same bacteria in order to overcome them. At some future time, of course, the defense could become the offense.

- *Increased biological hardiness.* Many harmful organisms adapted to live inside humans die upon contact with sun or air. As a result they cannot be sprayed from an airplane or released from a canister. Military researchers are seeking to make these terrible organisms survivable in the air, so they are viable when humans breathe them.

- *New organisms that can defeat vaccines or natural human or plant resistances.* Another avenue of research is to camouflage an organism so it defies diagnosis and therefore cannot be treated.

- *New vaccines.* A nation developing biological warfare agents needs also to create vaccines, theoretically to protect its own citizenry.

- *Increased virulence.* Creating bacteria that are, as Pillar and Yamamoto describe, "more powerful, faster-acting, [more] invasive and [able to] infect and kill more reliably."

- *Weaponization of innocuous organisms.* Making friendly bugs, like *E. coli,* now a normal occupant of human intestines, into killers.

- *Ethnic weapons.* Scientists believe that certain bacteria and chemicals can be made racially or regionally specific. The authors of *Gene Wars* cite valley fever: "Certain studies suggest that blacks are far more susceptible to valley fever than whites. It may be possible to prey on such ethnic or racial groups by targeting a combination of these genetic factors."

• *Hormonal weapons.* To affect human hormonal balance sufficiently enough to lead to death.

Most people who are aware of chemical and biological warfare erroneously assume that the 1925 Geneva Protocol and the 1972 Biological Warfare Convention produced some significant degree of protection. Those agreements only specify offensive research work. They do not prevent a nation from doing defensive work, which, alas, has identical implications and dangers.

In addition, according to Pillar and Yamamoto, the U.S. "historical record on CBW is replete with subterfuge, reckless experimentation, and rogue actions and is punctuated by violations of both domestic policy and international legal and moral norms. The modern record is no more reassuring." And, say the authors, if this is the record in the U.S., a country characterized by an active investigative press and a relatively high degree of public disclosure, what confidence could we have in other nations that operate without this level of pubic involvement?

It may be that in the present world climate, U.S. defensive research is exactly that: defensive. It may also be that Soviet research is defensive. But what happens if some nation develops an organism that cannot be detected or killed by current defenses? And what if this weapon had the potential for world domination that the atomic bomb had in the 1940s? Would the intent of the nation so blessed by this discovery remain defensive? It would depend upon who was in power in that nation and the world situation at the time. The only protection the world would have against a genetic holocaust would be the inclinations of a small number of people.

GUILTY UNTIL PROVEN INNOCENT

In 1986, when the United States Congress asked a few mild questions about certain aspects of genetic engineering, the genetics industry and its apologists began to moan about the prospect of legal restrictions on their inventiveness. One industry witness put it this way: "What you have here is people [the critics] saying 'we're scared.' Nothing [negative about biotechnology] has been proven . . . but 'we're scared.' Is Congress now going to say, for the first time, that here's a new technology that we're going to delay because we're going to presume it's bad until it's proven good?"

Chances are that Congress will not say any such thing. But of course that is precisely what it should say. *Guilty until proven innocent!* Here we have a new genre of technology that presents dangers as vast as those prescribed by any that preceded it, and that is advancing without safety measures, without controls over what it may put into the environment, and without thought about its social, spiritual, philosophical, or military implications. This is a classic case of a new corporate technology barreling through society without meaningful discussion about its possible effects. The genetics industry is aghast at any controls, and the liberal response is the same as it is to all new technologies: *It depends on how it's used.*

The book that best articulates the liberal perspective is *To Govern Evolution* by California writer and environmentalist Walter Truett Anderson. Anderson feels that it's necessary to exercise caution but that we should go forward with biotechnology. He points out that we have been altering nature for thousands of years, at least since the beginning of agriculture, and that biotechnology is only the latest example. He feels that given a balance between potential good and potential harm, genetic engineering is good, since so many aspects of it are useful to humans. He acknowledges risks, but is willing·to accept them. "No research or development in any field would be possible if we demanded absolute certainty," writes Anderson.

Anderson is interested in standards: "We should be asking some very serious questions . . . about what we should and should not do. As we rapidly increase our power to intervene in nature—to govern evolution—we need to develop a realistic ethical basis. There's no way we can prohibit biotech without setting up a police state with a cop in every lab. It's here; it won't go away; we have to learn how to cope with it. And we can't allow it to be guided entirely by the profit motive."

What makes Anderson's view a liberal rather than conservative one is that he speaks about the dangers of a police state, and the harmfulness of the profit motive as the guiding principle for development. But in all other ways Anderson's views are identical with conservative analyses of technology.

My own viewpoint differs in most details from Anderson's. That we have been intervening in nature all along hardly indicates that it was wise to do so. It wasn't. And it is even less wise when the scale and quality of intervention is of the sort that is now taking place. Biotechnology may benefit humans as Anderson says, but the benefits are probably only short-run, and limited to a few select humans. In any event, what benefits humans alone can no longer be the standard for measuring technology; a less anthropocentric view is required if the planet is to survive.

I agree with Anderson that there is risk, but I disagree that the risk is worth it. As for a police state, we are far more likely to create a police state with genetic engineering than without it, since it truly serves philosophies of social management. I agree that it's good to control the influence of the profit motive, but there is no evidence that such a reform is possible in capitalist society.

But my most significant disagreement is with Anderson's statement, "It's here; it won't go away; we have to learn how to cope with it," in which he voices the major apology of the last half-century (or more); the essence of our passivity in the face of the technological juggernaut.

Biotechnology is capable of utterly changing life on Earth, including human life. Accidents may wreak immeasurable havoc on a scale that only such diseases as AIDS can presently imply. Genetics may ultimately create an entirely new kind of racism or discrimination. The field is already creating and eliminating life forms and placing them under commercial control; it is destroying small farmers, reducing the genetic pool, and may eventually alter human beings to make them conform to a new techno-politics of hierarchical gene structures. "Designer babies"—the commercialization of generational reproduction—are nearly here. Tinkering with human "personality traits" is also gaining speed. Selecting genes and assembling new humans, as if with modules from a lumber yard, is imminent. Wars of devastation will also never be the same; they may leave buildings and machines intact while the biological basis of the planet is destroyed.

Given the current path of genetics, and its possible consequences, don't you believe it would be prudent to stop the process and ask that it prove itself innocent of these possibilities before we plunge into the abyss? Don't you think our entire society ought to engage in this debate, right now? Don't you think we all ought to ask if, on balance, we prefer the coming world to the one we have? Shouldn't we be asking what the trade-offs really are? Don't you think it is a matter of absolute urgency? And don't you think that if biotechnology proves to be more destructive than beneficial, that we have every right and obligation to stop it? If so, the first sentence to drive from our discourse is "It's here and it's not going away." The next step is to seek a means of stopping it.

10

IN THE ABSENCE
OF THE SACRED

IN MAY 1990, the *Washington Post* reported that the National Research
Council, an arm of the National Academies of Sciences and Engineering, had thrown its support behind a technical scheme to battle the greenhouse effect, or global warming, caused by excessive carbon dioxide in the
atmosphere.

Environmentalists have been arguing for over half a century that the
solution to the problem was simple: drastically cut the use of fossil fuels
and stop cutting down the earth's forests, which absorb carbon dioxide.
But the environmentalists' solutions have been considered unfeasible, since
they might interfere with industrial growth and profit, and would require
changes in Western lifestyles. So the scientific community has been seeking technical fixes that can accommodate continued industrial activity.

The plan supported by the National Research Council, which advises
Congress on behalf of the scientific establishment, proposes a massive
"iron enrichment" of the oceans; that is, spraying hundreds of thousands
of tons of iron powder onto the seas. This would in turn stimulate the
growth of giant blooms of marine algae to soak up carbon dioxide, as the
forests had previously done. The NRC called the plan "conceptually feasible" and suggested an expenditure of $50 to $150 million to begin research off the coasts of Alaska or Antarctica.

The scientific community became very excited by the idea. The *Post* quotes Roger Revelle, formerly of the Scripps Institution of Oceanography, as saying, "I see no reason why it shouldn't work. . . . I don't think there would be any negative consequences."

And Adam Heller, a chemical engineering professor at the University of Texas, said the plan would be cost-effective and he thought there was nothing "fundamentally stupid" about it.

A more cautious response was given by Anthony Michaels, a research scientist at the Bermuda Biological Station for Research. "It is an enticing idea that is being actively pursued," he said. But he added, "If you start playing God with the system, we don't understand it well enough to know what the outcome would be. The whole food web would be altered."

Michaels was reflecting on the fact that marine algae form the basic foundation of the ocean food chain. They feed the krill that are in turn eaten by fish, seals, penguins, and whales. Once human beings begin actively adjusting the balances, especially at the scale contemplated, there could be surprising ecological effects. According to *Washington Post* science writer William Booth, when the added iron nutrient is sprayed on the waters, "the marine plants should undergo tremendous growth, much like ordinary houseplants gorging themselves on plant food. . . . The researchers do not think their experiment could run amok because the marine algae would grow only so long as other nutrients such as phosphorus and nitrogen held out."

The "iron enrichment" solution is only the most recently advocated technical fix contemplated by science. Here are some others the *New York Times* reported in August 1988:

- A plan to cover the oceans with polystyrene chips, while painting all the roofs of the houses on Earth bright white. This would cause sunlight to be reflected rather than absorbed on the earth's surface.

- A project to create orbiting satellites made of a very fine material, equal in size to about 2 percent of the earth's surface, that would block sunlight and cast a shadow on the planet, reducing temperature. (Such a scheme is also proposed to cool Venus, so that we might contemplate colonization there.)

- Last but not least, a proposal by Dr. Wallace Broecker, a professor of geochemistry at Columbia, to load several hundred jumbo jets with sulfur dioxide to be released at high altitudes. This would simulate the effect of a large volcanic explosion of the kind that has, from time to time, blocked the sun's rays, thereby cooling the earth's surface. The negative aspects of this plan, Broecker said, include an increase in acid rain, and a change in the color of the sky from blue to whitish. "This is not a big expense," he argued, "compared to the impact on industry if we give up reliance on fossil fuels."

• • •

A second contemporary atmospheric problem that science is attempting to correct is ozone layer depletion due to the excessive release of chlorofluoro-carbons in the atmosphere. Again, environmentalists have offered a simple solution: Stop using CFCs for polystyrene, aerosols, and refrigeration. But again this would negatively affect industrial production. Science is seeking alternatives.

The *New York Times* quoted Princeton physicist Thomas H. Stix, who is promoting an idea called "atmospheric processing." He suggests aiming giant lasers at chlorofluorocarbons as they rise from the earth, shattering them before they get to the stratosphere. The only concern with this is whether it is possible to shoot the CFCs without also hitting other mole-cules, with unknown consequences.

Another suggestion was to shoot ozone bullets directly into the strato-sphere, where they would melt and replenish the depleted ozone. Leon Y. Sadler, a chemical engineer at the University of Alabama, would load a fleet of jumbo jets—presumably a different fleet from Dr. Broecker's—with ozone manufactured by an earth-based industry, carry it as high as possible, and pump it back into the atmosphere.

This idea has great merit for industry. First of all, it places ozone into the category of "renewable resource," like a forest. (Of course, forest prod-ucts, when cut down, are at least used for something, while ozone is de-stroyed for no purpose.) Dr. Sadler's plan would replace formerly unproductive atmospheric ozone with new ozone, produced in our fac-tories on Earth, thereby creating jobs, profits, and economic growth.

The *Times* quotes some scientists as cautioning that these ideas are still on the drawing board and may not prove feasible. Nonetheless they felt that as such proposals are publicized, as the *Times* was doing (and as I am doing), scientific creativity is stimulated.

What neither the *Times* nor the scientists say is that this manner of ap-proaching two planet-threatening problems—problems with very simple solutions (don't cut trees, don't use CFCs, reduce energy use, and apply an economic standard other than growth)—is perpetuating the very process that created the problem: more and bigger technological fixes for more and bigger technological problems. In my view, it is a form of obsessive insanity, rooted in our society's failure to grasp or respect the limits of the natural world.

MOLECULAR ENGINEERING

October 1988. My friend Mark Dowie telephones. He is the former editor of *Mother Jones* magazine and is now a freelance journalist focusing on the excesses of technology. His book *We Have a Donor* takes a blistering look at the organ-transplant industry. Dowie asks my opinion of the latest hot ticket on the technology frontier: nanotechnology. I tell him I've never heard of it.

"It's beyond genetics," Mark says. "Instead of merely redesigning the gene structures of living creatures, they're now into redesigning the molecular structure of absolutely everything. It's the new frontier, Jerry, working with the infinitely small. The guru for this movement was the physicist Richard Feynman [who died in 1988]. The idea is to zero down into the atomic structure of all materials and rearrange their molecules to get completely new forms, materials, and creatures. They barely make a distinction between what is an 'organic' material and an 'inorganic' material, since once you're down to the molecular level, it's all the same. I'm telling you, it's like the ultimate acid dream," says Dowie. "It's the 'new physics' all right, here and now. Once they can move the atoms around and redesign the molecular chains—and they're gaining on it—they will be able to redesign the whole world, molecule by molecule, and that's exactly what they intend. It's the technological fix to end them all. These nanotechnologists claim they will create new food, and end all famine. They have already designed tiny semiorganic engines called nanomachines that can enter your bloodstream and be programmed to destroy cancers or eat fat or make any cellular change you want. They're talking about other nanomachines called assemblers that will be superintelligent and will be able to build anything that's now made by workers in factories. These assemblers will just be thrown into a vat of specially chosen molecules and will rearrange them in such a way that they will interact with each other and cause an object to actually grow in that soup and emerge as a space capsule or laser weapon or hair dryer. If they're right, it's the end of the resource problem on Earth. We won't need resources anymore since the resources are the molecules themselves from which they can make anything: trees, houses, animals, weapons, people. Eventually, they promise to eliminate death. Jerry, nanotechnology will make the Industrial Revolution look like a hiccup."

By now I am sure that Mark is kidding me. He knows I'm skeptical about new technology. And this all sounds like science fiction. But he's not kidding. I tell him I don't know which would be worse, if they fail or they succeed. This much is for sure. They are fantasizing. They are living inside that best-case scenario frame of mind, although in the history of technology the best-case result has never once been achieved. I ask Mark who these people are.

"I've been all over the country interviewing them," says Mark. "I would say the main guy right now is a Stanford University lecturer named Eric Drexler, who wrote the bible of nanotechnology, *Engines of Creation*. He is hot. But Drexler is only one of them. There's another guy named Grant Fjermedal, who wrote *The Tomorrow Makers,* and a whole slew of them at IBM. They're all about forty and they're brilliant. They deeply believe they're doing something wonderful. It's like they're saying, 'Hey, this world is a mess. Technology has gotten out of control. We're heading for disaster. Let's wipe the slate clean and start all over. But this time, let's do it right, and let's not be limited by the way nature has chosen to organize things.'

"But Jerry, there's something missing from these people. I'm not sure what it is. These kids are the ultimate technology nerds. There's something cold and harsh in their perspective. Perhaps it's because they are the first generation of scientists born and raised in a world already totally overtaken by the high-tech vision. They really believe more in machines than people or nature. To them human beings are kind of out of date. The only thing really important is somehow finding a way to preserve their brains. They speak about *downloading* their consciousness into computers. I don't think they'd mind if their brains could be saved and the rest of their bodies—in fact, *all* human bodies—were thrown into the trash heap with the dinosaurs. They see their engines as an improvement over human brains, which have to be lugged around by clumsy bodies. It's the old sci-fi image of the disembodied brain. Or that old mad scientist flick where the scientist is ready to sacrifice all of humanity just to save some artificial creature he invented. At first I didn't think anyone would take them seriously, but unfortunately they are being taken seriously. Their work is being funded. The big universities are involved. They're making progress, Jerry; this is really important. We've got to write about them."

Dowie did. His article was called "Brave New Tiny World" and appeared in *California* magazine.

THE POSTBIOLOGICAL AGE

A few months after talking with Mark Dowie, I picked up a copy of Hans Moravec's *Mind Children*. Moravec is director of the Mobile Robot Laboratory of Carnegie Mellon University and his book was written to describe "the future of robot and human intelligence." To borrow Mark Dowie's phrase, it makes the Industrial Revolution *and* nanotechnology look like hiccups.

The author unashamedly presents a tightly reasoned, step-by-step argument in favor of a "postbiological" future: "It is a world in which the human race has been swept away by the tide of cultural change, usurped by its own artificial progeny."

Moravec calmly explains how within the next thirty years we will bypass the present limits upon artificial intelligence and robotic mobility, to the point where we will be able to "download" all of the content of our brains—which are now unfortunately stuck in decaying biological entities—into computers housed within mobile robots, thereby gaining "us" immortality, via these machines. The machines will "evolve" by their own design and, when given the collective knowledge of all the great thinkers on the planet, without the limitations and fragility of their flesh, will generate ideas and actions that will far exceed human achievement: "Such machines could carry on our cultural evolution, including their own construction and increasingly rapid self-improvement, without us, and without the genes that built us. When that happens, our DNA will find itself out of a job, having lost the evolutionary race to a new kind of competition. . . . The new genetic takeover will be complete. Our culture will then be able to evolve independently of human biology and its limitations, passing instead directly from generation to generation of ever more capable intelligent machinery."

Moravec bases his predictions on calculations that the human brain is capable of "performing 10 trillion (10^{13}) calculations per second." He continues, "This is about one million times faster than the medium-sized machines that now drive my robots, and 1,000 times faster than today's best supercomputers." So, according to Moravec, all that's required to match human calculating ability is a computer that operates at only 1,000 times the speed of today's supercomputers.

While acknowledging that his own calculations may be subject to criticism, Moravec predicts that a computer that can operate at the speed and capacity of the human brain, and that can include all elements of the brain (including the mechanistic equivalent of sense perceptions and emotions), can and should be achieved within the next thirty to fifty years. He reminds us that in only the last eighty years "there has been a *trillionfold* decline in the cost of calculation," so the changes he envisions are actually do-able, especially because of the burgeoning technologies of miniaturization, such as nanotechnology. "Atomic-scale machinery is a wonderful concept and would take us far beyond the humanlike point in computers, since it would allow many millions of processors to fit on a chip that today can hold but one. Just how fast could each individual nanocomputer be? . . . A single nanocomputer might have a processing speed of a trillion operations per second. With millions of such processors crammed onto a thumbnail-size chip, my human-equivalence criterion would be bested more than a millionfold!"

Moravec indicates that his work is driven by his fear that two other technologies—genetics and organ replacement—are simply insufficient to accomplish his futuristic vision. Genetics, which hold great promise for totally redesigning human beings to be more intelligent and efficient, if undifferentiated, is nonetheless limited by the flesh-and-blood factor; we can only live within climatic and atmospheric limits and eventually we die. As for organ transplants and artificial organs, Moravec has this to say:

> Many people are alive today because of a growing arsenal of artificial organs and other body parts. In time, especially as robotic techniques improve, such replacement parts will be better than any originals. So what about replacing everything, that is transplanting a human brain into a specially designed robot body? Unfortunately, while this solution might overcome most of our physical limitations, it would leave untouched our biggest handicap, the limited and fixed intelligence of the human brain. This transplant scenario gets our brain out of our body. Is there a way to get our mind out of our brain?

That's where "downloading" comes in. Moravec goes into exquisite detail on various ways this can be achieved. To give you one idea of his thinking, I will quote one of his descriptions entirely. It involves the operating procedure for a voluntary "downloading" of consciousness into a computer:

> You've just been wheeled into the operating room. A robot brain surgeon is in attendance. By your side is a computer waiting to become a human equivalent, lacking only a program to run. Your skull, but not your brain, is anesthetized. You are fully conscious. The robot surgeon opens your brain case and places a hand on the brain's

surface. This unusual hand bristles with microscopic machinery, and a cable connects it to the mobile computer at your side. Instruments in the hand scan the first few millimeters of brain surface. High-resolution magnetic resonance measurements build a three-dimension chemical map, while arrays of magnetic and electric antennas collect signals that are rapidly unraveled to reveal, moment to moment, the pulses flashing among the neurons. These measurements, added to a comprehensive understanding of human neural architecture, allow the surgeon to write a program that models the behavior of the uppermost layer of the scanned brain tissue. This program is installed in a small portion of the waiting computer and activated. Measurements from the hand provide it with copies of the inputs that the original tissue is receiving. You and the surgeon check the accuracy of the simulation by comparing the signals it produces with the corresponding original ones. They flash by very fast, but any discrepancies are highlighted on a display screen. The surgeon fine-tunes the simulation until the correspondence is nearly perfect.

To further assure you of the simulation's correctness, you are given a pushbutton that allows you to momentarily "test drive" the simulation, to compare it with the functioning of the original tissue. When you press it, arrays of electrodes in the surgeon's hand are activated. By precise injections of current and electromagnetic pulses, electrodes can override the normal signaling activity of nearby neurons. They are programmed to inject the output of the simulation into those places where the simulated tissue signals other sites. As long as you press the button, a small part of your nervous system is being replaced by a computer simulation of itself. You press the button, release it, and press it again. You should experience no difference. As soon as you are satisfied, the simulation connection is established permanently. The brain tissue is now impotent—it receives inputs and reacts as before but its output is ignored. Microscopic manipulators on the hand's surface excise the cells in this superfluous tissue and pass them to an aspirator, where they are drawn away.

The surgeon's hand sinks a fraction of a millimeter deeper into your brain, instantly compensating its measurements and signals for the changed position. The process is repeated for the next layer, and soon a second simulation resides in the computer, communicating with the first and with the remaining original brain tissue. Layer after layer the brain is simulated, then excavated. Eventually your skull is empty, and the surgeon's hand rests deep in your brainstem. Though you have not lost consciousness, or even your train of thought, your mind has been removed from the brain and transferred to a machine. In a final, disorienting step the surgeon lifts out his hand. Your suddenly abandoned body goes into spasms and dies. For a moment you experience only quiet and dark. Then, once again, you can open your eyes. Your perspective has shifted. The computer simulation has been disconnected from the cable leading to the surgeon's hand and reconnected to a shiny new body of the style, color, and material of your choice. Your metamorphosis is complete.

Moravec admits there may be some debate about whether *you* are merely your consciousness, which can be passed into the machine. He argues that our tendency to cling to our bodies, what he calls the "body-identity" position, is out-of-date thinking. He points out that the cells of our bodies are in a constant process of replacing themselves with new ones, and that within every seven years, *all* of our cells are new. He says it is absurd to believe that *you* have anything whatsoever to do with your body, your flesh. *You* are only your mind, or "your pattern," which, he argues, can be transmitted into a machine. In fact it can be transmitted into two or three or many machines simultaneously, not so much like a photocopy as a facsimile transmittal: teleportation, as in the "beam-down" machine in "Star Trek." In other words, the real *you* can be infinitely duplicated; so can the consciousnesses (the "patterns") of other intelligent creatures such as whales, dolphins, elephants, and giant squids. Moravec wants all of these transferred into machines where they will "live" permanently, producing an unimaginably greater, richer new society that can literally reach to the entire universe, without the awful limits of the flesh. Meanwhile, organic life as we have known it can, at last, be abandoned forever. Our collective suicide will give birth to a new, higher species.

THE MADNESS OF THE ASTRONAUT

I am not sufficiently versed in science to tell you whether the ideas of Hans Moravec in robotics, or the work of Drexler in nanotechnology, or the ideas of Broecker, Stix, and Sadler for solving our atmospheric problems, or for that matter, the work of the genetic engineers, can possibly prove practical and achievable. But I do know this. The greatest universities in this country—Stanford, MIT, Harvard, Berkeley, Princeton—provide these projects funding and housing and a platform to speak from.

The United States military—particularly the Navy—backs many of these researchers with multimillion-dollar grants. Giant corporations hunger to patent the concepts and exploit the finished products. Major publishers produce books extolling these ideas. Serious newspapers, journals, and magazines reverently review and report on the most recent advances.

All of these institutions can support these new modes of technological expression because the ideas are in every way consistent with the logic and the assumptions by which our society has operated for the past several centuries.

These were the same assumptions that were employed by the World's Fair planners of the 1930s, the ad agencies of the fifties and sixties, the Disney "imagineers" at EPCOT Center, and the people who envision uto-pian worlds of space colonies. Today's technological pioneers consider themselves original thinkers, but they are only the latest in a long line of advocates for the same set of propositions, the most prominent of which is that nature sets no limits on the degree to which humans may intervene in and alter the natural world. Manifesting the arrogance of Technological Man, the technopioneers assume they are authorized to go anywhere and rearrange anything, including alterations in the structure of human life, animal life, and now natural form itself.

In doing so, they are acting in service to the fundamental principle that has informed technical evolution in the modern era: *If it can be done, do it.* There are no boundaries, no rules, no sets of standards by which to moderate these activities. No sense of right or wrong, no taboos; there's only what will succeed in the marketplace. (Perhaps abandoning human biology will not *sell*—is that our only hope?)

The assumptions have been gaining strength for thousands of years, fed both by Judeo-Christian religious doctrines that have de-sanctified the earth and placed humans in domination over it; and by technologies that, by their apparent power, have led us to believe we are some kind of royalty over nature, exercising Divine will. We have lost the understanding that existed in all civilizations prior to ours, and that continues to exist on Earth today in societies that live side by side with our own; we have lost a sense of the sacredness of the natural world. The new technologists don't accept this notion; they live in a world that is removed from it; they themselves have lost touch with the source of that knowledge. They find it silly.

What is true for the new technologists has sadly become true for most people in the Western world. Having bought the idea that all problems can and should be solved by technology, never thinking back to any alter-native knowledge that could provide a point of contrast, and not even knowing that alternative knowledge exists, we too have spun outward, away from the source, off into space, isolated from that knowledge by concrete and machines. Each new level of technical invention has taken us further away from the source. Each invention has spawned others, placing us ever deeper within technical consciousness and further away from organic reality, to the point where we can seriously consider abandoning the planet, abandoning nature, abandoning our bodies. These ideas are discussed and considered by intellectual leaders, as if such notions are sane.

Our entire society has begun to suffer the madness of the astronaut; uprooted, floating in space, encased in our metal worlds, with automated systems neatly at hand, communicating mainly with machines, following machine logic, disconnected from the earth and all organic reality, without contact with a multidimensional, biologically diverse world and with the nuances of world views entirely unlike our own, unable to view ourselves from another perspective, *we* are alienated to the nth degree. Like the astronaut, we don't know up from down, in from out. Our world and our thought processes are confined to technical boundaries. In such a state many insane ideas and solutions can seem logical because there are no standards by which to compare them. All invention, if achievable, becomes plausible, and even desirable, since it is part of the commitment we have already made, even if the commitment leads logically to reorganizing our genes, our trees, and our skies; and possibly abandoning the planet and life itself.

MEGATECHNOLOGY

Given the scale of the technologically caused environmental problems we now face; and given the scale of the technological fixes that have been proposed; and given the scale and implications of the new technological forms, one would assume these subjects would be hotly debated. As we have seen, they are not. Technology continues to be introduced and described by the people who stand to benefit most from its acceptance, and who deliver their visions in utopian form. The public is uninvolved; there are no forums for argument. No pros and cons. No referenda. Presidential candidates only mention the issues in passing references to solving the acid rain problem, or limiting oil drilling. By the time the body politic becomes aware of problems with technology, it is usually after they are well installed in the system and their effects are too late to reverse. Only now, four decades after the introduction of computers, are there any rumblings of discontent, any realizations of their full implications. By the time the alarm finally goes off, technologies have intertwined with one another to create yet another generation of machines, which makes unraveling them near to impossible, even if society had the will to do it.

As the interlocking and interweaving and spawning of new technologies take place, the weave of technology becomes ever tighter and more difficult to separate. For example, without computers, it would be impossible to have satellites, nuclear power, genetics, space technology, military lasers, information technologies, or nanotechnology. And because of computers, all of these technologies are intertwined with one another. We continue to view them as if they were separate, discrete systems, but they aren't. Computers are at the base of them all, and also plug them into one another and into central systems of management and institutional control, made larger than ever before possible. In fact, the whole complex web of systems ought properly to be thought of as *one* technology that effectively encircles the globe, and that can instantaneously communicate with all its parts. Rather than a biosphere, we have a technosphere. Call it megatechnology.

•   •   •

There is no conspiracy here, at least not in the usual sense. Human beings did not set out to create such a worldwide, interlocked technological entity. But at each stage human beings followed the logic of technical evolution, which seeks to expand its power over nature, and to employ other technologies to be reborn into ever newer, larger, more impactful forms; to strengthen the web of connection.

It is true that there are human beings who sit near the hub of the process, and who make deals with each other, and who advertise the process at such places as EPCOT, and who benefit financially if they can steer the process a certain way. But they are not really in charge. Technological evolution leads inevitably to its own next stages, which can be altered only slightly. The invention of the computer inevitably implied the invention of the supercomputer and its ability to spawn a thousand other high technologies, with their vast social and political consequences. It didn't matter who put the money down to further the process. The people and the machine were *inside* the technical project together; they were the same. If there was a conspiracy here, it is only one in the Ellulian sense; a *de facto* conspiracy; a conspiracy of technical form.

In any event, the result is a worldwide technical creature that includes us in its functioning: the way our minds operate, the way we perceive alternatives, what we imagine are good and bad ideas. We have entered into a universe that has been re-formed by machines; we are a species that lives its life within mechanistic creations; our environment is a product of our minds. Locked inside our cities and suburbs, working in our offices, controlling and conceptualizing nature as a raw material for our consumption, and now even including *ourselves* as raw material suitable for redevelopment, we are at one with the process.

If we have a worldwide technical creature, then computers are its nervous system. Television is the way human minds are made compatible with the system and identical with one another; it is the sales system, and the audiovisual training mechanism. Genetics has the role of reworking the biological structures to maximize economic potential. And nanotechnology and robotics make the leap beyond biology.

All of these technologies result from and are in service to the overall utopian conception: a technological vision of a single world-machine that looks and feels something like EPCOT Center or the bubble domes of space stations. Everything figured out. Everything planned. Everything created. The apparent purpose of this machine is to eliminate human ailments and human unhappiness (assuming we still have humans), to expand the human potential, and to create a world of abundance for human enjoyment. But the unstated purpose is to fulfill the inherent drive of technological society to feed its own evolutionary cravings, to expand its domination of both Earth and space, and to complete the utter conversion of nature into commodity form—even the part of nature that remains wild within human genes and molecular structures.

That's the bad news.

The good news is that even "perfect" technological systems are showing signs of leakage and fraud. Technological society, during the past half-century, has demonstrably not achieved the benefits it advertised for itself. Peace, security, public and planetary health, sanity, happiness, fulfillment are arguably less close at hand than they ever were in the past. And the awful sacrifices that the planet has made to satisfy the cravings of the technological thrust are now becoming visible in oil spills, global warming, ozone depletion, toxic pollution, and deforestation, all of which affect our sense of well-being in everyday life.

As a society we have been slow learners, but there is an emerging awareness that we may have been led down the garden path by false advertising toward a fantasy world, created by romantics who had an economic stake in our accepting their dream. The question now is: Will the new skeptics and advocates of alternative paths become prominent enough to be sufficiently heard, and to create a critical mass of public opinion? We'll see. At this moment the situation is not promising. We still have not developed an effective language with which to articulate our critiques. This, in turn, is because we ourselves are part of the machine and so we have difficulty defining its shape and its direction. But even if we have this difficulty, there are societies of people on this planet who do not.

STATEMENT TO THE MODERN WORLD

Millions of people still alive on this earth never wished to be part of this machine and, in many cases, are not. I am speaking of people who have lived on the fringes of the technical world. They have remained outside of our awareness, either because they live in obscure places, or their resources have not been coveted by technological society, or because many millions of them have been murdered or otherwise silenced. But *they* are still aware of certain fundamental truths, the most important of which require reverence for the earth—an idea that is subversive to Western society and the entire technological direction of the past century.

These are people whose ancestors and who themselves have said from the beginning of the technological age that our actions and attitudes are fatally flawed, since they are not grounded in a real understanding of how to live on the earth. Lacking a sense of the sacred we were doomed to a bad result. They said it over and over and they still say it now.

The following is an excerpt from *A Basic Call to Consciousness, the Hau de no sau nee* [Iroquois] *Address to the Western World,* delivered at the 1977 UN Conference on Indigenous Peoples, published by *Akwesasne Notes*.

In the beginning we were told that the human beings who walk about on the Earth have been provided with all the things necessary for life. We were instructed to carry a love for one another, and to show a great respect for all the beings of this Earth. We were shown that our life exists with the tree life, that our well-being depends on the well-being of the Vegetable Life, that we are close relatives of the four-legged beings.

The original instructions direct that we who walk about on Earth are to express a great respect, an affection and a gratitude toward all the spirits which create and support Life. . . . When people cease to respect and express gratitude for these many things, then all life will be destroyed, and human life on this planet will come to an end.

. . . To this day the territories we still hold are filled with trees, animals, and the other gifts from the Creation. In these places we still receive our nourishment from our Mother Earth. . . .

The Indo-European people who have colonized our lands have shown very little respect for the things that create and support Life. We believe that these people ceased their respect for the world a long time ago. Many thousands of years ago, all the people of the world believed in the same Way of Life, that of harmony with the Universe. All lived according to the Natural Ways.

Today the [human] species of Man is facing a question of [its] very survival. . . . The way of life known as Western Civilization is on a death path on which their own culture has no viable answers. When faced with the reality of their own destructiveness, they can only go forward into areas of more efficient destruction.

The air is foul, the waters poisoned, the trees dying, the animals are disappearing. We think even the systems of weather are changing. Our ancient teaching warned us that if Man interfered with the Natural laws, these things would come to be. When the last of the Natural Way of Life is gone, all hope for human survival will be gone with it. And our Way of Life is fast disappearing, a victim of the destructive processes.

The technologies and social systems which destroyed the animal and the plant life are destroying the Native people. . . . We know there are many people in the world who can quickly grasp the intent of our message. But our experience has taught us that there are few who are willing to seek out a method for moving toward any real change.

The majority of the world does not find its roots in Western culture or tradition. The majority of the world finds its roots in the Natural World, and it is the Natural World, and the traditions of the Natural World, which must prevail.

We must all consciously and continuously challenge every model, every program, and every process that the West tries to force upon us. . . . The people who are living on this planet need to break with the narrow concept of human liberation, and begin to see liberation as something that needs to be extended to the whole of the Natural World. What is needed is the liberation of all things that support Life—the air, the waters, the trees—all the things which support the sacred web of Life.

The Native people of the Western Hemisphere can contribute to the survival potential of the human species. The majority of our peoples still live in accordance with the traditions which find their roots in the Mother Earth. But the Native people have need of a forum in which our voice can be heard. And we need alliances with the other people of the world to assist in our struggle to regain and maintain our ancestral lands and to protect the Way of Life we follow.

The traditional Native people hold the key to the reversal of the processes in Western Civilization, which hold the promise of unimaginable future suffering and destruction. Spiritualism is the highest form of political consciousness. And we, the Native people of the Western Hemisphere, are among the world's surviving proprietors of that kind of consciousness. . . . Our culture is among the most ancient continuously existing cultures in the world. We are the spiritual guardians of this place. We are here to impart that message.

PART III

SUPPRESSION OF THE NATIVE ALTERNATIVE

*S*INCE THE BEGINNINGS *of the technological juggernaut, the only consistent opposition has come from land-based native peoples. Rooted in an alternative view of the planet, Indians, islanders, and peoples of the North remain our most clear-minded critics. They are also our most direct victims. That technological society should ignore and suppress native voices is understandable, since to heed them would suggest we must fundamentally change our way of life. Instead, we say* they *must change. They decline to do so.*

I I

WHAT AMERICANS DON'T
KNOW ABOUT INDIANS

*I*N 1981, WHEN my sons Yari and Kai were attending San Francisco's
Lowell High School, they complained to me that their American History class began with the arrival of whites on this continent and omitted
any mention of the people who were already here. The class was taught
that Columbus "discovered" America and that American "history" was
what came afterward.

That same year, Ronald Reagan gave his first inaugural speech, in
which he praised the "brave pioneers who tamed the empty wilderness."
Still, I was surprised to hear that the wilderness was also empty for the
faculty at Lowell High, a school usually considered among the top public
high schools in this country.

The American History teacher asked my kids why they were so keen
on the subject of Indians, leading them to mention the book I was planning to write. This in turn led to an invitation for me to speak to the class.
As a result, I got some insight about the level of Indian awareness among
a group of high-school kids.

The youngsters I met had never been offered one course, or even an
extended segment of a course, about the Indian nations of this continent,
about Indian-Anglo interactions (except for references to the Pilgrims and
the Indian wars), or about contemporary Indian problems in the U.S. or
elsewhere. These teenagers knew as little as I did at their age, and as little
as their teacher knew at their age—or now, as he regretfully acknowledged to me. The American educational curriculum is almost bereft of

information about Indians, making it difficult for young non-Indian Americans to understand or care about present-day Indian issues. European schools actually teach more about American Indians. In Germany, for example, every child reads a set of books that sensitizes them to Indian values and causes. It is not surprising, therefore, that the European press carries many more stories about American Indians than does the American press.

In the sixty minutes I was allotted to speak to the Lowell class, I tried to communicate five points: 1) there were a lot of Indians living here before whites arrived; 2) they were not "savages" but lived in very well organized, stable societies spanning thousands of years; 3) the white European settlers killed most of the Indians on the continent, and massively stole from the rest; 4) nonetheless, there are still many Indians within the United States facing problems similar to those faced by their ancestors; and 5) there are millions of Indians (and other native people) all over the world.

I posted one of the excellent maps prepared by the Bureau of Indian Affairs (BIA), showing Indian land areas prior to the arrival of white colonists. The students were shocked to learn that nearly every acre of what is now the United States was once part of some Indian nation. I pointed out that by the time this map was drawn, some of the Indian nations had been in place for thousands of years. So much for "empty wilderness."

Some of the Iroquois tribes have been living in the northern U.S. for at least 5,000 years. In the Southwest, the Hopi Indians are estimated to have been living in what is now called the Four Corners area (the junction of Colorado, New Mexico, Arizona, and Utah) for at least 10,000 years. (Some archeologists have lately put the Hopi arrival as long as 40,000 years ago. The Hopi themselves say, as do many Indian nations, that they did not "arrive" at all; that their genesis was in the Grand Canyon.)

Whatever the millennium, Indian people were living on this continent thousands of years before the Hebrews came down from the steppes into what is now the Middle East; long before Christ, long before the establishment of European nations, and very long before Columbus.

By 1776, when the United States was established, about 100 Indian nations had survived the slaughter of the fifteenth, sixteenth, and seventeenth centuries, and some two to five million Indian people (depending upon whose estimate you accept) were living in the "lower forty-eight" states, speaking more than 750 distinct languages. In California alone— where climate and conditions were hospitable—more than 200,000 Indians lived in several hundred "subtribes," each with its own language. And in Hawaii in 1776, there were still, by the most conservative estimates, at least 300,000 natives. By 1830 the number was reduced to 80,000 because of massacres and diseases brought by the white followers of Captain Cook.

When I got to this point in my lecture, one of the students asked, "What do you mean by the word 'nation,' as applied to Indian tribes?"

The definition of "nation," by such international organizations as the United Nations and the World Court, includes the following components: common culture and heritage, common language, stable geographic locale over time, internal laws of behavior that are accepted by members of the community, boundaries recognized by other nations, and formal agreements (treaties) with other nations. By those standards, Indian "nations" were and are just that. Moreover, the colonial powers on this continent—the British, French, and Spanish—openly recognized the Indian nations as such and made treaties with them, affirming boundaries, mutual alliances, peace, and friendship, as well as land exchanges and concessions. The Indian nations also made thousands of treaties with each other.

From the late eighteenth to the late nineteenth centuries, the United States made 370 formal treaties with Indian nations, following the same procedure of congressional and presidential approval that was followed with France or Great Britain. There were no distinctions between Indian treaties and any others; all became the "law of the land" as the Constitution requires. The fact that we violated virtually all of these Indian treaties resulted from our feeling that we could get away with such violations, that the violations were acceptable in the eyes of the European community of nations, and that the U.S. would not be as heavily criticized as we would if we violated treaties with Spain or England. Clearly there was a sense that Indians are somehow not people in the same category as the English, and so deals with them can be made in a less earnest fashion.

European doubts about the peoplehood of Indians extend back to the murderous explorations of Hernando Cortez in the mid 1500s, among the Indians of Central America and Mexico. The fate of the Indians became the subject of fierce disagreements within the Catholic Church. The argument became focused in the historic sixteenth-century debates between Spanish scholar Juan Ginés de Sepúlveda and Dominican friar Bartolomé de las Casas, as to whether Indians had souls and ought to be saved for the Church, or whether they should be slaughtered or made into slaves. Sepúlveda argued the Aristotelian viewpoint that some people are born to slavery. De las Casas, who had traveled in Mexico with Cortez, and had been impressed with the Indians, was horrified at the invaders' brutality. He argued that murder and slavery contradicted the Gospels. Pope Pius V finally sided with de las Casas in 1566, ruling that Indians should be converted rather than killed. Apparently no consideration was given to permitting Indians to live as they had before the Spanish invasion.

By the eighteenth century, the case for Indian inferiority was no longer predicated on the issue of souls, but on the fact that Indians had no concept of private property: their religions were based on nature, they lived by subsistence economics, and they believed that rocks, trees, and the earth were alive. Such beliefs were held to be prima facie evidence that Indians were less evolved than Europeans and that they stood against the tide of history. That viewpoint has not fundamentally changed for the last 300 years.

Next on my agenda at Lowell High was a discussion of Indian governmental structures. Like most Americans, the young high-school students assumed that Indian or aboriginal people had no forms of government other than despotic chiefs, like the Shaka Zulu characterization we've seen on television. This lack of information about Indian governments represents another tragic omission from American education, since many Indian governmental forms were highly evolved and democratic. Some of them, notably the Iroquois, apparently had considerable effect upon concepts later incorporated into the U.S. Articles of Confederation and the Constitution. The systems of checks and balances, popular participation in decision-making, direct representation, states' rights, and bicameral legislatures were all part of the Great Binding Law of the Iroquois Confederacy, dating back to the 1400s, as will be described later. But there may not be one American in ten thousand who knows this.

Another shocking fact was that very few of the students were aware of the degree to which, or how recently, Indian lands had been expropriated. Between 1776 and the late 1800s, Indian land holdings were reduced by about 95 percent, from about three million to 200,000 square miles. This was accomplished in a variety of ways, from massacres to duplicitous treaty-making. Some treaties exacted land cessions in exchange for guarantees of safety and permanent reserves, but these treaties were soon violated. Usually the Indians were driven off because the settlers wanted gold or farmland or mineral rights or railroad rights. Wherever there was resistance, the cavalry insured compliance. All of this was in the cause of Manifest Destiny: God willed it.

My hour was nearly gone. I had only enough time left to say that, while ignoring the past reality of the Indians is bad enough, ignoring the current situation is worse. In this country there are still one and a half million Indian people, more than half of whom live on the lands where their ancestors lived thousands of years ago. Some of these Indians maintain traditions that have survived for millennia. But, when the U.S. government or a corporation seeks to get oil, coal, or copper from Indian land, they behave exactly as they always have. Since the Custer period, the methods have switched from violent assault to "legal" manipulations that separate Indians from their lands as surely as the guns once did. I gave the students three brief examples:

- *The Dawes Act (1887).* Provided that individual Indians could now own their own plots of land. Hailed as a liberal reform when introduced, the real purpose and effect of the law was to break the communal-tribal ownership of land. Tribes were rarely, if ever, willing to sell land. But individuals could be persuaded to sell, for cash, guns, or liquor. Millions of acres moved from Indian to white ownership.

- *The Indian Reorganization Act (1934).* Another liberal reform, it offered U.S. assistance in converting Indian governments to "modern democratic" systems. Like the Dawes Act half a century earlier, this law was designed to break the hold of traditional Indian governance—based on slow-moving consensus processes—because it invariably led to refusal to negotiate leases for oil, coal, gas, and other minerals that the U.S. was seeking. "Democracy" had nothing to do with it. In fact, as the new American-style governments were put into place, the great majority of Indians refused to participate in the voting. This enabled the Bureau of Indian Affairs to train and run its own compliant candidates—ready to make deals—who were elected by the tiny handful of Indians willing to participate in the alien process. As a result, corporations gained inexpensive access to Indian resources, and the new Indian tribal councils effectively became part of the U.S. bureaucracy, as most still are, though a sizeable resistance on many reservations now threatens this cozy arrangement.

- *The Indian Claims Act (1946).* Theoretically established to settle Indian grievances about stolen lands, in practice the Indian Claims Commission is a fraud. The commission refuses *all* requests to grant land title to Indians, offering only compensation for lands that it determines were lost by Indians (at per-acre rates that are often a century old). So Indians entering claims to land find that accepting payment amounts to a permanent extinguishing of their aboriginal title, which is the opposite result of the one they sought.

I ended my talk by mentioning that there are hundreds of millions of indigenous people all over the world who continue to live on their ancestral lands, and who experience varying degrees of domination by invading colonial interests. Most of these people are suffering even more violent assaults than were visited upon American Indians a century ago. As in the past, these acts are justified by an assumption of cultural and spiritual superiority and by the fact that the Indians stand in the way of the orderly progress of technological and industrial development.

The bell rang. The kids leapt up. Out the door to lunch.

THE MEDIA: INDIANS ARE NON-NEWS

That the Lowell High students should know nothing about Indians is not their fault. It is one of many indicators that this country's institutions do not inform people about Indians of either present or past. Indians are non-history, which also makes them non-news. Not taught in schools, not part of American consciousness, their present-day activities and struggles are rarely reported in newspapers or on television.

On the rare occasions when the media do relate to Indians, the reports tend to follow very narrow guidelines based on pre-existing stereotypes of Indians; they become what is known in the trade as "formula stories."

My friend Dagmar Thorpe, a Sac-and-Fox Indian who, until 1990, was Executive Director of the Seventh Generation Fund, once asked a network producer known to be friendly to the Indian cause about the reasons for the lack of in-depth, accurate reporting on Indian stories. According to Dagmar, the producer gave three reasons. The first reason was guilt. It is not considered good programming to make your audience feel bad. Americans don't want to see shows that remind them of historical events that American institutions have systematically avoided discussing.

Secondly, there is the "what's-in-it-for-me?" factor. Americans in general do not see how anything to do with Indians has anything to do with them. As a culture, we are now so trained to "look out for number one" that there has been a near total loss of altruism. (Of course American life itself—so speedy and so removed from nature—makes identifying with the Indians terribly difficult; and we don't see that we might have something to learn from them.)

The third factor is that Indian demands seem preposterous to Americans. What most Indians want is simply that their land should be returned, and that treaties should be honored. Americans tend to view the treaties as "ancient," though many were made less than a century ago—more recently, for example, than many well-established laws and land deals among whites. Americans, like their government and the media, view treaties with Indian nations differently than treaties with anyone else.

• • •

In fairness to the media, there are some mitigating factors. Just like the rest of us, reporters and producers have been raised without knowledge of Indian history or Indian struggles. Perhaps most important, media people have had little personal contact with Indians, since Indians live mostly in parts of the country, and the world, where the media isn't. Indians live in non-urban regions, in the deserts and mountains and tundras that have been impacted least by Western society, at least until recently. They live in the places that we didn't want. They are not part of the mainstream and have not tried to become part.

When our society *does* extend its tentacles to make contact—usually when corporations are seeking land or minerals, or military forces are seeking control—there is little media present to observe and report on what transpires. Even in the United States, virtually all Indian struggles take place far away from media: in the central Arizona desert, in the rugged Black Hills, the mountains of the Northwest, or else on tiny Pacific islands, or in the icy vastness of the far north of Alaska. The *New York Times* has no bureau in those places; neither does CBS. Nor do they have bureaus in the Australian desert or the jungles of Brazil, Guatemala, or Borneo.

As a result, some of the most terrible assaults upon native peoples today never get reported. If reports do emerge, the sources are the corporate or military public relations arms of the Western intruders, which present biased perspectives.

When reporters are flown in to someplace where Indians are making news, they are usually ill prepared and unknowledgeable about the local situation. They do not speak the language and are hard pressed to grasp the Indian perception, even if they can find Indians to speak with. In addition, these reporters often grew up in that same bubble of no contact/no education/no news about Indians.

To make matters even more difficult, as I explained at length in my TV book, it is also in the nature of modern media to distort the Indian message, which is far too subtle, sensory, complex, spiritual, and ephemeral to fit the gross guidelines of mass-media reporting, which emphasizes conflict and easily grasped imagery. A reporter would have to spend a great deal of time with the Indians to understand why digging up the earth for minerals is a sacrilege, or why diverting a stream can destroy a culture, or why cutting a forest deprives people of their religious and human rights, or why moving Indians off desert land to a wonderful new community of private homes will effectively kill them. Even if the reporter does understand, to successfully translate that understanding through the medium, and through the editors and the commercial sponsors—all of whom are looking for action—is nearly impossible.

So most reporters have little alternative but to accept official handouts, or else to patch together, from scanty reports, stories that are designed for a world predisposed to view Indian struggles as anomalies in today's technological world: formula stories, using stereotyped imagery.

PREVALENT STEREOTYPES AND FORMULAS

The dominant image of Indians in the media used to be of savages, of John Wayne leading the U.S. Cavalry against the Indians. Today the stereotype has shifted to *noble savage,* which portrays Indians as part of a once-great but now-dying culture; a culture that could talk to the trees and the animals and that protected nature. But sadly, a losing culture, which has not kept up with our dynamic times.

We see this stereotype now in many commercials. The Indian is on a horse, gazing nobly over the land he protects. Then there's a quick cut to today: to oil company workers walking alongside the hot-oil pipeline in Alaska. The company workers are there to protect against leaks and to preserve the environment for the animals. We see quick cuts of caribou and wolves, which imply that the oil company accepts the responsibility that the Indians once had.

The problem here is that the corporate sponsor is lying. It does not feel much responsibility toward nature; if it did, it would not need expensive commercials to say so, because the truth would be apparent from its behavior. More important, however, is that treating Indians this way in commercials does terrible harm to their cause. It makes Indians into conceptual relics; artifacts. Worse, they are confirmed as existing only in the past, which hurts their present efforts.

Another stereotype we see in commercials these days is the *Indian-as-guru.* A recent TV spot depicted a shaman making rain for his people. He is then hired by some corporate farmers to make rain for them. He is shown with his power objects, saying prayers, holding his hands toward the heavens. The rains come. Handshakes from the businessmen. Finally the wise old Indian is shown with a satisfied smile on his flight home via United Airlines.

Among the more insidious formula stories is the one about how Indians are always fighting each other over disputed lands. This formula fits the Western paradigm about non-industrial peoples' inability to govern themselves; that they live in some kind of despotism or anarchy. For example, in the Hopi-Navajo "dispute" (to which a part of Chapter 15 is devoted), the truth of the matter is that U.S. intervention in the activities and governments of both tribes eventually led to American-style puppet governments battling each other for development rights that the traditional leadership of each tribe does not want. But the historical reality of that case, and most Indian cases, is unknown to the mass media and therefore left unreported.

Another very popular formula story is the one with the headline INDI-ANS STAND IN THE WAY OF DEVELOPMENT, as, for example, in New Guinea or Borneo or in the Amazon Basin. These stories concern Indian resistance to roads, or dams, or the cutting of forests, and their desire for their lands to be left inviolate.

The problem with these formula stories is not that they are inaccurate—Indian peoples around the world most certainly are resisting on hundreds of fronts and do indeed stand in the way of development—but that the style of reporting carries a sense of foregone conclusion. The reporters tend to emphasize the poignancy of the situation: "stone-age" peoples fighting in vain to forestall the inevitable march of progress. In their view, it is only a matter of time before the Indians lose, and the forests *are* cut down, and the land *is* settled by outsiders. However tragic the invasion, however righteous the cause of the Indians, however illegal the acts being perpetrated against them, however admirable the Indian ways, reporters will invariably adopt the stance that the cause is lost, and that no reversal is possible. This attitude surely harms the Indians more than if the story had not been reported at all.

Finally, and perhaps most outrageous, is the *rich Indian* formula story. Despite the fact that the average per-capita income of Indians is lower than any other racial or ethnic group in the United States, and that they suffer the highest disease rates in many categories, and have the least access to health care, the press loves to focus on the rare instance where some Indian hits it big. Sometimes the story is about an oil well found on some Indian's land, or someone getting rich on bingo, but often the stories emphasize someone's corruption, e.g., Peter MacDonald, the former chairman of the Navajo Nation. This formula story has a twofold purpose: it manages to confirm the greatness of America—where *anyone* can get rich, even an Indian—and at the same time manages to confirm Indian leaders as corrupt and despotic.

A corollary to this story is how certain Indian tribes have gotten wealthy through land claims cases, as, for example, the Alaska natives via the Alaska Native Claims Settlement Act. As we will see, a little digging into the story—if reporters only would—exposes that settlement as a fraud that actually deprived the Alaska natives of land *and* money.

The press's failure to pursue and report the full picture of American Indian poverty, while splashing occasional stories about how some are hitting it big, creates a public impression that is the opposite of the truth. The situation is exacerbated when national leaders repeat the misconceptions. Ronald Reagan told the Moscow press in 1987 that there was no discrimination against Indians in this country and the proof of that was that so many Indians, like those outside Palm Springs (oil wells), have become wealthy.

INDIANS AND THE NEW AGE

While most of our society manages to avoid Indians, there is one group that does not, though its interest is very measured.

I was reminded of this recently during my first visit to a dentist in Marin County, an affluent area north of San Francisco. The dentist, a friendly, trendy young man wearing a moustache, looked as if he'd stepped out of a Michelob ad. While poking my gums, he made pleasant conversation, inquiring about my work. When he pulled his tools from my mouth, I told him I was writing about Indians, which got him very excited. "Indians! Great! I love Indians. Indians are my hobby. I have Indian posters all over the house, and Indian rugs. And hey, I've lately been taking lessons in 'tracking' from this really neat Indian guide. I've learned how to read the tiniest changes in the terrain, details I'd never even noticed before."

In this expression of enthusiasm, this young man was like thousands of other people, particularly in places like Marin or Beverly Hills, or wherever there is sufficient leisure to engage in inner explorations. Among this group, which tends to identify with the "New Age," or the "human potential movement," there has been a renaissance of awareness about Indian practices that aid inner spiritual awakening.

A typical expression of this interest may be that a well-off young professional couple will invite friends to a lawn party to meet the couple's personal Indian medicine person. The shaman will lead the guests through a series of rituals designed to awaken aspects of themselves. These events may culminate in a sweat ceremony, or even a "firewalk." There was a period in the seventies when you could scarcely show up at a friend's house without having to decide whether or not to walk on hot coals, guided by a medicine man from the South Pacific.

Those who graduate from sweat ceremonies or firewalks, as my dentist had, might proceed to the now popular "vision quests." You may feel as you read this that I am ridiculing these "human potential" explorers. Actually, I find something admirable in them. Breaking out of the strictures of our contemporary lifestyles is clearly beneficial, in my opinion, but there is also a serious problem. For although the New Age gleans the ancient wisdoms and practices, it has assiduously avoided directly engaging in the actual lives and political struggles of the millions of descendants who carry on those ancient traditions, who are still alive on the planet today, and who want to continue living in a traditional manner.

• • •

The roots of the current New Age Indian revival lie in the hippie period of the 1960s, and in early drug explorations. In that era, young people sought to define new modes of being that were non-acquisitive, spiritually oriented, non-hierarchical, tribal, communal. The hippie community did have some awareness of the political dimensions of Indian societies. In fact, many of the hippie activists, now thirty years older, continue to show up when a meeting is called by Indians trying to spread the word of a problem. It is still Wavy Gravy's Hog Farm that goes down to help the elders at Big Mountain on the Navajo reservation. It is still the Grateful Dead who play at the benefits.

It was also during the sixties that Carlos Castaneda offered, through his books, a window into a different reality construct. I was among the people in those days who found Castaneda's work fascinating and important. Castaneda did not avoid political realities. In each of his books, Don Juan, and sometimes others among the shamans, spoke passionately about the prejudices they experienced as children. But few reviewers commented on those passages; they were not the reason the books were devoured.

Castaneda was able to immerse millions of Americans in a system of logic truly different from our own. He created Indian heroes who were irresistible to middle-class whites seeking a pathway out of rigid Western modes of thinking. He led millions of readers through experiences designed to reveal unknown dimensions of our nature. And he did all this by imitating Indian storytelling style. Like the stories, myths, and histories Castaneda emulated, it scarcely mattered to what extent the characters were real or not real. They were teaching systems. They brought us a new way of mind, and they delivered experiences, images, and perspectives that ran counter to the prevailing imagery and paradigms of our society. In these ways, the books approximated Indian thought, and were subversive and political, even dangerous.

Americans went for them like dry roots seeking water. We still do. For like Castaneda himself, born of Indian heritage in an increasingly Westernized Peru, we are all caught between chairs. Drawn to the subjective, longing for the naturalistic, the moody, the sensory, the mythic, the magical, and desiring to integrate these elements in our lives, we are stuck in a world of concrete, time-bound, homocentric, mechanical logic. Castaneda's images, like firewalking and sweat lodges, offered pathways back to nature within ourselves.

But however enlightening this may be, confining our knowledge of Indians to their "spiritual" pathways continues to deny what is most important to the Indian people. While we experience and explore Indian-ness in ourselves, Indian people experience our culture in terms of its drives to expand and to dominate nature and natural people. We have managed to isolate one or two aspects of Indian life—the spiritual aspect and sometimes the art—and to separate these from the rest of the Indian experience, which is something Indian people themselves would never do. It is a fundamental tenet of Indian perception that the spiritual aspect of life is inseparable from the economic and the political. No Indian person could ever make the kind of split we wish to make for them. So why do we?

For one thing, it is a way that we can skim the "cream"—arts, culture, spiritual wisdom—off the Indian experience. We can collect it for our museums, while discarding whatever we find in it that challenges the way we live our lives. We can make ourselves feel good about "saving" something Indian, as if it were meaningful support for living Indians.

It is little wonder, of course, that we choose such a course. The average person does not seek information that will make him or her feel badly. In fact, if we ever became more personally engaged than at present, and let into our hearts and minds the full spectrum of horrors that Indian people have faced, and still face; if we ever accepted that American corporate and military interests and surely American commodity and technological visions drive the juggernaut, the pain of these realizations would be overwhelming. So instead, we avoid the subject, which allows us to avoid re-examining the premises upon which our current lives and this society are based, premises that sanction the destructive behavior against nature and native peoples that is now rampant.

CULTURAL DARWINISM

There is yet a deeper widespread rationalization for our avoidance of Indians and the news they bring us. On some level we think that however beautiful Indian culture once was, however inspiring their religious ideas, however artistic their creations and costumes, however wise their choices of life within nature, our own society has advanced beyond that stage of evolution. *They* are the "primitive" stage and *we* have grown beyond them. They have not adapted as we have. This makes us superior. We are the survivors. We are the "cutting edge."

A good friend of mine (who now works in television) put it this way: "There is no getting around the fact that the Indian way is a losing way. They are no longer appropriate for the times. They are anomalies."

In saying this, my friend was essentially blaming the Indians themselves for the situation that befell them. They failed to adapt their lifestyle and belief systems to keep up with changing times. Most importantly, they failed to keep up with technological change. They were not competitive.

This statement reflects a Darwinist, capitalist outlook of survival of the fittest, with fitness now defined in terms of technological capability. If you can use the machine better than the next fellow or the next culture, you survive and they die. This may be sad, the reasoning goes, but that's the way it is in today's world.

This view sees Western technological society as the ultimate expression of the evolutionary pathway, the culmination of all that has come before, the final flowering. We represent the breakthrough in the evolution of living creatures; we are the conscious expression of the planet. Indians helped the process for a while, but they gave way to more evolved, *higher* life forms.

Our assumption of superiority does not come to us by accident. We have been trained in it. It is soaked into the fabric of every Western religion, economic system, and technology. They reek of their greater virtues and capabilities.

Judeo-Christian religions are a model of hierarchical structure: one God above all, certain humans above other humans, and humans over nature. Political and economic systems are similarly arranged: Organized along rigid hierarchical lines, all of nature's resources are regarded only in terms of how they serve the one god—the god of growth and expansion. In this way, all of these systems are *missionary;* they are into dominance. And through their mutual collusion, they form a seamless web around our lives. They are the creators and enforcers of our beliefs. We live inside these forms, are imbued with them, and they justify our behaviors. In turn, we believe in their viability and superiority largely because they prove effective: They gain power.

But is power the ultimate evolutionary value? We shall see. The results are not yet in. "Survival of the fittest" as a standard of measure may require a much longer time scale than the scant 200 years' existence of the United States, or the century since the Industrial Revolution, or the two decades since the advent of "high tech." Even in Darwinian terms, most species become "unfit" over tens of thousands of years. Our culture is using its machinery to drive species into extinction in one generation, not because the species are maladaptive, but by pure force. However, there is reason to doubt the ultimate success of our behavior. In the end, a model closer to that of the Indians, living lightly on the planet, observing its natural rules and modes of organization, may prove more "fit," and may survive us after all. Until that day, however, we will continue to use Darwinian theories to support the assertion that our mechanistic victory over the "primitives" is not only God's plan, but nature's.

12

INDIANS ARE DIFFERENT
FROM AMERICANS

*I*N *The Death of Nature,* Carolyn Merchant, a professor of natural resource studies at the University of California at Berkeley, argues that
until the Age of Enlightenment in the 1700s, and the "scientific revolution" that accompanied it, the prevailing viewpoint among the peoples of
the earth was that the planet itself was a living creature. Most cultures
shared this belief, whether they were "Western" in orientation (such as the
Sumerians, the Greeks, and the Romans), or whether they still lived within
nature. They believed that the Earth was a being, with skin, soul, and organs. The skin was the soil, the soul was contained within the rocks and
bones of the dead, the organs included rivers (the bloodstream) and wind
(the lungs). Such categories were not meant as metaphors. Earth *was* alive;
we lived upon it as millions of tiny microorganisms live on human skin.

According to Merchant, most cultures up to the Enlightenment also believed that the Earth was a female being, the actual mother of life.

The "scientific revolution" changed all this. For the first time, the idea
was postulated that the earth is actually a kind of dead thing, a machine.
With that perspective came a new set of scientific paradigms that gave impetus to the idea of human superiority over other animals and over nature.
The seeds of such a notion had already been well implanted by the Judeo-
Christian tradition. But with the manmade technical machine spreading
itself rapidly across the landscape, we had physical demonstrations of our
power to alter nature, giving us "proof" of our superiority.

If human beings had maintained our original notions about the planet
being a living mother, perhaps human behavior subsequent to the "sci-

entific revolution" would have been different. On the other hand, in books such as *Woman and Nature,* feminist authors such as Susan Griffin have argued brilliantly that it is precisely because of the female nature of the planet that patriarchal, hierarchical, Western technological society has raped the earth with such alacrity.

In any event, I believe it is critically important for all Westerners to realize that the idea of the earth *not* being alive is a *new* idea. Even today, that view is far from universal and may represent a minority viewpoint, advocated mainly by people who live in Western technological cultures. Failing to see the planet as alive, they have become free of moral and ethical constraints, and have benefited economically from exploiting resources at the earth's expense. But if the majority of people in the United States, Western Europe, and the Soviet Union are comfortable regarding the earth as a huge, dead rock, this is emphatically not true of those Indians and aboriginal peoples throughout the world who continue to live as they have for thousands of years, in a direct relationship to the planet.

"MOTHER EARTH"

If you have ever spent time with American Indians, you have noticed that their resistance to resource development is expressed as an effort to protect "Mother Earth." It is not only American Indians who use the phrase. So do Aborigines of the Australian desert, natives of the Pacific islands, Indians of the Ecuadorian jungles, Inuit from Arctic Canada; in fact, I have yet to find a native group that does not speak of the planet as "mother." And they all mean it literally. Plants, animals, all life as we know it is nurtured at her breast. We have germinated within her, we are part of her, we burst into life from her, and we dissolve back into her to become new life.

Every culture that maintains this attitude about Mother Earth also has restrictions against any individual owning land, or mining it or selling it. Such ideas were unthinkable to native people until they met the invading Western cultures.

This fundamental difference in viewpoint between technological cultures and land-based native peoples—whether the planet is alive or isn't— is the root of many conflicts between the two groups. Americans, for example, have a particularly hard time grasping the notion of a living earth. We scoff at the idea, in fact, and at anyone who speaks of it seriously. I have seen white people laugh aloud when young Indian activists stand at meetings to denounce some mining development as a "desecration of our mother, the earth." We find it particularly hard to take when such words are spoken by the more radical young Indian leaders of today: street-smart tough guys with an aggressive urban style. We think they're using a ploy on us with that language, that they're not as sincere as their elders who have not been Americanized.

It is true that unlike their grandparents many young Indians did not grow up with the feelings they now have. Many of the young activists I have met were born on reservations but fled early to the cities. They did so for the same reason as many other people: to be nearer the action. Once in the cities, however, they did not fit in. Aside from the racism directed at them, they found they could not merge with the speed and abstraction of urban life. It is sadly typical that they often sank into drunkenness. A large percentage eventually returned to their reservations, sometimes experiencing a reawakening of pride in their heritage. They began to accept themselves as Indians and a desire grew to improve the circumstances of their people. It is then they sought out the old people and, for the first time, they listened.

The relationship between grandparents and grandchildren is one of the most critical elements in the maintenance of Indian culture. For young people, the elders are windows to the roots of their own identity, to the visions of Earth and life that came before modern times. The sharing of knowledge between the elders and the young is what makes survival possible.

For the elders, the notion of a Mother Earth is totally integrated into their beings. And young activists today realize the importance of that perspective. So they verbalize such concepts, which, even if new to them, are ancient nonetheless. They recognize that Indians are the authentic guardians of such ideas, and they are ensuring that the lineage of understanding is preserved.

That white folks have a hard time accepting this is logical, since the concept is as alien as the people who speak of it. And yet it behooves us to at least entertain the possibility that the idea of a living planet, a concept that has endured for millennia, just might be true.

Lately some scientists have emerged who are ready to argue on behalf of the whole planet as a living system. Notable among them are biologists Lynn Margulis and James Lovelock, authors of *The Gaia Hypothesis,* which describes the planet and the atmosphere as a unified biological entity. Their work in particular became the focus for numerous conferences on the issue, including the one organized by James Swan titled "Is the Earth Alive?" in Mill Valley, California, in 1986, which considered the point from both traditional native and Western scientific perspectives.

However, it will take many such conferences and many more books before there is any change in the dominant Western view of the issue, since such change could prove subversive to our culture. If such an idea were taken seriously, the United States would be hard-pressed to continue existing in anything like its present form.

Many authors, notably Carl Jung and Aldous Huxley, have stated that Western societies fear, hate, destroy, and also revere Indians, precisely because they express the parts of our personal and cultural psyches that we must suppress in order to function in the world as we do. How could present-day America possibly exist if great numbers of people believed that the minerals in the ground, the trees and the rocks, and the earth itself were all alive? Not only alive, but our equals? If our society suddenly believed it was sacrilegious to remove minerals from the earth, or to buy and sell land, our society would evaporate. Nor could it exist if Americans believed in an economic life organized along steady-state, collective-subsistence forms, as most Indian societies are. Therefore it is logical, normal, and self-protective for Americans to find the philosophical, political, and economic modes of Indian culture inappropriate and foolish.

TABLE OF INHERENT DIFFERENCES

The concept of an organic female earth is basic to native societies, and is also a basic difference between native peoples and the people of technologized societies. Believing that the earth is alive leads to a world view utterly unlike the one that emerges when you believe the planet is dead, or that it is a "machine." Is it possible, then, for the two societies to coexist? To look at that issue, I thought it would be helpful to create a chart that compares the two societies in various aspects of life. The more detailed the comparisons, the more obvious it becomes that in almost every category Indian and Western societies are at virtually opposite poles. Beyond "opposite," they are in contradiction.

During the years I worked on this book, I kept an informal list of various characteristics that seem to be inherent in all (or most) native societies. Though it is by no means complete, and does not pretend to be scientific, I think it reveals the near impossibility of assimilation. The two cultures are profoundly at odds. To attempt to merge them does not produce coexistence or integration, but death for one or the other, which is already happening.

The following chart is not universally applicable to all Indian societies or all Western societies. There are differences among Indian tribes just as there are among Western societies. For example, though the Aztecs and Incas were Indians, they were more like modern Americans than the majority of other Indians. In fact, it is because of the ways in which the Aztecs and Incas were similar to us—they created a "state," they had hierarchical authority (which most Indian societies do not), and their architecture was built for permanence—that we speak of them as "an advanced civilization."

In fundamental ways, however, Indian tribes and aboriginal peoples, whether they live in the far north or in tropical forests, are more alike than not. The Inuit, the Navajo in the southwestern U.S., and the Aborigines in Australia all share very similar attitudes toward nature. To the degree that they have not been overtaken by Westerners, they still engage in collective production, share commodities, and live in extended families. They have similar ideas about art, architecture, time, and dozens of other dimensions of life. Their religions are nature based; they believe in a living planet. Also important, they share the fact that Westernized nations are behaving toward each of them in exactly the same fashion. This in turn is because despite all our differences, most Westerners are also more alike than different. In both the Soviet Union and the U.S., we wear ties and wristwatches, drive cars, live in nuclear families in permanent structures alongside pavement walkways. We work for fixed hours of the day for years at a time for a person we call "boss." We use money to purchase commodities. We share an attitude about our level of superiority to nature and to non-technological humans.

What follows, then, is a rough description of tendencies, loosely comparing technological cultures on the one hand and native cultures on the other. It is meant as a vehicle for exploration and discussion. (Some of the points will be amplified in later chapters.)

Technological Peoples	Native Peoples
ECONOMICS	
Concept of private property a basic value: includes resources, land, ability to buy and sell, and inheritance. Some state ownership. Corporate ownership predominates.	No private ownership of resources such as land, water, minerals, or plant life. No concept of selling land. No inheritance.

Technological Peoples	Native Peoples
Goods produced mostly for sale, not for personal use.	Goods produced for use value.
Surplus production, profit motive essential. Sales techniques must create "need," hence advertising.	Subsistence goals: no profit motive, little surplus production.
Economic growth required, especially in capitalist societies, hence need for increased production, increased use of resources, expansion of production and market territories.	Steady-state economics: no concept of economic growth.
Currency system—abstract value.	Barter system—concrete value.
Competition (in capitalist countries), production for private gain. Reward according to task/wages.	Cooperative, collective production.
Average workday, 8–12 hours.	Average workday 3–5 hours.
Nature viewed as "resource."	Nature viewed as "being"; humans seen as part of nature.

POLITICS AND POWER

Hierarchical political forms.	Mostly non-hierarchical: "chiefs" have no coercive power.
Decisions generally made by executive power, majority rule, or dictatorship.	Decisions usually based on consensual process involving whole tribe.
Spectrum from representative democracy to autocratic rule.	Direct participatory democracy; rare examples of autocracy.

Technological Peoples	Native Peoples
Operative political modes are communist, socialist, monarchist, capitalist, or fascist.	Recognizable operative political modes are anarchist, communist, or theocratic.
Centralization: most power concentrated in central authorities.	Decentralization: power resides mainly in community, among people. (Some exceptions include Incas, Aztec, et al.)
Laws are codified, written. Adversarial process. Anthropocentrism forms basis of law. Criminal cases judged by strangers (in U.S., western Europe, Soviet Union). No taboo.	Laws transmitted orally. No adversarial process. Laws interpreted for individual cases. "Natural law" used as basis. Criminal cases settled by groups of peers known to "criminal." Taboo.
Concept of "state."	Identity as "nation."

SOCIOCULTURAL ARRANGEMENTS AND DEMOGRAPHICS

Large-scale societies; most societies have high population density.	Small-scale societies, all people acquainted; low population density.
Lineage mostly patrilineal.	Lineage mostly matrilineal, with some variation; family property rights run through female.
Nuclear two- or one-parent families; also "singles."	Extended families: generations, sometimes many families, live together.
Revere the young.	Revere the old.
History written in books, portrayed in television docudramas.	History transmitted in oral tradition, carried through memory.

Technological Peoples	Native Peoples

RELATION TO ENVIRONMENT

Living beyond nature's limits encouraged; natural terrain not considered a limitation; conquest of nature a celebrated value; alteration of nature desirable; antiharmony; resources exploited.	Living within natural ecosystem encouraged; harmony with nature the norm; only mild alterations of nature for immediate needs: food, clothing, shelter; no permanent damage.
High-impact technology created to change environment. Mass-scale development: one-to-millions ratio in weaponry and other technologies.	Low-impact technology; one-to-one ratio even in weaponry.
Humans viewed as superior life form; Earth viewed as "dead."	Entire world viewed as alive: plants, animals, people, rocks. Humans not superior, but equal part of web of life. Reciprocal relationship with non-human life.

ARCHITECTURE

Construction materials transported from distant places.	Construction materials usually gathered locally.
Construction designed to survive individual human life.	Construction designed to eventually dissolve back into land (except for pyramids built by minority of Indians); materials biodegradable in one lifetime.
Space designed for separation and privacy.	Space designed for communal activity.
Hard-edged forms; earth covered with concrete.	Soft forms; earth not paved.

Technological Peoples	Native Peoples

RELIGION AND PHILOSOPHY

Technological Peoples	Native Peoples
Separation of spirituality from rest of life in most Western cultures (though not in some Muslim, Hindu, or Buddhist states); church and state separated; materialism is dominant philosophy in Western countries.	Spirituality integrated with all aspects of daily life.
Either monotheistic concept of single, male god, or atheistic.	Polytheistic concepts based on nature, male and female forces, animism.
Futuristic/linear concept of time; de-emphasis of past.	Integration of past and present.
The dead are regarded as gone.	The dead are regarded as present.
Individuals gain most information from media, schools, authority figures outside their immediate community or experience.	Individuals gain information from personal experiences.
Time measured by machines; schedules dictate when to do things.	Time measured by awareness according to observance of nature; time to do something is when time is right.
Saving and acquiring.	Sharing and giving.

It is important to note that the characteristics on each side of this chart form an internally consistent logic. In politics, for example, hierarchical power makes a great deal more sense for operating a large-scale technological society in widely separated parts of the world than does a consensual decision-making process, which is much too slow to keep pace with machinery, electronics, and the need to grow and expand. In relation to the environment, the notion of "humans above nature" is more fitting for technological cultures, and for capitalism in particular, than "humans within nature," which throws wrenches in the wheels of progress.

It has proven unfortunate for the survival of Indian nations that their way of viewing the world is so drastically at odds with the views of American technological society. Indigenous systems of logic have not led them to emphasize expansion, power, or high-impact technologies of violence. Meanwhile, several aspects of the industrial system, especially in capitalist societies, do celebrate and even require the goals of expansion, growth, and exploitation and the development of the technologies appropriate to those goals. When the two world views come into conflict, we in the industrial cultures have the brute advantage of the violent technologies to help wipe out indigenous cultures; we then interpret this so-called victory as further evidence of our greater fitness to survive.

It is clear from this big picture of both cultures that they are incompatible. They do not and probably cannot mix. They ought rightly to be viewed as antitheses of each other, or as each other's shadow. They are both branches on the tree of human life, but they have grown very far from each other. Author Dee Brown has suggested that the Indians have always known about this schism, and the inevitable conflict that comes with it. Case after case of Indian-white interaction documents that Indians were never interested in assimilating with white culture.

Indians do not want to be Americans. They have historically tried to negotiate with us as to what was theirs and what was ours; they never wanted to be part of us, and many still do not want to be. For these reasons the new Indian leadership puts great emphasis on political separation, and on reclaiming Indian identity, land, and sovereignty. They see assimilation as an absurdity.

This may be the most important and yet most difficult point for Americans to grasp: that Indians in this country and elsewhere are different from other "oppressed" or "underdeveloped" Third World peoples who seek to share the fruits of our society. In fact, many Indians speak of themselves as a Fourth World. They do not wish to become like us. They are fighting to avoid that outcome, struggling to maintain their land base and to live as they have always lived.

Contrary to our prevailing paradigms, which assume that indigenous peoples throughout the world wish to participate in our economy, many Indians do not see us as the survivors in a Darwinian scenario. They see themselves as eventual survivors, while we represent a people who has badly misunderstood the way things are on the earth. They do not wish to join the technological experiment. They do not wish to engage in the industrial mode of production. They do not want a piece of the action. They see our way as a striving for death. They want to be left out of the process. If we are going over the brink, they do not wish to join us.

Throughout the world, whether they live in deserts or jungle or the far north, or in the United States, millions of native people share the perception that they are resisting a single, multi-armed enemy: a society whose basic assumptions, whose way of mind, and whose manner of political and economic organization permit it to ravage the planet without discomfort, and to drive natives off their ancestral lands. That this juggernaut will eventually consume itself is not doubted by these people. They meet and discuss it. They attempt to strategize about it. Their goal is to stay out of its way and survive it.

"WE ARE HELPING YOU"

On December 6, 1986, in San Francisco, a group of non-Indian activists gathered to strategize about Indian issues. Present were about sixty representatives of civil rights, human rights, religious freedom, anti-nuclear, anti-colonialist, and environmental organizations. Also in attendance were a dozen Indians, most of them Hopi and Navajo, invited to inform the meeting about their fight to prevent the forced removal of 10,000 Indians from their ancestral homes in order to make way for coal and uranium mines, and other forms of development.

The first question the conferees faced was why they had never convened about Indian issues before. Clearly, Indian struggles were directly related to the work of each of the represented organizations; yet collaboration with Indians had rarely been included in organizational agendas.

The conference was in its second day when the mood suddenly shifted. By then there had been panel discussions on the role of media, the law, and legislation; there had been historical overviews; there had been scholarly comparisons with prior historical aggressions against Indians. Next on the schedule was a presentation of the environmental implications of certain Indian questions. But before it could begin, a young Navajo man, Danny Blackgoat, stepped forward to gently interrupt the process.

Blackgoat began speaking to the assembled group of activists: "The Indian people here have been listening quietly while you have been talking for two days and we have been waiting to hear what's going to happen, and if any of you are going to be able to help us. We've been here a pretty long time now and we still don't know what's going to happen. We think it would be good now if you heard what the Indian people have to say because so far you've heard from everybody but the Indians."

At this point one of the environmentalists issued a protest. If we interrupt the schedule, he said, which was already running an hour and a half late, we would fall hopelessly behind. But he was immediately shouted down by the rest of the people. Then Blackgoat added, "I think the first thing we better do right now is that everybody should take off their watches and put them in their pockets." He then invited the other Indians to join him in the front of the room.

The mood of the meeting instantly changed. The assembled liberal do-gooders, myself included, realized our role had changed. Our authority had diminished. We were now an audience to the eight Indians who went forward and sat facing us. One by one each told his or her story. They began with their Indian names, the clans they belonged to, and a discussion of the ways in which they understood their religious teachings. They spoke quietly, slowly, and directly.

Looking at their faces I was thrown back twenty-one years to 1965—the first time I was in such a situation with Indians. The Hopi Tribal Council (which is not considered a legitimate government by most Hopi, but rather a puppet government controlled by the U.S.) had leased a portion of Black Mesa to Peabody Coal Company for a strip mine. In doing this the tribal council had ignored the pleadings of the traditional village political and religious leaders, who argued that Black Mesa was one of the Hopi's most sacred places. The tribal council was not concerned about that since most of its members were Americanized, progressive-type Indians that the Bureau of Indian Affairs had in its pocket. In fact most of the tribal council were not so much Hopi as they were Mormons.

I had been invited to meet the religious leaders by an ethnomusicologist from Santa Fe, Jack Loeffler, who was helping the elders in their fight against the mine. Loeffler introduced me to many of the leaders, and eventually I wrote an advertisement on their behalf, with the headline LIKE RIPPING APART ST. PETER'S IN ORDER TO SELL THE MARBLE. That advertisement included a quote from John Lansa, a Hopi elder, who had been the first to explain to me what was motivating the Hopi resistance:

> Nature is everything important to the Hopi. It is the land, all living things, the water, the trees, the rocks—it is everything. It is the force or the power that comes from these things that keeps the world together. This is the spiritual center of this land. This is the most sacred place. Right here on this mesa . . . before the white men came, all the Hopi were happy and sang all the time. The Hopi didn't have any class structure at all—no bosses, no policemen, no judges—everyone was equal. There weren't any politics then. . . . In those days the air was clear and everyone could see far. We always looked to the Earth Mother for food and nourishment. We never took more

than we needed. Our lives were very rich and humble. We lived close to the earth as laid out by the Great Spirit. When the white men came, everything started to get out of balance. The white brother has no spiritual knowledge, only technical. . . . Now there is a big strip mine where coal comes out of the earth to send electricity to the big cities. They cut across our sacred shrines and destroy our prayers to the six directions. . . . Peabody Coal Company is tearing up the land and destroying the sacred mountain. . . . It is very bad. You can't do things like that and have nature in balance.

Lansa has since died, as have many of the other elders of that time. But many years later, I was sitting in a room in San Francisco hearing similar words from a new generation of Indians. I was realizing that the most astounding fact about Indian people today is that despite what they face and what they know, they continue to express themselves in exactly the same terms. They are uncompromising, speaking of values alien to the dominant culture. And yet they continue.

Following Danny Blackgoat, each of the other Indians rose to speak. One said that "religion is the most important thing in our lives, and the struggles for the land are religious struggles." Another spoke of the importance of the land: "If you were born on the land, that land is your home. That cannot be taken away from you. Tribal councils, relocation, American education—all of this is intended to get us away from our culture and our way of life."

A young western Shoshone Indian, Joe Sanchez, spoke about the failure of Americans to grasp the Indian struggles:

For most Americans, land is a dead thing. It means nothing. But to disconnect from land is unthinkable to Indians. The land is everything. It's the source of our existence. It's where the ancestors' spirits live. It is not a commodity that can be bought or sold, and to rip it open to mine it is deeply sacrilegious to all Indian people. Nowadays most Americans live in or near cities. They have no connection with the dirt, with the earth. They have no way of identifying with the most essential feelings that define Indian experience and values. So they don't take us seriously. When our elders try to explain that Indian people die if they are removed from the land, Americans don't know what they're talking about. The schools and media don't help. The public pretty much assumes we're all dead and gone. We are invisible to Americans and so are our causes. To Americans we are just part of some story about the past, somehow connected to their own pioneer heroics.

The next speaker was an Inuit woman, a veteran activist in native causes:

I am watching the first generation of my people [from Alaska] be forced to give up their traditional nomadic ways; the first generation that had to move into settlements because of oil development. It's been many years, but I was also resettled from the North down here to the States, and I would never do such a thing to anyone. . . . I go home now every year and see that the people there still have the joy of living . . . the joy of taking care of each other. But I don't think it will last. There is no justice in America. Indians in prison are not even permitted to pray in their traditional ways. Treaties with Indians are supposed to be the law of the land but the U.S. ignored them. I am here to help the traditional Indian people, those who still have their land. They are still strong. That way of life is natural. That way of life is good.

The final speaker was a young Menominee Indian woman, whom I know as Ingrid Washinawatok, but who also uses her Indian name, Opēgtaw Matāēmōh:

My first name means Flying Eagle Woman. My second name means The Spirit Watches Over. I am one of those Indians who lives between worlds but I know the one I prefer. I go back and forth from the reservation [in Wisconsin] to my job in New York City. When I fly over the land in a plane I can see a big dark spot and I know that's where the reservation is. Everywhere else has been clear-cut for dairy land and farming and for timber. The reservation is the only place where the people try to leave the land in its natural state. . . . Americans have really strange notions about what's an Indian. If you're a traditional Indian they tell us we don't belong in the world anymore and they ignore us. If we wear blue jeans and drive a pickup truck they say we're not really Indians. . . . My kid was watching TV and he started talking about power. He saw a commercial where power was associated with a toy gun. I told him that wasn't power. I told him to come back to the land and I'd show him what power is. . . . The traditional Indian people are protecting something that is important for everyone. They are trying to keep the land alive, and the world in balance. Sometimes I get the feeling that you [looking at the audience] don't really get the point. You are not really helping us. We are helping you.

13

THE GIFT OF DEMOCRACY

JOHN BOORMAN'S POPULAR 1985 film *The Emerald Forest,* set in the Amazon rainforest, may come closer to describing the contemporary Indian problem in certain parts of the world than any other film. It is not a perfect film by any means. The acting is awkward and the attempt to portray authentic Xingu Indian dances, arts, and rituals (performed by actors from Rio) makes it self-consciously "realistic." But the film gets an A+ on a few counts. First, the situation it describes—an Indian tribe being pushed off its land by the construction of a huge dam that causes massive destruction to the forest—is typical of what is happening to the Xingu and the Yanomamo Indians of South America, as well as Indian nations throughout the world. Second, the film accurately depicts the intertribal conflict that ensues when one tribe is pushed from its own lands into territories of other tribes. Third, the destructive role of Western technology—bulldozers, dams, guns—is clearly portrayed, as is the inexorable drive of Westerners to expand without regard for the forest or the peoples within it.

The Emerald Forest is also unusual in its effort to show white people from the point of view of Indians. The Indians call the whites "the termite people," because of how they destroy the forest; white society is "the dead world," because of the concrete environments it creates, where nothing grows.

That the film describes a *current* situation distinguishes it from the usual media portrayal of Indian issues as part of the past. *The Emerald Forest* is as topical for Indians as *The China Syndrome* was for anti-nuke activists.

But for me, the most interesting moment in the film is a fleeting one that I never saw mentioned in reviews or articles, though it authentically portrays a fascinating aspect of Indian governance. It happens during a conversation between an American engineer who has wandered deeply into the jungle searching for his lost son, and a chief of the Invisible People. The engineer has been pushing the chief to order that one of the young men of the tribe undertake a certain exploration that no one had volunteered to do. The chief declines, explaining to the American, "If I tell a man to do something he doesn't want to do, then I wouldn't be chief anymore."

● ● ●

In the years I worked on this book, the most surprising revelations concerned the political and governmental forms of native peoples. Like most Americans I was raised with the idea that American constitutional democracy represented a new and unique political system, a utopian system that has proven itself workable in actual practice. I held the usual prejudices against other structures of government, especially socialism and Marxism, but it never passed through my mind that "primitive" peoples might have something to offer in the way of democratic government. Such a possibility was never mentioned in schools or in the media. Indian government systems, like all other dimensions of Indian life, were described with clichés about "anarchy" or despotic chiefdoms. Indian governments were described as representing an earlier stage of political development, of which we are the advanced form.

Describing Indian governments in such negative terms, or else declining to mention them at all, was and still is convenient for Americans and Westerners. It is yet another way we justify our interventions of past and present as having benefit for them: *we* bring the gift of democracy. More than hubris, this is a direct distortion of historical truth. It turns out that many Indian nations around the world, especially the Indians of the Americas, practiced a very high form of participatory democracy for thousands of years; and many nations continue to do so today.

In fact, there is a large and growing body of evidence among scholars of Indian-U.S. history that a pre-Columbian governmental form—the Great Binding Law of the Iroquois Confederacy—may have been the primary model and inspiration for the U.S. Articles of Confederation and for the Constitution itself. This possibility was not even mentioned as part of the official celebration of the Constitution's bicentennial in 1987, which represents a scandalous disregard for the role Indians played in the for-

THE GIFT OF DEMOCRACY

mation of our country, and our debt to them. I will come back to this later in this chapter.

Of course not every Indian government was democratic, and no one description of a particular tribal government can apply to the many thousands of native governmental systems that have existed around the world. Sadly, we can no longer observe these traditional forms because the tribes themselves are gone, or have been forcibly destroyed or so manipulated by Western intervention that the original traditional systems have disappeared. Nonetheless, it seems abundantly clear that the majority of native nations on this continent, as well as most in South America, Australia, New Zealand, the Arctic, and Africa were small, non-imperial, non-hierarchical, usually matriarchal, and democratic societies. (Notable exceptions to this are the Aztec, Inca, and perhaps Zapotec societies, which tended toward large imperialist theocracies.) This generalization applies to tribes that were nomadic (such as the Navajo and Sioux in North America) and those that were more sedentary, as well as to tribes that lived in deserts or mountains or in the frozen north.

What's most significant, perhaps, is that virtually all traditional tribal people share three primary political principles: 1) all land, water, and forest is communally owned by the tribe; private ownership of land or goods beyond those of the immediate household is unthinkable; 2) all tribal decisions are made by consensus, in which every tribal member participates; and 3) chiefs are not coercive, authoritarian rulers, as we tend to think of them; they are more like teachers or facilitators, and their duties are confined to specific realms (medicine, planting, war, relationships, ceremonies).

On the North American continent (as elsewhere) these three factors were the source of much conflict with the colonists and later with the American government, as they conspired to frustrate American expansionist dreams.

For example, communal ownership of land, combined with consensus decision-making, made it profoundly difficult for Americans to make deals or buy land from Indians, or even to trade for land, because all members of the tribe needed to agree. Direct military action, therefore, became a more viable option. In recent times, more legalistic means have been found to subvert traditional Indian government forms, as we'll see in later chapters.

In addition, the fluidity of a chief's role was incomprehensible to Western invaders, who had come from a Europe that had only known monarchies. Here they found no single authority with whom to negotiate, and who could then exercise authority over everyone else. Many tribes had several chiefs; some, such as the Plains Indian tribes, had dozens. At certain times of year, the ceremonial chiefs would gain prominence. At other times it might be those with knowledge of agriculture. It was only during wartime that war chiefs would emerge, but even their position would subside as things calmed. None of the chiefs had lifetime tenure, reigning in their roles only so long as they were trusted and supported by the tribe, as in the example from *The Emerald Forest*. If a chief's wisdom or performance was found wanting, another person would emerge or be placed into that role.

(Early contacts with white colonists disrupted some of the fluidity of the power arrangements within Indian tribes. Typically a white military force might make first contact with a tribe, and be greeted, appropriately, by the warrior chiefs. To the invading peoples the warrior chiefs seemed like monarchs, and were treated in that manner. This gave the warriors a political importance within the tribe that they might not have had before. Meanwhile, the arriving invaders never recognized the other chiefs, especially those responsible for such subtle matters as medicine, agriculture, or relationships, many of whom might have been women.)

RULE WITHOUT COERCION

The seminal work on the true nature of Indian chiefdom is *Society Against the State* by French anthropologist Pierre Clastres, in which he reports on his travels among several South American tribes. He also refers to research among tribes in areas of North America, Africa, Siberia, and the South Sea Islands that continue to live by traditional subsistence ways, that are outside the market economy, and that maintain their ancient forms of governance.

Clastres concludes that the Western idea of the Indian chief as a mini-king is totally erroneous:

> The chief has no authority at his disposal, no power of coercion, no means of giving an order. The chief is not a commander; the people of the tribe are under no obligation to obey. . . .
>
> The chief has to rely on nothing more than the prestige accorded him by the society to restore order and harmony. . . . What qualifies a man to be chief is his technical competence, his oratorical talent, his expertise as a hunter, his ability to coordinate . . . and in no circumstance does the tribe allow the technical superiority to change into a political authority. . . .

. . . The oldest chronicles leave no room for doubt on this score: if there is something completely alien to an Indian, it is the idea of giving an order or having to obey, except under very special circumstances such as prevail during a martial expedition.

Describing the duties of a chief, Clastres says, "The chief must be responsible for maintaining peace and harmony in the group. He must appease quarrels and settle disputes—not by employing a force he does not possess, but by relying solely on the strength of his prestige, his fairness and his verbal ability. More than a judge who passes sentence, he is an arbiter, who seeks to reconcile. . . . A second characteristic is generosity, which is both a duty and a bondage."

Clastres quotes Francis Huxley on practices of the Urubu people: "It is the business of a chief to be generous and to give what is asked of him. In some Indian tribes you can always tell the chief because he has the fewest possessions and wears the shabbiest ornaments. He has had to give away everything else." The point of the giveaway process is to maintain economic equality among the people, as with the potlatch ceremonies of the Kwakiutl and others.

Speaking specifically of North American Indian societies, Clastres adds: "One is confronted by a vast constellation of societies in which the holders of what elsewhere would be called power [chiefs] are actually without power; where the political is determined as a domain beyond coercion and violence, beyond hierarchical subordination, where no relationship of command-obedience is in force. This is the major difference of the Indian world, making it possible to speak of the American tribes as a homogeneous universe despite the extreme diversity of cultures moving within it."

Clastres is not alone among anthropologists who have noted this phenomenon of chiefs without power. But astonishingly, most of them conclude that this indicates the inferiority of "primitive" governance. Rather than celebrating communities capable of living happily for millennia without using coercive power, most anthropologists denigrate these governments, calling them "embryonic," "nascent," or "poorly developed," while decrying that most Indians did not "advance" sufficiently to develop "states."

The notion that coercive power is somehow "higher" than systems that function without it is debatable, to say the least. So is the notion that the "state" is an advancement over more informal nationhood, given that the term "state" lumps together democracies and monarchies and dictatorships of all kinds.

But the creation of such a standard does serve one important purpose for Western anthropologists: It becomes another thread in the fabric of standards by which we confirm our imagined superiority.

OUR FOUNDING FATHERS, THE IROQUOIS

One of the greatest irritations for American Indians today is how American society refuses to acknowledge that the flow of influence between our societies over the centuries has not been entirely one-directional. That *we* had a major impact on Indians—mostly destructive—cannot be denied. But virtually no credit is given the Indian contribution to Westerners. Occasionally, begrudging recognition is given the fact that the Indians taught the early arrivals to these shores what to eat, how to farm, and how to survive in the harsh, cold woods. And nowadays, because of the recent work of groups attempting to protect the rainforests of the world, we are hearing about forest Indians' knowledge of medicinal plants. We are beginning to grasp that modern pharmacology is rooted in the ancient knowledge of forest plants, and that we have barely begun to tap the Indians' full knowledge in these matters. And yet that knowledge is on the verge of being totally lost as the forests are destroyed and the Indians are killed or removed from their lands.

In his book *Indian Givers,* anthropologist Jack Weatherford lists numerous areas where Indian contributions have not been acknowledged, particularly in agriculture, food, architecture, and urban planning. But to me, the most important area where the Indian role has been ignored, or hidden, is their influence on democratic government. It is surely one of the most closely guarded secrets of American history that the Iroquois Confederacy had a major role in helping such people as Benjamin Franklin, James Madison, and Thomas Jefferson as they attempted to confederate a new government under democratic principles.

Recent scholarship has shown that in the mid-1700s Indians were not only invited to participate in the deliberations of our "founding fathers," but that the Great Binding Law of the Iroquois Confederacy arguably became the single most important model for the 1754 Albany Plan of Union, and later the Articles of Confederation and the Constitution. That this would be absent from our school texts, and from history, and from media is not surprising given the devotion Americans feel to our founding myth: Great men gathered to express a new vision that has withstood the test of time. If it were revealed that Indians had a role in it, imagine the blow to the American psyche.

• • •

Please try to imagine what it was like in the mid-1700s, when the colonists were desperate to free themselves from oppressive English control. The major urban settlements of the time—Albany, Philadelphia, Boston, New York—were nothing like they are today. Albany, the capital of New York, and site of the most important meetings about confederation, had only some 200 houses in 1754. Its population was under 3,000. Philadelphia, which was to become the U.S. capital, was the largest city in the colonies, with a population of 13,000. These places were really tiny towns, with mud roads, separated from one another by hundreds of miles of forest and several days' travel. Within those forests were Indians! In fact, the Indians were still, at that time, the stronger society, having yielded only a small part of their coastal territories. The Iroquois Confederacy (of New York, Pennsylvania, Ohio, Tennessee, and Ontario) had yielded practically nothing.

The colonists were still quite vulnerable. It was exceedingly important to them to get along with the Indians, who were all around. They often met to discuss mutually important issues: safe passage, commercial trade, land agreements (treaties), and military alliances. The Iroquois were especially important to the English colonies militarily, since alliance with the Iroquois against the French was critical to survival.

If the Iroquois had not finally fought on the side of the English colonies, we would all now be speaking French, and would probably be part of Quebec. Dealings with Indians took place on an everyday basis, and, according to many scholars, most negotiations were "in the Indian manner," that is, they were held as part of Indian councils, and followed Indian rules of discussion, procedure, and contact. So the colonists who negotiated with the Indians had significant knowledge of Indian decision-making and governance and went to considerable pain to accommodate the Indian processes. Even the selection of Albany as the site of many meetings was at the behest of the Indians.

It is fair to say that good relations with the Indians of that period were as important to the colonists as, say, present-day U.S. relations with Canada or the Soviet Union. In the 1700s, "foreign policy" was largely about relating to the Indians.

In addition to having day-to-day contact with the Indians of the mid-1700s, and carrying on negotiations in the Indian mode, the men who were striving to achieve independence, confederation, and democracy were struggling under another great burden: Nowhere in their own experience was there a working model of a democratic confederation of states. All of Europe at that time was under the rule of monarchs who claimed their authority by Divine Right. There *were* stirrings of democratic ferment in Europe, in the writings of Montesquieu, Locke, and Hume, who were being studied and discussed. And the Greeks provided a model, although it was 2,000 years old, only a partial democracy, not a confederation, and existed in an utterly different geopolitical context.

Meanwhile, living side by side with these aspiring federalists, in constant negotiation with them, was an Indian nation that, beyond theory or historical abstraction, was an actual living example of a successful democratic confederation, united under a single law that had already survived for many centuries: the Great Binding Law of the Iroquois Confederacy.

Although some Western scholars assert that the Great Law was created in the early 1400s, the Iroquois themselves argue that the Great Law existed for hundreds of years before Columbus's arrival. There is little doubt, however, that the Great Law arose from circumstances very similar to those faced by the separate colonies. The law was designed to form a peaceful federation among five previously separate, disputatious Indian nations—Onondaga, Oneida, Mohawk, Seneca, and Cayuga (joined later by Tuscarora)—who resided for millennia in adjoining areas that extended from what is now Tennessee to most of Ontario. The Great Law articulated the manner in which the confederated nations would thenceforth relate to one another as a single body. It also articulated the rights that would be reserved for the individual nations (states' rights). The Law described a system for democratically electing representatives to a Grand Council, divided into separate deliberative bodies (multi-cameral legislature). And it included, in great detail, descriptions of the legislatures of individual nations, as well as rights of universal suffrage, popular selection and removal of chiefs, and the manner in which all the members of the population should participate.

That the model was successful was apparent by the mere fact that it was already many centuries old, during which time the separate nations had cooperated peacefully on federal matters, yet remained separate. In fact the Iroquois Confederacy is still functional today among the six member nations, and the Great Law remains as the system of governance.

Given all of the above, it is preposterous to assume that the colonists were not influenced by the Iroquois. And yet it has been an uphill struggle for historians who have argued this point against the founding myths of American society.

Foremost among the maverick historians is Professor Donald Grinde, Jr., of the University of California at Riverside. In his book *The Iroquois and the Founding of the American Nation,* Grinde argues that the Iroquois were a significant influence on colonial leaders, who had nowhere else to turn. He quotes George Clinton, then governor of New York, as observing in 1747 that most American democratic leaders were "people of republican principles who have no knowledge of democratic governments." Grinde continues, "The tribesmen of America seemed to many Europeans to be free of such abuses [as were generated by the European monarchs]. . . . The colonists saw freedom widely exercised by American Indians. Even the cultural arrogance and racism of English colonists could not fully disguise their astonishment at finding Native Americans in such a free and peaceful state."

Grinde points out that James Madison made frequent forays to study and speak with Iroquois leaders. William Livingston was fluent in Mohawk, and visited and stayed with Indians over extended periods. John Adams and his family socialized with Cayuga chiefs on numerous occasions. Thomas Jefferson's personal papers show specific references to the forms of Iroquois governance, and, says Grinde, "Benjamin Franklin's work is resplendent with stories about Indians and Indian ideas of personal freedom and structures of government." University of Nebraska professor Bruce Johansen has added that Franklin, who was in the printing business, was especially intimate with Indian thinking since he "had been printing Indian treaties since 1736 and not only was he acquainted with them, he set the type." Franklin was also present at an important meeting among Iroquois chiefs and several colonial governors in Lancaster, Pennsylvania, in 1744, at which the chiefs recommended that the colonists stop fighting among themselves and form a union.

By 1754, when most of these men and others gathered to create the Albany Plan of Union, the first try at confederation, they invited forty-two members of the Iroquois Grand Council to serve as advisors on confederate structures. Benjamin Franklin freely acknowledged his interest in the Iroquois achievement in a famous speech at the Albany Congress: "It would be a strange thing . . . if six nations of ignorant savages [*sic*] should be capable of forming such a union and be able to execute it in such a manner that it has subsisted for ages and appears indissoluble, and yet that a like union should be impractical for ten or a dozen English colonies."

According to Grinde, Franklin convened meetings of Iroquois chiefs and congressional delegates in order to "hammer out a plan that he acknowledged to be similar to the Iroquois Confederacy."

In a 1989 interview with Catherine Stifter of National Public Radio,

Grinde referred to the considerable resistance in the academic community to the idea of the Iroquois role in the formative stages of American history. According to Grinde, as recently as fifteen years ago people considered the idea a "fantasy," but there has since been considerable progress:

> People have [now] accepted the fact the Iroquois were at the Continental Congress on the eve of the Declaration of Independence and they're having to deal with the fact that John Adams was advocating the study of Indian governments, and that Adams observed that others among the founding fathers were advancing Indian ideas on the eve of the Constitutional Convention. But people have been led kicking and screaming into these realizations. . . . The promise and the vision that Indian societies provided to Europeans was that democracy did not die 2,000 years before in ancient Greece, [to be followed by] Divine Right monarchy as the evolution of government. In North America and in other places in the world there were people that were living without kings or landed nobility and who had systems of government that were clearly less coercive than those in Europe. . . . Some people [still] deny this. I believe for some people this is a problem. . . . It's difficult to entertain the idea that the founding fathers were relating to, talking about, and evaluating the ideas of non-white peoples . . . it goes against the conventional wisdom of our society.

If Indian influence upon American constitutional democracy is a tough pill for Americans to swallow, there is yet another minor aspect to the story that can only create still greater anxiety. There's a case to be made that the Iroquois model was also influential in Europe, particularly upon Frederick Engels and Karl Marx.

At the time when Marx and Engels were struggling to create models for an egalitarian, classless society, which later evolved into communism, Engels was strongly influenced by the eighteenth-century work of anthropologist Lewis Morgan, particularly his reports on the Iroquois. Engels was so impressed that in his work *Origin of the Family, Private Property and the State,* the Iroquois were used as the prime example of a successful classless, egalitarian, noncoercive society.

And so we have the bizarre situation that while Westerners continue to assume that the flow of influence was simply from the more "advanced" Western societies to the Indians of the Americas, it is arguably the case that the two dominant political systems of the past century were both at least partly rooted in the wisdom of the Great Binding Law of the Iroquois Confederacy. If so, both the U.S. and the U.S.S.R. would do well to ac-

knowledge the connection, study the original document, see where each
went wrong, and try to get it right the next time.

THE GREAT BINDING LAW
OF THE IROQUOIS CONFEDERACY

According to Iroquois history, the creation of the Great Law is attrib-
uted primarily to the work of two men: Hiawatha (Mohawk) and Dekan-
awida (Onondaga), who spent several decades wandering together across
what is now the eastern U.S. and Canada hundreds of years before Columbus landed, with a plan to unite the Mohawk, Oneida, Cayuga, Onondaga, and Seneca. (The Tuscarora joined much later, in 1715.)

The Great Law was transmitted orally from generation to generation,
with its tenets recorded only on wampum belts and strings. Many of these
wampums have since been lost, and those that remain were the subject of
bitter lawsuits during the 1980s between the Iroquois and the State University of New York, which housed them. The university finally returned
them to the Indians in 1989.

One of the early translations of the Iroquois constitution was by the
turn-of-the-century anthropologist Arthur H. Parker, and is contained in
Parker on the Iroquois, edited by William Fenton. In addition to Parker's
commentaries on Iroquois life, the book contains Parker's English translation of the entire constitution: 115 pages of text.

Parker comments that "The Great Law as a governmental system was
an almost ideal one for the stage of culture [*sic*] with which it was designed
to cope. . . . By adhering to it the Five Nations became the dominant native power east of the Mississippi and during colonial times exercised an
immense influence in determining the fate of English civilization on the
continent." Iroquois members today credit the Great Law as the main reason for their continued coherence as a viable nation, more successful than
other American Indians in resisting domination by white society.

● ● ●

Certain features of the Great Law, as reported in Parker's book, are instantly recognizable for their similarity with the U.S. Constitution: the establishment of a federation with separate powers for federal and state
governments; provisions for the common defense; representative democracy at the federal and local levels; separate legislative branches that debate
issues and reconcile disagreements; checks and balances against excessive

powers; rights of popular nomination and recall; and universal suffrage (although this last provision took Americans another 150 years to achieve).

But the features the colonists declined to introduce are just as interesting as the features that resemble our Constitution. For example, the Iroquois had no executive branch, no rulers or presidents; the colonists couldn't bear to get too far away from their monarch. Many of the powers to appoint and remove chiefs for the Iroquois were held by the women, another dimension of checks and balances that the United States did not include, along with the principle of consensual decision-making at each level of government and in each legislative branch.

According to Parker, the Great Council of the Iroquois Confederacy, the federation's legislature, consisted of fifty *rodiyaner* (civil chiefs, as opposed to war chiefs) divided into three distinct "houses" according to tribal membership. Each of the "houses" debated issues separately, eventually reporting their decisions to the Onondaga, who were not part of the other legislatures, but served as "firekeepers." The Onondaga determined if a consensus had been reached among the houses. If not, they would return the question to the houses and demand that they reach the unanimity required for the passage of any policy.

The only executive person was a temporary "speaker," appointed by acclamation, who served for one day only.

The right to nominate chiefs was hereditary, held only by clan mothers of certain clans from each tribe. After nomination, the candidate was then ratified in stages by the whole clan, the national council, the Grand Council of the Confederacy, and then finally by all the people. The women also had the power to remove the chiefs from office if they proved not to have "in mind the welfare of the people," as the Law says. They could also remove a chief "who should seek to establish any authority independent of the jurisdiction of the Great Law." If the women removed a chief, they also nominated the replacement.

The procedure for removing chiefs was spelled out in exquisite detail, as were all rules of the Great Law, including the exact words the women used to deliver a warning to the offending chief, then follow-up warnings and removal.

In addition to the chiefs nominated by the women, the Law permitted the recognition of "Pine Tree Chiefs" who spontaneously sprang from the community. According to the Great Law these are people "with special ability [who] show great interest in the affairs of the nation, and [who] prove themselves wise, honest and worthy of confidence." Such chiefs participated in all council deliberations.

The duties of the chiefs were spelled out in great detail:

[They] shall be mentors of the people for all time. The thickness of their skin shall be seven spans, which is to say that they shall be proof against anger, offensive actions and criticism. Their hearts shall be full of peace and good will and their minds filled with a yearning for the welfare of the people of the confederacy. With endless patience they shall carry out their duty and their firmness shall be tempered with a tenderness for their people. Neither anger nor fury shall find lodgement in their minds and all their words and actions shall be marked by calm deliberation. . . . [They] must be honest in all things . . . self-interest must be cast into oblivion . . . [They shall] look and listen for the welfare of the whole people and have always in view not only the present but also the coming generations, even those whose faces are yet beneath the surface of the ground, the unborn of the future Nation.

Deliberately Slow

The Great Law contains one rule that I found particularly extraordinary for its democratic import and the degree of trust it reveals for the people of the member nations. The Law says that when an "especially important matter or a great emergency is presented before the council, and the nature of the matter affects the entire body of the Five Nations," then the council is not permitted to act without first going back to all of the people in the confederacy. The chiefs "of the confederacy must submit the matter to the decision of their people and the decision of the people shall affect the decision of the confederate council. This decision shall be a confirmation of the voice of the people."

What is remarkable is that this rule describes a way of doing things that is exactly the opposite of our own. In the United States the most apocalyptic decisions, especially military ones, are always made by government, quickly—often secretly—without consulting the people. This speed and secrecy is justified precisely because of the importance of the matter and by the need for rapid action. Often this reflects how technology has accelerated the pace of events, creating situations such as "launch on warning."

In the United States, the president makes all war decisions. The constitutional principle that only Congress can declare war is a farce, as was most recently obvious in the U.S.-Iraq situation. For although Congress finally gave its (divided) approval for war, it came only after President Bush had maneuvered 450,000 troops to the front lines *without* approval, and issued a level of verbal invective against Iraq that made war impossible to avoid. And in preceding years, we saw U.S. presidents bomb countries

(Vietnam, Cambodia, Laos), invade countries (Grenada, Lebanon, Panama), and undertake indirect military actions (Nicaragua), all without congressional approval, let alone the approval of the people.

I don't know of any native society in which any war chief could undertake military action without long meetings of the entire tribe, which could take days or even weeks. Even when a military response was approved, warrior recruitment was voluntary. If an insufficient number of warriors showed up, there was simply no war, or else the war chief would have to go out there alone, as occasionally happened. The Iroquois Confederacy institutionalized this rule, making the war decision slower and much more difficult.

States' Rights

Several rules in the Great Law were created to ensure the continued sovereignty of each member nation of the confederacy. For example, one section stated, ". . . The five Council Fires shall continue to burn as before and they are not quenched. The [chiefs] of each nation in the future shall settle their nation's affairs at this council fire [though] governed always by the laws and rules of the council of the Confederacy and by the Great Peace."

Sound familiar? It is very close to the model adopted by Franklin and Jefferson for the United States Constitution.

According to Arthur Parker, in addition to ensuring sovereignty for each member nation, there were also rules ensuring sexual equality, as well as the rights of local communities to determine their own affairs:

> The men of every clan of the Five Nations shall have a Council Fire ever burning in readiness for a council of the clan. When it seems necessary for a council to be held to discuss the welfare of the clans, then the men may gather about the fire. This council shall have the same rights as the council of the women.
>
> The women of every clan of the Five Nations shall have a Council Fire ever burning in readiness for a council of the clan. When in their opinion it seems necessary for the interest of the people they shall hold a council and decisions and recommendations shall be introduced before the Council . . .
>
> All of the Clan Council Fires of a nation or of the Five Nations may unite into one general Council Fire, or delegates from all the Council Fires may be appointed to unite in a general council for discussing the interests of the people. The people shall have the right to

THE GIFT OF DEMOCRACY

make appointments and to delegate their power to others of their number. When their council shall have come to a conclusion on any matter, their decision shall be reported to the Council of the Nation or to the Confederate Council, as the case may require.

The Great Law also contained specific articles concerning the rights and duties of war chiefs, the rules of consanguinity, the official symbolism of the tribes, laws of adoption, and laws of emigration and immigration (including political asylum). The rights of foreign nationals were spelled out, as well as many passages containing the exact words and procedures to be used for "raising chiefs," funeral addresses, installation songs, and all ceremonies. For example, at the opening ceremonies before each council meeting, the Onondaga were required to "offer thanks to the Earth where men dwell, to the streams of water, the pools, the springs and the lakes, to the maize and the fruits, to the medicinal herbs and trees, to the forest trees for their usefulness, to the animals that serve as food and give their pelts for clothing, the great winds and the lesser winds, to the Thunderers, to the Sun, the mighty warrior, to the moon, to the messengers of the Creator, and to the Great Creator who dwells in the heavens above, who gives all the things useful to men, and who is the source and the ruler of health and life."

IROQUOIS NATION, 1991

Two hundred years after the founding of the United States, the Iroquois Confederacy is rare among American Indian nations in its successful resistance to U.S. efforts to dismantle the traditional government in favor of a new government created under the Indian Reorganization Act (IRA). The Six Nations credit the clarity and cohesiveness of their Great Law as the reason they have become the leaders among American Indian nations on issues of sovereignty, maintenance of traditional governments, and protection of land rights.

The Onondaga, the "firekeepers" of the Iroquois, exert particular leadership on the sovereignty issue. Now living in a small territory outside of Syracuse, New York, the Onondaga steadfastly maintain that neither New York State nor the United States has legal sovereignty over them. Onondaga chiefs are frequently invited to visit and advise other Indian nations about maintaining and recovering their traditional governments. By now it is clear to most American Indians that the IRA governments have failed to protect traditional Indian cultural and spiritual values, and serve instead as an arm of the U.S. bureaucracy, making deals with the mining and development interests that the native peoples abhor.

Prominent among the militant Onondaga leadership is Oren Lyons, Faithkeeper of the Turtle Clan. I visited Lyons at his home several times to learn more about the subtleties and power of the Great Law.

Now in his early sixties, as handsome as a movie star, Lyons lives alone in a small log house on the reservation. As a younger man, Lyons had lived in a far more affluent manner in non-Indian society. He had a successful career in New York City, as planning director for Norcross Greeting Cards, and as an illustrator for books and advertising. The experience left him with a unique ability, among Indians, to speak with ease to upper echelons of the non-Indian world.

Lyons told me that he left his marketing career in 1967 to return to the reservation when he was "called by the clan mothers of the Turtle Clan" to replace a Turtle Clan chief who had died. He also represents the Onondaga on the Iroquois Grand Council.

Chiefs don't get paid, so Lyons partly supports himself by directing the Native American studies program at the State University of New York at Buffalo. He also paints paintings of traditional Indian subjects, and he's coach of the Iroquois Confederacy national lacrosse team. (At Syracuse University, Lyons had been an all-American goalie on the same lacrosse team as Jim Brown, better known for his football exploits. Lyons's dream is to have the Iroquois compete in the Olympics as a separate nation. The Iroquois team did compete in the 1990 World Games of the International Lacrosse Federation.)

In 1977, Lyons was selected by the American Indian delegation to the United Nations Conference on Indigenous People to be one of the official spokespersons for all the Indians of the Western Hemisphere. The selection was extended to Lyons in recognition of the role the Six Nations has played among American Indian nations as the leading advocate of traditional Indian governments and sovereign rights. Lyons is also on the steering committee of the Global Forum of Spiritual and Parliamentary Leaders for Global Survival, an international ecumenical organization of religious and political leaders, formed to address the relationship between the world's environmental and spiritual problems.

During my visits with Lyons, and in later correspondence, my goal was to gain further insight into the history of the Great Law, as well as its present-day workings within the Iroquois (Hau de no sau nee) governments.

Lyons cautioned me to remember that "the Great Law is [essentially] an oral law and [will] remain that way. In 1974, the Grand Council of the Hau de no sau nee rejected all written versions," said Lyons, including that of Arthur Parker. While many of Parker's passages are not objectionable, Parker's use of such devices as articles and numbers to define the sections has nothing to do with the oral version, and Parker's use of words such as "Lords" to describe the members of the Council is actually offensive to Indians. Lyons told me that the Indians are constantly engaged in study, discussion, and interpretation to ferret out nuances of the Great Law's meaning, and that much subtlety is lost in the English translations of the spoken versions. The opening prayer of thanks, for example, that I quoted earlier from Parker, has at least three different oral versions; according to Lyons, "the shortest version is about fifteen to twenty minutes long; the long version can take up to an hour and a half.

"I think it is fair to say the Hau de no sau nee council of chiefs may be the last of the traditional governments in North America that have control of their territories," said Lyons. Of the six confederated nations, only the Mohawk have seen their traditional system succumb to an American-imposed governmental form, which has led to disastrous events on the Akwesasne (Mohawk) Reservation in New York State. "That is where the government instituted gambling operations without the consent of the people, and they've been fighting among themselves ever since."

According to Lyons, the basic strength of Iroquois governance comes from its trust in and dependence upon the participation of all the people. "The word *chief* is an English word," said Lyons. "The Indian word *hoyawnah* means 'the good mind,' the peacemaker. We [the chiefs] are servants. With our nations, the leaders are directly accessible to the people. In nation-states like the U.S. you develop an entity separate from the people with accompanying power structures—for example, executive committees or central committees. In our government, national consensus is paramount. There is no process for voting. We have a system of discussion and council that requires agreements from all sides of our council fire; all must finally agree on the subject before them. All meetings are public. We cannot have a closed meeting in the long house. There are no executive [presidential] decisions."

In all council meetings, "every adult member of the tribe is permitted to speak for as long as he or she wishes, unless they raise their voice too loud. There are strictures against attempting to dominate the meeting, or to use any measure of force, even verbal force. The idea is for everyone to have a say, and to say everything they wish.

"Discussion continues until consensus is reached," Lyons said. "It's a very slow process. Sometimes it takes days or weeks, but we're not in a hurry, especially about important things." Lyons added that only in machine-oriented societies is there pressure to get human matters processed quickly, because society is moving at machine speed.

"If everyone has spoken and still there's no decision, then the question is put off to the next meeting. If the issue is discussed at three meetings and there's still no decision, then we decide that there will be no decision. We stop discussing it. We figure it will come up again some other time."

At first I was shocked by this idea of just dropping something that cannot be agreed upon. But eventually I realized that the Indian decision-making system is biased toward the idea that things don't really have to be changed. They can stay the way they are. If some step really is needed— say there's an attack of some kind—then a consensus *will* be reached and steps will be taken. The equivalent principle in American terms is "If it ain't broke, don't fix it."

It's not as if decisions are not made at all. While I was present, for example, the tribe decided to evict several white families who had, by various means, insinuated themselves into houses on the reservation. Although the intrusion of non-Indians onto the reservation was a violation of treaties with the U.S. and with New York State, appeals to those governments for enforcement had produced no action. After three months of discussion, it was decided that Indians would do the evictions, and they did.

Lyons told me that unlike many Indian nations, especially those governed by U.S.-style IRA governments, the Onondaga "do not have to this day a police force or army to carry out any orders by the chiefs. Therefore it is elemental that the people agree before any change takes place, because they are the ones to carry it out." New York State police and federal agents are not permitted to take action on Onondaga land without the invitation of the Onondaga Council. (Because of this rule, fugitive Sioux Indian leader Dennis Banks was able to remain safe with the Onondaga, even though the FBI knew where he was. "He was under the protection of the Grand Council," said Lyons. New York police and the FBI attempted to negotiate with the chiefs for Banks's release, but did not succeed. So Banks remained, though he could not set foot off the Indians' land. Eventually Banks decided to return to South Dakota and completed his jail term.)

I asked Lyons about the principles used to make decisions about tribal matters. What happens, say, if there is an act of violence by one Indian against another on the reservation? Lyons told me that in matters affecting the whole Iroquois Confederacy, questions are discussed in the Grand Council and its rules are followed. But in local matters, "All I can tell you is that every situation is seen as entirely different. We really don't have the kind of specific rules or laws that you have. Nothing is ever written down.

Well, we do have a few rules. If you rape or murder somebody, you are banished from the tribe for life. But we've only had one such case in thirty years [unlike many Indian tribes]. If you write the rules down, then you have to deal with the rule rather than figuring out what's fair. We're interested in principle. The principle is to be fair. We know everybody, we know their families, what they like, what they don't like, what's troubling them, what the kids may be going through. We have all the problems any community has. When one member intrudes on another, we have a situation. We meet and just keep talking until there's nothing left but the obvious truth, and both families agree on the solution."

I asked Lyons to tell me more about the role of the chiefs. He told me they do not function the way Westerners think. It is true that in the end they seem to decide what's going to happen, but this comes only after the whole nation has spoken for many hours and has reached an agreement. The chiefs only confirm what is already obvious. The chief is a kind of facilitator, according to Lyons, an employee. If the people don't like the way the chief is acting, he is removed. Technically speaking, the chiefs are "appointed for life," but there are standards for chiefly behavior among the Onondaga. If they stray from that behavior, they can be removed immediately by the clan mothers.

"A chief can de-horn himself [the symbol of a chief's authority is a set of deer antlers] by certain crimes like murder, rape, or arson, or crimes against children," as well as other behaviors that are spelled out in the Great Law. "The clan mother is the one to remove the chief," said Lyons, employing a carefully articulated three-step process that first involves a warning from the women, and then actions by the other chiefs.

Arthur Parker's translation of the Great Law suggests that a chief who refuses to leave can be killed, but Lyons strongly disagrees. "That sounds spectacular and makes good reading," he said, "but it is not true. The process of removing any chief is painful enough. . . . The law says if a leader cannot obey the tenets of the Great Law he is banished from the nation and he is ordered to take his followers with him. This is not applied to personal misconduct, but conduct that attacks the law itself and its structure." Lyons adds that Parker's mistranslation of that element of the law "is the best example of why the chiefs refuse to allow English translations, [preferring to keep it] only in the native tongue."

I asked Lyons to tell me what are the specific qualities sought in people selected to be chiefs. "Well, they're spelled out in the Great Law," he said. "I would say the most important ones are compassion, patience, commitment to natural law, commitment to process rather than goal [you don't stop the talking from running its course], courage, fairness, generosity, commitment to and love for the seventh generation of unborn children, and dedication to the way of the long house [the spiritual path]. Chiefs cannot be Christians or of any other faith. Another quality is a kind of benign nature. Not too pushy."

I wondered about this last point, concerning the chiefs' levels of aggressiveness or the use of verbal force. "It's difficult to define," he answered. "You can be very powerful if you are right and can persuade [the people]. Ordered thought, logic, are the persuasive tools of Six Nations' meetings. [But equally important] is respect for other points of view and opinions, and the power and patience to listen and understand."

I finally gathered that it was a subtle point, a matter of degree. Good orators have an influence, but the power of oratory *itself* should not be used to overcome rationality and full discourse.

In thinking this issue over, I remembered a meeting I had in the late 1960s with some of the *kikmongwis,* the religious leaders of the Hopi Nation in Arizona. I had come to ask permission to make a film about the strip-mining of sacred sites on Hopi land, and expected to be able to make my case to the group and get a quick answer. Instead, I experienced a meeting unlike any I'd ever been part of before. The first half of the meeting lasted all morning, during which the *kikmongwis* (there were ten present) sat in a circle engaging in a very slow conversation, in Hopi. My translator, without revealing exactly what was being said, told me in general terms that they were discussing previous experiences with white outsiders who had come to them with projects, and how the issue was viewed from the perspective of Hopi teachings. It wasn't until midday that I was able to speak. I delivered my proposal in a well-organized snappy fashion, which took about twenty minutes. For the next several hours, the Hopi elders continued to discuss the matter in Hopi. It was the *style* of their discourse that amazed me, even more than the duration. Each speaker spoke in quiet, modulated tones, punctuated by very long silences. Meanwhile, the others sat very still, often with their eyes closed. Sometimes they seemed to be asleep, but I have since realized, from several such experiences with Indians, that there is among oral cultures a unique way of listening and remembering. They were not asleep; they were alert in a way that was difficult for me to see. Most of all, I was astonished that no speaker attempted to use any degree of persuasion on any other, except insofar as they expressed their own understanding of Hopi teachings on the matter at hand. It seemed to me to be a process of peeling away layers of consideration until nothing but a clear agreement remained. They were all equals in this process.

In the end, the Hopi *kikmongwis* told me they hoped I would come back again and meet with them whenever my own thinking on the project was further developed. They never did answer yes or no, and I never did the film, although I did do an advertisement on their behalf about the mining at Black Mesa.

I don't think the Iroquois process is precisely like the Hopi, but the effort to achieve consensus is absolutely at the heart of the Iroquois decision-making process, as it is, in fact, among most Indian nations of the Americas. According to Oren Lyons, the strength of consensus is the unanimity it eventually produces. Unlike decisions made by majority rule, in which there is always a dissatisfied, resistant minority, once a position is reached by consensus, the solidarity that emerges is awesome to behold.

For example, the Onondaga have decided, irrevocably I'd say, that they will never give up more land. "Land is the most important thing the Indians have," said Lyons. In fact, they are committed to regaining much of the treaty land that they believe was fraudulently taken from them.

A few years ago they refused a cash offer of several hundred thousand dollars from a power company that wanted to put power lines along a fifty-foot right of way across the reservation. "One old woman stood up," Lyons told me, "and asserted, 'Not one more foot, ever,' and there was unanimous agreement right there. That one didn't take long."

The Onondaga have turned down large amounts of money to lease a tiny piece of land to New York State for a highway cloverleaf. And they turned down money to build a garbage-processing plant on their land.

The Onondagas have also refused to give the names and addresses of the children living on the reservation to the New York State Board of Education. "Our treaty with New York says that in return for ceding some land eighty years ago, New York is to provide us schools and the money to run them, forever. That's how they got some of our land. But lately they've asked us for the names of the kids. We are never going to give up those names," said Lyons.

For Oren Lyons, and the Onondaga chiefs, it's a question of maintaining the strength of native governance and sovereignty. "For the whole history of the Iroquois we have maintained that we are a separate nation. We have never lost a war. Our government still operates. We have refused the U.S. government's reorganization plans for us. We have kept our language and our traditions, and when we fly to Geneva to UN meetings, we carry Hau de no sau nee passports. We made some treaties that lost some land, but that also confirmed our separate-nation status. That the U.S. denies all this doesn't make it any less the case."

14

LESSONS IN STONE-AGE
ECONOMICS

*I*F ONE FRAUDULENT justification for Western aggression upon native lands has been that we bring the gift of democracy, an equally fraudulent justification is that we bring freedom from toil.

Our mythology has been that native peoples live with the awful oppression of "subsistence economics"—a term that by its mere utterance invokes feelings of pity and images of squalor. Our machines, our technology, and our superior systems of economic management offer freedom from backbreaking labor, the opportunity for leisure, and protection against the arbitrariness of nature's cycles. Pre-technological peoples, living hand to mouth in a never-ending search for food and protection from the elements, need and want what Western society brings. So goes the story.

Given this logic, most Westerners are shocked to find that the majority of native peoples on the earth do not wish to climb onto the Western economic machine. They say their traditional ways have served them well for thousands of years and that our ways are doomed to fail. These views came forth in Canadian jurist Thomas R. Berger's book *Village Journey,* which describes a tour through Alaskan communities faced with the onslaught of Western economies. Berger's book offers extensive testimony from native Alaskans who are resisting the Western economic way.

Suzy Erlich of Kotzebue, Alaska:

> I came from a subsistence family. I grew up that way. I am very proud of it. I want my children to grow up that way. It brings strength to us as Inupiats. It is something different than going to the store. Our grocery store is millions of acres wide, and it brings us pride.

Bobby Wells of Kotzebue, Alaska:

I remember our fathers, how they survived in this world, in strong winds, in cold temperatures. . . . They were taught to share, they were taught to help each other. . . . This time, we are fighting to survive among different people, among different races in this Western civilization. What does this Western civilization have to offer? Business.

Alice Solomon of Barrow, Alaska:

The people are happy . . . they caught a whale. They get really excited, and it goes all the way, deep inside. And when you go into the house that caught the whale, there's that happiness, that excitement, that crying for joy, because they are glad they have been given that gift.

On the rare occasion when Westerners hear such views as these—it was a point of Berger's book that native peoples are hardly ever asked—we tend to relegate native opinions to mere ignorance. We are so thoroughly convinced of the rightness of the Western technological project that we are determined to "improve" the native condition, even over their objections.

And so it has been for hundreds of years. Western attitudes today on such matters are no different than they have been since the seventeenth century. Our sense of superiority justifies the continued expansion of our economic system, of digging up, cutting down, and paving over the natural world, without guilt toward the native peoples' lands we destroy in the process. Our mythology supports this, our economic system is based on it, and our financial institutions—from your local bank to the World Bank—aggressively seek to ensure that these ways continue.

The system never questions itself on these points. Only recent campaigns by groups such as Rainforest Action Network and Earth First! have begun to challenge such attitudes and policies. But if our society ever really questioned its assumptions about the viability of native economies and asked the people within those societies how they felt about them, we would surely have to reassess our views.

PRE-TECHNOLOGICAL LEISURE

The publication of Marshall Sahlins' *Stone Age Economics* in 1972 should have exploded most of the operative paradigms by which we define the beneficial aspects of our technology. A University of Chicago professor, Sahlins uses field research from tribes all over the globe to argue powerfully that, contrary to the prevailing wisdom, "primitive" societies (particularly hunter-gatherer communities like those in Alaska) enjoyed a great amount of "leisure time," satisfied their material desires and survival needs with little difficulty, did not work very hard, and consciously chose "subsistence economics": They *deliberately* did not accumulate surpluses.

Sahlins writes, "Almost universally committed to the proposition that life was hard in the paleolithic [era], our textbooks compete to convey a sense of impending doom, leaving one to wonder not only how hunters managed to live but whether, after all, this was living." Sahlins lists some of the commonly used terms of denigration: "mere subsistence economy," "limited leisure," "absence of economic surplus," and the need for these societies to survive by putting out a "maximum energy from a maximum number of people." Sahlins calls such attitudes "the first distinctly neolithic prejudice," created deliberately to depict the hunter's relationship to land and resources in the manner that would be "most congenial to the historic task of depriving him of the same."

Stone-age peoples were not prisoners of hard labor, says Sahlins. To the contrary, "a good case can be made that hunters and gatherers work less than we do; and, rather than a continuous travail, the food quest is intermittent, leisure abundant, and there is a greater amount of sleep in the daytime per capita per year than in any other condition of society."

BANKER'S HOURS

In his book, Marshall Sahlins quotes a 1960 study by Frederick D. McCarthy and Margaret McArthur of aboriginal communities in Western Arnhem Land, Australia. The researchers added up all the time spent in all economic activities—plant collecting, food preparation, and weapon repair—over a span of several months, finding that the average male worked three hours and forty-four minutes per day, while the average female worked three hours and fifty minutes per day. "The most obvious immediate conclusion," said Sahlins, "is that the people do not work hard. . . . Moreover they do not work continuously."

According to McCarthy and McArthur, "Apart from the time spent in general social intercourse, chatting, gossiping, and so on, some hours of the daylight were also spent resting and sleeping. If the men were in camp, they usually slept after lunch from an hour to an hour and a half, or sometimes even more. Also, after returning from fishing or hunting they usually had a sleep. . . . The women, when out collecting in the forest, appeared to rest more frequently than the men. If in camp all day, they also slept at odd times, sometimes for long periods."

The Dobe Bushmen of southern Africa offer an example from a different continent. Sahlins cites research by Richard Lee demonstrating that the average Dobe Bushman's work week is approximately fifteen hours— two hours and nine minutes per day. What's more, only 65 percent of the population worked at all.

Sahlins comments on this: "One man's labor among the Bushmen will support four or five people. Taken at face value, Bushmen food-collecting is more efficient than French farming was in the period up to World War II, when more than 20 percent of the population were engaged in feeding the rest. Confessedly, the comparison is misleading, but not as misleading as it is astonishing." Such a comparison with our own society today would show American farmers, only 5 percent of the population, feeding the rest of the country, thanks to technology. But in primitive societies those who feed the others do so by a cooperative arrangement—sharing turns of work and sharing food—that frees the rest of society to not work at all. In our own society, in which there is virtually no sharing, and virtual dependence upon dollar purchases of food, the non-farming 95 percent are not freed from work; they are strapped to some economic machine other than farming to produce the money they need to pay for food.

According to Richard Lee, "A woman gathers in one day enough food to feed her family for three days, and spends the rest of her time resting in camp, doing embroidery, visiting other camps, or entertaining visitors from other camps. During each day at home, kitchen routines, such as cooking, nut cracking, collecting firewood, and fetching water, occupy one to three hours of her time. This rhythm of steady work and steady leisure is maintained throughout the year. The male hunters tend to work more frequently than the women, but their schedule is uneven. It is not unusual for a man to hunt avidly for a week and then do no hunting at all for two or three weeks. During these periods, visiting, entertaining and especially dancing are the primary activities of men."

DIETARY INTAKE

A common misconception is that primitive societies survive at only the bare minimum of existence, yet research proves otherwise. The Arnhem

Land hunters, for example, do not like a monotonous diet; they work to ensure themselves a wide diversity of food well beyond sufficiency. According to researchers McCarthy and McArthur, the dietary intake of the hunters was adequate according to today's standards of the National Research Council of America. Mean daily consumption for several aboriginal communities was above 2,130 calories per day, which is a better nutrition level than is enjoyed by 15 percent of the U.S. population.

Like the Aborigines, the Dobe Bushmen enjoyed a caloric intake of more than 2,100 calories per day. However, according to the calculations of one researcher, judging by the Bushman's average body weight, people only required about 1,900 calories per day. The surplus food, says that researcher, was given to the dogs.

"The conclusion can be drawn," says Richard Lee, "that the Bushmen do not lead a substandard existence on the edge of starvation as had been commonly supposed."

Marshall Sahlins summarizes by saying, "Hunters keep banker's hours, notably less than modern industrial workers," and yet, he points out, their food consumption is varied and adequate. They eat as much for pleasure as sustenance.

DELIBERATE UNDERPRODUCTION

In primitive societies, unlike modern industrial societies, the people choose not to produce at maximum levels. Incredible as it may seem to Western minds, "there is a conscious and consistent disregard for the notion of 'maximum effort from a maximum number of people,'" according to Sahlins. He goes on: "Labor power is underused, technological means are not fully engaged, natural resources are left untapped . . . production is low relative to existing possibilities. The work day is short. The number of days off exceeds the number of work days. Dancing, fishing, games, sleep, and ritual seem to occupy the greater part of one's time."

As labor is underused, so are environmental resources left to "go to waste," a fact that drives Westerners into a frenzy to get at those "wasted resources." The immediate environments of many hunter-gatherer communities could easily support triple their populations, but deliberate control of population growth, and deliberate underuse of the environment's full economic capacity, has kept the ratio of people to resources very small. Rather than using up the productive potential of the environment, stone-age communities chose to let some of the fruit fall to the ground, and some of the animals exist in peace. The people, meanwhile, are content to hang out, sleep, dance, flirt, and engage in the rituals and relationships that have meaning within these societies. "Maximum effort" indeed.

THE CHOICE OF SUBSISTENCE

The Western assumption is that nomadic hunter-gatherers, especially those who are still functional today (numbering in the tens of millions), would love to be free of their "subsistence" economy. But Sahlins argues that these people have clearly chosen their lifestyle. Even when neighboring tribes convert themselves from hunter-gatherers into stable agricultural communities, sometimes using "advanced technological tools," many hunter-gatherer communities refuse that choice on the ground that it would require them to work harder. Richard Lee quotes the Bushmen: "Why should we plant when there are so many mongomongo nuts in the world?"

Hunter-gatherers are often called "culturally inferior" for failing to produce a surplus that could protect them from the whims of nature. Sahlins suggests four reasons why they eschew surpluses. First, they are optimists. When there is food they tend to eat it all, even gorging themselves. The attitude seems to be that since food is abundant in nature, storage is not necessary; nature itself stores food here and there in the plants and animals, if you know where to find it. So even when storms or accidents deprive a community of food for a period of days or weeks, the results are rarely disastrous and you can always move on to the next place.

Second, hunter-gatherers are nomadic by choice. If they stored or carried food they would be tied to a specific place, or have their movements seriously slowed. For nomadic hunter-gatherers, "It is truly said that his wealth is a burden," says Sahlins. The fact of movement "rapidly depreciates the satisfactions of property."

In *Lost World of the Kalahari,* author Laurens van der Post has written about his inability to give gifts to the Bushmen: "Almost everything seemed likely to make life more difficult for them by adding to the litter and weight of their daily round. They themselves had practically no possessions: a loin strap, a skin blanket, and a leather satchel. There was nothing that they could not assemble in one minute, wrap up in their blankets or carry on their shoulders for a journey of a thousand miles. They had no sense of possession." (In modern society, of course, "possession" may be our central passion.)

Third, an economy based on storage would increase the Bushmen's impact on the environment beyond the present-day ethic of underuse. Surplus would also lead to population growth, which would threaten the community's mobility and increase vulnerability to natural calamities.

Fourth, the hunter's self-esteem is based on hunting. To accumulate surpluses would diminish the cultural and psychological importance of the hunter. It might also downplay the training of the young and produce a lazier society with fewer skills.

Sahlins does not argue that stone-age cultures are invulnerable to food shortages, but he does argue that hunter-gatherers are no more vulnerable than any other society. "What about the world today?" he asks. "One-third to one-half of humanity are said to go to bed hungry every night. Some twenty million [are] in the U.S. alone. In the Old Stone Age, the fraction must have been much smaller. *This* is the era of unprecedented hunger. Now, in the time of the greatest technical power, is starvation an institution. Reverse another venerable formula, the amount of hunger increases relatively and absolutely with the evolution of culture."

THE CREATION OF "POVERTY"

The Bushmen's lack of material wealth, which we call "poverty," is put into a different perspective by Sahlins:

> Possession of the necessary tools is general and knowledge of the required skills common. . . . Add in the liberal customs of sharing, for which hunters are properly famous, and all the people can usually participate in the going prosperity. . . . But of course this prosperity depends upon an objectively low standard of living . . . that the customary quota of consumables be set at a modest point . . . want not, lack not.
>
> Poverty is not a certain amount of goods, nor is it just a relation between means and ends; above all it is a relation between people. Poverty is a social status . . . it was not until culture neared the height of its material achievements that it erected a shrine to the Unattainable: Infinite Needs.

To bring the point to the present, it is worth noting the viewpoint of the Yupik (Eskimo) people of Alaska. In a publication by the Association of Village Council Presidents, edited by Art Davidson, *Does One Way of Life Have to Die So Another Can Live?* there was this comment on how modern economic systems have affected the creation of poverty:

Poverty has only recently been introduced to Native communities. . . . for thousands of years people subsisted from the land and ocean along the west coast of Alaska. It was a hard life, but it had none of the frustrations and stigmas of poverty, for the people were not poor. Living from the land sustained life and evolved the Yupik culture, a culture in which wealth was the common wealth of the people as provided by the earth. Whether food was plentiful or scarce among the people. This sharing created a bond between people that helped insure survival. Life was hard then, but people found life satisfying. Today life is getting easier, but it is no longer satisfying.

. . . With the first Russian traders came the idea of wealth and poverty. These new people added to the process of living the purpose of accumulation. Whether it was furs, money, land or the souls of converts, lines were drawn between people on the basis of what they had accumulated. . . . The new economic system . . . began replacing food and furs with cash, cooperation with competition, sharing with accumulating.

The Yupik give a recent example of what happened to them at Bristol Bay when the subsistence economy was replaced by a new cash economy:

Originally people subsisted from the land and sea; the tremendous salmon runs provided a reliable source of food. [Then] commercial fishing began with an attitude of get what you can. It was only a matter of time before urban politicians and outside economic interest permitted the salmon runs to be exploited nearly to extinction. The local people were left impoverished. Then the government became concerned. Then fishery research was called for, [and] "limited entry" demanded. Then food stamps were passed out to people who used to fish. Somehow or other Native people were expected to adapt their traditional ways to this western economic system. . . .

White men brought diseases like measles and syphilis, which killed thousands of our people. . . . It is not so well known that the economic impact of western civilization was every bit as devastating to the well being and spirit of the people . . . these new ways of doing things can be as disturbing to the life of a person or of a culture as the measles infection is to the life of a body. Fortunately a cure has been found for measles. A cure has not been found for our "poverty". . . . The attempted cures have involved ever-increased doses

of the western way of life in the hope that the new system will somehow successfully replace the old.

FAST FORWARD:
LEISURE IN TECHNOTOPIA

In the United States today, according to figures from Louis Harris and
Associates, the average work week is forty-seven hours. This is up from
forty hours, the average of a decade earlier. More than one-third of the
male employed population works longer than the average. According to
the U.S. Department of Labor, nearly six million men and more than one
million women work more than sixty hours per week at paid jobs. (This
does not include the added unpaid domestic work of most women.)

In certain job categories, such as self-employed farmers, entrepreneurs,
and professional people, the typical work week is sixty hours. The heads
of corporations average more than sixty hours of work per week.

• • •

The figures quoted above represent a marked improvement over the situation in 1850, the usual time period with which such figures are compared. At that time, the average work week was seventy hours, working
conditions were far worse, and the standard of living was much lower. So
compared with 1850, we are far better off today. But is that an appropriate
comparison? It was around 1850 that the worst excesses of the new industrialization were being visited upon workers, and created a new class
of urban working poor. Compared with 1850, we are bound to look good.

Going back to the Middle Ages, according to French sociologist Alain
Caillé, the average workday was 8½–16 hours, depending on the season.
But urban workers also had about 130 days of *no work:* holy days and vigils,
plus Sundays and some Saturdays. "In the countryside," said Caillé, "there
[were] only 180 days of real work." And "living standards" were arguably
as good for workers then as in the grim 1850s. As for Roman times, there
were some 150–200 public holidays per year. And back in the stone age?
(See Sahlins.)

So have things really improved? Those of us who enjoy the fruits of the
technological juggernaut have more stuff in our lives. We are cleaner and
we live longer. But if we compare ourselves to preindustrial societies, it is

arguable that we work harder than they did. In addition, our devotion to gathering and caring for commodities has created an extraordinary modern paradox: a scarcity of time, *loss* of leisure, and increase of stress amidst an environment of apparent abundance and wealth. A *decrease* in the quality of life and experience.

• • •

This paradox was addressed in a provocative series of articles in the *Los Angeles Times* entitled "The Harried Society," by reporter Kent MacDougall. He argued that modern times have not increased the amount of leisure in our lives, but diminished it:

> Back in 1609 when the Algonkin Indians discovered Henry Hudson sailing up their river, they were living off the fat of the land. They lived so well yet worked so little that the industrious Dutch considered them indolent savages and soon replaced their good life with feudalism. Today, along the Hudson River in New York, supposedly free citizens of the wealthiest society in the history of the world work longer and harder than any Algonkin Indians ever did, race around like rats in a maze, dodging cars, trucks, buses, bicycles, and each other, and dance to a frantic tempo destined to lead many to early deaths from stress and strain. . . . What went wrong? How, in the process of acquiring so much material wealth, did Americans manage to lose so much leisure?

MacDougall quotes the late anthropologist Peter Farb: "The fact is that high civilization is hectic, whereas primitive hunters and collectors of wild food . . . are among the most leisured people on Earth." And, says Farb, "they are among the best fed people on Earth and also among the healthiest."

MacDougall continues: "Work consumes as much of the average wage earner's time as it did a generation ago [actually, it takes more time now], while commuting to and from work takes more. And higher material living standards have so complicated Americans' lifestyles as to require them to spend more time at shopping, maintenance, and housework, leaving them less time to enjoy all the goods and recreational opportunities at their disposal. . . . In an age of high living standards, longer vacations, faster transportation, and supermarkets stuffed with convenience items, Americans somehow have wound up feeling more harried than ever."

THE ALLEGED SUPERIORITY OF MODERN
RESOURCE MANAGEMENT

On August 14, 1987, at the Big Cypress Seminole Indian Reservation, Florida, the trial began for Seminole Chief James Billy. He was charged with shooting a Florida panther while on a night hunt. The United States has charged that killing a Florida panther is a violation of the 1973 Endangered Species Act, and is punishable by one year in jail and a $10,000 fine. The Seminole tribe argues that since it is a sovereign nation, recognized as such by treaties with the United States, it can determine its own rules about taking wildlife. Secondly, says the tribe, the treaties that arranged for the Seminoles to cede land to the U.S. also guaranteed the Indians the right to continue their traditional subsistence activities at their own discretion. (Hundreds of treaties with American Indian tribes guaranteed that Indian hunting and fishing would not be subject to U.S. law. This condition was of major importance in getting the Indians to cede land, as it assured the continued viability of the traditional economy. Now, however, most such guarantees are under assault by commercial fishing or ranching interests and by U.S. agencies, which claim that Indians should be bound by the same rules as the rest of Americans, and that the treaties are ancient history. That the treaties are not as "ancient" as many binding real-estate agreements dating back to the early 1800s is considered irrelevent. Treaties with Indians are not given the same respect.)

In the Seminole case, the United States now denies, as it has in other cases brought against Indian hunting and fishing rights, that Seminole law can supersede U.S. law. The U.S. argues it needs to control hunting and fishing to manage and protect wildlife population. But, in an interview with NPR radio, Chief Billy pointed out, "Our tribal laws existed for hundreds of years before the U.S. existed. We are a sovereign nation; the United States has acknowledged this [in treaties and other proceedings]." Billy says that when he shot the animal, he was just shooting two eyes in the dark, thinking it was another kind of cougar. He adds that in any event, the Endangered Species Act is an absurdity when it comes to Indians: "Indians are the best conservators of any natural resource and we have been for thousands of years. . . . The government is attempting to blame the Seminoles for the destruction of a species, but the real reason the Florida panther is endangered is the overdevelopment of south Florida. The reason is all these condominium communities, and the construction of Freeway I-95 right through the swamp, and then the highway across the Everglades. It has nothing to do with our hunting practices. It has to do with yours."

•   •   •

It seems quite obvious—almost self-evident—that native cultures that have lived successfully in one place for millennia have been abiding by successful economic practices, including wildlife and resource conservation. But if we listen to our Western scientists and governments, we would think that native societies can barely manage another day without computers, quotas, satellite mapping, and "maximum sustainable yield" analysis. How, I wonder, do scientists rationalize how natives have survived for thousands of years? Instinct?

The assumption that our modern system of wildlife and resource management is more efficient—despite the fact that we "manage" without any understanding of the environment or the way the people have managed prior to our arrival—is not only hubristic, but racist.

In Chapter 4 I mentioned how computer models are being rapidly introduced for resource management in the Arctic North. A high percentage of American and Canadian government "aid" to the Indian and Inuit peoples of the Arctic regions now comes in the form of computer training. That this mode of wildlife and resource management has a regrettable negative effect on the traditional relationships between native peoples and animals is rarely considered.

Once an intimate knowledge based on close observation and centuries-old teachings, the relationship among humans and animals is now based on computer printouts, and has thus become a fast-paced, objective, abstract, quantitative kind of knowledge. This is destructive to Indian cultures and traditions. Within a generation, it is likely to shatter a mode of knowledge that survived for millennia. But beyond the damage done to cultures, recent evidence suggests that the objective-scientific-quantitative computer management systems rarely improve upon the native conservation and management systems. In fact, the modern systems often prove disastrous.

University of Alberta anthropologist Milton M. R. Freeman is among a growing number of scientists who have begun to organize resistance to the idea that our system of economic management has a great deal to offer traditional native communities.

Freeman is particularly peeved at wildlife biologists. Speaking at the 1984 meeting of the Western Regional Science Association (in Monterey,

California), Freeman said: "An explicit faith in the correctness of the scientific method is so integral a part of the professional formulation of wildlife biologists that the limits of that particular system of belief are only learned, often much later in life, as a result of experience gained in the non-professional world." Freeman recounts instances in which wildlife biologists ignored traditional practices, only to find them a more effective way of maintaining viability among animal species.

One example concerned caribou hunting on the Ellesmere Islands of Arctic Canada. Canadian wildlife managers told the Inuit that they should hunt only large and/or male caribou, and only a few animals from each herd. The Inuit argued that this practice contradicted their traditional relationship with the animals and would destroy the caribou herds, but their pleas were ignored. The result was as the Inuit predicted. Though their new limit was only twenty-six kills per year—far less than the Inuit had hunted before—the formerly abundant population dropped sharply. Why?

According to Freeman, "The Inuit hold that each small group of Peary caribou is a social group and there is good reason for those particular animals being together. Inuit hunters point out that given the marginality of the environment for herbivores, older/larger animals are important to the survival of the group. These older animals have experience and they have the physical strength enabling them to dig through the snow for food. Old animals are also more passive relative to the more nervous younger animals or pregnant females and this behavioral trait has a calming effect on the younger animals in the group."

A second example concerns the proposal to permit sport hunting of musk-ox in the Arctic. Again, only the male musk-ox would be harvested; since the best "trophy animals" were the old, biologically "superfluous" bulls, the managers were sure the hunting would not negatively affect the musk-ox population. The Inuit said otherwise. They argued that the musk-ox are highly social animals. The old males are not "surplus" at all. They play an important social role at certain times of the year, becoming the regathering point after periods of dispersal during rutting. They function like "elders," according to the Inuit. Again, the Inuit turned out to be correct: The government policy was eventually reversed.

Freeman points out that this "native critique of the management proposal was based upon essentially esoteric knowledge," from direct observance and traditional belief, since the Inuit did not actually use the musk-ox for meat or for anything else. Simply by sharing the land with the animals for thousands of years, they got to know their habits and social structures:

For our present purposes, it is sufficient to observe that as in the case of the Peary caribou example, behavioral knowledge of the species was the critical point of the Inuit position, contrasted with an inexact quantitative perspective proposed by the game management service. . . . In reality both Native systems and western science rest on the same foundation—namely empirical evidence. Both systems place value on the systematic accumulation of detailed observations and the abstraction of norms from disparate data sets. At this point, however, the two systems begin to diverge. The Native system assesses deviation from the norm in a qualitative sense: e.g., animals become fewer, or fatter, or more excited, there are fewer calves in the herd, more injured bulls, more barren cows, etc. . . . The sum total of the community's empirically based knowledge is awesome in breadth and detail, and often stands in marked contrast to the attenuated data available from scientific studies of these same populations.

The native management systems are also deeply ingrained in cultural practice, passed down from generation to generation. I have previously quoted from Dr. H. A. Feit concerning the exquisitely detailed management of wildlife resources practiced by the James Bay Cree of northern Ontario, including the appointment of "stewards" and the careful study and division of hunting regions.

Dr. Feit has also studied some of the more subtle practices, including the proper rituals used in killing and cooking an animal. Most of the rituals are designed to demonstrate "reciprocity between man and animal . . . which includes respect for the needs of animals to survive as a population, and which is complemented by animals respecting the needs for humans to subsist and survive as well."

Dr. Feit described the Cree methods of hunting beaver as a further demonstration of respect, as well as impeccable conservation practice. One method of hunting the beaver was during daylight, by trapping. The second method, at night, was to surround a beaver lodge, where 50 or 100 may reside, and to drive them out to the waiting hunters. The first system was not as efficient in terms of man-hours per beaver caught. But, said Feit, "the important finding was that while waking the beaver could permit the capture of more beaver in total, it was used only under special circumstances, relatively rarely . . . a clear indicator that hunters' choices limit their harvests, rather than inability to harvest more beaver. . . . More beaver could be caught if [the second] technique was widely used." The Cree were deliberately underusing their resources, according to Feit, for

conservation purposes, and ingraining this practice with traditional teachings about when to make one choice or another.

• • •

Professor Freeman argues that the main problem with Western wildlife
biology, as with most scientific interventions in age-old economic management systems, is that the basic operating assumptions are inappropriate
to the situation at hand. For example, says Freeman, most Western biologists—college trained, usually white, and usually lacking direct knowledge of the environment or cultural group they are researching—will tend
to view wildlife as a resource, and the harvesting of animals as strictly an
economic activity. They adopt the capitalist terminology of "maximum
sustainable yield" (the number beyond which a herd might begin to diminish). The biologist essentially acts as a resource manager, like a corporate functionary, whose goal is to maximize production and contribute
to profit. No effort is made to become sensitive to alternative views stem-
ming from native traditions and culture.

To native people, animals are never viewed strictly in quantitative
terms, or as "resources." They are part of a web of living systems that includes relationships among themselves and between them and human
beings. These systems are passed on among natives through historical
teachings and stories; they are further articulated through religious rituals;
and they are part of native systems of social structure, status, and psychology. The ebbs and flows of the animal population, therefore, are inseparable from the continuous activities of the people. While it is possible
that the scientific "maximum sustainable yield" might turn out to be very
close to the numbers of animals the natives finally kill and use, the conceptual relationship to the animals, and processes involved in making
those decisions, are entirely different. Furthermore, for native societies to
adopt the Western conceptual processes could cause grave injury to the
continued vitality of native culture and tradition, since their economic
well-being is inexorably linked to their religious, social, and cultural
practices.

When native societies decide to accept the advice of Western biologists,
and employ Western-style wildlife management techniques, we tend to
consider them to be acting rationally. American institutions become willing to invest. The World Bank offers development funds. And yet the
Western mode, by failing to include the more holistic dimensions of native
thought and practice, may ultimately prove to be the less rational approach. It is surely less rational, in the long run, for native people.

As discussed earlier, indigenous societies tend to not maximize production, and for very good reason. They deliberately underproduce. In fact, according to Professor Freeman (in basic agreement with Marshall Sahlins), when fortuitous circumstances do result in a surprise surplus, the favored manner of dealing with it is *not* to store it or trade it. Instead, it is consumed as a feast. "Widespread sharing and community feasting is a characteristic feature of all hunting and fishing societies," says Freeman. "Moreover, in such societies there are values and sanctions to expressly guard against individual accumulation or hoarding of resources, and such societies have elaborate systems of kinship and social relationships that prescribe the channels along which the resources shall flow so that equanimity prevails in the face of the threat posed by unequal access to valued resources." Unlike industrial and technological societies, where the primary purpose of economic activity is to maximize profit, "the purpose of nearly all economic activity in such foraging societies is directed toward the reproduction of the social group." So, where capitalist management systems emphasize numbers and individual gain, native management emphasizes relationships among humans and animals, believing that balance is what feeds people and helps animals thrive. There is no such thing as "maximum sustainable yield" in the native economic outlook.

• • •

In order to support native communities in their efforts to maintain traditional economic practices, Dr. Milton Freeman helped organize the Working Group on Traditional Knowledge, Conservation, and Rural Development, of the International Union for the Conservation of Nature and Natural Resources. Based in Geneva, this group may be the first effective organization of scientists who take seriously the traditional methods of managing wildlife and resources.

Though the organization has only existed for a few years, it has shown tremendous vigor. A long list of programs are underway; their study projects include traditional knowledge of coastal systems, traditional fisheries management among South Pacific islanders, ecological and hunting practices of peoples of the Northern Circumpolar region, traditional agroforestry and conservation practices among the tribal peoples of New Guinea, practices of microclimate management among farming peoples, the preservation of the traditional knowledge of Native Alaskans, and the use of fire in agriculture among the Aborigines.

The urgency of the task at hand was articulated by Working Group member Dr. Bob Johannes:

Much of what we know about the nature and management of natural resources in developed countries can be found in libraries.
[Among native communities], however, much of it resides only in
the heads of older men and women in the villages. Scientists have
come to realize within the past few years that such knowledge concerning the forest, the garden, the plains, and the sea, is both ency-
clopedic and of major scientific value, particularly as it relates to
natural resource management. But it is being lost rapidly as a result
of westernization, industrialization, urbanization, and the concom-
itant alienation of the young from their traditions. . . . Recording
this knowledge is an urgent matter. Allowing it to vanish amounts
to throwing away centuries of priceless practical experience.

Johannes warns of certain pitfalls, however, including the fact that
many researchers do not exhibit respect for the peoples they are studying,
often rushing to get answers and causing the communities internal conflict
about whether or not to participate.

Also, according to Working Group member Diane Bell of Australian
National University, in certain societies such as the Aborigines, much information is the province of women, who tend to refuse to report it to
men.

Finally, there is the major issue cited by the Working Group of scientists' failure to recognize the rights of the native peoples they deal with.
When Western researchers have discovered, for example, a medicinal
herb's curative powers, the scientists have often sold the information for a
large profit to Western corporations without any corresponding benefit for
the natives. In fact, the scientists usually leave the scene and do not return
to aid the same native peoples when their lands are assaulted by outsiders.
Many examples of this can be found among the native peoples of the Amazon. Though many scientists gleaned profitable information from the Indians of the region, few have stood up to defend the natives who are now
under direct assault.

When they ignore the concrete political situations that Indians face,
Western scientists are merely mimicking corporate amorality. Indians,
their knowledge, and their environment fall within the Western definition
of "resource," and are thus subject to exploitation. The idea that Western
intervention is somehow improving the lot of the natives—their government, their health, their economics—is self-aggrandizement at best. More
likely it is a public relations mask designed to shield the scientists, the corporations, and you and me, from a true recognition of the horror of what
is happening.

PART IV
WORLD WAR AGAINST
THE INDIANS

*I*N THE LATER *stages of an epic worldwide struggle, the forces of Western economic development are assaulting the remaining native peoples of the planet, whose presence obstructs their progress. In some places the assault is violent; elsewhere, as here in the United States, it is legalistic. Given the lack of public awareness and the misreporting by the media, a "final solution" for the native problem is deemed likely. Upon the ultimate outcome of this battle will depend whether a living alternative world view, rooted in an ancient connection with the Earth, can continue to express what is insane and suicidal about the Western technological project.*

15

THE IMPERATIVE TO DESTROY TRADITIONAL INDIAN GOVERNMENTS

The Case of the Hopi and Navajo

THE PREVAILING VIEW that native peoples are too backward to create democratic governments has been a primary rationalization by
which Westerners have historically justified intervening in their societies.
Our stated goal has been to raise the "primitives" to our own higher level.

However, as discussed in Chapter 13, the evidence actually shows that
most of the governmental systems of the Indian nations of North America
were non-imperial, non-hierarchical, and democratic. This applies to traditionally nomadic nations as well as sedentary agricultural nations. Outside intervention into these democratic systems was not to help them; it
was to destroy them.

From an American viewpoint, there were three problems with nearly
all traditional Indian governments: 1) communal ownership of all land
and religious strictures against selling it, 2) consensual decision-making,
and 3) lack of a central hierarchical authority, who had power to make
binding deals. When Americans made contact with Indians, we wanted to
make deals for land and for resources. And we wanted the deals *now*. The
traditional forms of Indian governance represented a roadblock to our
deal-making and expansion: They were slow, they were democratic, and
they would never agree to give up land. So they had to go.

During some periods of American history, we used military force to overpower Indians and drive them off the lands we wanted. Later, we succeeded in coercing the Indians into treaties, which we then broke or ignored. Recently, we have subverted traditional Indian governments through manipulations, in which we act as if we are helping, but we aren't. In certain ways, every story in this book about Indian-white interaction is an example of the attempted disruption of Indian sovereignty and autonomy. But this chapter explores the issue in detail, using the examples of the Hopi and Navajo of the American Southwest. I discuss these two nations for three reasons:

- First, they represent contrasting traditional governmental systems, appropriate for very different lifestyles. The Navajo are traditionally a nomadic people, and their government system is typical of nomadic communities throughout the world. The Hopi, on the other hand, were (and are) stable village dwellers with an agricultural base who have lived in a series of independent city-states.

- Second, outside intervention has thrown these two societies into an apparent conflict, which has been wildly misreported in the American press as a conflict between tribal peoples. It is actually a conflict between "puppet governments," created and controlled by the United States.

- Third, the Navajo and Hopi peoples are presently suffering one of the most atrocious acts against Indian people ever to take place on this continent: the forced removal of 10,000 Navajo and Hopi from their ancestral homes. That this displacement, which is having horrible consequences upon the people, could happen today—more than a century after General Custer and Andrew Jackson—reflects the essential continuity of American attitudes to this time.

DECLARATION OF INDEPENDENCE

On October 28, 1979, a community of Navajo Indians who live in and around a place called Big Mountain, in the northern desert of Arizona, issued a declaration of independence from the United States, the State of Arizona, and the Navajo tribe as it is officially recognized by the United States government. That this declaration of independence was scarcely reported in the United States press (as compared, say, with similar declarations from Latvia, Lithuania, Estonia, and other Eastern European nations) is further indication of the problem Indians face with the media.

The precipitating issue was U.S. Public Law 93-531, which requires the relocation of some 10,000 Navajo and Hopi Indians from land they've been occupying their entire lives, which has also been occupied by their grandparents and many generations of ancestors going back hundreds of years. The new law changes the status of what has been called the Joint Use Area (JUA) in which Big Mountain is located and which the Hopi and Navajo have shared. Under the new law, half the JUA becomes part of the Hopi reservation and half becomes Navajo. Whoever is on the wrong side of the new partition line has to move, usually to off-reservation border towns such as Winslow, Gallup, and Tuba City.

The people who live in the Joint Use Area are among the largest self-sufficient communities still existing within U.S. boundaries. They have lived in a traditional subsistence manner, raising sheep and growing what they need. Many are old; many do not speak English. Most have never held a wage-earning job; they barely relate to the money economy.

To move these Indians will ultimately cost U.S. taxpayers about a quarter of a billion dollars in direct costs, plus another three-quarters of a billion dollars in indirect social costs. Among the Indians who have already been relocated, the rate of death, sickness, alcoholism, depression, suicide, and poverty is extraordinarily high. They bitterly miss their desert homes. They have never lived in cities, or paid gas bills, or dealt with welfare agencies. Some have already lost their new homes to loan sharks. Others simply abandon them and return to the desert, only to find their prior homes bulldozed, and to face yet another forced relocation.

The United States government portrays itself in this issue as a peacemaker, and blames the problem on an "age-old land dispute between the Hopi and Navajo." Whenever an occasional press report has appeared, it has accepted the official line on the story, sporting headlines such as INDIAN RANGE WARS, and featuring bitter quotes from Hopi and Navajo tribal chairmen attacking each other.

But if you actually go to that desert, which is about as far as you can get from the United States (save Alaska) and still be within it, you will not find conflict between the Hopi and Navajo who live there. What dispute exists is not among them, but between the U.S.-created Tribal Councils.

To the people living at Big Mountain, and to all traditional Hopi and Navajo, these tribal councils are as alien as George Bush is to a Micronesian islander. In traditional Hopi and Navajo government systems there was no such thing as "tribal councils" or any central governmental authority. The traditional people don't recognize the authority of these councils; instead they say the councils are artificial inventions of U.S. policy. What's really going on, say the natives, is that the U.S. and the puppet councils want to kick people off the land to make way for large-scale ranching, coal strip-mining, and uranium exploration.

"There's no dispute between the Navajo and Hopi," according to Hopi elder Thomas Banyacya, "it's the Tribal Councils and the big energy companies and the U.S. government who are in dispute against the Navajo and Hopi who live on the land. The Great Spirit didn't want that land dug up to create nuclear weapons. If you were born on that land then that land is your home. . . . The [Hopi] prophecies say the Navajo will intermarry and trade with us, and we'll hold the land together."

The declaration of independence was signed by sixty-four elders of the Independent Dine Nation at Big Mountain, with Roberta Blackgoat as chairperson. An excerpt of it reads as follows:

> The U.S. government and the Navajo Tribal Council have violated the sacred laws of the Dine [Navajo] Nation . . . [dividing] the indigenous people by boundaries of politics, Euro-American education, modernization, and Christianity. The U.S. denies our right to exist as indigenous people on Mother Earth. . . . Our sacred shrines have been destroyed. Our Mother Earth is raped by the exploitation of coal, uranium, oil, natural gas and helium. . . . We speak for the winged beings, the four-legged beings, and those who have gone before us and the coming generation. We seek no changes in our livelihood because this natural life is our only known survival and it's our sacred law.

FIRST CAME THE HOPI

American anthropologists like to make a big deal of the cultural differences between the Navajo and the Hopi. One well-published anthropologist once told me, "There's a greater cultural difference between a Navajo and a Hopi than between either of them and a New Yorker." He made the remark with such certainty that I took it on faith. But after I'd spent enough time out there in the desert it dawned on me that colonizing cultures like to exaggerate the differences and conflicts among the colonized. It makes it somehow okay for us to be there. It rationalizes our military intervention, and makes *us* the good guys.

This is not to say there are no differences. Most obvious is that the Hopi, for at least a millennium, have been stable village dwellers who live by agriculture, while the Navajo have been nomadic sheepherders. But as we will see, the similarities are greater than the differences.

The Hopi people are directly descended from the Anasazi cliff dwellers who inhabited Mesa Verde (in the southwest corner of Colorado) and, before that, Chaco Canyon (in New Mexico), for at least 10,000 years, according to most archeologists. There they built their spectacular multistory apartment villages, some of which are still standing. For reasons that are unclear (the presently prevailing assumption is drought), the Anasazi people left Mesa Verde and headed south and west, eventually forming some twenty pueblo communities in what is now Arizona and New Mexico. The group that became the Hopi have been living in what is now central Arizona since at least 1000 A.D. The Hopi village of Old Oraibi, built in 1100 A.D., is believed to be the oldest continuously occupied community in North America. Other Hopi villages are clustered within about fifty miles on three high mesas in the desert, where the beauty and efficiency of the traditional pueblo-style apartments still amaze visitors.

The Hopi farmlands surround the villages within a five- to ten-mile radius. Most Hopi farmers commute to the fields in the traditional manner of Pueblo people: They run.

The Hopi are often described as "the world's most proficient dry farmers," since for centuries they have been successfully growing corn, beans, and squash in a desert that receives less than ten inches of rainfall annually. The Hopi credit their improbable success to their spiritual practices, which place all of life within a cycle of Earth-related ceremonies and activities that help them know exactly when to plant, how to place the seeds, and exactly where the seed will be able to draw from the underground water table. Hopi ceremonies, they say, not only bring abundance from the sand but also "keep the whole world in balance."

Traditionally, the Hopi keep only the number of animals needed for their immediate family. In fact, one distinction between the traditional Hopi and the new breed of "progressive" Hopi is that the latter practice large-scale herding and ranching on "private" land. Another distinction is that most of the new ranchers are Hopi who have converted to Mormonism, and have abandoned traditional cultural and religious practices.

Hopi City-States

In the traditional Hopi system, there was no such thing as a "tribal council." Nor, for that matter, was there any kind of central government that united all of the Hopi people. Since at least the tenth century, each Hopi village has been a totally autonomous self-governing entity. The bonds among the villages are cultural and spiritual but not "political" in the sense that we tend to think of it. The villages are bound together, but in ways unfamiliar to us.

Each Hopi village contains one to four distinct clans and each clan has a *kikmongwi,* the nearest thing to a leader or chief that the Hopi know. This *kikmongwi* is selected by a partially secret process, based on religious training, knowledge of the ceremonial cycles, possession of certain objects, heritage, and consensual agreement of all the people of the village. Though the Hopi reckon descent and property ownership by matrilineal means, the *kikmongwi* is usually (but not always) male. There is no real authority vested in the *kikmongwis,* except insofar as they are respected as teachers, wise persons, and reliable sources of traditional religious knowledge. They cannot order anyone to do anything. Decisions are made in community meetings, in which the *kikmongwis* play a facilitating role.

All of the Hopi clans gather together many times each year for religious events and celebrations. Each clan has a very specific and distinct role to play in each event, which means that all of the clans are needed to complete the entire Hopi religious cycle, and all the clans are equally interdependent. So the Hopi Nation is actually a collaboration or collection of disparate clans, for the purpose of religious, cultural, and political activity.

When there are matters of great importance that affect all of the Hopi people, the *kikmongwis* meet to talk things over. There is no leader in this process. The *kikmongwis* are there to share information and to develop a shared understanding of the situation. They do not take any kind of unified action, except occasionally to join forces to make a public statement.

As for laws, the Hopi say that the only laws are "nature's laws," which they claim to protect, on behalf of all the people on the planet. These laws can never be changed. One such law is that land is never sold. Another is that land is never opened up to take anything from within it. Those particular laws, which traditional Hopi continue to observe, are most threatening to the United States of America. Similar laws among the Navajo are similarly threatening.

ARRIVAL OF THE NAVAJO

The Navajo are an Athabascan people, directly related to the Apache and to the Dene Indians of northern Canada, from whom they descended. The Navajo and Apache migrated from what is now Canada in about 1400 A.D. While the Apache continued southward, the Navajo adopted a range to the east of the Hopi villages, and to the north and west of the other Pueblo peoples who already inhabited New Mexico.

Like some other nomadic peoples, the Navajo were given to raiding. During the first century of their presence in New Mexico they had skirmishes with several of the southern Pueblo peoples, though apparently not with the Hopi.

When the Spanish showed up around 1500, they conquered the Pueblos, under the guise of protecting them from "marauding Athabascans." The Spanish were also "peacemakers."

"Such explanations were often used to justify Spanish conquest," according to Roxanne Ortiz, author of *Roots of Resistance,* "yet the Pueblo people frequently went to live with the Navajo during times of crisis, and some of the Navajo wintered with the Pueblo. . . . There is ample evidence to show that the two peoples were not enemies."

By contrast, *everyone* hated the Spanish. By 1690, the Navajo were hosting a series of secret meetings among all the tribes, which resulted in the Navajo joining with the Pueblo and the Hopi in a simultaneous revolt that overthrew Spanish rule and temporarily reestablished the sovereignty of the individual tribes. Even after the Spanish reasserted their domination two decades later, relationships among the tribes were peaceful and cooperative.

The Spanish were finally eliminated from the scene altogether at the conclusion of the U.S.-Mexican War, when the Treaty of Guadalupe Hidalgo was signed in 1854. Among the notable elements of that treaty (not taught in U.S. schools) was that all the Pueblo peoples, including the Hopi, were officially recognized as sovereign independent nations. But as soon as the treaty-makers went home, white settlers, most of them Mormons, began encroaching onto sovereign Hopi lands. This led to serious friction between the Hopi and the whites.

Hopi resistance is usually expressed passively. But such is not the case for the Navajo. Navajo bands repeatedly attacked the white settlements until General Kit Carson led a huge cavalry brigade against them. In a series of horrible scorched-earth actions that destroyed all the Navajo animals and orchards, Carson eventually trapped some 8,500 Navajo in a canyon and starved them. Thousands died; finally the survivors yielded, culminating in the forced "Long March" of 1864, across New Mexico to an internment camp at Fort Sumner.

Most of the Navajo remained there for four years. Some, however, had evaded Carson's capture. Others escaped and fled west toward Hopi country, creating the first significant pressure on the Hopi from the Navajo in more than four centuries of contact.

When the rest of the Navajo were finally released from internment, they were given two sheep each, told to give up being nomads, and placed onto the most barren region of the southwest desert, on a tiny, dry reservation. Unable to survive on this land the Navajo headed toward their fellow clanspeople who had moved near the Hopi, thereby increasing pressure upon the agricultural people.

Despite all this, the Hopi *kikmongwis* were less concerned about the Navajo, with whom they had worked things out in the past, than they were about the white settlers on Hopi farmlands in the desert, and about the U.S. government's increased meddling. The Hopi argued that their status as an independent nation was guaranteed by the Treaty of Guadalupe Hidalgo, and that the United States should live up to its pledge to keep the whites out. But this was the era of Manifest Destiny. Instead of ejecting the white intruders from Hopi land, the government response was to unilaterally create a reservation for the Hopi. They ignored the Treaty of Guadalupe Hidalgo, defied Hopi sovereign status, and reduced Hopi territory by 60 percent. What's more, *a portion of the land that the U.S. declared a Hopi reservation was actually land that the Navajo were living upon.* This is the same land that, many years later, became a Joint Use Area for the two tribes, to the chagrin of the Hopi. This is the very area that is currently in dispute. The U.S. never did anything to recover Hopi land that was illegally occupied by whites.

HOPI-NAVAJO SYMBIOSIS

Throughout this period, relations between the Navajo and Hopi, thrown into uncomfortably close quarters by decisions of the United States, remained surprisingly good. The most exhaustive and scholarly study of their relations, a 1978 Indian Law Resource Center report titled *Report to the Kikmongwis,* found that as late as 1884 the Bureau of Indian Affairs (BIA) agent in the region was reporting the following to Washington: ". . . Trifling quarrels arise between members of the two tribes; these are usually caused by careless herding of the young Navajos who allow herds to overrun outlying Hopi gardens . . . but the best of good feeling generally exists between these tribes; they constantly mingle at festivals, dances, etc. . . . The Hopi barters his surplus melons with his old pastoral neighbors for their mutton and wool."

The differences between the Navajo and the Hopi actually created a complementarity that brought them closer. Where traditional Hopi life is connected to farming, Navajo spiritual and economic life is intertwined with the health and well-being of their animals—horses, goats, and especially sheep. This created an organic symbiosis between the tribes: Meat, wool, and woven goods were exchanged for corn, squash, melons, and pottery. It was a business connection, which also became social. Considerable intermarriage ensued.

The nomadic Navajo eschewed the mesa-top Hopi villages, but moved their families and herds through the desert from one strategically placed hogan (the traditional Navajo round wood-mud shelter) to another, along routes chosen for the location of hundreds of sacred sites: wells, rock formations, and places where certain medicinal and religious herbs were known to grow.

While the Hopi and Navajo economies were different (but complementary), in more subtle areas, the cultures were (and are) actually quite alike. For example, both Hopi and Navajo cultures place religious practices at the heart of everything in life. Both invest enormous spiritual power in the land, and regard it as a living being. For both tribes, to open up land to obtain minerals, or to disfigure the earth, or to attempt to exploit it for personal use, were unthinkable acts—until they were performed by whites. (In this respect all American Indian cultures are alike. The land itself is alive and it sustains all creatures, including humans. All people hold the land, water, animals, and forests in common; no one owns them.)

The political structures of the Hopi and Navajo also have much in common. Like the traditional Hopi, the traditional Navajo never had anything remotely resembling a "tribal council." Like the Hopi, all Navajo political power was local, decentralized, fluid, and consensual.

Among the Navajo, the main political unit is the autonomous extended family, which may number from 20 to 300 people who collaborate on all economic and spiritual aspects of life. Each extended family has a "headman" (a BIA term) who is actually almost always a woman. As with the Hopi, descent among the Navajo is reckoned matrilineally. Navajo households, sheep, and general family welfare fall within the domain of the Navajo women. Even today, among traditional families, it's the women who control the herds. It is not surprising that the three major violent incidents against United States agents, attempting to enforce various stages of the relocation, involved women over sixty years old carrying rifles.

Like the Hopi, the Navajo Nation had no central authoritative power. Navajo relate strongly to each other as a people, but their cohesion is based upon common roots, language, culture, ceremonies, geography, and economy. There are often "tribal" gatherings for celebration, trade, or common defense, but within this nation, decision-making was traditionally decentralized, and spread out among all the extended families. At least that's the way it was until 1923, when the United States government directly intervened in the traditional governmental process, creating a totally artificial

Tribal Council. The council was desperately needed, not by the Navajo, but by the United States. Its only function was to "legally" approve the leasing of oil and minerals to Standard Oil, something the traditional governance system would never have permitted.

THE AMERICANIZATION OF INDIAN GOVERNMENTS

The United States had a big headache. We wanted to get at the gold, coal, oil, copper, tin, minerals, and land. We wanted to work things out with the Indians but it was difficult to deal with nations that had no central authorities, no one to make binding decisions for the whole population. It was hard to find out where all the people met and who was in charge. Who could sign on the dotted line? These governments, such as they were, were so very slow, and they operated by "natural laws" that were immutable; and they viewed the land as Being or Spirit, never to be sold or bartered. It was clear the situation needed to change, and we set out to do that in a variety of ways. It began with the children.

Step 1. Removal of the Children

The United States undertook the forced removal of Indian children from their families, and placed them in distant boarding schools, for "the benefit of the Indians." We argued that this would help the children break away from boundaries of a culture that diminished the children's ability *and desire* to partake in American society. In each part of the country, the policy was executed in slightly different ways. Among the Hopi, it began in the 1880s when the cavalry moved the kids to BIA schools at Keams Canyon, Arizona. There the Hopi children were forbidden to speak the Hopi language, to wear Hopi clothes, or to keep their traditional long-haired styles. They were given English names to replace their Hopi names and all Hopi customs were outlawed. All Hopi children were required to undergo religious indoctrination, much of it by Mormons. (Mormonism is now the dominant religion among the "progressive" [non-traditional] Hopi.)

Mormonism teaches, among other things, that dark skin is a punishment from God. The *Book of Mormon* says, ". . . after they [the Indians] had dwindled in unbelief, they became a dark, and loathsome, and a filthy people, full of idleness and all manner of abominations." If Indians accept the Mormon church, however, ". . . many generations shall not pass away among them, save they shall be a white and delightsome people." In other words, accept Mormonism and you start turning white.

When Hopi parents resisted sending their kids to schools, the cavalry tore the children from their parents' arms and then arrested the parents. This policy continued into the 1930s.

The forced separation of Indian children from their parents was very successful from the United States' point of view. It created a whole generation of Indians trained to hate their Indian-ness, and indoctrinated them with American religious, social, and economic values. These children were the Indians the United States would later reward with "tribal leadership."

Step 2. The Dawes (Allotment) Act of 1887

While the kids were being torn from their parents' arms, the land ownership question was addressed very bluntly by the Allotment Act of 1887. Also known as the Dawes Act, it was named after the congressman who made no bones about its purpose: ". . . breaking up of the tribal land mass."

The Dawes Act, which applied to most of the Indian tribes in the country, took the remaining tribal lands and divided them into 160-acre parcels. The parcels were then to be applied for by individual Indian families, who would thenceforth own the land in their individual names, and could sell it as well. Surplus land, i.e., tribal land left over from the 160-acre allotments distributed to individual members, was controlled, leased, and sold by the U.S. government, invariably to whites.

Amazingly, the Dawes Act, like the boarding school removal policy and most other Indian-related acts right up through the Alaska Native Claims Settlement Act, was considered a liberal reform that would benefit the Indians. In the late nineteenth century, the solution to "the Indian problem" was "assimilation," which in turn required the development of individualism and a sense of competitive economic self-interest among Indians. Such arguments were actively voiced by the leadership of a growing "Friends of the Indians" movement throughout the country, of which Dawes was an outspoken member.

Another leader of "Friends of the Indians" was Dr. Merrill E. Gates, the president of Amherst College. In *The White Man's Indian*, Robert Berkhofer, Jr., quotes a speech by Gates about the virtues of individual private property for Indians:

To bring [the Indian] out of savagery into citizenship . . . we need to awaken in him wants. In his dull savagery, he must be touched by the wings of the divine angel of discontent. . . . Discontent with the teepee and the Indian camp . . . is needed to get the Indian out of the blanket and into trousers—and trousers with a pocket in them, and with a pocket that aches to be filled with dollars!

Here is an immense moral training that comes from the use of property. Like a little child who learns the true delight of giving away only by first earning and possessing what it gives, the Indian must learn that he has no right to give until he has earned, and that he has no right to eat until he has worked for his bread. Our teachers upon the reservations know that frequently their lessons . . . are effaced and counteracted by the [Indians'] old communal instincts and customs. . . We have found it necessary, as one of the first steps in developing a stronger personality in the Indian, to make him responsible for property. Even if he learns its value only by losing it, and going without it until he works for more, the educational process has begun.

Senator Dawes himself used similar language to explain his sponsorship of an act that had, as its principle virtue, the creation of selfishness. He is quoted in *Blood of the Land* by Rex Weyler:

The head chief [of the Cherokees] told us that there was not a family in that whole nation that had not a home of its own. There was not a pauper in the nation, and the nation did not owe a dollar. . . . Yet the defect of the system was apparent. They [the Indians] have got as far as they can go, because they own their land in common. . . . There is no enterprise to make your home any better than that of your neighbor's. There is no selfishness, which is at the bottom of civilization. Until this people consent to give up their lands and divide them among their citizens so that each can own the land he cultivates, they will not make much progress.

The "progress" the Dawes Act finally achieved among Indians in this country was considerable. It lost them more than 60 percent of their tribal land base, plus most of the individually held allotted lands, due to fraud by white buyers. It created poor economic management, such as the need to sell to pay off debts, in an economic system that was alien to them. If you add to this the Indian lands that have been leased to white economic interests, the estimated total loss of the Indian land base was about 90 percent.

The Allotment Act may have been the greatest single blow to Indian sovereignty ever in this country, since it struck at the heart of the fundamental collectivism of Indian economic and political life. Once the traditional collective ways were broken, the individual Indian was easier to manipulate and coerce. That process is being repeated now in Alaska via the Alaska Native Claims Settlement Act, as we will see in the next chapter.

Curiously, the Allotment Act did not have as much effect upon the Hopi and Navajo as among other Indian nations. Communal landholding was so ingrained among the Hopi in particular that when allotment surveyors came out to measure off the Hopi plots by day, the Indians would surreptitiously remove the stakes and markings at night. As for the Navajo, the land they were given following their release from Kit Carson's concentration camp was an area of desert so barren that no whites were interested. But other processes proved just as subversive to both the Hopi and Navajo.

Step 3. The Creation of Puppet Governments

The next stage of U.S. assault took direct aim at Indian governmental structures. Among the Navajo, the key date was 1921, when Standard Oil found oil on Navajo land. Up to that time, most mineral and oil explorations were very small-scale and tentative. An 1880s law was still on the books, which stipulated that all mineral and oil prospectors needed to obtain leases from "the authority of the council speaking for the Indians." But among the Navajo, with their fluid, traveling, clan-oriented, decentralized government, there was no such authority to make lease agreements. So the Bureau of Indian Affairs would literally create fictitious councils for the specific purpose of approving a lease.

The process was described by historian Lawrence Kelly in *The Navajo Indians and Federal Indian Policy:* "The calling of a Navajo council in these early years of the twentieth century was a routine and even casual event. The local agent would issue a call for all adult males to convene at the agency's headquarters on a given date. . . . Once a council had been held, the Indians disbanded."

The Bureau of Indian Affairs did not mince words about the purpose of this process. In its 1915 position paper on the subject the Bureau said, ". . . so long as the council can be used and controlled it should be a great benefit to the Indians . . ." The Navajo didn't think so, however. Another BIA document pointed out that "It's been with considerable effort that we have been able to restrain the Indians from taking vigorous action against the prospectors."

And so in 1921 when Standard Oil asked for approval of its exploration plans, the Bureau of Indian Affairs started searching for a bunch of Navajo who could come together and provide "official" approval. Finally seventy-five male Navajo did gather but, in a surprising expression of revolt, voted seventy-five to zero to refuse Standard Oil's request. Nonetheless, since the Bureau of Indian Affairs considered each of these councils temporary, it just created another one, which also refused to grant the lease. A third council, picked with great care, finally did okay it.

By now it was clear to the BIA and to the oil companies and mining interests that this creative BIA process was a bit too creative, informal, and unpredictable. The Bureau decided to convene a new council, but this time the BIA would get it to vote permanent "broad-based authority to the BIA itself." After two years, the BIA agent finally formed a new Navajo council that included regions not formerly represented, and anointed it with a continuous existence. In fact, it became the embryo of today's Navajo Tribal Council.

According to Lawrence Kelly, the first act of the new council in 1923 was to give away all of its own leasing authority to the Bureau of Indian Affairs, which thenceforth made all deals without approval of the tribe: "One of the reasons for the Navajo acceptance of the Department's prepared resolution [to give away its own power] appears to have been the assurance that in return . . . the Indians would receive government aid in securing new lands. . . . The BIA commissioner was not above coercing them with the argument. The Navajos, he explained, would suffer more than anyone else if they failed to grant a consent." So they consented. And they did get some new land, which was taken from—guess who? The Hopi.

So the new Navajo Tribal Council—the predecessor of today's Navajo Tribal Council—was born as a creation of the Bureau of Indian Affairs. Its main purpose was to give away the tribe's traditional rights to control what happens on tribal lands. As its reward, the Tribal Council got a piece of Hopi land, which is part of the land that the Hopi Tribal Council (also a BIA creation, as we will see in a moment) now wants back.

The creation of the Navajo Tribal Council as an arm of the United States bureaucracy was achieved sixty years ago. From the U.S. government point of view, the result has been excellent. There are now four coal strip mines on the Navajo reservation and five giant coal-fired power plants. There are also thirty-eight uranium mines and six uranium mills.

From the point of view of the Navajo people, an area once considered to have the cleanest air in the United States now has heavy black smoke and soot. Uranium miners—most of them Navajo—suffer a lung-cancer rate several times higher than the national average. Groundwater tables have been drastically lowered because the water has been pumped to serve the coal slurry lines; this, in turn, has made it more difficult than ever to grow corn in the desert. Groundwater tables have also been irradiated as a result of numerous uranium spills; there are instances of horses and sheep dying from drinking runoff water. Uranium tailings have been left in huge uncovered heaps all over the reservation. Some Navajo have built hogans made from these tailings. Children play in them.

What's more, under the Bureau of Indian Affairs' financial management, the deals that were made on behalf of the tribe for coal, oil, and uranium were among the worst ever made in this country and the whole world. In one case the Navajo tribe received a royalty of fifteen cents per ton of coal—one-tenth the $1.50-per-ton price that applied on non-Indian land.

And the Tribal Council? Until recently it remained little more than a rubber stamp for the BIA, as it was originally intended to be. But things changed a decade and a half ago with the election of Peter MacDonald to the chair of the Council. However one feels about MacDonald—who, in my opinion, was a kind of dictator—he was the first tough negotiator the tribe ever had, and he succeeded in wresting back some power from the Bureau of Indian Affairs and renegotiating some of the more outrageous deals. On the other hand, MacDonald was gung-ho for American-style development on the reservation, and was a leader among all American Indian Tribal Councils, urging them to develop in that manner. As a result, he probably did more to lead Indians away from traditional paths than any Indian before him. In 1989 MacDonald was indicted and later convicted on numerous counts of corruption involving kickbacks and embezzlement; perhaps he learned Dawes' lessons of "selfishness" a bit too well.

• • •

What was achieved by coercion in dealing with the Navajo was accomplished by simple fraud with the Hopi. The instrument was the 1934 Indian Reorganization (Wheeler-Howard) Act. Like the Allotment Act fifty years earlier, the IRA was praised as yet another great reform. Instead of dismembering Indian tribes, the Act promised federal aid to tribes that would abandon their traditional governmental structures and replace them with Tribal Councils elected by American-style majority rule. This was called "liberal" because it would bring democracy to Indians who, theoretically, had none before.

The constitutions for these new democratic governments were written, not by the Indians, but by the United States Department of the Interior, which then supervised their submission to tribal referendum. A stipulation of the constitutions was that the tribal decisions would be subject to U.S. approval. So what was being sold as self-government was really subversive to that goal.

Because of the massive economic aid that was promised to tribes who voted favorably—and because the Indians' traditional economic subsistence base and land base had been decimated—the IRA governments looked appealing. Also that new generation of "progressive" boarding-school Indians saw this government as a step toward sharing a piece of the American pie. Of the Indian nations that voted, 67 percent voted approval. One hundred seventy-two tribes adopted the new governments.

Among the Hopi Indians, however, there was strong resistance. From the moment they heard of the plan, the Hopi *kikmongwis* were against it. In a letter to the BIA Commissioner, one *kikmongwi* said: "As to the matter of forming a self-government, we already have that, handed down from generation to generation up to this time." When the referendum was held on the Hopi reservation, the *kikmongwis* led a boycott, which the overwhelming majority of Hopis joined.

The United States government was fully aware that among the Hopi Indians, the traditional expression of disapproval was refusal to participate. A strong non-vote was really a "no" vote. Oliver LaFarge, the BIA's Hopi agent, explained it to his Washington superiors:

> It is alien to the Hopis to settle matters out of hand by majority vote. Such a vote leaves a dissatisfied minority, which makes them very uneasy. Their natural way of doing is to discuss among themselves at great length and group by group until public opinion as a whole has settled overwhelmingly in one direction. . . . In actual practice this system is democratic, but it works differently from ours. Opposition is expressed by abstention. Those who are against something stay away from meetings at which it is to be discussed and generally refuse to vote on it.

On the day of the referendum, 519 Hopi (21 percent) voted "yes" while 305 (12 percent) voted "no." And 1,714 Hopi (67 percent) refused to vote at all. LaFarge told Washington that this result "should be interpreted as a heavy opposition vote." But the BIA superintendent announced that as far as he was concerned, abstention counted as "yes."

And so, after ten centuries of decentralized, consensual self-government that had sustained them very well, the Hopi joined the Navajo and most other American tribes in being governed from a central authoritative Tribal Council, empowered to execute laws and make deals in the name of the whole tribe under U.S. supervision. In other contexts we have learned to label the creation of these puppet governments as "neocolonialism."

Whereas the *kikmongwis* found the idea of selling, leasing, and mining to be repugnant, the new Tribal Council, now composed mainly of "progressive" Mormon BIA Hopi, felt quite the opposite. According to *Report to the Kikmongwis,* it was at the BIA suggestion that the Tribal Council hired an attorney from Salt Lake City, John S. Boyden, a former bishop in the Mormon church, to handle Hopi-corporate negotiations. In short order, Boyden made deals with Kerr-McGee, Tenneco, and a string of other companies.

The *kikmongwis* protested at every stage. They even filed suit in United States District Court in Arizona, charging that the Tribal Council had no authority to make leases. The suit was dismissed on the astounding grounds, considering the U.S. manipulations that had created the situation, that the Hopi Tribal Council represented a sovereign state and so could not be sued.

Of course, the Indian governments created under the Indian Reorganization Act represented a *loss* of sovereignty. Had there been true sovereignty, the tribes would have been free to choose their own forms of governance, without outside interference. Furthermore, the powers of these governments would not have been limited and controlled by the United States Department of the Interior, as they still are today.

Alvin Josephy, writing in *Now That the Buffalo's Gone,* presents a good summary of the results of coercing Indian nations into acceptance of the IRA:

> Instead of enabling each tribe to choose its own form of government, which in many instances would have meant a revival or adaptation of a traditional system conforming closely to the cultural heritage of the people, the implementation of the Act resulted in the government unilaterally imposing on the Indians an unfamiliar system that guaranteed continued non-Indian control. . . . The [new] governments were given no real power. The matters with which the councils could deal were strictly circumscribed, and all their decisions and actions were subject to the approval of the BIA.

Josephy points out the "Reservation Superintendent"—an employee of the BIA (something like a colonial governor)—"still had full control over the property and financial affairs of the tribe and of individual Indians, as well as almost every aspect of their daily lives, and could veto anything they or their government did."

Josephy describes the specific case of the Oglala Sioux:

Since the [new] constitution failed to provide true freedom, and in some cases threatened nonrecognized but still existing traditional forms of government—such as those guided by clan or spiritual leaders—many people boycotted the voting. Others abstained because of confusion, fear of power-seeking fellow tribesmen, or an inability to get to the voting places. . . . Only 13 percent of the eligible Oglala voters accepted the IRA. Twelve percent voted against it. The other 75 percent failed to vote or, from the Indians' point of view, voted in the negative by boycotting the procedure. But a majority of those who voted had said "yes," and a minority of 13 percent was thus used to foist upon the other 87 percent a form of self-government that white men had chosen for them.

The results could have been foreseen. . . . Once they were in office, those who went along with the BIA were accorded favors, honors, and opportunities to benefit financially and build petty political machines of friends and relatives who would loyally serve the BIA's purposes . . . [and became] less accountable to the membership of the tribe. The latter, in turn, felt contempt for those who were profiting at their expense from the white men's government and in large numbers ignored them and continued to boycott the elections. . . .

As the gap between the politicians and the grass-roots people widened, the latter looked increasingly to their spiritual teachers and other traditionalists for guidance and leadership. Though the traditionalists and their followers, who were often the majority on a reservation, had nothing to do with the BIA or the recognized tribal council, their presence was a constant irritant and threat to the council and its officers. . . .

Until the 1960s, the system effectively kept decision-making out of the Indians' hands. Policies and programs were established by Congress and the Department of the Interior in Washington and were imposed on the tribes by BIA officials and superintendents on the reservations. Both the policies and the programs usually applied to all, or many, of the reservations, and ultimately almost all of them failed.

The Navajo and Hopi experiences, and that of the Sioux, are typical of what has happened wherever the IRA "puppet" governments were established in Indian nations. As bidders of the development-oriented BIA, they dutifully abandon traditional economic and spiritual practice in favor of mining, drilling, agribusiness, and other schemes in concert with American corporate interests.

Meanwhile the frictions these non-traditional governments create, with both traditional leadership and the rank-and-file Indian people, result in devastating schisms and conflicts within tribes. They also help create conflict between tribes—as with the Hopi and Navajo—where the voracious new Tribal Councils fight against each other for resources, just as American corporations would do.

It's a tragedy that, in circumstances like these, the American media cannot grasp and report on what is actually happening. They continue to call it a dispute between tribes, and fail to mention the colonial policies and puppet regimes that are actually at the root of the problem, thus feeding the fire.

The paradoxes involved here were well described by the late Dan Bomberry, a Cayuga-Salish Indian who founded the Seventh Generation Fund, an all-Indian organization that continues to struggle on behalf of the traditional Indian viewpoint. He told me this:

"They're calling it a Hopi-Navajo dispute, but it's a U.S. law that's forcing the removal of the people, it's Americans that are paying the bills, and it's a United States agency that is actually moving the people. It was the U.S. that shoved the Navajo toward the Hopi 120 years ago, after killing their animals and putting the Navajo in a concentration camp. And if you want to blame the Hopi Tribal Council for its land-grabbing efforts, you've got to realize that the Hopi Tribal Council, just like the Navajo Tribal Council, are not Indian institutions. They're American institutions. They were put there by the U.S., created in that form for the very purpose of doing what they're doing: exploiting the land and the minerals.

"Those so-called Tribal Councils are really just extensions of the U.S. bureaucracy. Putting Indians off the land to get minerals and grazing rights makes perfect sense in American corporate logic. The Hopi Tribal Council are just being good colonial Americans. Now if you want to ask about Indians, you've got to turn to the old people, the traditionals, and the large number of young people who are joining forces with them now. The traditional Hopi and the traditional Navajo—especially the ones who live out on the land—are completely in support of each other. Leave them alone and they'll work everything out. I don't see how you can ignore their wishes and then call it an Indian problem, or an Indian solution."

CURRENT EVENTS

As this book goes to press (July 1991), about 75 percent of the Navajo and Hopi slated for relocation from the Joint Use Area have been moved. This leaves roughly 2,500 people (some 400 families) still refusing to go. These are the most militant families who can be expected to physically resist if efforts are made to remove them. Already there have been several instances where Navajo women have fired warning shots at relocation workers.

Of the families that have been moved, only 25 percent have received the benefits the government promises as incentives: $5,000 to $10,000 cash, new homes, and help in training for and finding some kind of livelihood away from the Indians' traditional lands. They now face social problems as well as economic hardship, typical of relocated peoples forced away from self-sufficient lifestyles: psychological disorientation, illness, alcoholism and drug abuse, and suicide.

Meanwhile, the removal policies of the U.S. Relocation Commission seem to have been altered in recognition of the fact that the remaining families will not be moved without a struggle. The government seems eager to avoid page-one photographs of U.S. marshals dragging elderly people across the sand to concrete-block houses hundreds of miles away; that is one eventuality that might actually create interest within an otherwise passive media. The new government policy boils down to attrition. It continues economic sanctions against the people on the land—restricting the number of animals, preventing new agricultural projects or new construction—in hopes that the old people will eventually give up or die.

As for the official U.S.-recognized Tribal Councils, the old people have little faith in either the Hopi or the Navajo councils. Recent Navajo chairmen Peterson Zah, Peter MacDonald, and Leonard Haskie have all given lip service to the Big Mountain residents, but have done nothing concrete. There was some hope for a "land swap" between the Hopi and the Navajo, which would allow most of the remaining residents to stay, but Hopi chairmen Ivan Sydney and Vernon Masyeseva have not, in their successive terms, been interested in that possibility. Anyway, according to the Big Mountain elders, both Tribal Councils are now committed to mining.

Meanwhile in Washington, D.C., the continued nonvisibility of Indian issues has made legislative solutions all but impossible. Proposed legislation by Senator Alan Cranston and Congressman Tom Bates (both of California) to create a moratorium on forced removal of the Navajo or Hopi has languished badly, especially since Cranston's tenure was threatened by the savings and loans scandals of 1990. There now seems little chance of a congressional remedy.

Legal challenges have similarly not been fruitful. The most hopeful case was one based on First Amendment religious-freedom rights, but this case, like all other Indian cases making similar arguments, received a shattering blow in 1990 with the infamous G-O Road decision of the U.S. Supreme Court. The Court essentially held that Indian religions cannot be used as legal restraints against government actions. (This case will be described in greater detail in Chapter 18, concerning Native Hawaiian religion.)

On the international front, the Hopi-Navajo issue receives much greater media attention and more public support than in the United States. The International Indian Treaty Council has repeatedly brought the case to the attention of the United Nations Subcommittee on Human Rights in Geneva, as well as to the Organization of American States. The goal is to eventually have U.S. policy labeled as "genocidal," within the common definition used in international law. At this time it seems likely that both the UN and the OAS will condemn U.S. policy and cast world public opinion further against the forced removal program. However, the U.S. government has repeatedly ignored the findings of international courts and agencies when they contradict U.S. wishes, as happened repeatedly during the U.S. anti-Sandinista war of the Reagan years.

Meanwhile any lingering doubts about the true motives for the forced removal are fast disappearing. In 1989, the *Gallup Independent,* a New Mexico newspaper, reported on a "secret" meeting between officials of the Peabody Coal Company and the Hopi Tribal Council, in which Peabody requested official approval of a new coal strip mine directly south of the present mines at Black Mesa. The new area would include Big Mountain and was claimed to contain some 300 to 500 million tons of high-quality coal, which would double Peabody's production.

The newspaper quoted conversations at the meeting in which Peabody urged rapid removal of the remaining residents because the company did "not want to become involved in the Navajo-Hopi land dispute," as if it were not already. According to the paper, Peabody hopes to begin mining in the south mesa area between 1997 and 1999. The coal's eventual destination is Japan.

Only two things now stand in the way of the massive mine program: 1) the lack of sufficient groundwater in the desert to create new slurry lines to move the coal for processing (the existing Black Mesa mines have dangerously depleted the water table throughout the region, seriously threatening Hopi and Navajo farms and the Hopi mesa communities); and 2) the continued resistance of the few hundred old people and their families who believe they have the right to remain on their ancestral lands, to maintain their traditional life, and to oppose the desecration of their holy places. They seem prepared to die rather than yield.

16

THE IMMINENT THEFT
OF ALASKA

*I*HAVE DISCUSSED the corporation as a kind of machine, more perse-
vering than the human actors within it, that operates by its own rules.
This chapter describes the effects of the imposition of corporate structure
upon a society that, for thousands of years, had organized its economic
activity in a far different way. To the Aleut, Yupik, Inupiat, Athabascan,
and other native peoples of Alaska, the corporation may prove just as fatal
a technology as the machine gun was to Indians of the American plains
100 years ago.

The alien corporate form was introduced to the native populations by
the Alaska Native Claims Settlement Act of 1973 (ANCSA). Like so
many congressional acts before it, ANCSA was hailed as a new dawn in
U.S.-Indian relations, claiming to offer a fair deal: full value and permanent protection of native land and culture. But just like the Allotment Act,
the Indian Reorganization Act, and the Indian Claims Commission Act,
ANCSA was a fraud in concept and in execution. It was created by a Congress that was essentially acting as a surrogate for U.S. oil, mineral, and
fishing companies. In terms of effective, efficient robbery and scale of de-
ception, ANCSA makes the Allotment Act look like a dimestore burglary.
That it's happening right now defies the notion that Americans have
learned from the past, or plan to behave differently in the future. That's
the bad news. The good news is that since this situation is current, some
of its most dire consequences may still be altered.

FROM COMMUNAL TO CORPORATE

Few Americans are aware that until the Alaska Native Claims Settlement Act was passed in 1973, the native people of Alaska had legal title to virtually *all* of that state. Many lawsuits had confirmed native ownership on the basis of "aboriginal rights." By U.S. law, native populations maintain their aboriginal ownership except under certain circumstances: 1) they are conquered in war, 2) a treaty agrees to cede land, or 3) a simple act of Congress *extinguishes* "aboriginal rights."

U.S. courts have also held that natives can lose their "aboriginal rights" if they no longer live on or make use of lands that can then be "encroached" upon by newcomers. But this is far from settled law; in each instance, the definition of "use" is debatable. Do subsistence societies, who hunt and gather through an entire ecosystem, "use" the land? Or do they physically have to live on the land or develop it?

In the overwhelming majority of cases involving the United States and American Indians, one of the above three acts of title extinguishment has occurred, thereby "legalizing" the taking of Indian lands. But in several instances, where land was not considered valuable and no one was hungering after it, no such congressional act occurred. The case of the Western Shoshone Indians of the Nevada desert is one example to be described in the next chapter. The Alaska natives represent another.

• • •

The native people of Alaska have long argued that the entire assertion that the United States owns Alaska is based on a false assumption: The U.S. believes it legitimately purchased the land from Russia. The Russians themselves were scarcely ever present in Alaska. Except for a few groups of fur traders on the Aleutian Islands and along the south coast, there were no Russians in Alaska; surely not in the vast interior. The great majority of native people never met a Russian nor knew that their land was claimed by a foreign nation. Despite this, the United States paid $7.2 million to the Russians in 1867, and then announced that all Alaska was ours. As for the people who had lived on that land for 4,000 years, nobody asked them anything.

From the time of the U.S. purchase until gold was discovered at the turn of the century, and invading miners became a problem, most of the Alaska native population continued to live without threat. Following the gold rush, some American fishing industry developed along the coast, and there was logging in the southern forests. But even through the 1960s, the native lifestyle was not seriously threatened. Hundreds of communities of native people lived in small villages, hunting, trapping, fishing, living off the land and the sea. The Yupik and Inupiat people were interspersed along the northern and western coastlines; various Athabascan peoples were settled in widely dispersed communities in the interior mountains and forests.

One notable exception to this peaceable pattern was among the Aleut people in the Aleutian Islands. During the Russian reign, the Aleut had been forced to abandon their traditional subsistence lifestyle to capture fur seals for European trade. The Russians forced many of the Aleut to leave their homes and move northward to the Pribiloff Islands, where huge fur-seal rookeries were located, and still are. When the U.S. took over, rather than reversing this forced servitude we maintained it up until the Second World War. Then when the Aleutian Islands were threatened by the Japanese, the Aleut were moved to internment camps. Returning home after the war, the Aleut found their villages decimated. Then they found they had to battle animal rights groups who told them to give up the only economy they ever knew on the bare islands that were not their traditional home. "They don't even want us to hunt the seals to eat," one Aleut leader said. "They suggest we get our meat from Chicago, with all those pesticides." Only recently have the Aleut achieved a compromise which allows subsistence hunting of sea mammals.

Most of the native population first felt a major U.S. presence during World War II. American soldiers were stationed on new bases carved out of the Alaskan wilderness, which caused the development of an infrastructure sufficient to accommodate resource explorations. Disputes first arose when the government or corporations sought to designate Alaskan lands as U.S. National Forest (so they could be logged) or as private lands. But the courts consistently ruled that legal title remained with the native populations, because of "aboriginal rights," which frustrated development and exploitation. When oil was discovered at Prudhoe Bay in 1968, it became critical for U.S. commercial interests to "clarify" the question of native title. Oil companies needed clear title before they could justify investing in drilling and pipeline construction. The idea of a negotiated settlement with the Indians took on new dimensions; the U.S. Congress got involved.

In an unusual alliance, the oil companies were joined by many environmental groups and by the State of Alaska. All wanted to finally decide who owned what. The State of Alaska and the oil interests favored development; the environmentalists, seeing the writing on the wall, wanted the land preserved as national park land, or under another protected status. By the late 1960s, economic activity and environmentalist pressure upon native communities caused them to feel that they too should clarify the issues. Most believed that they would eventually maintain their traditional title, at least to *most* of their homelands, as well as the right to carry on their traditional culture and economy. They were wrong.

Details of the Alaska Native Claims Settlement Act

The most authoritative work on the history and implementation of the Alaska Native Claims Settlement Act was produced by the celebrated Canadian jurist Thomas R. Berger, at the behest of the Alaska Native Review Commission.

Published by Hill and Wang as *Village Journey, the Report of the Alaska Native Review Commission,* it concluded that the so-called negotiations toward a settlement of native land claims was less a negotiation between Native Alaskans and the U.S. government than it was a federally mandated ruse.

Berger reports that the negotiations did not include the participation of any of the leaders of the 200 Alaska native communities that were to be affected. Neither were tribal governments involved; in fact they were excluded with a vengeance. There were no hearings in the communities, no testimonies, no votes taken among the native people to ratify or veto the agreement. Nor were there negotiations with the Alaska Federation of Natives, the one organization that the natives themselves had set up as their lobbying group and public representative. Instead the negotiations were conducted with the leadership of federally funded community programs, such as economic development, drug and alcohol treatment, and family services—administrators whose salaries came from federal funds. After six years of this "negotiation," an agreement was announced. Because of the dollar amounts involved and the apparent protection for large Indian land holdings, the agreement was hailed by Congress, the oil companies, and the environmentalists as breaking new ground. The natives' welfare would apparently be assured, which was a radical departure from previous double-dealing.

The new agreement had several principal terms:

1. "Aboriginal land title" was permanently extinguished. This, of course, was the primary purpose of the settlement—to destroy native title.

2. Aboriginal hunting and fishing rights were also extinguished. Not to worry—these rights would be protected in another way, per below.

3. The native peoples got title to 10 percent (44 million acres) of Alaska. This was one of the act's "liberal features": native people would get

title and control of a huge parcel of land (10 percent, whereas they formerly owned 100 percent). But as it turned out, this "title" was seriously qualified.

4. The federal government got 60 percent (197 million acres) of Alaska. This land was to be divided among various departments: the National Park Service, Forest Service, the military, the Bureau of Land Management, the Fish and Wildlife Service, and so on. Some of the land was to be preserved, and some to be developed. (The fate of each of these parcels has since been the subject of fierce battling and suing among environmentalists, corporations, and the government, especially as to the possibility of oil drilling within the "protected" Arctic National Wildlife Refuge.)

5. The State of Alaska got 30 percent (124 million acres). This acreage was earmarked for development.

6. The native populations were to be compensated for the loss of 90 percent of Alaska (321 million acres) at $3.00 per acre, or a total of $962.5 million. This figure was described as a "huge" cash settlement benefiting the natives. But . . .

7. Not one dollar nor one acre of land was actually placed in the control of any native person. Instead, native lands were divided among twelve regions, each under the control of a native-owned corporation, with rights to mine and otherwise develop that region for a profit. The native people received shares in this corporation. The people would get some money if and when the corporation made a profit, by developing the wilderness (as the non-natives wanted them to do). They would never again, as a people, own or control any land. The only control they had was through these corporations—institutions that operate by far different rules and with very different goals than the traditional tribal economies.

8. In addition to the twelve regional corporations, each native village became a separate corporation, thus replacing the traditional governmental structure of the village. The village corporation maintained the surface rights to the land, but the subsurface rights were controlled by the regional corporation, which also owned the land around the village.

9. Stock ownership in these new corporations was divided among the native populations of each Alaskan tribe, with every living member sharing equally. However, native people who did not live within a village received shares only in the regional corporations. This was the

only stock distribution. No consideration was made for future generations.

10. All shares in the new corporations were to be held by natives, and are nontransferable to non-natives until 1991. From 1991 on, the land was to be up for grabs for anyone. It was the old Allotment Act ploy replayed half a century later. The alienation of the natives from their homelands and from their age-old source of survival would have been achieved. (By 1991, however, the natives had fully grasped the potential of this stipulation and successfully lobbied a change in the law. Now shares can only be sold with the approval of 50 percent of the shareholders, thus making the transfer to non-natives still possible, but more difficult.)

THE REQUIREMENTS OF CORPORATE PROFIT

By assigning corporations to control all of the land and all the cash settlement due the native people of Alaska, the Alaska Native Claims Settlement Act had several predictable results. First, corporate management robbed the traditional native leadership from both village and tribal control of their peoples' economic future. Although the managers were themselves natives—at least at first—they were very different people from the former tribal leaders. These managers were obliged to operate by corporate goals, which often placed them in direct conflict with the desires of their own communities. The native peoples of Alaska had lived for 4,000 years almost entirely by subsistence activity—hunting, fishing, agriculture, trapping, and trading—and wanted very much to maintain their way of life. The desire to protect that life was what drove them to seek a settlement ensuring that their land was preserved for future generations.

Second, ANCSA made sure that the profit-making abilities of the resource-managing corporations directly determined land ownership, and the dollar value of the natives' awards. If the new corporate management failed to turn a profit, the shares of stock held by the native people would diminish in value (as they now have). The native stockholders would eventually be tempted to sell them in order to recover at least some part of their award. If this should happen, the traditional native lands would be forever removed from the control of the people who lived on them for millennia.

Third, the demands of profit required that the new management team be capable of successfully managing a complex competitive enterprise.

This skill is rare among native peoples, especially those who have lived in isolated regions free of the training and values of Western businesspeople. So the inexperienced native managers found they had to turn to highly paid non-native consultants—mostly out-of-state lawyers, accountants, bankers, and managers—to operate their businesses. At the time of this writing, more than 50 percent of the management of Native Alaskan corporations (and 50 percent of the employees) are non-native.

In addition to their own inexperience, the new native managers had to deal with a dearth of start-up capital, inadequate infrastructure for business development, a lack of trained staff for business operations, the anti-native bias of the Alaska non-Indian community, and unrealistic native shareholder expectations.

Fourth, to have a chance to be successful, the new corporate leadership had to adopt corporate values. Profit, growth, expansion, and conversion of natural resources to dollar-producing income were now the managers' driving motives. It was quickly obvious to the new class of native businesspeople that traditional subsistence activity would not turn a profit—unlike cutting down forests, mining for minerals, drilling for oil, servicing oil development, directly selling land, and promoting high-impact tourism. So, these native managers, themselves one generation from being whalers and trappers, were totally absorbing corporate ideology. In an article called "ANCSA in Perspective," Professor Monroe Price comments: "In a sense, the gospel of capitalism has gripped the leadership of the regional corporations just as in another day, [the Christian] gospel was introduced for its educative and assimilative influence . . . The profitmaking mandate has become a powerful driving force. The [new] corporate executives will be those who are willing to forgo subsistence activities, to place a higher priority on board meetings than on salmon fishing, and to spend time talking to lawyers and financiers and bankers, rather than the people of the village."

Fifth, the necessity to seek profit drove the regional corporations into fierce conflict with many of the village corporations, who were more interested in maintaining the traditional way of life. Though the villages were themselves set up as corporations, local control meant that the people with an interest in maintaining the older ways had a say in making choices. Most villagers did not want development, but since huge regional corporations owned the land surrounding the village corporations and the resources underneath the villages, unprecedented fierce battles developed among the natives. Even the local village corporations have suffered from the pressure to abide by corporate laws totally alien to their experience. Just to fulfill the legal obligations of corporate and tax laws in Alaska and the United States, the villagers were required to spend $60,000 to $80,000 per year for accountants and lawyers. At the village level, therefore, corporate structure required that villages find means to produce income, to avoid going bankrupt and losing their land.

So the Alaska Native Claims Settlement Act, the great liberal achievement that promised to benefit Natives as no act had done before, and to affirm native control over traditional native lands, and to break with the United States' past by paying the highest cash settlement ever, was a fraud. It made the formerly secure native holdings highly precarious. It directly disrupted traditional village economies and political structures. It instantly changed the hierarchical arrangements among the native people themselves. And it made available to outside corporate interests—some of the most economically voracious organizations in the world—a treasure chest of previously inaccessible resources. All of this without firing a shot. The corporation, a technology far more subtle than guns, did the job just as well and with far greater public-relations potential.

"SOCIAL ENGINEERING"

When you look through the corporate eye, our relationship to the land is altered. We draw our identity as a people from our relationship to the land and to the sea. This is a spiritual relationship, a sacred relationship. It is in danger because, from a corporate standpoint, if we are to pursue profit and growth, and this is why corporations exist, we would have to . . . exploit these resources to achieve economic gain. This is in conflict with our traditional relationship to the land. We were stewards, we were caretakers, and we had respect for the resources that sustained us.—*Mary Miller, Nome*

As we all know, these corporate officers . . . may not have as much conviction as others on the issues of subsistence living and retention, which seems to be the main concern of most Natives I know. We shouldn't expect corporation officers to represent our interests. —*Natalie Susuk, New Stuyahok*

I believe that if the vast majority of Alaska Natives were given the opportunity to either kill or die for their land, most of them would do just that . . . Now, when they are coming in after the land they come not with soldiers, but with people carrying briefcases. If you shoot somebody carrying a briefcase . . . then you are just a criminal, not [making] an act of war. That means there isn't any clear way for the people to protect their land.—*Paul Ongtooguk, Kotzebue*

These remarks are among thousands of similar statements that were published by Thomas R. Berger as part of the report of the Alaska Native Review Commission.

Justice Berger's field hearings while touring Alaska's villages were the first to permit natives to express their points of view about ANCSA.

Berger argues that the U.S. Congress did not hold its own field hearings as it never intended to permit native communities to continue their traditional uses of the land, or to maintain their subsistence economy. The Congress's overriding goal was to ensure that the State of Alaska would develop rapidly. The rationale was that all Americans need to benefit economically from Alaska's rich resources. If in the end the natives had to change their ways, so be it.

Berger quotes congressional staff assistant William Van Ness, who worked for the late Senator Henry Jackson, the chief architect of ANCSA. Van Ness called the act "a very radical effort at social engineering, [which] was done on a very calculated basis." Professor Douglas Jones, formerly an assistant to Senator Mike Gravel of Alaska, also used the term "social engineering." It's amazing that they were so willing, and so proud, to put it that way.

In Berger's analysis he states, "Although Congress recognized the necessity of a land base for the native subsistence economy, it nevertheless insisted that economic development of the land must become the principal means of improving social and economic conditions in village Alaska. Congress intended native people to go into business and to participate actively in the economic development of Alaska." But according to Berger, the results have been negative:

> Native people who had little money before 1971 have little money today. . . . Where there was unemployment, there is still no work. Where unemployment has been alleviated, it is not because of ANCSA. . . . The imposition of a settlement of land claims that is based on corporate structures was an inappropriate choice, given the realities of native life in village Alaska. The serious changes that ANCSA has introduced to native life are becoming ever more apparent with the passage of time. ANCSA has affected everything: family relations, traditional patterns of leadership and decision making, customs of sharing, subsistence activities, the entire native way of life. The village has lost its political and social autonomy.
>
> [Congress declined to] take into account the strengths of the native culture, economy and government. ANCSA is a domestic application of theories of economic development that had been applied

to the Third World. . . . The central thesis is that, with large-scale economic development, the modern sector of the economy will expand to incorporate persons still active in the traditional sector and, in this process, the traditional sector will gradually disappear. . . . Congress was not altogether ignorant of conditions and life in rural Alaska, but it did not wish to acknowledge the legitimacy of native ways of life. Alaska Natives were a problem to be solved, and Congress thought it knew how to solve it. . . . ANCSA is an attempt to re-create Main Street on the tundra.

ANCSA'S EFFECT ON THE YUPIK ESKIMOS

From the natives' point of view, one of the more subtle elements of ANCSA—the government's new authority to regulate hunting and fishing throughout the state—is causing some of the greatest hardships. The U.S. and the State of Alaska sought for decades to gain these regulations through the courts, but were thwarted by aboriginal rights rulings. Now there are no aboriginal rights. The state and federal governments decide who will hunt and fish and what quotas prevail. (Even on the 10 percent of Alaska's land that native corporations now own, the government sets the quotas, though only natives can hunt in those places.)

This change in status for Alaska's lands has delivered another blow to traditional subsistence economic practices, since government agencies are far less responsive to subsistence protection than to commercial interests. Native fishers must suddenly compete with commercial firms in a race to deplete resources. Meanwhile, even subsistence hunting and trapping have become the target of animal protection organizations who oppose hunting for any purpose whatsoever.

One native group that has been seriously affected by this change are the Yupik Eskimo people, who have lived a stable life in the Yukon-Kuskokwim delta region for the past 4,000 years.

Shocked by the sudden impact of ANCSA and the government agencies that have begun to directly intervene in their lives, the Yupik have been seeking to slow down the process, arguing that their subsistence economy is valid on its own terms. In *Does One Way of Life Have to Die So Another Can Live?* (edited by Art Davidson), the Yupik leaders comment on the ways the Yupik have been excluded from the decisions that affect their lives:

When Russia claimed Alaska as its territory, the Yupik people were not involved. When the United States bought Alaska, the Yupik

people were not involved. When large wildlife refuges were established on the Delta, the Yupik people were not involved. When fish
and game regulations were formulated, the Yupik people were not
involved. Even when the Alaska Native Claims Settlement Act was
passed, the Yupik people were not involved. . . .

Please try to fathom our great desire to survive in a way somewhat
different from yours. . . . If the [U.S.] law prohibits hunting . . . the
people will hunt even against the law. . . . Every one of us is Eskimo
around here. We all have to eat our own native food [as opposed to
store-bought food] and there is no question about it. We cannot possibly go without it.

The Yupik argue that their subsistence activity has never threatened
wildlife populations. Yupik culture is based on a mutual respect between
humans and animals, and the relationship has remained in balance for
4,000 years. The problems have arisen only recently, say the Yupik, because
the U.S. government and the State of Alaska have encouraged rampant
commercialism, resulting in severe depletion of the salmon population
and the death of many sea mammals as a by-product of commercial fishing procedures. The Yupik say that the habitat is being suddenly overpowered by newly introduced commercial hunting and fishing ethics.

The government response to the environmental crisis in the region has
been to create a "limited entry permit" system for fishing and hunting.
This has made subsistence hunting and fishing nearly as expensive as commercial fishing. Meanwhile, the government tells the Yupik to "come out
of the Stone Age" and participate in the corporate cash economy. But the
Yupik argue, as do most other Alaska native groups, that their economic
structure cannot be separated from every other aspect of their lives: their
religion, their family structure, their political structure, and their value
systems of sharing, joint effort, land use, wildlife management, even education. To them, subsistence is an entire way of life. From *Does One Way
of Life Have to Die So Another Can Live?*:

The Yupik culture, like other Native American cultures, depends
upon a subsistence resource base for which there are no alternatives.
The relationships are really very simple. If the fish and seal and beaver and birds were to disappear, we could no longer hunt and fish.
Our culture would die. Our way of life and our people would disappear. All precedents predict this will happen to us. . . .

Today public policy decisions are almost invariably made on the
assumption that we are going to be drawn into the mainstream and
one day become like everyone else. This assumption is made . . . de-

spite the intention of most Yupik people to continue their hunting and fishing way of life.

The Alaska Native Claims Settlement Act created a new pattern of land ownership and management among native corporations, village corporations, and the state and federal governments. Ownership and rights of use have now been fractured into thousands of small parcels, which confuses the natives and makes the continuity of traditional land use impractical. Yupik elder Alena Nikolas explains (from the Yupik report *Does One Way of Life Have to Die So Another Can Live?*):

> When I was growing up, we didn't know any white people, and all the food we had was from the land. We would go out in a canoe and go fishing and never waste any part of it. Everything we used for hunting and fishing was made by the people. The women would go berry-picking with their backpacks, and their buckets were made from bark. . . . In my time there weren't such things as regulations, or land planning commissions. In my time people lived happily together. Nobody would come around and say this is my land, and that is your land. These lands were everybody's. People weren't coming in and saying you do this, and you use the land for this, you use the river for this. These little lines and areas drawn up on the map by so and so—there weren't such things as those. People were happy then.

The editors of the Yupik report agree:

> The villager's use of land cannot be broken into pieces if his way of life is to continue . . . the rivers flow through the various pieces of the ownership puzzle. The fish and game migrate from one area to another. The geese and ducks, and salmon and moose don't live by boundaries. They don't check the land office in Anchorage to see whose land they are on. And as the fish and game move through the whole land, so the hunter must be able to move through the whole land if he is to survive.

William Tyson, testifying before the State Land Use Planning Commission, said this about the traditional Yupik relation to land (from the Yupik report):

> I don't know of any other way of making a living besides living off the land and working together with my neighbors. If we see somebody to help, we go down and help him . . . there used to be some woman coming up and picking berries right outside of our house. My wife would open that door and say "Hey, the coffee is good,

won't you come in and have some coffee with me?" The woman who picked berries right outside of my house would come into my house and have coffee with my wife in the house. That was before we got cautious.

Then, after we were told that we had to have a boundary around our property, then anybody comes and tells us, that one is trespassing and I can do as I please with him. Okay. I'm not helping him no more, just driving him away. That is not preserving the land the way it should be.

RESISTANCE TO CASH ECONOMY

One of the most illuminating sections of *Does One Way of Life Have to Die So Another Can Live?* has to do with the Yupik's strong resistance to a cash economy. Referring to a University of Alaska study, the report says that half of the Yupik people still depend solely on subsistence. Of thirty-eight families interviewed, researchers found that half lived entirely by subsistence hunting and gathering, making their own clothes, and living off the land. Seventy-five percent of the families were primarily dependent upon subsistence. Only 15 percent of the families were solely supported by wages.

Another study attempted to measure the cash value of the elements in the subsistence economy—animals, birds, plants—as if the people had been required to purchase them in a store. For food alone, the annual dollar equivalent was more than $3,000 per person, or $15,000 for a family of five. (Most families are actually larger than five.)

Since the average per capita cash income among native families in the region is only $800 per year, it is clear that if they give up their subsistence economy, natives would have to find new jobs, ones that pay much higher wages than are now available, just to maintain their present standard of living. Even with the massive industrialization brought on by ANCSA, finding these jobs is unlikely.

From the Yupik standpoint, even full cash equivalency earnings would not satisfactorily replace the subsistence economy, which offers more subtle benefits. The subsistence hunter does not have to deal with inflation, for example, or with the inconsistent availability of imported foods. Subsistence foods contain no pesticides or additives, unlike imported, store-bought foods, and commercially processed foods may be lower in nutritional value. Finally, certain foods, such as seal meat or moose, are impossible to buy in a store.

Dr. Bradford Tuck, an economist who worked with the Federal-State Land Use Planning Commission, has commented on the quality of subsistence as opposed to commercial food: "It is important that the equating of dollar cost or dollar equivalent not be interpreted as representing equal value. The value is the same only if the satisfaction from consuming the pound of store meat is the same as the satisfaction derived from consuming a pound of moose meat. If the moose meat is preferred over store meat, then the substitute value is underestimated by using only dollar equivalent." (The above quote and the two below are from *Does One Way of Life Have to Die So Another Can Live?*)

Margaret Cooke (Yupik) puts it more directly: ". . . believe me, my body must have seal oil. I eat it almost daily. . . . I have never been in jail or arrested in my life, but if this bill passes [which would outlaw subsistence seal hunting] I will become a criminal. My body is used to seal oil and must have seal oil . . . no matter what."

Guy Mann (Yupik) explains further: "We Eskimos use seal oil like this. In spring we hunt seals. Then skin dry up. When dry we put oil in seal skins. Then save it for winter. Then after season we fishing. The fish dry. Then smoked. After smoked we put dry fish into the seal skin with seal oil and we save it for winter. And all summer we not seal hunt. And in September we start seal hunt again. Then we seal hunt all winter because we Eskimo like to eat all kind of oil from ocean. Every time when we eat we take a seal oil. Please, please help us. We don't want to stop seal hunt. And when we eat something without seal oil, our stomachs kind of sick."

REINSTATEMENT OF NATIVE GOVERNMENTS

It cannot really be doubted that a grave injustice, typical of those performed against native people for the last century and a half, is now being perpetrated against the Alaska natives. ANCSA was a lie from the outset, created by interests whose goals were to steal the natives' land and feed it to industrial-corporate society. The U.S. Congress was the effective actor in creating the problem. The corporation was and is the major weapon. The regulatory agencies are in place to ensure that the social engineering of "Main Street on the tundra" is achieved.

Now that the cat is out of the bag, what is to be done? The native people's goals include reestablishing tribal control over the land, reestablishing tribal governments, and preserving the subsistence economy.

Their testimonies, unheard by Congress, but repeated hundreds of times in Justice Berger's book, are eloquent on these points:

> This act was done for our future benefit, but it has hurt us, our children and grandchildren and those that are yet to be born. If we do not do anything about this, that is exactly our future. —*Mike Albert, Tununak*

> Our subsistence way of life is especially important to us. Among other needs it is our greatest. We are desperate to keep it. —*Paul John, Tununak*

> Profit to non-natives means money. Profit to natives means a good life derived from the land and sea. . . . This land we hold in trust is our wealth. It is the only wealth we could possibly pass on to our children. . . . Without our homelands we become true paupers. —*Antoinette Helmer, Craig*

> The government we have, the tribal government, has existed and was a legal government when Columbus supposedly discovered America. . . . There has been a crying need to re-establish the tribal government. The government that now exists, specifically the federal government and the state government, is not our way of government. The elders are saying re-establish your tribal governments. Make your own laws, practice your self-determination as your ancestors have practiced it. —*Willie Kasayulie, Akiachak*

In order to reverse the problem in Alaska, many natives feel the first and most important step is to remove native land (10 percent of Alaska) from the control of corporate entities and return it to traditional tribal governments. If corporations maintain ownership, their land-use policy will directly conflict with native traditions and desires. Eventually the natives could lose even their corporate ownership—through the sale of native shares—and wind up with neither land nor stock nor money. Converting corporate lands back to tribal ownership would instantly boost the traditional subsistence economies.

The second most essential step would be to diminish U.S. agencies' authority over tribal lands. Natives must be given at least equal partnership with state and federal authorities in regulating access to and use of areas not owned by tribes. The idea that native resource management skills are not up to such a task is ridiculous, as was pointed out in previous chapters. Spud Williams, president of the Tanana Chiefs Association, put it this way: "The state needs us as much as we need them to manage fish and game resources. They've got to be willing to recognize tribal governments for effective management in rural Alaska. They cannot police this country. The only police force out there that can do it are the people, and we are probably more strict than the state because [to us] it's not 'fish and game,' it's *food*."

If the creators of the Alaska Native Claims Settlement Act had ever once consulted the native villagers, or had hearings out on the land, reality (and publicity) would have forced the U.S. Congress to see that the American solution opposed the native peoples' desires to maintain their traditional economy. Instead, Congress acted secretly and duplicitously to steal their land and their rights.

Justice Berger concluded his report with this remark about the Alaska natives:

> After visiting sixty villages, I know the depth of feeling about the land that exists among the Native people of rural Alaska. . . . At every hearing witnesses talk of the corporations, shares, profits, sometimes even of proxies, but then, emerging from this thicket of corporate vocabulary, they will talk of what they consider of most importance to them—the land, subsistence, the future of the villages. . . . Alaska Natives now realize that ANCSA has failed them and that its goals are at cross-purposes with their own. Today they are trying to strengthen their subsistence economy and to restore their tribal governments. . . . It is their profound desire to be themselves, to be true to their own values, that has led to the present confrontation. Far from deploring their failure to become what strangers wish them to be, we should regard their determination to be themselves as a triumph of the human spirit.

17

THE THEFT OF NEVADA

The Case of the Western Shoshones

*I*N 1979, THE U.S. Indian Claims Commission announced that the
Western Shoshone Nation in Nevada had been awarded $26,145,189—
one of the largest "land-claim settlements" in history. The award was
called "compensation" for some 24 million acres of aboriginal Western
Shoshone land in Nevada and California, which the U.S. says it "took"
from the Indians in 1872, following 10,000 years of undisturbed Western
Shoshone occupancy.

The Indians have refused to accept the money. They say their land was
never taken. They say that the assertion that the land was taken results
from a deal between a claims attorney, whom the Indians had fired, and
the United States, which has a strong desire to assert that the Indians no
longer own the land.

"Nothing happened in 1872. No land was 'taken' by the government.
That's just a made-up date," asserts Glenn Holley, then spokesperson and
chair of the Temoak Bands of the Western Shoshones, the officially named
Indian representative in the claims case. "We never lost that land, we never
left that land, and we're not selling it. In our religion it's forbidden to take
money for land. What's really happening is that the U.S. government,
through this Claims Commission, is stealing the land from us right now."

For the five years preceding the "award," the Indians tried to stop the
claim, which, they say, was fraudulently made in their name. Though they
had fired Barker, their attorney of record, he refused to withdraw from

the case, and the Claims Commission insisted on recognizing him. The Indians appealed to the president of the United States, the Court of Claims, and the U.S. Supreme Court, asking each to vacate or stay the claim.

The Shoshones insist that the 1863 Treaty of Ruby Valley remains in effect. That treaty between the United States and the Western Shoshones was one of "peace and friendship," which did not concede any lands to the United States. In fact, the point of the treaty was to confirm Indian title to specific territories, while also gaining the Indians' agreement for "safe passage" for Americans traveling through the Western Shoshone Nation to California. The treaty also permitted a small amount of non-native mining and ranching in specific areas. The boundaries of the Western Shoshone Nation were established as including most of what is now central and southern Nevada, as well as a small portion of California, including Death Valley.

One of the Shoshones' new attorneys, John O'Connell, told me at the time of the claims "settlement" that there had never been any act by the United States to extinguish Indian title to the land—no act of Congress; no assertion of eminent domain; nothing.

"We have asked the government over and over again in court to show evidence of how it obtained title to the Shoshone land," said O'Connell. "They start groping around and can't find a damn thing. In fact, the relevant documents show that the U.S. never wanted the Nevada desert until recently. There's not a doubt in my mind that the Western Shoshones still hold legal title to most of their aboriginal territory. The great majority of them still live there and they don't want money for it. They love that desert. But if the Claims Commission has its way, the United States may succeed in finally stealing the land 'legally.'"

Just before the Claims Commission had announced its award, the Western Shoshones had offered a compromise. They had suggested that the secretary of the interior, who was then Cecil Andrus, invoke a clause of the Treaty of Ruby Valley by which the Indians would agree to "give up their wandering ways" and accept a three-million-acre reservation (about one-tenth of their former territory). This would have been accompanied by a much smaller cash settlement. The compromise was enthusiastically received by mid-level government officials. But to everyone's amazement, Andrus suddenly broke off all negotiations without a counteroffer. His only comment came in a letter that said, "It would not be in the best interests of the Indians."

Two weeks later, President Carter announced that the first-choice location for deploying the MX missile basing system was the "public land" in the Nevada desert. Also proposed for this "public land" was the U.S. underground nuclear testing program, as well as the nation's low-level radioactive waste storage facility. All of these "public lands" activities fall squarely within the boundaries of the Treaty of Ruby Valley, and are bitterly opposed by the Indians.

LAND OR MONEY?

That a small number of Indians would refuse a huge amount of money for mostly arid desert may seem crazy, particularly since the average family income among the Shoshones is only about $3,000 a year. "The grass is so sparse there," one official of the Interior Department told me, "the cows have to graze at forty miles per hour just to get enough to eat."

As an occasional driver on Interstate 80, my own experience of the Nevada desert was typical of most people's—all I could see was hour after hour of dull, brown wasteland from Reno to Elko. Then once in 1978 I hiked off the highway into that desert world of juniper and sagebrush flats and strange, bare, folded mountains. I found that the light is alive there as it is nowhere else in this country except in parts of the New Mexico desert. The moods and colors change dramatically from hour to hour. Soon, the power of the land begins to dominate urbanite preconceptions. "All of this land, everything in it, is medicine," one old Shoshone woman told me.

The nuances of the desert are not obscure to the Shoshones. They have been sustained by this "wasteland" for more than 400 generations, roaming through it in small bands. Hidden in the valleys and on ridgetops are large pine nut (pinyon) forests that provided the staple food as well as forest cover for the deer and small animals that contributed to the Indians' subsistence.

When the whites intruded four generations ago, all of this started to change. But the major recent development came less than twenty years ago. The Bureau of Land Management took it upon itself to destroy more than one million acres of these pine nut groves, and killed the trees in a most terrifying manner by pulling them down with gigantic iron chains dragged between bulldozers. After clearing the pinyons, the BLM planted grass in hopes of attracting white ranchers.

This destruction of the Shoshones' subsistence base forced them to seek support from white society. While some of the Shoshones have been able to continue living off the land, many have moved into settlements, appropriately called "colonies," adjoining the white communities. The men work as miners or on ranches when work is available. The women hire out as domestics or waitresses. Though unemployment figures are slightly misleading when applied to a culture that partially sustains itself on the land, the U.S. government estimates unemployment among the Shoshones at 30 to 50 percent. Many are on welfare. Glenn Holley himself is a former copper miner, now partially living on disability payments due to a mining injury. Despite their "poverty," the Indians have refused to accept cash for the desert land that they say is legally theirs and that provides their cultural, economic, and spiritual identity.

INDIAN CLAIMS COMMISSION:
PLOT AGAINST THE INDIANS

The Indian Claims Commission Act of 1946 was considered a liberal reform. At last a mechanism existed "to settle finally any and all legal, equitable, and moral obligations that the U.S. might owe to the Indians." It sounded good, but as usual, there were some subtle wrinkles.

First, the law provided only one method of grievance resolution: cash payment for lost lands. Instead of helping Indian nations to enforce their treaty rights, or to recover lands that had been encroached upon illegally, the law only allowed Indians to ask for money by asserting that their lands had been taken from them. Once money was awarded, Indian land title was permanently lost and the Indians were barred from seeking further redress.

Second, the law dictated that any tribal member could sue on behalf of the entire tribe. This claimant, or rather this claimant's attorney, then became the sole representative of the tribe. As a result, those Indians who did not wish to file for the monetary awards, but did wish to fight for treaty rights or for confirmation of land titles, had no means to prevent the commission's process.

The third and probably the worst element of the law was the stipulation that claims attorneys who represented Indians before the commission were awarded 10 percent of the settlement amount. This provision produced a new breed of attorney, who got very rich by seeking out individual Indians willing to file claims. It also gave lawyers a compelling incentive to persuade Indian governments that the only viable course for their many grievances was to make cash claims.

The Indian nations were slow to recognize the limitations of the Claims

Commission process, or the true role of their claims attorneys. Often, Indian claimants began the claims processes thinking that they might gain confirmation of their aboriginal land title. Though claims attorneys knew this was impossible, they would sometimes fail to correct their clients' erroneous assumptions, at least until the process was too far along to reverse, and their legal fees were assured. Eventually, the Indians saw that instead of recovering land title, they were effectively giving up their claims for land, or selling lands they wanted to fight to keep. The Claims Commission finally revealed itself as yet another effective fraud upon the Indians.

The commission was essentially a mopping-up operation, established to clarify ambiguities about land ownership that still remained after a century of white assault. It simply asserted that the Indians *had* lost land that they often had not, and gave them money as a panacea. Usually these claims awards were dutifully hailed in the American press—as was the case with the Passamaquody and Penobscott cases in Maine—as if the U.S. were generously giving down-and-out Indians a gift, when actually the opposite was the case.

By now, however, many Indian nations have gotten wise to the way the commission works. In addition to the Western Shoshones, at least twenty-two other Indian nations are refusing settlements made in their names by claims lawyers who effectively work as arms of the government.

Most notable among the refuseniks are the Oglala and Rosebud communities of the Sioux Nation, who are refusing two settlements, one of $103 million and another of $40 million, for the alleged "taking" of the Black Hills in 1877. The Sioux say that the land was not taken and that they would never sell it. But the commission pushed through the settlements and twenty-seven corporations have filed for uranium mining rights to the Black Hills.

Energy resources on Indian lands are at the root of many U.S.-Indian land struggles that are played out in the Indian Claims Commission. Sixty-five percent of the U.S.'s known uranium reserves are located on Indian reservations or on treaty lands, as is over 35 percent of the strippable coal and 5 percent of natural gas. Former Energy Secretary James Schlesinger once called Indian lands "America's energy ace-in-the-hole," but this is only the case while the Indians are compliant. Increasingly they are not.

According to the late Dan Bomberry of the Seventh Generation Fund, "When the U.S. succeeded in forcing the Indian Reorganization Act (IRA) upon tribes, installing puppet governments, the ultimate U.S. aim was to make Indians a resource colony, like Africa was for Europe. Sometimes the issue is coal or uranium and sometimes it's just open land for

MX missiles and nuclear testing. The role of the Indian Claims Commission is to get at the lands of tribes who do not have puppet governments, or where the traditional people are leading a fight to keep land and refuse money."

"WE SHOULD HAVE LISTENED TO OUR OLD PEOPLE"

The Western Shoshones' case began with a very clear grievance. Since 1910 they had been asking the United States to stop calling the Western Shoshone treaty lands "U.S. public domain." Their protests were consistently ignored, and eventually they sought legal advice. By the 1930s the Shoshones had hired a legal advisor, Ernest Wilkinson of the Washington, D.C., law firm of Wilkinson, Cragen, and Barker. Wilkinson advised the Shoshones to join him in lobbying a new law through Congress by which Indians could obtain cash settlements for lost land. (This law later became the Indian Claims Commission Act.) The Shoshones refused to participate. They pointed out that they never lost their lands to begin with, and only wished to confirm that fact. At some point after the Indian Claims Commission Act was passed, Wilkinson's partner, Robert W. Barker, advised the Indians that now their only viable course was to seek a cash claim. A group of Shoshones, including the Temoak Bands tribal council, as it was then constituted, agreed to let him proceed.

Barker filed the claim in 1951, asserting that the Western Shoshones had lost not only their treaty lands, but also their aboriginal land extending into Death Valley, California. He put the date of loss as 1872 (only nine years after the Treaty of Ruby Valley), and he included in the twenty-four-million-acre claim some sixteen million acres that the Shoshones insist were not occupied by anyone but Indian bands, and that were never in question. But the U.S. Justice Department accepted Barker's contention. Since opposing attorneys agreed, the Claims Commission did not investigate or seek other viewpoints. They awarded the Shoshones $26 million, based on an 1872 land value of $1.05 per acre, plus some unpaid mineral royalties. (An average acre of Nevada desert now brings about $250.) When this claim was finally paid, Wilkinson, Cragen, and Barker received $2.5 million.

"We should have listened to our old people," said Raymond Yowell, a member of the Temoak tribal council who once supported the claim.

"They told us that Barker was selling out our lands. It took me years to realize it."

Another Shoshone elder who felt misled by Barker was Saggie Wil liams of Battle Mountain: "All we wanted was for the white men to honor the treaty. I believed the lawyers we hired were to work for the Indians and to do what the Indians asked. But they didn't. They did as they pleased and told us that we didn't have any land. At that time we didn't talk about selling our land with the lawyer because we had the treaty, which settled the land question; it protected the lands."

In a 1978 article in the *Native Nevadan,* Yowell attempted to show how Barker had engineered paper support from a tribe that was basically op posed to what he was doing. At a 1965 mass meeting called to get tribal approval of a loan needed to pursue the claims, Yowell said, "A majority of the people present objected to the way Barker was giving up the re maining rights to our lands and walked out. . . . Soon after at an Elko meeting about 80 percent of the people showed their opposition by walk ing out. It is important that at these meetings Barker insisted that we had no choice as to whether to keep title to some lands or give them up for the claims money. The only choice was to either approve or disapprove the loan. And if we disapproved we would get nothing. After the majority left, those Indians remaining, about twenty-five or thirty, elected me and Jackie Woods members of the Claims Committee," which approved Barker's loan. (Tragically, traditional Indian people tend to express disapproval by boycotting meetings, walking out, and refusing to vote. This is logical among Indians themselves, who recognize a boycott for what it is, a neg ative vote. But when dealing with whites and white legal systems, the ef fect has been to leave the voting and deal-making to those who remain; i.e., those who want to make deals.)

While I was working on a story about the Shoshone case for the *Village Voice* in 1979, I called attorney Barker to get his side of the story. "Ever since the beginning of this case," Barker said, "I have told the Indians that if they could find a way of getting the land back we would not stand in their way. We have been very patient. These delays have already cost $5.5 million in interest. But we have a contract with the claimants and the re sponsibility to proceed with the claim. We had to tell the Indians that in our opinion, and in the opinion of all responsible parties, Indian title had been extinguished by the government. Aside from seeking cash, their only option was to try to get Congress to pass a bill giving them land. We even drafted one for them in the fifties but they couldn't find a Nevada con gressman to introduce it." I asked Barker what other "responsible parties" had agreed that Indian title had been extinguished. He named the Justice Department and the Indian Claims Commission itself.

The legal records of the case cast doubt on Barker's statement that he did not stand in the way of Indians who wanted to assert continued title.

In 1974 Glenn Holley and others formed the Western Shoshone Legal Defense and Education Association, which hired John O'Connell as attorney. O'Connell filed a petition to intervene with the Claims Commission, charging Barker with collusion with the government. Barker responded that the collusion charge was merely a technical point to allow the Shoshones to argue their case.

But according to Glenn Holley, "Most of our people never understood that by filing with the Claims Commission we'd be agreeing that we lost our land. They thought we were just clarifying the title question. Barker kept saying the claim was for land we had already lost—that we weren't selling anything. We wanted to show we hadn't lost the land."

Shoshone elder Clarence Blossom from Elko, Nevada, who was a signatory to the actual agreement with Barker, concurs with Glenn Holley. According to Blossom, "The land claim was never explained to the people. The old people do not even understand English. It was years later that I read that once you accept the money, you lose your land. The government pulled the wool over our eyes. If I had known what was going on, I never would have signed the attorney contract." Despite such sentiments, Barker fought hard against the Shoshones' petition to intervene with the Claims Commission. He continued to insist that he had done nothing wrong.

"I always tried to stay out of internal controversies in the tribe," said Barker, "but I had to oppose the association on the grounds that this matter had been exhaustively discussed back in the thirties, forties, and fifties. I always sought the judgment of the Shoshones as a whole as to whether or not to seek to restore their lands and we always discussed alternatives. Holley's group is just a small but vocal minority." When they lost the petition, O'Connell appealed to the Court of Claims, and Barker fought the appeal. The court agreed with Barker that the Temoak Bands had chosen long ago to give up the land for money and that it was "too late to upset the apple cart after the fruit has been so carefully collected and piled."

By 1976, the Temoak Bands had gone through a complete revolution and voted to seek a stay of the claim until the land question could be considered. Barker fought them again. The court denied the stay. Finally, the Temoak Bands fired Barker, and he fought the firing. The court continued to recognize him as attorney of record, so he eventually reaped the economic benefits of his thirty years of advice and counsel.

In 1977, new Shoshone attorneys proposed the three-million-acre compromise mentioned earlier, which, despite enthusiasm by many government people, was mysteriously rejected by Interior Secretary Cecil Andrus. The appeal to the Supreme Court argued that the Shoshones were prevented at every stage from presenting their case on land title. Like every court before it, the Supreme Court refused to hear arguments. Meanwhile, however, another Shoshone land case was working its way slowly through the court system.

THE DANN SISTERS' CASE

Mary and Carrie Dann are Shoshone sisters who live with their brother and with Carrie's children on a ranch outside of Crescent Valley, Nevada. In 1974, the Dann sisters were herding cattle near their home when a Bureau of Land Management ranger stopped them and demanded to see their grazing permit. The Danns replied that they didn't need a permit since this wasn't U.S. land, but the land of the Western Shoshone Nation. They were charged with trespassing. "I have grazed my cattle and horses on that land all of my life," Carrie Dann told me, "and my mother did before me and her mother before her. Our people have been on this land for thousands of years. We don't need a permit to graze here."

The trespassing case went to the U.S. District Court in Reno. The Dann sisters convinced attorney John O'Connell to invoke their aboriginal rights. O'Connell challenged the Justice Department to show evidence demonstrating how and when the U.S. had obtained title. The U.S. could produce nothing. Instead, in a typical Catch-22, the U.S. referred the court to the Claims Commission, which found that the land had been "taken" in 1872. But in reality the Claims Commission had not "found" anything of the sort. It had merely accepted Robert Barker's assertion of title extinguishment. Still, this was enough for the Reno judge, who ruled against the Danns, fined them $500, and ordered them off the land.

O'Connell appealed to the Ninth Circuit Court of Appeals, repeating that there was no evidence anywhere, including in the claims case, that the Indians had lost title. In a tremendous victory for the Western Shoshones, the appeals court agreed with the Danns, and on March 15, 1978, remanded the case to the lower court for trial on the land-title question.

In the intervening year and a half, the Danns repeatedly tried to bring their case to trial but were met with delays by the court. "The judge never wanted that trial," said O'Connell. "At one point I accused the government of deliberately delaying the Dann case long enough to get the Indian claims check written, under the theory that once the payment was received Indian title would have been extinguished and the Danns would have been prevented from asserting it. The judge admitted on the record that he was 'sympathetic with the government's strategy.' "

O'Connell turned out to be right. Once the Indian Claims Commission announced that the Indians had been awarded $26 million, and that the money was placed into a trust account on their behalf (since the Indians would not accept the money), Judge Thompson made his decision. In another masterful Catch-22, Thompson ruled that the Danns did have title after all, based on aboriginal rights—up until 1979; but that once the Claims Commission Award was made in 1979, Shoshone title was extinguished.

In other words, a $26 million payment to Indians who never sought it, tried to stop it, and refused to accept it—payment for lands that were alleged by the payer to have been "taken" in 1872, but which the courts have finally affirmed were never "taken" at all—is now itself being used as the instrument to extinguish Indian title.

MX MISSILE

October 1979. A meeting is called in Elko, Nevada, by Glenn Holley and Raymond Yowell to tell the people that the government plans to put the MX missile on Shoshone aboriginal land. About 100 representatives of Shoshone communities around the state are in attendance. Also present are representatives of several environmental and disarmament groups, including SANE and Clergy and Laity Concerned.

Holley and Yowell explain in intermittent Shoshone and English that the MX is the largest construction project in U.S. history and that it will bring some 20,000 new people onto their land. The government plans to pave 10,000 miles of roads through the desert. Construction will require 3.15 billion gallons of water, endangering an already overused water table. Two hundred nuclear warheads will be moving around on trucks. Holley's speech becomes impassioned, and reveals the depth of traditional Indians' abhorrence of technical intrusions onto land they regard as sacred:

> Water is life. Water is not just used for consumption; it is also used
> in spiritual ways for purification, like in sweat ceremonies. Another
> thing the MX will destroy is the natural vegetation: the herbs like

the babeda, doza, sagebrush, chaparral, Indian tea. All these things will be destroyed. Not only the herbs but other medicines like the lizard in the south, which we use to heal the mentally sick and arthritis. There will also be electric fences, nerve gas, and security people all over our lands. It will affect the habitat of the eagles and the hawks, the rock chuck, ground squirrel, rabbit, deer, sage grouse, and rattlesnake. If this MX goes through, it will mean the total destruction of the Shoshone people, our spiritual beliefs and our ways of life. The MX would destroy our relationship to the five directions: 1) the universe—the skies, 2) the south, where the warm winds blow, 3) the east, where the sun appears, 4) the west, where the sun sets, and 5) the north, where the moist air comes from and brings moisture to vegetation. Everyone who leads a spiritual life gives offerings to these five directions. The Great Spirit is the only one who can determine the existence of living things. The MX will totally destroy the whole meaning of this concept. It is in violation of all natural laws of the Mother Earth.

Another man, Corbin Harney, stands up to represent the Duckwater community in northern Nevada: "Now we are witnessing the real reason why we are being forced to accept money for lands. We don't need their money. We need to keep these lands and protect them." Carrie Dann adds, "We have to be completely clear. We must not allow them to destroy Mother Earth. We've all been assimilated into white society but now we know it's destroying us. We have to get back to our ways." A resolution against the MX is passed unanimously. The statement expresses anger at the government for "assuming the land belongs to the U.S." and blames the MX for Interior Secretary Andrus's cutoff of negotiations.

VISITS WITH THE GOVERNMENT

After the meeting I approached John O'Connell to ask him why he thought negotiations were canceled. Did he believe that someone might have laid an arm on Andrus, because of the MX? "I doubted it at first," he said, "but I don't know—Andrus acted awfully suddenly and against a lot of advice."

I decided to try to speak to the relevant government people. First I called Major Art Forester at the Air Force Information Office. "Yes, the Air Force does know about the land dispute with the Indians, but no, there have been no attempts to talk with either Justice or the Department of the Interior about it."

I then visited four different bureaucrats at the Department of the Interior in Washington, D.C., and three at the Department of Justice, all of whom had been involved at various stages with the Shoshone case. None of them admitted to having heard the MX mentioned, although one who asked not to be named called it "extremely plausible" that Andrus was contacted, "probably by the National Security Council."

I tried and failed to reach Andrus himself. I did reach Andrus's assistant, who informed me that the secretary "was not involved in the case and doesn't know much about it." So who actually made the decision? "Leo Krulitz."

Krulitz was the Interior Department's chief lawyer at that time, and its second most powerful man. He had been described to me in several quarters as being totally devoted to "clarifying" all Indian title issues in favor of the U.S. I reached Krulitz on the phone and asked him why the negotiations for a reservation had been cut off.

"Well, I wasn't that comfortable with the claim that the Indians still seem to possess title," he told me, "but really I didn't give the legal issues much thought. They were so complex that I addressed it as a policy question." I asked him what a "policy question" was.

"Under no circumstances was I going to recommend that we create a reservation without first going to Congress. But the Indians can always do that themselves."

I reminded him that the Treaty of Ruby Valley gives the Interior Department clear authority to establish a reservation, and that practically speaking, since the Nevada delegation is one of the more conservative in the country, the Indians had no real chance to go that route.

"I saw my job," Krulitz responded, "as assessing the resource needs of the Shoshones, but I couldn't recommend that we establish a reservation." I asked him what he meant by "in the best interests of the Indians," which was the phrase Secretary Andrus used in his letter to the Shoshones (actually written by Krulitz), refusing the negotiated compromise and land settlement. "What I meant is that this money is sitting there in the Claims Commission and it's a lot of money, you know. You have to realize these are very poor people, living in disparate communities. I just thought they ought to have the money."

I thought about asking Krulitz if he'd ever discussed the matter with an actual Shoshone, but I already knew that he hadn't. Instead I asked his opinion of the Shoshone allegations that their attorney misled them into seeking money instead of land. "I can't get into a discussion about their lawyers," he said. "What about the MX missile?" "No, that came along much later." I knew this was not exactly true. The Andrus letter had preceded the MX announcement by only a few weeks, but by this time I had lost interest in the fine points of secret MX dealings. I realized that deploying the MX is only slightly different from the prior destruction of the pinyon groves, and that both are just symptoms of the larger crime the Shoshones have been trying to broadcast since 1910. The U.S. *is* stealing Shoshone land! The bureaucrats involved are not really concerned about the legalities of the matter or what the Indians have to say about it. They are just following a set of rules, a procedural logic, begun a long time ago, that obscures to the world (and even to themselves) the knowledge of what they're actually doing. By now, it just seems right to tie up the loose ends.

Finally, I asked Krulitz if he had any personal feelings about the injustices being visited upon the Western Shoshones. He seemed shocked at the question. "Certainly there's been no injustice from anyone in the Interior Department," he said.

• • •

Following my visits to the Interior Department, I had one more appointment with an old friend who had achieved a high post in the Carter administration, with some involvement in Indian land cases.

I had known this man best during the 1960s when he was one of the country's top environmental lawyers. He had bravely fought and won epic battles against corporate polluters. I expected a warm reception from him and I got it. We had a drink at his apartment at Watergate and then he took me out to dinner. We talked about the "old days" and about the new programs his office had instituted under Carter. Everything was very pleasant until I came around to the Western Shoshone case, and the fact that I was writing an article for the *Village Voice* about them and other Indian tribes who were refusing settlements.

My friend became tense and angry. "These Indian cases make me so damned uncomfortable," he said. "I wish I didn't have to work on them at all. I really can't understand what these people want. Their lawyers get them great settlements—the Shoshones were awarded $26 million, and the Sioux may get $143 million for the Black Hills—and damn if they don't turn around and start talking about land."

I was surprised by the bitterness of his tone. I attempted to explain that many of the claims lawyers acted without clear authority from the tribal membership. In any event, the lawyers have been oblivious to what the

Indians truly want, which is to retain land rather than be paid money. The land is the Indians' economic, cultural, and spiritual base, I explain to my friend. Maintaining land is what permits them to remain Indians. The lawyers, however, seem always to go for the money.

My friend stares at me. Then, he says, "I'd really like to help these people, Jerry, but let me tell you one goddamn thing. There's no way we're ever letting any of the Indians have title to those lands. If they don't take the money, they'll get nothing," he says.

CURRENT EVENTS

As this book goes to press, the Western Shoshones, like the Oglala and Rosebud Sioux, have not given up. They still refuse payment for their lands, though the interest-bearing trust account is now over $60 million.

Led by the Dann sisters and Raymond Yowell, the Indians continue to graze cattle on the disputed lands, and to hunt, gather, and fish without paying grazing fees.

Meanwhile, the MX missile basing system, which was killed by Congress during the Reagan years, has re-emerged under George Bush, with the Western Shoshone treaty lands among the possible sites. The huge new radioactive waste dump is still very much in the cards. And underground nuclear testing continues unabated in southern Nevada, despite frequent large demonstrations by peace activists.

On this latter issue, there are some positive developments. Many of the peace groups have belatedly recognized the Indian issue and now request permission from the Western Shoshone Nation to demonstrate on their land. The Indians, in turn, have been issuing the demonstrators "safe passage" permits and have agreed to speak at the rallies. The Western Shoshone National Council has called the nuclear testing facility "an absolute violation of the Treaty of Ruby Valley and the laws of the United States."

Peace activists are instructed that if they are confronted or arrested by U.S. government officials while on Shoshone land, they should show their Shoshone permits and demand to continue their activities. Furthermore, in case of trial, the defendants should include in their defense that they had legal rights to be on the land, as granted by the landowners.

On the legal front, however, things are very bleak. A new strategy was hatched to sue the government for mineral fees and trespass fees from 1872 to 1979. The logic of the argument was that since the courts recognize that the Shoshones did have legal title until the Claims Commission took it away in 1979, they were entitled to mineral and trespass fees for 109 years. This would amount to billions of dollars due the Shoshones; it was hoped that this amount was sufficient to cause the government to negotiate. But the court rejected this new intervention on the technical grounds that the specific interveners were not parties to the original claim. This suit may yet re-emerge.

As for the Dann sisters, their earlier victory on the land-title issue turned to defeat. The Ninth Circuit Court somehow confirmed the Catch-22 decision that the 1979 Claims Commission award wiped out the Danns' aboriginal rights, along with the rights of all the Western Shoshones. The Supreme Court concurred. The Danns, however, remain undaunted. They are heading back into court with a new suit based on their hundreds of years of "continued use and occupancy'" prior to the authority of the Bureau of Land Management, which began in 1935. They hope to carve a hole in the earlier decisions, which might reaffirm their rights to a traditional livelihood and reopen a doorway for the rest of the Western Shoshones.

Meanwhile, the resolve of a growing number of Western Shoshones is beginning to weaken. The steady pressure of the government agencies, combined with the wall of opposition that the Justice Department and the courts have put against them, have caused an already poor people to exhaust their resources and their energy. Compromise solutions are emerging.

One hope is that a new bill can be introduced in Congress to give new life to the 1978 plan—a reservation and some cash—that Secretary of the Interior Cecil Andrus had mysteriously rejected. But the Shoshones who would compromise are running into hostility from those who remain adamant in their opposition to giving up any land at all. The result is an internal split in the tribe that is becoming increasingly harsh. Given the continued disinterest of the media, the absence of public understanding and support, and a legal and court system that has bent over backward to give the government preposterous, absurd victories, Western Shoshone optimism is on the wane.

One of the current attorneys for the Western Shoshone National Council, Tom Luebben, very experienced in fighting for Indian causes, put it to me this way: "It is clear that one of the main strategies the government uses in these cases is simply to wear out the Indians over decades of struggle. The government has unlimited resources to litigate. If the Indians win one victory in court, the government just loads up its legal guns, adds a new, bigger crew of fresh lawyers, and comes back harder. It's the legal equivalent of what the cavalry did a hundred years ago. There's simply no interest in justice. It's hardball all the way. The government has all the time in the world to achieve its goals. The Indians run out of money, they get tired of fighting, they get old, and finally, after ten to twenty years, somebody says, 'The hell with it; let's take what we can.' It's really understandable that it finally works out that way, but it's disgusting and it's wrong."

Contemplating such an outcome, Western Shoshone educator Glenn Wasson said this (from *Newe Sogobia: The Western Shoshone People and Land*):

> In Indian terms there is no equation in dollars for the loss of a way of life . . . you cannot equate dollars to lives. The redmen are the last people on Earth who speak on behalf of all living things. The bear, the deer, the sagebrush have no one else to speak for them. The animals and plants were put here by the Great Spirit before he put the humans here. . . . There is a story that the old people tell about the white man. That they are like children. They want this and that, they want everything they see, like it's their first time on Earth. The white men have all these tools but they don't know how to use them properly. The white people try to equate national defense with human lives. There can never be an equation between the dollar bill and living things—the fish, the birds, the deer, the clean air, clean water. There is no way of comparing them. . . . The white people have no love for this land. If we human beings persist in what we are doing, we will become like a bad cancer on Mother Earth. If we don't stop ourselves, something will stop us. We are destroying everything. The way things are fouled by nuclear waste, nothing can live on it. After we have made the earth uninhabitable, will the human beings take this to other planets? If we take these ways of destruction to other planets, we will be the worst cancer in the universe. The universe will be programmed for destruction. We will wipe out the whole galaxy with our filth.

18

DESECRATION OF
SACRED LANDS

The Case of the Native Hawaiians

THE UNITED STATES *is supposed to guarantee freedom for all religious worship but it looks like it doesn't apply to every religion. The Hawaiian religion, which thousands of us still observe, is different from Christianity or Judaism or Buddhism. Like Native Americans, our religion is in nature. Our Gods and Goddesses are alive and with us. On the Big Island of Hawaii, the Goddess Pele appears to us daily in all her forms. She is the volcano, the lava, the steam, the heat. Her family is present in the ferns, certain shrubs and native trees. She is the land itself. We pray to her daily. Many of our chants and hula are for Pele and about her. We believe that some of us are descended from her. This is the way we have believed for thousands of years. For us it is a sacrilege for an energy company to come along and drill holes in Pele's body, to capture her steam for geothermal power, to destroy her rainforests, all so a few people can make money. Such things should never be allowed in sacred places. But when we argue that point in courts or commissions they don't take us seriously. We are ignored. This is not right. It's not respectful of our religion or of Native Hawaiian people. It is also a violation of American law protecting religious worship. We have to keep fighting to stop the geothermal drilling of Pele.*
—NEW YORK TIMES, SEPTEMBER 21, 1988—
ADVERTISEMENT FOR PELE DEFENSE FUND, BIG ISLAND, HAWAII

That there even exists such a thing as a Native Hawaiian activist movement comes as a surprise to most Americans. Most of us have been hidden from real contact with Hawaii's native population, just as we have from American Indians. Our sole contacts with Hawaiians tend to be with the tourist hotels' cocktail lounge entertainers, or hula dancers. Few Americans know the history of native-white interactions in the islands. Fewer still are aware that the word *aloha,* so loudly trumpeted by the Hawaii Convention and Visitors' Bureau, is a distortion of a native concept, *aloha aina,* meaning "love, reverence, and care for the land." Nor do we realize that Hawaiian activists view the tourist economy of hotels, condos, and golf courses as a direct violation of native land use, culture and religion, and of *aloha aina.*

In fact, today's Native Hawaiian community, which now accounts for less than 20 percent of the state's population, is a remnant of a great Polynesian nation that thrived on the Hawaiian Islands for 1,200 years, and numbered at least 300,000 people. (Some Native Hawaiians put the population closer to one million.) The ancient Hawaiians lived within a sophisticated system of laws and religious practices, as well as enjoyed economic abundance based on agriculture and fishing. It's only been during the last century that the Native Hawaiians' land was stolen, their economic base destroyed, and their culture reprocessed and sold to tourists in an aberrant form.

Native Hawaiians now suffer the highest rates of unemployment, ill health, alcoholism, and incarceration of any racial group in the state. These factors have produced an anger among them that has found occasional expression in assaults against newcomers and tourists. More recently, however, the frustration has been given a creative outlet through a burgeoning number of activist groups that concentrate on recovering native lands, revitalizing the native economy, and preventing the further desecration of native culture and sacred places. Two of the largest grass-roots groups are the Protect Kahoolawe Ohana, which has been waging a long battle against the U.S. Navy's bombing of the sacred Kahoolawe Island, and Pele Defense Fund, which opposes geothermal energy development on the Big Island, considering it a direct humiliation of the Goddess Pele and the earth.

THE FOURTH OF JULY, 1980

My involvement with Native Hawaiians began on Independence Day 1980, when my family and I were met at the Molokai airport by a prominent Native Hawaiian physician, Dr. Emmett Aluli. Director of the Molokai Clinic, Aluli has been one of the leaders of both the Protect Kahoolawe Ohana and Pele Defense Fund. Accompanying Aluli was Colette Machado, a Molokai native educator, rural economic development worker, and leader of the grass-roots resistance to tourist development on Molokai.

After the usual welcome greeting, with leis, hugs, and kisses, Aluli and Machado took us on a tour of Molokai. We found that it does not have the overdeveloped feeling of Maui, Oahu, or Kauai. On Molokai, the majority population is still native and the traditional culture is alive.

As we drove along the south shoreline, Machado explained that the major battles have been to forestall the huge resort hotel and condo developments envisioned for the entire western edge of the island, "where the beaches have white sand. . . . That's what the *haoles* like: white sand, surf, and sun," she said.

Indeed, since that visit, Machado has told me that Japanese investors have bought the enormous west-end development area and proposed six to eight golf courses and eight to ten major hotels, "with artificial lagoons and white sand, to improve on Molokai's rural character."

When our little tour turned inland, we learned that the central highlands of Molokai are devoted to one-crop agriculture. Once pineapples, the crop is now coffee; about 10 million coffee-bean trees grow on Molokai's plantations. "All this land was originally owned by the monarchy," Machado told us, but "when the U.S. overthrew the queen it also seized a majority of the crown lands."

Three decades later, in 1920, the federal government passed the Hawaiian Homes Commission Act, setting aside 187,000 acres of Hawaiian land for homesteading by Native Hawaiians. These lands were considered least desirable by the large sugar and pineapple planters, who got first choice. When statehood was granted in 1959, the lands were transferred to state ownership, with the proviso that they would be used for Native Hawaiian settlement. But it has not worked that way. "Every once in a while a Native Hawaiian will be awarded a homestead on Hawaiian Homes land," Machado said. "But over 18,000 names are on the waiting list, and the average wait is thirty years." Many applicants die before their names come up.

Machado believes that the federal and state governments are stonewalling on homestead claims because "by law, Native Hawaiians have 'superior rights' to the water. This issue alone would stop west-end tourist and resort development on Molokai," as well as similar developments on other islands, as the Hawaiian natives would tend to use their land and water for traditional subsistence agriculture, especially taro growing.

Eventually, our tour took us back to Dr. Aluli's house. Surprising for its modesty, nothing like a typical American doctor's home, the house was little more than a three-room wooden shack, enclosed by screens, with no locks on the doors, about ten feet from the Maui Channel, facing Lanai. The house was surrounded by mango trees, from which fruit was continually falling, as in paradise. "Molokai is probably the only place in the world where you don't ever feed the dogs," Aluli said. "They eat the mangoes."

Alongside the house was an open workshop area covered by a piece of corrugated tin. Within, a long plywood board was set upon six barrels: the dining room. And a few feet in front of that, along the water, was a stone fire pit with a large bucket of fish nearby. "We caught those about four hours ago," said Aluli, "right out there in the fish pond." Aluli pointed toward a semicircle of rocks that extended several hundred feet into the shallow water.

"That fish pond was probably built 700 years ago," Machado added. "The entire southeastern end of Molokai is lined with these fish ponds; nearly fifty of them. In ancient times, they were used on a daily basis. The people stocked the fish ponds with baby fish, and others would swim in between the tiny cracks in the rocks. They'd hang out, grow big, and then couldn't get back out. You could use a baseball glove to catch fish in those ponds, the fish are so plentiful," Machado said. "It was a way of life not based on a money economy. But over there"—she pointed across the twelve-mile channel toward Maui—"the fish ponds are gone. Dredged and filled for resort complexes. This has also happened on Oahu and at Kona. Since most of the productive agricultural lands are [now] used for coffee, pineapple, sugar cane, golf courses, and resort development, Native Hawaiians have had to fight to protect our [remaining] water rights [and land] for the cultivation of taro. With no fish and no land, the people are forced to work for the hotels, or to collect welfare, or to sit around getting drunk and mad."

I asked Aluli about his medical practice. Why had he eschewed a high-income practice on Maui or Oahu to move to Molokai? "I wanted to be a country doctor," he said, "and Molokai needed doctors. But also this is where the Hawaiian culture is still thriving. I wanted to be part of that."

Aluli has begun an ambitious project interviewing most of the oldest natives on Molokai, in order to preserve their knowledge of the ancient society and religion. "It's like with the American Indians," he said. "The culture is embodied by the old people, and the young need to seek them out. We are placing emphasis on the *kahuna,* the traditional religious practitioners, because we can't separate the political struggle here, or the fight to regain our land and traditional economy, from the religious teachings. In Hawaii the land *is* the religion and so is the sea. Fighting for land rights is religious work, just as with American Indians."

By now, the afternoon had begun to merge with the evening. Colette Machado came over and jokingly told Emmett to stop talking and start cooking the fish. Neighbors and friends started to arrive. Beer was brought out by the case. Emmett introduced us to an old man and woman, accompanied by a young ethnomusicologist from Chicago. Aluli explained that the two were *kapuna,* elders who are also celebrated artists, among the islands' top singers of ancient Hawaiian songs. I was fascinated by their appearance. The man sported a shock of white hair and an astounding black coral necklace hanging around his neck, over his white polyester shirt. The woman was huge, about seventy-five years old, and had a way of rolling her head that seemed—how to put it?—ecstatic.

After we all consumed great amounts of fish, the two *kapuna* pulled out guitars and ukuleles and began their chants to the waves, to the mountains, to the mangoes, and threw in a fair number of rowdy songs about sex and fighting. The gathered crowd roared with laughter. Then suddenly, we heard the sound of explosions from across the water. There was a full moon that night, so we could clearly see the outlines of Maui across the channel. My son Kai shouted, "Fireworks!" We had forgotten. It was the Fourth of July. The Maui resorts were putting on a fireworks show to celebrate American independence. How odd. Sitting with these Native Hawaiians around a fire, singing ancient songs, while in the distance came the sounds and colors of U.S. Independence Day celebrations. Was this America or wasn't it?

THE GREAT MAHELE

The Hawaiian people migrated from the southern and western Pacific in roughly the sixth century A.D. Though there are some 132 islands in the Hawaiian archipelago, the eventual population of 300,000 to one million lived on only the eight largest: Hawaii (the Big Island), Oahu, Maui, Kauai, Molokai, Lanai, Niihau, and Kahoolawe, which make up 99 percent of the total Hawaiian land area.

After the arrival of Captain Cook in 1778, the population was decimated: Within fifty years it was reduced to 80,000, then to 54,000 a half-century after that. Cook, and the fleets that followed him, brought cholera, mumps, influenza, and venereal diseases. And guns. All had major roles in population reduction, as did the forced imposition of Western economic and religious concepts.

Prior to white arrival, Hawaiian society was organized into hundreds of small, self-sufficient, autonomous communities—little city-states. Unlike similar autonomous communities among American Indians, the Hawaiian villages had hierarchical governments. Chiefs and priests held personal powers said to be given them by the myriad of gods and goddesses who were apparent everywhere to the Hawaiians: in the running waters, the hills, the volcanoes, the wind, the land, the plants, the clouds, the air, and the forests. An elaborate system of laws, *Kapu,* dictated proper behavior toward these chiefs and their assistants, and also among the people. Certain rule violations could be met with harsh punishments, including banishment and death.

Though the chiefs had great ceremonial and coercive military power, and held certain lands for themselves, most of the land was held communally. Work was performed collectively and the output was shared. In these latter respects, Hawaiian society did resemble Native American societies, except that in Hawaii the agriculture was especially rich and abundant. All of this was duly noted by Captain Cook in his diaries, and by subsequent arriving Westerners, who then set out to destroy the communal land-tenure system, and with it the glue of Hawaiian culture and economy.

I have mentioned the role of guns. Certain village chiefs grasped the potential of firearms and made huge investments in guns by trading pigs and foodstuffs. Skirmishes among Hawaiian communities, which had been frequent even before Cook arrived, became much larger and far deadlier once the arms race began. By 1810, one chief, Kamehameha I, who effectively used gunboats and cannons in especially bloody encounters, became the first chief to unify all the Hawaiian islands and communities under his rule. He then granted himself the Western title of king. His dynasty lasted nearly a century.

Just as mainland white Americans had found it helpful to destroy traditional Indian governments, and to bring decentralized communities under one central authority, a Hawaiian king was also good for the white man's business. With only one customer to concentrate upon, white trading companies could convince Kamehameha of the potential benefits to him of a change in traditional economic activity. In a sharp departure from the past, the king ordered his people to abandon their farms, and to cut down whole forests of sandalwood for export.

Missionaries also made inroads by converting the king's wife, Kaahumanu, to Christianity. She then carried the gospel to the islands and paved the way for missionary schools. The missionaries began literacy programs but only used Christian texts, filled with Western concepts of morality and economics. They persuaded the people to wear clothes and adopt chastity and monogamy, arguing that it would halt the spread of the venereal diseases sweeping the islands since the whites arrived. The missionaries also gave lessons in "private property," as something more godly than communal property. Many of the increasingly corruptible chiefs took this news to heart.

By the 1840s, under the rule of Kamehameha III, the missionaries and businessmen had sufficient control to assault the communal land system directly. They pressured the king to change the system, telling him that businesses would not enter Hawaii in full force unless they could be assured secure land title. The king finally agreed and instituted "The Great Mahele," arguably the most significant step ever in the alienation of the Native Hawaiians from their land and culture.

"The Great Mahele" of 1848 divided the kingdom into three parts: 1.5 million acres were set aside for the 245 chiefs and their aides; 1 million acres, referred to as Crown Lands, were reserved for the king and his heirs; the remaining 1.5 million acres were reserved for the Hawaiian government. All of this land could now be bought and sold. None of the land was held communally anymore, though for a while agriculture continued as before on "government land."

The king also established a parliamentary system under a constitution, while retaining veto power. In 1850, the new parliament passed a law permitting Hawaiian "commoners" to claim lands on which they lived and worked as their individual private property. (This act was similar to the Allotment Act and the Alaska Native Claims Settlement Act, which converted communally held land into a saleable commodity.) Fewer than 30,000 acres—only 1 percent of the total lands—were actually claimed by natives, as they didn't understand how to deal with the new bureaucracy. Also, the whole idea of individual ownership of small plots of land defied their traditional way of working communally.

With the natives confused and in turmoil from all the changes, non-Hawaiians, particularly the missionaries, worked feverishly to acquire and expand their personal holdings. They bought and leased land whenever they could, intermarried with Native Hawaiians, and used fraud to get their way. With the land thus usurped by private ownership, traditional self-sustaining agriculture gave way to cash-crop plantations (mainly sugar cane and pineapple) for export. By the 1800s, a handful of non-Hawaiians owned the vast majority of lands that were once the domain

of ordinary people; they also owned a substantial portion of the land that
had been set aside for the Crown and the chiefs.

With their communal land-tenure system destroyed, and without private plots of land, Native Hawaiians found themselves having to accept
jobs as laborers, working for miserable wages on the same lands they used
to own and work collectively. Some refused to do this work, so the plantation owners imported Chinese, Filipinos, Japanese, and Koreans willing
to work for low wages under terrible conditions. This threw the Native
Hawaiians into an even more unworkable position, competing with new
immigrant classes for the lowest rungs on the economic ladder.

The final assault on Hawaiian sovereignty came in the late 1800s. In
1887, white plantation owners demanded and obtained the Reciprocity
Treaty between the Hawaiian government and the United States, which
eliminated all tariffs on Hawaiian sugar exports. The U.S., in turn, got
ownership of Pearl Harbor. Soon after, an army financed by plantation
owners militarily coerced King Kalakaua to scrap the old Hawaiian constitution, and in its place establish a new one that gave voting rights only
to large property owners (now mostly whites) and eliminated the king's
veto power. This was called the Bayonet Constitution, which effectively
disenfranchised Native Hawaiians from self-rule.

One last stand was attempted in 1893 by Queen Liliuokalani. She tried
to overrule the Bayonet Constitution and recover authority. In response the
whites recruited an army of foreigners aided by U.S. troops, which forcibly deposed Liliuokalani and declared the new Republic of Hawaii. Annexation followed in 1898, at which point all Hawaiian government lands
were ceded to the United States government. This left the Native Hawaiians landless, save for the few parcels reserved for the Crown, the chiefs,
and their aides. From start to finish, from "The Great Mahele" to annexation, the alienation of Hawaiians from their lands took fifty years.

Since annexation, the only opportunity for Native Hawaiians to bid for
lands they formerly owned came with the Hawaiian Homes Commission
Act of 1920. As indicated earlier, it turned out to offer far less than it
seemed. Though the law reserved 187,000 acres of land for homestead
claims, heavy lobbying by the sugar, pineapple, and ranching industries
exempted the highest quality agricultural lands. So while Native Hawaiians might claim a homestead, it was only on the poorest land, very difficult to farm.

Nonetheless, the Hawaiians have been trying to obtain some of this
promised land. The law states that anyone with 50 percent Hawaiian
blood is qualified to apply. But in all this time only 2,000 families have
secured a Hawaiian Homes ninety-nine-year lease. Eighteen thousand

other applicants remain on the waiting list. Many have waited for decades. A complex set of rules has effectively thwarted successful applications. One rule, for example, requires that applicants show financial means sufficient to obtain mortgages to build homes on the land. Since most applicants are very poor—which is why they want the land—this rule alone is sufficient to block them.

The net effect is that Hawaiians are virtually landless in their own homeland, while the state continues to promote itself as a paradise, based on Native Hawaiian concepts of love of the land.

THE INVASION OF KAHOOLAWE

It was in this depressing context, the destruction of the Native Hawaiian land base, that the direct actions in 1976, on the island of Kahoolawe, became a cause célèbre for the native community.

"The American Indians had the takeover of Alcatraz in the 1970s to catalyze their movement; we had Kahoolawe," said Dr. Emmett Aluli. "For the past thirty years that island, one of the most sacred places to Native Hawaiians, has been used for bombing practice by the U.S. Navy and other nations of the Pacific Rim. It has been a visible, tangible slap in our face to use these sacred lands in this way. Beginning in 1976, we started fighting back and it has re-energized the entire native movement here."

Few tourists are even aware of Kahoolawe, though it sits directly across an eight-mile channel from the Kihei coast of Maui. Five miles long by three miles wide, Kahoolawe can be seen from the crowded beaches as a bright red dome rising mysteriously from the ocean. Now unpopulated because of the military actions, Kahoolawe was first settled in the sixth or seventh century A.D. Attesting to its role in Hawaiian life are the recent discoveries of some 544 archeological sites, adze quarries, fishing shrines, temples, petroglyph fields, housing complexes, and burial grounds.

Kahoolawe fell out of native hands during "The Great Mahele," and was operated as a ranch by a small number of whites until 1941. After the Japanese assault on Pearl Harbor, the Navy requisitioned Kahoolawe for military exercises and practice bombings. After the war, in 1953, President Eisenhower issued an executive order that officially seized the island for the military. (The American military holds 6 percent, or 259,000 acres, of Hawaiian land, a greater total percentage of land holdings than in any other state.)

Until very recently, Kahoolawe was the primary site of the Rimpac (Pacific Rim) Games. These were bombing exercises by the U.S., Canada,

Australia, South Korea, France, New Zealand, and ironically, Japan, that involved dozens of warships, hundreds of military aircraft, and some 20,000 personnel. The bombings and shellings would occur daily for about a month. During bombing practice days, you could sit on the beach at Kihei and believe you were watching a rerun of World War II.

The effect on Kahoolawe has been to destroy its forest cover, lateralize the soil, cause terrible erosion, blow out of existence many of its historic and religious sites, and to drive a spike into the spirit of the Native Hawaiians who revere Kahoolawe as a sacred place.

By 1976, Aluli and other Native Hawaiians were so enraged by the bombing, and by the Navy's refusal to allow native access to the island, that they undertook a sensational act of civil disobedience. Several dozen Hawaiians boarded six fishing boats at Maui and headed toward Kahoolawe, intending to land a group as an "occupation force," and thereby force a delay in the bombing.

Nine of the party, including Aluli, made it to shore, but the Coast Guard quickly rounded up seven of them. Aluli and another Hawaiian, Walter Ritte, managed to evade capture for two days and nights, succeeding in delaying the bombs.

When word of the "invasion" hit the media on the larger islands, a wave of pride and hope swept the native communities. When Aluli and Ritte returned, after becoming the first natives to explore the island in nearly a century, they reported that they had found hundreds of ancient sites of temples, petroglyphs, and shrines. "The Navy had told us for years that there was nothing out there," Aluli told me. "They said there was nothing of ecological or historic importance. We never believed that, but the public did. We proved they were lying. Even after all their bombs, we found hundreds of signs of our ancestors. . . . Kahoolawe is a *piko* to Native Hawaiians, an umbilical cord, connecting us to our ancestors. The whole island is a kind of temple for us. For the Navy to be keeping us off the island, while dropping bombs on it, is sickening and sacrilegious."

Aluli went on to form the Protect Kahoolawe Ohana, and "everything good has followed from that," Aluli said. "We gained strength to ratchet up the struggle for Kahoolawe but also to begin new battles for agricultural lands, shoreline access, and to fight hotel development on lands that are supposed to be ours. It was our first big consciousness-raising effort. We learned we had the power to make something happen to recover our culture and our rights. We didn't have to be passive anymore."

Aluli also filed suit in federal court. In *Aluli v. Brown*, Emmett Aluli asked that an environmental impact report and a survey of archeological sites be completed before any bombing resumed. The suit led to a negotiation that won the following for Native Hawaiians: 1) that the Ohana (which means "extended family" in Hawaiian) be permitted access to the island once each month for a four-day encampment, 2) that the Navy agree to remove live bombs and ammunition from encampment sites, 3) that teams of researchers be permitted to explore the whole island to map the religious and historical sites, and 4) that the Navy agree to stop bombing such sites as were discovered. In a separate action, the native community succeeded in having Kahoolawe placed on the National Historic Site Register of the U.S. government, surely the only such historic place that the government continued to bomb.

The Ohana simultaneously began lobbying in Congress to block the bombing completely and began a campaign of letters and personal visits to foreign governments attempting to gain their agreement to withdraw from Rimpac. While the efforts in the U.S. Congress languished from disinterest, Japan, New Zealand, and Australia soon ceased to participate in the games, leaving only Canada, South Korea, and the United States continuing their assaults.

• • •

July 6, 1980. Aluli has invited my family and me to a four-night Kahoolawe encampment. At 3 A.M., with about 125 other people, we board a huge trimaran at a Maui pier, and we are off.

By dawn, the outlines of Kahoolawe are in view, looking like a giant sleeping human lying sideways. Two mountains rise where the shoulder and hip might be. In the early morning sun, the mountaintops are bright red.

Because of the rocky shoreline, the boat sets anchor about 300 yards offshore. For the first time, I realize that we are all expected to swim the remaining distance through a rough sea, though nonswimmers can board a small rubber Zodiac that commutes back and forth with supplies. I get up my courage and make it to shore, straggling behind my kids.

The encampment is within a low forest of *kiawe* trees, alongside a dry riverbed. Nearby stands an impressive, half-constructed ceremonial long house, built by previous monthly Kahoolawe access groups using materials brought over by boat. Construction is in the traditional manner: poles lashed together with bark and a floor made of small, round sea stones. One of the encampment's major tasks is to complete the floor, which means that each of us is expected to lug dozens of baskets of heavy stones up the beach from the sea.

Nearby we see fire pits for cooking, a kind of amphitheatre constructed with a stage area of palm fronds, and several large gardens where taro, sweet potato, and various greens had been planted and seem to be thriving. We express amazement that these gardens flourish, since no one is on the island between the monthly encampments, and a population of voracious feral goats will eat anything they can find. Fences around the gardens must be built well enough to withstand a month's worth of animal assaults. The Hawaiian campers have also devised an ingenious system of drip irrigation designed to last exactly one month, using a water supply laboriously brought over by boat.

After supplies are unloaded, Aluli and Machado gather the entire group for prayers—Christian and Hawaiian—and to explain the rules, tasks, and explorations. One very strict rule is that no one is permitted out of the encampment area—about 300 yards square—without a guide, because of the live ammunition lying buried in the sand. Hiking parties are limited to twenty-five people at a time, with two ammo experts supplied by the U.S. Navy accompanying the groups, at the front and rear.

The first hike begins before 6 A.M., with Aluli in the lead. We walk first through dense forest, opening into gorgeous grassy hillsides. After about one mile, we climb uphill out of this unbombed area and find ourselves on a mountainside of bare, smooth, hard red earth stretching in all directions—the product of decades of bombing. Littered everywhere for miles around are spent shell casings, craters, and twisted metal remains of jeeps, tanks, and assault vehicles from mock invasions.

With no trees, the heat becomes intense. Our walk is straight up the side of a 1,400-foot mountain. I quickly become tired, but Aluli, who walks barefoot, seems to actually gain energy from his excitement.

At the first peak, we are greeted by a breathtaking view of Maui, the volcanoes on the Big Island, Lanai, Molokai, and Oahu in the distance. Aluli explains how this peak is directly aligned with the main Hawaiian islands and with Tahiti, 1,500 miles south. This explains, Aluli says, Kahoolawe's importance as a navigational and ceremonial center for ancient ocean travelers.

From there we walk down through a saddle and find another miraculously untouched field of lush green meadows. Aluli then leads us past an ancient adze quarry and several ruins of ancient *heiau* (temples), now surrounded by rusting military equipment. The approach to the second peak is through another dismal terrain of scorched, destroyed lands. But near the top of the peak we find numerous wild tomato plants. My son Yari gathers several handfuls and remarks with amazement at how they could have survived such destruction.

• • •

Back at the campsite, activities include garden work, strategy meetings, stone carrying, and the constant preparation of meals for 125 people. The meals are voluminous and fabulous. Hawaiian, Japanese, and Chinese cooks prepare traditional pig baked underground, chicken in curry and coconut, and massive amounts of *poi*. The entire group then gathers in the amphitheatre around a campfire for reports. We hear about the genealogical research by which Hawaiians are attempting to prove their 50 percent Hawaiian blood, so as to qualify for Hawaiian Homes land. We hear about efforts to block tourist hotels on Kauai, updates on negotiations with the Navy for expanded access, and about lobbying in Congress to stop the Kahoolawe bombing.

Several archeologists are present at the encampment, having gained permission to leave the regular hiking trails. They tell the group about some new sites of significance.

The director of the garden project reports on his discovery of a new well, which might solve the problem of a two-month break in scheduled accesses.

There is a long discussion about the difficulties of persuading young Hawaiians to be more active in Ohana projects. One elder, Harry Mitchell, speaks about the Hawaiian inferiority complex: "Growing up Hawaiian, even though these were my islands, I was always called stupid by the non-Hawaiians, and for the first forty years of my life I believed that." I realize that in accepting colonialist definitions of themselves as valid, the Hawaiians have much in common with Native Americans.

For me, one of the most enlightening presentations is by a young Hawaiian attorney, Mililani Trask.

Trask is among the leaders of a wing of the Native Hawaiian movement that seeks sovereign status, similar to that of other Native Americans: self-government under a Native Hawaiian constitution and court system, control of traditional lands, right to sue in federal and state courts to protect trust assets. Trask's organization, *Ka Lahui Hawaii,* envisions a Native Hawaiian government that combines an elected executive, elected legislature, separate judiciary, and *Alii nui,* or traditional chiefs. The organization, which now claims more than 7,000 members, believes that sovereign status will give the Native Hawaiians greater leverage in dealing with *haole* governments, as well as more accurately reflect the historical reality of Hawaiian nationhood.

On this evening around the Kahoolawe campfire, Trask speaks on a more subtle political subject, the work of the Native Planters Association in encouraging Native Hawaiians to return to taro growing. Trask describes the importance of taro to Hawaiian culture and identity: "Hawaiian stories tell us that the first child of *Wakea* (Sky Father) and *Ho' oho' Kukalan* was stillborn, and was placed into the ground, where it became taro. The second child became the first human. The Hawaiian concept of extended family (*ohana*) is derived from the word *oha* and refers to the rings of cormlets that encircle the parent plant. Taro has the same relationship to Hawaiians that corn does to the Pueblo Indians. It's our main nutritional staple, but it's also our psychological staple."

Trask points out that for a thousand years, Hawaiians were the world's foremost cultivators of taro, developing complex irrigation and hydraulic systems that are still visible on some mountainsides today. But now, Native Hawaiians "are losing our remaining taro fields; the land and the water are going to developers . . . which means survival for Hawaiian culture is becoming more difficult. We are trying to make a wedge into the juggernaut with a new lawsuit based on Native Hawaiian walking trails, a suit with the possibility of holding off development in some places. In some ways, native rights come down to being able to live on the land, pick up your fishing pole, and walk to the beach to fish. But if you do that today, you might be arrested. So all of you, remember," Trask says, "when you head to the beach to catch some food, you are asserting ancient Hawaiian rights."

THE DESECRATION OF PELE

In the years following the Kahoolawe trip, I heard occasionally from Aluli. He would stop in San Francisco on his way to Washington or to various conferences on native rights. He seemed especially interested in the possibilities of running advertising on the mainland to break the political logjam in Hawaii. "They are ignoring us in Hawaii. But if we can show them some impact on the mainland, and scare them back home, maybe we can change the atmosphere," he said.

Aluli felt the best issue for advertising was the proposed geothermal development project in the East Rift Zone of Kilauea volcano on the Big Island. To the native population, the drilling was a violation of their religion, a sacrilege of unprecedented proportions. It was also the most environmentally destructive project in the history of the Big Island, since it would destroy several pristine rainforests and fuel an expanded tourist industry, as well as create a brand-new heavy industrial complex to process ocean ores, which would cause severe toxic waste problems.

On several visits, Aluli was accompanied by a fisherman from the Big Island, Palikapu Dedman, cofounder and driving force of Pele Defense Fund. Dedman had been attempting to block the drilling by legal means for years. He explained that the Goddess Pele is still very much alive to the native people. "My mother and grandmother raised me in Pele religion," Dedman told me. "We would go to the volcano and to places in the forest to pray, and people still do that. We hear people say the old religion is gone but it isn't. Some people won't admit they still practice because the missionaries made them ashamed, but what the people say in the day is different from what they do at night. Go to the volcano's edge some nights and you will see a hundred people saying prayers and leaving offerings for the Goddess. You can find the offerings in the morning. That's why this campaign is so important. We have to tell the Hawaiians as much as the whites that our religion is as good as anybody else's and should be respected. . . . The white people can't get it, that for us Pele is all the land. She's the volcano and everything that grows there is her. The steam and the vapor and lava are all parts of her body, and her family is all the forest plants and the life in the sea. You can't go shoving drills into her body like that. The old people say it will injure Pele and stop her creative force. And it will cause spiritual and psychological damage for the people who worship and live with her.

"We have been trying to argue with commissions that grant those drilling rights, and with the courts. Sometimes they don't even let us testify because they say nobody practices Pele religion anymore, but that's bullshit. Then other times they say it's not a sacred site, but that's bullshit too, because all of the volcano is her and is sacred, and the whole island of Hawaii has been made by her lava. You can't drill geothermal anywhere and not violate her sacred body. And I'm not even talking about what all that energy is going to be used for. There'll be a metals smelting plant that will dump toxics on the fishing grounds. There's going to be some kind of Cape Canaveral on another sacred site at South Point. And we're going to have more tourism than ever before with Hawaiians getting jobs as maids and busboys, instead of getting our land back like they promised. We have a right to maintain our traditional ways and to stop them from ruining this island. We're tired of getting pushed around. The courts are ignoring us. Let's go for it. Maybe if we can tell our story in ads on the mainland, someone will pay attention."

• • •

In June of 1987, we went back to Hawaii for the last set of discussions about the ad. We were met at the Kona airport by Lehua Lopez, who, with

Dedman and Aluli, was the third member of Pele Defense Fund's leadership. As we drove around the south shore of the island, Lopez described her work with the Rainforest Action Network, which was now becoming directly involved in the anti-geothermal campaign, recognizing that the principal drilling sites are within some of Hawaii's last untouched rainforests.

We joined Aluli and Dedman at a quiet black-sand beach near where Dedman's family had lived for generations, then headed for the Kilauea Rift Zone to observe the latest series of eruptions, already going on for two weeks. The eruptions were at the 2,000-foot level of the volcano, causing lava to flow down across highways and houses. From our vantage point we could see how the lava settled into a huge gray lake seamed by boiling red fissures. Some of the boiling mass burst over the edges of the lake and poured down toward Highway 137 and the village of Kalapana; other flows entered natural "lava tubes" to the sea. There, the contact with the ocean caused great clouds of steam to rise high above the shoreline.

Later we visited the main Kilauea caldera (crater), inactive since 1976, when in a spectacular show lasting several weeks (that was broadcast on television), it sent plumes of flame 200 feet into the sky. Now, the three-mile-wide crater was quiet. We decided to hike across. When we got to the crater floor, we entered an otherworldly scene: a solid gray ocean of lava, with some areas flat and calm and other areas with swirling, silent, frozen whirlpools, all as if caught in a photographic frame, in mid-movement. The only sound we could hear was ourselves. Nothing was growing anywhere, making the place feel dead, and yet as we walked there was the constant awareness that not far below our feet a vast molten sea was boiling and actually emerging only a few miles away. That connection to the mountain's hidden life brought us closer to understanding the native viewpoint.

The following day began at 7 a.m. with a tour of a small rainforest, led by local biologist Bill Mull. "Ninety-nine percent of the flora and fauna found in Hawaiian rainforests are found nowhere else on Earth," said Mull. "To destroy them with such short-term projects as geothermal plants is unconscionable."

From the rainforest we were whisked off to Kalapana Beach to see a traditional hula performance. Though we had seen hula performed at hotels, this was very different, in both content and performers' attitude. Lehua Lopez explained to us that for Hawaiians hula was not particularly entertainment; it was a primary expression of Hawaiian religion. The woman leading the performers was Pualani Kanehele, who is not only one of the islands' top hula masters, but is also among the leading scholars and authorities of Pele religion in the state, holding teaching posts in Hawaiian Studies at the University of Hawaii campus in Hilo and at Maui Community College.

Lopez told us that during the battle against geothermal drilling, Pualani had often been called as an expert witness to testify before various commissions concerning the question of whether the physical land—the mountain, the volcano, the lava, the rainforests—could be considered "sacred." Lopez showed us the text of some of Pualani's extraordinary testimony.

Pualani Kanehele explained to the commissioners that she came from the ancient tradition of *Hula Kahiko,* like her grandmother and, she hoped, like her children. She then went on to explain and sing chants about the Goddess Pele's migration to the westernmost Hawaiian island, Kauai, and how she moved from island to island, "creating land":

> Pele is the creator. She has to be given her time in the land to create. She is not through creating here, and that's why we have the steam. As long as the steam exists, she is not through creating. And we must give her that time to create. We cannot just cut her off by putting a cap on the steam and sending it off somewhere else. Once you put a cap on the steam, you're putting a cap on the Hawaiian culture.
>
> Because we live on this island, we are very, very close to that deity. . . . We smell her every day. We see what she has done for us. And we know that once you put that cap on her, she's gone. She has not been given enough time to develop here, and drilling will cut off that time . . . and you will have the responsibility of cutting off that part of the culture and Hawaii will be dead. And for the Hawaiians who will be living, this may as well be New California. Because we'll all be *haoles* with the same goals as the *haoles:* make money. We would like to keep this part of our culture alive for our children. Please give us that chance.

In her testimony, Kanehele spoke directly to the question of sacred places, explaining that the ancient hula chants contain that information. They describe how Pele moved from island to island until she arrived on the Big Island, entered the crater, and decided to stay; how her bowels move beneath the crust of the earth; and how she dwells everywhere, even down to the sea.

> As far as we are concerned, the areas established in the chants are the areas that belong to Pele. [One chant] about the movements of the water . . . it's not really the movement of the water they are talking

about, but the movement of the deity herself. . . . All of these intimate movements of this deity are described as water, because many
people can relate to the water. . . . We can exchange that thought of
water to being the lava itself, that's the way the lava flows. The chant
talks about the beauty of how the lava flows to these geographical
areas. And so [Pele] is establishing a boundary where she flows. And
the boundary as far as we're concerned goes all the way to Puna,
where the geothermal drilling is under way.

Kanehele sang other hula chants about Pele's beauty, her smoke and
sulphur, and the moment that the lava contacts the sea. One chant described Pele's cautious invitation:

> You're welcome; come see my display,
> Come see the movements that I do,
> Come to view my inner parts and how I dance and how I move,
> But you are not welcome to take what is mine.
> Whatever is hot here is mine.
> Whatever is hot here is sacred.

According to Lehua Lopez, the commission members were stunned by
Pualani Kanehele's extraordinary testimony. But when the time came to
vote, they gathered themselves together and did as every other court and
commission has done: They ruled that threats to Hawaiian religious practice were not sufficient grounds to stop geothermal drilling.

●   ●   ●

While we were in Hawaii, Aluli, Dedman, and Lopez took us to a potluck
dinner party and meeting arranged with a group of environmental activists in the beautiful community of Volcano, built literally within a rainforest. The people of Volcano had successfully blocked an earlier
geothermal drilling plan nearby, by agreeing to a compromise that moved
the drilling about six miles southeast to Puna. Pele Defense Fund had been
part of this original coalition, but pulled out when the compromise was
struck: Although it saved Volcano from the noise, traffic, and fumes, the
agreement simply moved the problem to someone else's neighborhood,
did nothing about the eventual consequences of this massive new energy
supply, and was utterly unresponsive to the religious issues that Pele Defense Fund was raising. "Let me put it to you bluntly," Lehua Lopez had
told us on the way to the meeting. "These people protected their own
backyard but they did not go out on a limb to help Native Hawaiians."

Why, then, were we going to meet them? Lehua responded logically, pointing out that some of them remain active supporters, that their organizational connections were helpful for spreading the word, and that Pele Defense Fund needed non-Hawaiian friends.

It was an impressive group. Present were about twenty people from the Sierra Club, Audubon Society, Wilderness Society, and others. After dinner, Lehua made a brief speech describing the history of the battle against geothermal drilling, mentioning the work of many people in the room. She diplomatically avoided mentioning the rift with Pele Defense Fund. Instead, she attempted to enlist renewed support for the Fund's activities. Many agreed to re-engage.

• • •

The ads were finally placed in the fall of 1988, and caused an immediate shock wave within Hawaii. Placed in the *New York Times* and the *San Francisco Chronicle,* the headline read COME TO HAWAII, SWIM IN POLLUTED WATER, SEE UGLY ELECTRIC TOWERS, BREATHE TOXIC FUMES, and featured drawings of the ecological mess the geothermal project would cause. The ad also described the threats to the rainforest and, of course, to the "desecration of Pele," the native religion. In addition, the ad was placed in all the major papers of the State of Hawaii, but using a different headline: UGLY, TOXIC, COSTLY AND SACRILEGIOUS.

Readers were asked to send coupons and letters to the mayor of Hawaii County, to the governor of Hawaii, and to Senator Daniel Inouye, who was not only senior senator from Hawaii but also chair of the Senate Subcommittee on Indian Affairs. (According to a *Washington Post* exposé that appeared just before the ad ran, Inouye was also the prime behind-the-scenes mover in support of the geothermal project.)

The Hawaii Convention and Visitors' Bureau was aghast, as were all the leading public officials who united in a chorus condemning Pele Defense Fund for trying to threaten tourism. The controversy instantly ignited media interest, and a story that had languished on the back pages of even the Hawaii press was now front-page news. Major feature stories appeared in the *Los Angeles Times,* the *San Francisco Chronicle,* and the *New York Times.* Network television news teams were flown to Hawaii to interview Palikapu Dedman as he fished off his black-sand beach, and to show Native Hawaiians making midnight offerings at the edge of the volcano. Suddenly the power dynamics of the issue began to change.

Native Hawaiians rallied around Aluli, Dedman, and Lopez for having taken a stand for Hawaiian religion. Rainforest Action Network became the first non-Hawaiian group to make a major commitment to supporting geothermal resistance, and came through with mass mailings to its 30,000 members asking them to complain to the powers-that-be in Hawaii and in Washington. Later the organization undertook several direct-action protest demonstrations at the drilling sites.

Financial and energy experts from the mainland noticed the issue for the first time and voluntarily flew to the Big Island to study the situation. They issued new assessments that contradicted the state's claims on cost and feasibility, and finally stated that the project was little more than a boondoggle for a small number of investor groups. An enraged Senator Inouye issued telephone threats to Pele Defense Fund leadership, saying that he would not tolerate much more of their opposition. The mayor of Hawaii County, who had denounced Pele Defense Fund, was defeated at the polls in the 1989 election, the Fund's first direct political victory. Soon after, the state's governor showed a new willingness to open discussions toward a compromise solution, though a *compromise* on geothermal drilling has never been something Pele Defense Fund would accept.

CURRENT EVENTS

Most recent events concerning Native Hawaiian issues have been positive, but there was one stunning setback that hit every native group in the United States seeking to use religious freedom arguments to block developments within sacred areas. In the devastating 1989 Gasket-Orleans ("G-O Road") decision of the United States Supreme Court, three northern California Indian tribes lost in their attempt to block construction of a U.S. Forest Service road within the Six Rivers National Forest. The Forest Service contended the road was needed to support timber harvesting; the Indians argued the need for the road was speculative, and that it would run directly through a sacred place used for vision quests and ritual purification ceremonies, and that the area was thereby protected under the First Amendment.

The Supreme Court ruling came as a shock. The Forest Service's own expert anthropologist had agreed that the road would destroy "the very core" of Indian religious practice and had come out against the road. Two lower courts had ruled to protect the sacred sites. But the Supreme Court delivered what one attorney, Steven Moore, of the Native American Rights Fund, called a "life-threatening blow to Indian religion . . . [by permitting federal agencies to manage lands] in such a way as to unilaterally subordinate Indian religious values to the economic interests of timber, mineral, and water-power developments." Moore didn't specifically mention other native groups, but the finding was just as devastating to Native Hawaiian legal efforts to block geothermal drilling, as it was to the Big Mountain Navajo legal attempt to stop coal development or the forced removal of thousands of Indians from their ancestral lands.

The Supreme Court held that the use of federal land is an internal decision of the government and no one else, but more important, that only actions that directly and *intentionally* coerce religious practice are prohibited. So any plaintiff has the burden of proving that the *purpose* of a development is to deliberately destroy religious freedom, which of course is impossible to prove.

The court also indicated its disbelief that Indians "worshipped in nature" as they say they do, or that their manner of worship qualifies as religious. Justice Sandra Day O'Connor, for example, argued that since some Indians say they do not worship in this forest, doubt is thrown on the Indians' religious argument, as if unanimity were the test. It is like denying Catholics protection for a cathedral because not all Catholics worship there.

"What message does this decision send to Indian people?" attorney Moore asked. "That the American constitutional democracy does not respect their unique religions and cultures? . . . The effect is to strip Indians [and Hawaiians] of all constitutional rights for the protection of sacred sites."

In reaction to this decision, a new coalition was formed in 1990, including the National Congress of American Indians, the Association on American Indian Affairs, the National American Indian Council, and the Native American Rights Fund, to give "teeth" to the American Indian Religious Freedom Act of 1978. Until now, the act has been only a statement of policy. The goal of the coalition is to directly limit the actions of federal agencies on sacred lands.

Meanwhile, Pele Defense Fund lawyers are pursuing other legal avenues. Perhaps the most promising is a suit in the Hawaii State Court that alleges that a land exchange some years ago, which included the present geothermal drilling sites at Puna, was illegal, since it involved land that the State was holding in trust for Native Hawaiians.

• • •

On other fronts, events look far more promising. With the higher media visibility of the geothermal issue, new support has emerged from *haoles* on the islands of Maui and Oahu, who have finally grasped the implications of both this new energy source and the underwater cable shipment of electricity to their own islands. With Oahu and Maui already on the brink of overdevelopment, homeowners—especially new arrivals from the mainland—are complaining that their quality of life will be diminished. Pele Defense Fund has welcomed this unlikely new support group.

Meanwhile, Greenpeace has joined the Rainforest Action Network and Pele Defense Fund in direct-action campaigns at the drill site. The groups have staged nearly a half-dozen events, including one involving 1,500 protestors, 144 of whom were arrested for trespassing on the site. All of these actions have received front-page news coverage in the islands.

There have also been several new political victories on the geothermal issue. A federal appropriation of $15 million was blocked in the House of Representatives' Appropriations Committee; if this can be sustained in subsequent rounds, the entire project will be in danger. The governor of Hawaii has publicly admitted the importance of that appropriation, and has shown signs of looking for cover on the geothermal issue.

As for Kahoolawe, there has been a major breakthrough. Public pressure against the bombing became sufficient to make it a major issue in the U.S. senatorial election of 1990. Republican candidate Patricia Saiki convinced George Bush, who claimed he had known nothing about the bombing, to take a new look at the issue. And though Saiki lost to Democrat Daniel Akaka, the federal government did finally declare a bombing moratorium of two years and four months.

A three-person commission was established to hold hearings and to make proposals for the island's cleanup and its eventual conversion to other uses. One of the commission's members is Emmett Aluli.

A major struggle remains to be fought among contenders for the island's future. Possible outcomes include: 1) its partial development for tourism or for parkland, 2) its return to Native Hawaiians for cultural activities or settlement, 3) some combination of the preceding, or 4) depending on world events, its reversion back to being a military target.

Another promising development is the creation of an unusual new coalition of all the islands' activist environmental groups and Native Hawaiian groups. Called the Aloha Aina Action Congress, the organization is unique in equating environmental protection and native rights. If the group can sustain its breadth and its commitment to native values, a sharp turnaround for Native Hawaiians is possible. Palikapu Dedman has indicated a higher level of optimism than ever before: "With all this new help we are getting, I think we can win on Kahoolawe and on geothermal and some other things too. There've been lots of changes already. I was really lonely at the beginning of all this ten years ago, but not now."

19

WORLD NEWS BRIEFS (I):
THE PACIFIC BASIN AND ASIA

*T*HEFTS OF NATIVE lands, imposition of alien political and economic structures, and assaults upon native culture and religion have been the main themes of the American native experience, as described in the preceding chapters. They are also the themes of the brief reports that follow later in this chapter and the next.

Though assaults upon indigenous peoples occur all over the world, the styles of attack vary from region to region. In the United States and Canada, attacks on native cultures have "advanced" to being more "legalistic" than military. The objective is still the same: to break up the native communal land holdings and to separate the natives from their ancestral lands. "Legalistic" theft procedures are also the rule in the United States' colonial holdings, such as Micronesia, as well as in other countries, notably Australia, New Zealand, Japan, and parts of Europe. But in much of Southeast Asia, China, Tibet, and parts of Africa, South America, and Central America, the outside political and economic intrusions on native peoples are blatantly violent, as is the resistance to it.

Perhaps the ugliest war right now is in Indonesia, where the natives of Irian Jaya (West Papua) are engaged in a fierce battle to stave off the destruction of their rainforest homes and the forest itself. They are opposing an enormous Indonesian military force trying to clear them out of the way, so that several million Indonesians from Java can be transmigrated to new settlements in Irian Jaya. The goal is to turn the new settlers into a labor force to cut down the forest, and to develop the huge reserves of oil, copper, silver, tin, molybdenum, and other minerals of interest to multinational corporations. Ten thousand natives have already died in the resistance and tens of thousands have been forced to flee their ancestral lands.

The man in charge of the resettlement program on the natives' lands is Indonesia's minister of transmigration. As quoted in *Lords of Poverty* by Graham Hancock, the minister put the goals very clearly: "The different ethnic groups of Indonesia will in the long run disappear . . . and then there will be one kind of man."

Such an attitude is usually unstated by government officials but is nonetheless apparent from their actions, wherever on the globe native peoples are faced with the technological juggernaut.

"FOURTH WORLD" WARS

In *Cultural Survival Quarterly,* University of California at Berkeley Professor Bernard Nietschmann wrote that of the 120 military conflicts in the world (as of 1987), three-fourths involved *native nations* seeking to hold off or free themselves from larger, occupying *nation-states,* as is the case with the natives of Irian Jaya resisting the intrusions of the central Indonesian government. Nietschmann argues that the mass media's failure to grasp the true nature of these wars has effectively fanned their flames.

Nietschmann makes a critically important distinction between nations and states. He argues that some 3,000 native nations are presently contained within the borders of fewer than 200 states, which assert control over them. Under international law, Nietschmann asserts, a nation comprises peoples of common heritage, language, geography, culture, political system, and desire for common association. Nietschmann offers the examples of the Karens of Burma, the Mayans of Guatemala, the Tamils of Sri Lanka, the Miskito of Nicaragua, the Palestinians in Israel, the Kurds of Syria, Turkey, Iran, Iraq, and the Soviet Union, the Oromo of Ethiopia, the Basques of Spain, the Sami of Scandinavia, and the Latvians, Lithuanians, and Estonians of the Soviet Union, in addition to the hundreds of native nations in the United States, Canada, Latin America, Africa, and the Pacific.

"There are two very different geopolitical mappings of the peoples and countries of the world," says Nietschmann. "The first is the common one of [the large, recognized] states and their attendant peoples, often described in terms of 'three worlds'; the second is a quite different one of more than 3,000 enduring peoples and nations . . . peoples that exist beneath the imposed states. Nation peoples consider themselves to be members of distinct nations by virtue of birth and cultural heritage; they may not consider themselves to be citizens of some intruding state government, made up of other peoples from other places," as, for example, most American and Canadian Indians do not.

Nietschmann argues that fully one-third of the world's population falls within this definition, and that conflicts between nations and states constitute a "world war . . . hidden from most people's view because the fighting is against peoples and nations that are often not even on the map."

Nietschmann's criticism of the media centers on its mischaracterization of these conflicts as "civil wars," and its misidentification of native groups:

> Pick up a newspaper, and try to find the nationality of the peoples shooting at each other in Ethiopia, Sudan, Angola, Afghanistan, Indonesia, Burma, Bangladesh, Nicaragua, Guatemala, or in any of the rest of the world's wars. Nation peoples are rarely identified by their own names; instead they are referred to as rebels, separatists, extremists, dissidents, insurgents, terrorists, tribal minorities, or ethnic groups. How can a people be an ethnic group in its own nation?
>
> The autonomous Karens and their nation were termed a "Burmese hill tribe" [by the press] whereas the Burman people—only one of a dozen nations in the British-created state of Burma—became the ruling regime of a mythical "Burmese people." . . . Nation peoples are almost always misidentified as either members of the very state they are fighting against (the Oromo are called "Ethiopian rebels") or by the propaganda terms used by the invading state, e.g., "terrorists."
>
> Almost none of the world's more than 3,000 distinct peoples are recognized internationally. Their existence, territories, nationalities, and defensive struggles are largely invisible. Instead, multinational state populations become internationally recognized as "peoples" and "nations," even though they have none of the characteristics.

Following Nietschmann's logic, it is clear that terms such as "American people" are absurdities. The United States is a nation-state that gathers under one banner hundreds of peoples and nations, including at least two hundred Indian nations. Similarly, Canada, fighting to keep Quebec from splitting off as a separate nation, rarely acknowledges that it also has more than one hundred Indian nations within its borders, with separate languages and cultures, and with desires to be considered autonomous on land they occupied long before there ever was a Canada.

The situation is similar in many other states: Burma contains eleven separate native nations; China has fifty-five; Indonesia has three hundred; and the Soviet Union, more than one hundred.

Not surprisingly, Nietschmann says, the larger nation-states invariably side with each other on issues involving independence movements of the smaller contained nations. Even within organizations such as the United Nations, the large countries understand their commonality of interest. To grant independence to the small nations would subvert the worldwide development scheme, as designed by institutions such as the International Monetary Fund and the World Bank. This development scheme presupposes that a relatively few large, stable countries agree to work for "market economics," and to make over the world in the image of Western technological society. Even the cases of Lithuania, Latvia, and Estonia are not really exceptions to the rule, though Western countries did support their efforts for independence. In those cases, the anticommunism and dedication to "market economics" of the breakaway nations assured they would support the dominant, Western world view.

On the other hand, many Indian and other native nations are not interested in supporting the industrial-technological juggernaut or its lifestyle, since they see it as destructive to their own cultures and to nature. This ought to be clear from many of the following examples.

• • •

I regret that the reports that follow in this chapter and the next are far from complete. They leave out many important native struggles around the world. This is not because some struggles are less important than others; it's more the limitations of space, the fact that I personally know more about some issues than others, and that some stories are too complex to describe briefly. Of course all these stories are too complex to tell briefly, spanning as they do many centuries and many turns of events. There is also the problem of time lapses between when I write the reports and when they are published and when you read them. Nonetheless, in the interest of showing the commonality of native struggles all over the planet, I think it better to have these brief summary reports than none at all.

THE PACIFIC BASIN

Oceania

Although the Pacific Ocean covers an area three times the size of the United States, the total land mass of its 3,000 tiny islands covers less area than the state of Indiana. Upon these small islands—some of them volcanic and others mere coral atolls only one or two feet above sea level—live 1.5 million Polynesian, Melanesian, and Micronesian peoples. Politically and economically self-sufficient for at least 1,000 years, and in some places for 4,000 years, traditional activities of lagoon fishing and small-scale agriculture made survival extremely easy in these paradisiacal tropical and semitropical environments.

By now, however, few Pacific islands have been left untouched by the heavy impact of the outside world's military and economic activities. As with their cousins in Hawaii, Pacific islanders face certain common problems: the technological countries' urgency to exploit undersea resources and feed the industrial juggernaut; the ravages and humiliations of tourism; and, most important, the wars and war preparations among the larger countries that have overrun these tiny societies like the ocean's tidal waves.

The Pacific was first colonized in the sixteenth century by Magellan and the Spanish explorers, who were followed soon after by Germany, England, France, Japan, and the United States. But the most terrible scars of colonialism occurred during World War II, when U.S. nuclear testing in the Marshall Islands, combined with island-to-island combat between American and Japanese forces, ravaged the Gilberts, the Carolines, the Marianas, the Marshalls, Fiji, and others. The legacy of that fighting is still visible on hundreds of Pacific islands: Thousands of rusted airplanes, tanks, and landing barges lie on the land as testament to the brutality with which invader countries treated the fragile islands and the native peoples who lived on them.

For Pacific islanders the war did not end in 1945; in fact the Pacific islands may be one place on Earth on which nuclear weaponry had as great an impact as it did on Japan. Since 1945, more than 200 nuclear test-bombs have been exploded in the Pacific by the United States (about 100 tests), France (more than 75), and England (about 10). Even today, the French continue to test bombs near Tahiti, despite serious destruction to the region's coral-reef ecology, radioactive pollution of the waters and undersea life, and a growing antitesting protest movement among the islanders.

The U.S. testing program, in combination with preparations for Pacific wars (which involve U.S. military bases throughout the western Pacific), has had nearly apocalyptic consequences for the native people. Whole populations have been forced to leave their ancestral homes, the islands have been absolutely destroyed, there are terrible rates of radiation sickness and cancer, and the traditional economic and political autonomy the natives enjoyed for millennia has been shattered.

Micronesia

If I had to pick the worst example of recent U.S. behavior toward a native society, I would cite the case of Micronesia. Awarded to the U.S. in 1947 as a United Nations "strategic trust territory," Micronesia includes the Mariana Islands, the Caroline Islands, and the Marshall Islands—2,000 islands spread out over three million square miles.

The UN mandate called for the U.S. to promote the health and economic self-sufficiency of the inhabitants, to regulate and control the use of natural resources, to protect the inhabitants against loss of their lands, to improve transportation and education, and to "protect the rights and fundamental freedoms of all elements of the population without discrimination." The UN also mandated that within twenty-five years, the U.S. would give up its trust arrangement and permit self-governance under terms dictated by the people.

Forty-four years later, we have not complied with that regulation. Given our grim history in Micronesia from the 1940s to the 1970s, no one should be shocked that we have now refused to give up control.

It was in Micronesia in 1946, on Bikini Atoll, that the U.S. began its massive Pacific nuclear testing program. Our military persuaded the Bikini Islanders to "temporarily" move to Rongerik Atoll, so we could use their island for the "cause of peace." The islanders found that Rongerik offered very poor fishing, insufficient fruit and coconuts, and no government services. Within six months, starvation and malnutrition set in and the Bikini elders demanded to return home. But by then, nuclear explosions had made their home uninhabitable; fifty years later the island is still too radioactive to permit the natives to return. So a formerly self-sufficient, peaceful, happy society has been reduced to a myriad of welfare cases. The miracle is that their traditional tribal structure has somehow been maintained and Bikini's traditional chiefs continue to fight for a cleanup of their homeland. Their pleas have thus far been met by awesome indifference in the military and in Congress.

One hundred miles *downwind* from Bikini, on Rongelop Atoll, the population was *not* moved during the Bikini tests. Rongelop's natives are now suffering higher rates of radiation sickness, cancer, and malformed and stillborn children than anywhere else on Earth except for Japan, and among the Navajo uranium miners of Arizona. Representatives from Rongelop have sued the U.S. for increased medical care and compensation. But as the U.S. does not want to admit culpability (as with suits based on nuclear tests in Utah and Nevada), all appeals have been stonewalled.

In 1947, after we accepted UN trusteeship, the second major testing ground went into operation at Enewetok Atoll. We removed the people from their homes, and more than forty explosions rocked the island.

By 1956, the entire food supply of the northern Marshall Islands— fruits, coconuts, and undersea life—was too radioactive to eat. The natives were told to eat only U.S. government issue: canned spaghetti and tuna from the mainland. Malnutrition, starvation, and bitterness spread rapidly through the islands.

In 1960, the U.S. added the people of Kwajalein Atoll to its list of displaced dependents. The Kwajalein story is particularly tragic since that lagoon is one of the Pacific's largest, most beautiful, and most bountifully inhabited by fish, crabs, and other undersea species. Once the people were moved, the lagoon became the "splashdown" target for the U.S. Pacific Missile Range. Now missiles from as far away as Vandenburg Air Force Base in California are targeted at this once glorious place.

Meanwhile the Kwajaleiners have been trying for thirty years to survive on the tiny island of Ebbeye, with seventy acres, no lagoon for fishing, and no room for agriculture. By 1978, the population of Ebbeye was 7,000— twelve times the population density of Washington, D.C., with comparable slum conditions and social problems. The Kwajaleiners have protested mightily, going as far as undertaking a mass sit-in on their home island's airport runway. Thus far the only concessions have been some increased financial aid.

In 1975, after completing more than 100 nuclear tests, dislocating the populations of a dozen islands, causing tremendous radiation contamination, and making urban-slum welfare societies out of formerly productive self-sufficient communities, the United States began its long-overdue negotiations on Micronesian independence by demanding certain concessions. One demand is that Micronesia accept U.S. "protection" against foreign invaders; that we be permitted to construct larger military bases for our nuclear weapons, B-52 bombers, and Trident nuclear submarines. Micronesians are resisting these basing plans, feeling they will become little more than U.S. military dependents.

The greatest resistance comes from the Micronesian state of Belau, where the U.S. wants a military base that would occupy one-third of all Belauan territory. Having borne the brunt of World War II, Belauans want no military presence, and especially no nuclear presence. They voted 90 percent for an anti-nuclear constitution, submitted for referendum in 1979. The U.S. rejected their vote and demanded another referendum, which had the same outcome. That was also rejected.

A few years later, the president of Belau, a leader of the anti-nuclear sentiment, was mysteriously assassinated and replaced with a pro-nuclear

president. Public opinion on Belau holds that it was a CIA job—I think
so too.

The situation today is at a standoff, though U.S. strategy has changed.
We are now going in for bribery in a big way, promising massive financial
aid, road-building, U.S.-style housing, government jobs, economic development contracts, and better medical facilities. We are also counting on
attrition. As time passes and one generation gives way to the next, and as
the power of traditional chiefs begins to wane, and as the continued presence of U.S. military personnel erodes the culture, there are signs that Belauan resistance is declining.

On the other hand, Belau has received strong moral support from the
new Nuclear Free Pacific Movement among other island nations. It includes Vanuatu, Kiribati, the northern Marianas, the Solomons, the Marshalls, and New Zealand, as well as the native movement in Hawaii. All
of these have joined an informal alliance that meets annually and attempts
to chart a unified course against the intrusions of the major world powers.
In response, the Reagan administration issued a kind of Pacific Monroe
Doctrine, stating that we have the right to intervene in the affairs of any
Pacific island republic that makes deals of which we do not approve. President Bush supports that doctrine.

Australia and New Zealand

Aboriginal populations in both Australia and New Zealand are experiencing a rebirth of activism born out of a common resistance to mining
activities on native lands.

New Zealand's Maori are in a better position than the Aborigines of
Australia because they represent 10 percent of the country's population,
are well organized, and have treaties guaranteeing certain lands and
rights. The Maori also have a tradition of resistance, having fought militarily against the invading Europeans in the 1800s.

In some ways, the Maori experience is similar to that of American Indians. Much of their land loss resulted from "legal" subterfuge, designed
to alienate them from their communal land base. The minister of justice
of New Zealand in 1872 admitted this was the motive of the Native Lands
Act, written to "destroy the principle of communalism upon which their
social system was based, and which stood as a barrier in the way of all
attempts to amalgamate the Maori into our social system." From 1890 to
1920, Maori land holdings were diminished from 11 million to 2 million
acres.

Maori activism reawakened in the 1960s. According to Julian Burger's

Report from the Frontier, the Maori "feared mining activities would destroy the fishing grounds, disrupt lifestyles, interfere with recreation, and desecrate sacred sites. The objections were founded on the idea that mining companies did not share the same spiritual attitudes to land and water as the Maori, rather than any material pre-occupation about royalties." Having forged links with other progressive movements in New Zealand, such as the anti-nuclear and labor movements, the Maori political and economic situation is now improving.

• • •

Australia's Aborigines are only 200,000 in a country of 10 million people. Horribly brutalized, confined to the least desirable parts of the Australian desert (in miserable reservations first created by missionaries), the Aborigines' status is grim. A large percent live as "fringe dwellers" on the edges of cities. There they suffer poor medical care, a high death rate, malnutrition, unemployment, and despair.

However, discoveries of bauxite, manganese, oil, natural gas, and uranium on Aborigine lands, once considered wastelands by whites, have given the natives new leverage. For religious reasons, they are deeply opposed to any mining; the Aborigines say mining activity disrupts their ancient "song-lines" by which they reckon their spiritual connection to the land and the cosmos.

Recently they have gained support from anti-nuclear groups, and also from liberal whites who point to the disgracefully poor lease arrangements by which Australian mining interests have exploited the native lands. From all this, the Aborigine leadership has gained strength, even undertaking civil disobedience activities completely out of character with their historical passivity.

Japan

In 1980, the Japanese government declared to the United Nations that "there are no minorities in Japan," thereby exempting itself from UN rules about freedom of language and religion for minorities. Soon after that statement, Prime Minister Yasuhiro Nakasone stated that the reason the education level in the U.S. is low is because minorities such as blacks and Hispanics drag it down. This comment caused an uproar in the United States, resulting in an apology from Nakasone. It also created outrage from Japan's minority populations, whose existence the government doesn't acknowledge.

Minorities in Japan include Okinawans, and immigrant Filipinos,

Chinese, and Koreans, all of whom are met with significant discrimination. There are also two nonimmigrant minorities who fare little better than the immigrants. One is the "untouchable caste," the Buraku people. Little known outside Japan, they represent about 3 percent of the population. Discrimination against the Burakumin dates back to the Samurai period, when they were employed as meat-cutters and leather workers in a society with religious strictures against handling animal flesh. Despite new anti-discrimination laws, the Burakumin still cannot find decent housing outside their own ghettos in Osaka, Kyoto, and Tokyo, and they have difficulty gaining access to higher education, or employment, or marriage outside their caste.

More to our purposes, however, is the situation of the Ainu, the original native population of the Japanese islands. The Ainu now number about 50,000 and are concentrated on the northern island of Hokkaido. Their culture and story closely resemble that of some American Indian societies: They have a totem-oriented religion, in which bears, owls, and other animals are considered sacred; lineage is reckoned matrilineally; and their traditional economy is based on hunting, gathering, and fishing from stable villages. They lived in that manner for some 4,000 years before the invaders arrived in great numbers from Central Asia 2,000 years ago. By the seventeenth century, a series of bloody wars forced the Ainu to abandon all of Japan except Hokkaido in the north, where they were able to maintain their traditional life for several hundred more years, until the 1899 Law for the Protection of the Former Aborigines of Hokkaido. Like other laws with similarly friendly titles in the United States, Canada, Australia, and other places, it was anything but protective. Passed without any input from Ainu, the law outlawed traditional Ainu hunting, salmon fishing, and even the gathering of wood. It offered the Ainu individually allotted homesteads—another assault on communal land ownership—and demanded that the Ainu become farmers. If allotted land was not used for farming, it was confiscated.

Since the law effectively destroyed the Ainu economy, as well as their culture and religion, few Ainu applied for land. Instead, they dispersed, leading them to social isolation and discrimination that continue to this day. "Ainu are discriminated against on sight," says militant Ainu woman Mieko Chikkap. "We are technically citizens of Japan, but we have no rights at all."

Part of a new breed of young Ainu determined to recover cultural rights and land, as well as demand the respect of the majority population, Chikkap made a major political splash in 1988 when she won a lawsuit against a famous Japanese anthropologist and his publisher. The suit argued that photos of dug-up Ainu graves, Ainu artifacts, and Ainu people, including Chikkap herself, were published without permission. "They would never have dug up the graves of any other Japanese and taken pictures of them," Chikkap told me when I met her in 1987. She was especially furious that the author had called Ainu "a dead culture," thus characterizing present-day Ainu as little more than artifacts or curiosities. "By our actual presence, and our cultural practices, and our ceremonies, dancing, and weaving, it is obvious that we are not dead. They thought they could get away with showing my picture in that context without even asking because I am only an Ainu, and Ainu have no power in Japan." Chikkap gained the support of a feminist attorney who worked for low fees and succeeded in achieving an extraordinary settlement suggested by Chikkap: A cash settlement went to fund new Ainu educational and cultural activities, and the publisher issued a formal written apology to the Ainu people, an extraordinary gesture in Japan.

Chikkap's victory was front-page news in Hokkaido and elsewhere in Japan. It rallied the Ainu for renewed efforts to regain their rights. They are now considering lawsuits demanding that Japan deliver the promised homestead lands to those Ainu families that did accept the 1899 offer, but who had their lands confiscated nonetheless. They are also fighting a proposed new dam on Hokkaido, which would submerge some lands now owned by Ainu farmers, and at the same time they are trying to get the government's ban on Ainu salmon fishing lifted.

To overcome entrenched discrimination against them, the Ainu are insisting on the establishment of secondary education courses in Ainu language and culture, and university courses in Ainu Studies.

Under the auspices of the World Council of Churches, a new coalition has been formed combining the struggles of the Ainu with the Burakumin, the Okinawans, and the immigrant Koreans, Filipinos, and Chinese.

Indonesia and the Philippines

Indonesia and the Philippines are excellent examples of Bernard Nietschmann's thesis: Both countries are amalgams of literally hundreds of separate indigenous nations, speaking hundreds of languages, spread out over thousands of islands, having no reason to be lumped together in federations except out of convenience for some colonial administration. Having all these individual nations combined as one political entity made military control and trade management more efficient.

Even when granting "independence," the colonial powers chose only *one* cultural or national group for this dubious distinction. In Indonesia, the Dutch selected the Javanese as the dominant political authority. In the Philippines, it was first the Spanish and then the United States that directed the process. Now we have so-called Indonesian and Philippine "peoples" when no such "people" ever existed.

The result of such forced amalgamations is predictable: war. In both Indonesia and the Philippines, indigenous peoples seeking to retain their separate identity and autonomy have been pitted against the dominant nation-state, resulting in decades of bloody warfare.

• • •

The Indonesian government admits to a native population of two million, representing more than 100 separate native nations. In Molucca, Kalimantan, East Timor, and West Papua, huge populations are forced to submit to the development models of the central Javanese administration, egged on by international bankers and the Western technological countries.

As mentioned earlier, the hottest spot right now is Irian Jaya (West Papua), New Guinea (lumped within Indonesia), where one million natives, representing dozens of tribal nations, many of whom had no contact with the outside world until two decades ago, are engaged in a war against Indonesia (or more precisely, Java). President Suharto, a Javanese, instituted the policy of mass transmigration. Residents of Java are offered free land, technical aid, and cash incentives if they move to Irian Jaya, to assist with clearing the rainforest and developing mining. As of late 1990, more than a quarter of a million families have moved.

The Indonesian central government considers transmigration good policy because it relieves overpopulation in Java, provides a new cheap work force, and puts pressure on the natives of Irian Jaya to get out. In an area rich in oil, copper, nickel, cobalt, tin, silver, molybdenum, and gold, multinationals such as Shell, Conoco, Texaco, Total, and Chevron have leapt at the chance to stake their claims. The International Monetary Fund and the World Bank are smoothing the path for them by urging Indonesia to clear the rainforests (for cash to repay prior bank loans) and to restructure Irian Jaya for voracious development. The victims of this process are the peoples who have lived within those forests.

Julian Burger, in *Report from the Frontier,* writes, "It is possible with legitimacy to talk about genocide elsewhere—the Mayans in Guatemala, the Ache in Paraguay, the Chakma in Bangladesh—but even in the context of such violence the destruction of the West Papua [Irian Jaya] people has few parallels. . . . The invasion of the Americas and Australia are being reborn [today] in West Papua."

West Papua development policy has caused thousands of native people to flee across the border to relative safety in Papua, New Guinea, though tens of thousands are staying behind to fight in a full-scale war. The native resistance, which may be 20,000 strong, is no match for the huge Indonesian army, supplied with U.S. helicopters and sophisticated weaponry. Though the media continues to describe this as a "civil war," it is *not* a civil war. By any sensible definition, it is a series of bloody massacres by an invading outside power acting on behalf of an alien development model created by international banks and corporations. To call it a civil war shields the public from truly understanding what is going on.

• • •

In the Philippines, fifty "minorities" represent about 6.5 million people out of a total population of 16 million. Most of these live in the forested Cordillera region of northern Luzon—the Isneg, Kainga, Bontoc, Ifugao, and Ibaloy—and the southernmost island of Mindanao, where the Maranao, Yakan, Tausag, and Bangsa Moro peoples live. The rest of the population is descended from the Spanish or are of mixed blood. *Those* are the "Filipinos."

During Spanish rule, from 1521 to 1896, little effort was made to assault most of the Indian tribes. But after the Spanish American War, the U.S. created laws of "eminent domain," which made communal tribal lands available for the first time to Filipino and American private interests for sugar cane, pineapple, and banana plantations. As in Hawaii, U.S. corporations were involved: Del Monte, Castle and Cooke, and United Fruit, among others. The afflicted native nations thus either moved further north or south to the extremities of their prior lands, or they stayed to become plantation laborers, as in Hawaii.

In the 1960s, the Philippine government, under Ferdinand Marcos, announced that all forest land was henceforth "public domain" and began clear-cutting. One-third of the Philippine forest is now gone, exported to the United States and Japan; many of the indigenous peoples who lived in these forests now have no homes.

One corporate contract alone, to Cellophil Corporation, directly affected 150,000 tribal people, among five northern tribes in the north central highlands. Even greater devastation will result upon the completion of thirty-one dams, financed by the World Bank and the Asian Development Bank, that will flood the lands of 1.5 million tribal people in the north. Given the situation, it is little wonder that the natives have responded so enthusiastically to the armed resistance.

A slightly different situation exists in the south, on Mindanao, where the Bangsa Moro tribe, numbering more than two million people, has suc-

cessfully resisted military invasions begun by Marcos in 1972. Nearly
100,000 people have died so far in this twenty-year war, which is also called
"civil war" by the media, though it is most definitely an invasion. The
Bangsa Moro have never considered themselves part of the Philippines
and, in fact, have never been conquered. They have managed to maintain
sovereignty over their own lands throughout their history. When the media calls this a civil war, it effectively achieves the annexation of the Bangsa
Moro, which the Philippine army has otherwise not been able to do.

When Corazon Aquino was elected, there was some hope that negotiations with tribal peoples might begin. But that prospect diminished almost immediately when the entrenched landowners and the military
turned against Aquino and rendered her ineffective, leaving the situation
in stalemate.

ASIA

To attempt to convey the scope and depth of the problems of native
peoples in Asia is profoundly frustrating; a decent discussion of the situations in India or Burma or China or the Soviet Union would each require
a separate book. So, again, it's with regret that I offer only a brief listing
of numbers and a few paragraphs about a few locales.

According to organizations such as the Minority Rights Group and
Cultural Survival, the Asian continent is home to roughly 200 million native people, divided into several thousand linguistic and national group-
ings. (I am including Indonesia and the Philippines in the chart, though
they have already been discussed above.)

Country	Native Population
Afghanistan	about 10 million, including 6.7 million Pathan people, and 3 million Koochis (represents about 70% of total population)
Bangladesh	1.5 million
Burma	about 11 million (represents about 30% of total population); largest group is 6 million Karens
China	67 million, among 55 tribal groups

Country	Native Population
East Malaysia (Borneo and Sarawak)	500,000 people (represents 50% of total population)
India	51 million, among 200 tribal groups
Indonesia	1.5 million
Malaysian Peninsula	71,000
Pakistan	2.5 million
Philippines	6.5 million
Soviet Union	29 million (non-European nationals), including 22 million Turkic people, 6 million Kazakhs, and 1 million Eskimos and other Arctic peoples
Sri Lanka	2,000
Taiwan	310,000, among 10 tribal groups
Thailand	500,000, among 6 tribal groups
Vietnam	1 million

Not included above are the 15 million Kurdish people, as their unique situation does not lend itself to a chart. What was once the single nation of Kurdistan has been militarily subjugated and is now divided among at least five nation-states: Soviet Armenia, Turkey, Syria, Iran, and Iraq, none of which is sympathetic to recognizing the Kurds as a separate nation. In fact, in each of the countries that control them, the Kurds are the object of hatred and brutality. In one famous episode in 1988, the Iraqi government slaughtered an entire Kurdish village with poison gas, because of the village's separatist activities. More recently, some one million Kurds fled their homes to escape the assaults of the Iraqi military, only to be met by cynical indifference among the world's powers, and no support for their nationhood.

India

In its report on the Naga tribespeople of India, the London-based Minority Rights Group begins by asking, "What is India?" and then answers,

"There is not, and never was, an India, or even any country of India, possessing—according to European ideas—any sort of unity, physical, political, social or religious: no Indian nation, no people of India."

Until its independence, India was only a combination of management units—paperwork in English headquarters. For in reality, "India" was a wild amalgam of 200 native nations, as well as quite a few religious and political minorities. Mahatma Gandhi, in one of the few acts of his life with which I disagree, fought to maintain this fictional unity, despite its continuous and natural tendency to fall apart at its very weak seams. The Muslim leader Mohammed Ali Jinnah did manage to create a separate Muslim Pakistan; the Sikhs tried to do likewise, and are continuing to try, but thus far have succeeded only in causing extreme bloodshed in the northern provinces. Neither did the Justice Party succeed in establishing a separate Dravidian state in the south.

But in the remote Naga lands, where about half a million people live in the extremely steep, rugged terrain of the Assam region of northeastern India, a degree of autonomy has been maintained.

Though the British never occupied any part of the Naga homelands, they tacked it onto their Indian administrative apparatus. It was as if they couldn't figure out what else to do with this otherwise unaccounted-for region: They couldn't decide whether it should have been part of Burma or India, so some paperwork settled the case. But every effort of the British to actually enter the Nagan hills was met with fierce resistance up through the 1800s. Eventually the British gave up trying to assert physical control and, in 1929, informally agreed that the Nagas would remain sovereign.

Before India was granted independence, the Nagas received assurances from Gandhi and from Jinnah that Naga sovereignty would be respected, and in 1947 they declared themselves an independent nation. However, Jawaharlal Nehru did not see it that way. He insisted that the Nagas could have "autonomy" only under the rule of the Assam provincial government, within India. This led to periods of full-scale warfare between India and the Nagas, with no decisive victories. At this time, the Nagas and the Indians have carved out a compromise: The Nagas have a separate state within the province of Assam, but nominally remain part of India.

Vietnam

The Vietnamese peninsula is the traditional home of at least fifty native nations, including the Cham, the Khmer, and the 800,000 Montagnards of the highland areas, who also include the Nung, the white Tai, the black

Tai, the Tho, Muong, Yao, and Meo. The Montagnards, survivors from at least the Bronze Age, are skilled agriculturalists, capable of sophisticated irrigation to grow rice on steep, terraced fields.

When the French colonists arrived in the nineteenth century, they promised that the various tribes would have control over their own regions, including actual deeds of land ownership. But following the Geneva conference of 1954 and the establishment of South Vietnam, dictator Ngo Dinh Diem decided to assimilate all native people within one Vietnamese culture. According to a Minority Rights Group report, Diem's policies "meant a slow and systematic destruction of the way of life of the Montagnards and their cultural identity, designed to rob them of their land and make them disappear as a people. . . . Montagnards were driven from the land of their forefathers and their properties were distributed . . . [even] the official use and teachings of the Montagnard languages were prohibited," as were Montagnard hair styles.

Despite their treatment, the Montagnards fought for the South Vietnamese government and the American army in the Vietnam War, which has further complicated their lives. When the war was lost, thousands of Montagnards fled to the United States. They are now attempting to re-create their agricultural lives in California's Central Valley, where they are facing American-style racism.

Burma

Reading about the political upheaval in Burma in American newspapers, one is hard pressed to find a single reference to the fact that the political resistance to the brutal military dictatorship of the last three decades is led by the Karen tribe. When the British controlled Burma, the Karens insisted on maintaining their separate nationhood. The English hedged on the promise and created Burma, another fictitious entity made up of at least eleven separate nations now dominated by the Burman tribe. General Ne Win took over as dictator and created a new constitution that was rigidly centralist and recognized no rights of other tribal peoples. Consequently, the six million Karens formed a 20,000-strong army under a complete political organization, with a prime minister, a committee of Karen elders, and ministers of state. In 1976, the Karens and the eight other largest tribes formed an alliance to overthrow the Burmese and establish a new federation that would allow social and cultural autonomy for all indigenous groups. Their coalition succeeded in winning an election in 1990, but as this book goes to press the military has not yielded control and has kept opposition leaders under house arrest.

The Soviet Union

With so much media attention on Russian "ethnic minorities" these days—not from any devotion to minority rights, but rather from glee at the breakdown of communist rule—I will only briefly mention a few facts that tend to not be reported. In addition to the Lithuanians, Estonians, Latvians, Armenians, Ukrainians, and Georgians, all of whom *are* in the news, there are some 22 million Turkic peoples in Central Asia, about 6 million Kazaks living near the Chinese border, Kurdish people adjoining their own tribes across the arbitrary borders of Iran, Iraq, and Syria, and a profusion of Arctic peoples, including Eskimos and nomadic Chuckchi reindeer herders, cousins of the Sami of Scandinavia.

The northern peoples of the Soviet Union have been impacted by a policy that, though not officially called transmigration, has the same effect. Hundreds of thousands of Russians have moved north to find jobs mining nickel, tin, copper and coal, iron and oil, natural gas, gold, and diamonds. Though this policy has not met with violence in the Soviet Union—which has granted greater cultural recognition to tribal minorities than most other countries of the world—native groups are finding it increasingly difficult to maintain cultural and economic autonomy.

China and Tibet

There are fifty-five officially recognized "national minorities" (what we have been calling native nations) within China's borders today. They represent roughly seven percent of the total population, or about 67 million people. Included in the figures are the Zhuang (10 million), the Hui (6 million), the Uygar (5 million), the Miao (4 million), and the Tibetans (nearly 4 million). Several of these "minorities," as well as other smaller groups, have fought bloody wars to resist incorporation into China. In the past 200 years the Turkic peoples have revolted at least three dozen times against rule by the majority Han Chinese. More recently news reports have concentrated on fierce resistance in Tibet.

Many of China's so-called minorities have had glorious pasts, notably the Mongols, whose thirteenth-century empires reached westward to Europe, and the Tibetans, whose civilization has lasted at least two millennia and who are considered among the world's most refined people, psychologically, socially, spiritually, and artistically.

Chinese policy towards these separate cultures has gone through many changes, but in recent history the significance of the communist revolution is paramount. While fighting Chiang Kai-shek the communists promised the Mongolians, Tibetans, and Turkics complete autonomy. But once in power, the position was modified. Though all "national minorities" are guaranteed "equality," and certain elements of autonomy were instituted in five regions, in practice regional regimes were forced to adhere to central economic and cultural directives.

During certain periods "national minorities" were directly assaulted. In the 1950s Eastern Turkestan peoples, who follow Muslim religion and have a very distinct culture from the Han Chinese, found themselves the target of forced assimilation. According to Julian Burger's *Report from the Frontier*, some 360,000 Turkics were executed and half a million were sent to labor camps. Then the Han Chinese transmigrated to Turkestan, which made the native population a minority, unable to influence the central government's decisions to exploit uranium, coal, and petroleum reserves for development purposes.

The most well-known of today's conflicts is taking place in Tibet. Chinese armies invaded Tibet in 1950, after centuries of refusing its separate nationhood. Since then more than one million Tibetans have died resisting the invaders. In an open effort to forever suppress the elaborate and celebrated Tibetan culture, the Chinese have destroyed more than 6,000 monasteries, which also housed most of the Tibetan nation's art, religious artifacts, and books.

According to John Avedon in his book *Tibet Today*, 60 percent of Tibet's philosophic, historical, and biographical literature has been burned, one out of ten Tibetans has been imprisoned, and two-thirds of the original Tibetan territory has been appended to China. Only parts of central and eastern Tibet now remain as the so-called Tibetan Autonomous Region. At this time, over 100,000 Tibetans are in exile, another 100,000 are in labor camps, and more than 250,000 Chinese soldiers are stationed on the Tibetan Plateau. The Tibetan people are permitted no freedom of movement, given insufficient education and health services, and suffer fourteen hours of daily labor and political re-education meetings. In addition, entire mountainsides have been deforested, and Tibet's unique wildlife species, including herds of gazelle and wild ass, as well as flocks of bar-headed geese, have been obliterated. "In sum, a 2,100-year-old civilization was essentially destroyed in a mere twenty years," said Avedon.

Perhaps most insidious is China's transmigration policy, designed to make Tibetans a minority population in their own land. Some 7.5 million Chinese (mostly Han) have been moved to Tibet, where they outnumber the native population of 6 million. According to Avedon, "This population manipulation is the very means by which the PRC has overcome opposition in every other minority area. In Manchuria the ratio of Chinese to native inhabitants is about thirty-five to one, in Mongolia five to one. In Eastern Turkestan or Sinkiang there are now 15 million Chinese to 7.5 million East Turkestanis. . . . Within two to five years a point of no return may well be crossed in Tibet itself. The infrastructure that China is currently building will then be ready for a truly massive migration to commence."

That's the bad news. The good news is that Tibetans are among the few native peoples to be getting significant support from Westerners, particularly Americans and Europeans. This is due to the Western interest in Tibetan Buddhism, the activism of such groups as Humanitas and Amnesty International, and the immense influence of the 1989 Nobel Peace Prize winner, the Dalai Lama, as he travels and speaks throughout the world. "The struggle of the Tibetan people is a struggle for our inalienable right to determine our own destiny in freedom . . . a struggle for our survival as a people and a nation. . . . A future free Tibet will seek to help those in need throughout the world, to protect nature, and to promote peace," the Tibetan leader has said.

20

WORLD NEWS BRIEFS (2):
CANADA, EUROPE, AFRICA,
LATIN AMERICA

CANADA

In Chapter 16 I described how the United States press called the Alaska Native Claims Settlement Act a financial bonanza for the state's natives, when actually it was one of the most sophisticated frauds in two centuries of duplicitous dealings between the U.S. and the Indians.

Now in 1991, the Canadian press is using similar language to praise the "huge financial awards" being reaped by the Eskimo (Inuit), the Dene, and the Metis of the Northwest Territories in settlement of their "land claims." The Canadian deal is actually quite different from the American deal—there's no corporate intervention—but the outcome is identical. The press praises the government's apparent generosity, and the Indians are described as land and cash rich. Neither turns out to be true. Because of this acclaimed new settlement, the Indians may actually lose title to most of their lands, while the oil and gas companies will have greater ability to invade without fear of legal challenge.

Negotiations first began with the Inuit, the Dene, and the mixed-blood Metis when the natives sought to control development on their lands. They wanted confirmation of aboriginal title to all of the Northwest Territories, where they have lived for millennia. They wanted Canada to establish two new autonomous provinces, Denendeh and Nunavut, and to grant them self-government and full control of resources. (See also Chapter 6.)

The Canadian government feared that if natives owned the land, they would continue their traditional economy—trapping, hunting, fishing—rather than adapt the development economy the government preferred. But when early legal challenges seemed to confirm the native claim to aboriginal title, the government came to the bargaining table to seek compromise. In the end, the natives compromised more than Canada did.

The natives were finally offered four separate draft agreements that confirmed title to about 660,000 square kilometers within the Northwest Territories, as well as an award of $1.5 billion. This sounds generous until you realize that, if all the agreements are ratified, the natives will give up about 80 percent of the lands they arguably have owned until now, and will agree not to seek to reclaim title to any of those lands.

The natives were granted few of the self-governance options they sought in those negotiations. The only bones thrown to them were some promises of "equal participation" on advisory panels and management boards controlling resources and economic development. These panels will include representatives of the Canadian government, the territorial government, and the land claimants. The natives also stand to share some of the royalties for oil, gas, and mining. (The only exception was that the Eastern Arctic Inuit were given hope for a self-governing entity of some kind, for which negotiations have begun.)

As for the $1.5 billion in cash, that doesn't really go to the natives. It will be paid in installments over fifteen years into government trust accounts held on behalf of the tribes. Money will be parceled out from the *interest* for projects that the tribes wish to undertake, subject to government approval.

So rather than achieving a financial bonanza, the native peoples of the north may finally lose title to most of their lands, have their sovereignty denied, and be set up for an industrial penetration that will seriously threaten traditional economies, environment, and culture.

• • •

Elsewhere in Canada, other Indians are also causing controversy. The Meech Lake Accord was to have granted the Province of Quebec "special status," because of its distinct culture and language. The agreement was blocked, however, when several Indian groups, especially from Manitoba, demanded similar "special status" based on their prior occupancy and had sufficient political clout in their provinces to thwart the national consensus.

The Indians were roundly criticized for their action, since it could eventually cause the secession of Quebec. But one native leader, interviewed by the Canadian Broadcast Corporation, put it this way: "They're happy to give special status to Quebec because of its culture and language, but we have a culture and language and history here that precedes the Quebecois by thousands of years. We've been trying for special recognition since we were invaded. Why should we now just go along with Quebec's sovereignty dreams when they won't recognize ours?"

The Indians' successful demonstration of power in blocking Meech Lake may have been the impetus for the Mohawk Indian action outside Montreal in early 1990. When a suburban town began to expand its nine-hole golf course to eighteen holes, on land the Mohawk have traditionally claimed as theirs, the Indians roadblocked an important bridge, causing massive traffic delays for several months and producing a show of force by the Canadian army. As this book goes to press, the situation is at a standoff, but negotiations have begun.

Meanwhile, not far away, other Mohawk are involved in a complex battle essentially created by the arbitrary division of the Mohawk Nation into American and Canadian reservations: Akwesasne on the American side of the border, and St. Regis in Canada. As with native nations elsewhere on the planet, such a division is intolerable to a people who were once united.

The discord accelerated in 1989 after the government on the Akwesasne Reservation, created by the U.S. through the Indian Reorganization Act, instituted gambling casino operations. This created a split within the Mohawk, many of whom didn't want outsiders on the reservation for gambling. The rift soon spilled over the border, involving relatives in Canada. Matters were made worse by the fact that the casinos were privately owned. Since the profits were great, a quasimilitary was created by the owners to enforce their wishes. When violence broke out, the New York State Police, the FBI, the Canadian Mounties, and representatives of other agencies all became involved, causing a mass of confusion and hostility typical of situations where traditional authority has been usurped by occupying powers.

In the *Toronto Globe and Mail,* a former resident of Akwesasne, Kahn-Tineta Horn, argued that the fault for the hostilities lay with "legal systems that not only differ from each other but are alien to the native tradition." She indicated that similar problems in the past had only been settled when the natives abandoned foreign legal systems and returned to the "political and social institutions of the Iroquois Confederacy." Horn pointed out that "the traditional approach hasn't been given a chance. Its influence is growing but outside interference hasn't gone away. The Canadian and U.S. governments still impose their laws and deal exclusively with the [recognized] chiefs and elected band councils . . . puppet governments bypassing the traditional Iroquois forms of government. . . . The answer to the problem is to make the family whole again and let the Mohawks settle it themselves."

EUROPE

We tend not to think of European countries as containing any native nations, even when newspapers carry reports of Basque "separatists" in France and Spain, or of Serbians, Croats, and Slovenians in Yugoslavia, or Lapps in Scandinavia, or Bretons in France, or Frieslanders in northern Europe. They are all characterized by the media as "ethnic minorities," which ignores the fact that all were once separate nations. Some of these nations have histories going back thousands of years. The Frieslanders, for example, occupied the entire northern coast of continental Europe at the time of Christ, but are now divided among Holland, Belgium, and Germany. Few people are aware that the English language is linguistically more closely related to Frisian than to any other tongue. Or that in 1782 Friesland was the first European nation to grant official recognition to the new United States of America.

More to our purposes perhaps is the situation of the Sami people (Lapplanders), whose nation is also divided: 35,000 live in Norway, 17,000 in Sweden, 4,000 in Finland, and 2,000 in the Soviet Union. Despite this separation, their culture, heritage, and economic practices are still very much alive.

A Caucasian people, the Sami have roamed across the northernmost reaches of the world for at least 5,000 years, living by reindeer herding and small-scale agriculture. They were fortunate to be left alone for most of their history, because the climate in which they live is so forbidding and harsh. But lately, the crush for resources to feed the industrial machine, and the fallout of our technological society—as well as the literal nuclear fallout from Chernobyl—have threatened the Sami survival as never before.

In an article in *Whole Earth Review*, journalist Jon Stewart summarized the Sami situation:

Like the American Indian, the Sami is indivisible from the land, which for many centuries has provided the grazing pastures for immense herds of reindeer, which still constitute the central symbol of Sami culture and economic life. Though a number of treaties over the last 200 years have guaranteed the Sami sovereignty over their lands, today the Sami resources—like those of the American Indian—are simply too valuable for the central states to ignore. The most valuable resource of all is water, for energy generation, and it is the struggle over that commodity that has galvanized the Sami into an extraordinary political movement in the last few years.

Though more than 100 recent water-diversion schemes in northern Scandinavia have now flooded Sami valleys, their major struggle has concerned the proposed Alta-Kautokeino Dam, which would destroy a valley inhabited by 30,000 reindeer. In 1978, some 8,000 non-natives joined the Sami in a 104-day blockage of the project. The protest was eventually met by a level of police brutality rarely experienced in Norwegian history. Public outrage over the police action, combined with new policies from several successive environmentally oriented Norwegian governments, have sent the dam project into limbo, and left the Sami more politicized. According to young Sami leader Ande Goup, as quoted by Jon Stewart, "If we are to have a future we must gain control over our own lives and our land. But the colonizers have been standing on our toes for so long that they get angry when we try to lift our feet."

The Sami suffered a major setback in 1988, with the terrible events at Chernobyl. Clouds of radiation were blown directly westward from the plant over to Lappland, leaving the entire northern tundra radioactive. Most of the reindeer that were saved when the Alta-Kautokeino Dam was blocked had to be destroyed for having eaten radioactive grasses.

Despite their difficulties, the Sami are pushing ahead, demanding that new laws be made to protect their lifestyle and language, and that further water-development projects in the north be halted. They have joined forces with other groups opposing Norway's entry into the European Economic Community in 1992, for fear of the development pressures that would bring. Meanwhile, they are attempting to repopulate the northern reindeer herds.

AFRICA

Here we have a paradox. Except for South Africa and Namibia, indigenous groups are in power in most African countries, which has brought an end to the colonial period. The countries themselves, however, were created along geographical boundaries that have more to do with the needs of the old colonial administrations than with Africa's hundreds of precolonial native nations.

According to the Minority Rights Group, "Almost all African states are geographically the creation of Europeans: That is to say they are artificial in that they are the product, not of their own people's history, but of the rivalries of distant European powers. Because of this, almost all of them suffer from serious internal divisions." The Sudan and Ethiopia are good examples.

Sudan

In the Sudan, a horrifying war is now taking place between the peoples of the southern Sudan and the peoples of the north, none of whom should ever have been jammed into one political unit. The responsible colonial powers in this case were the Egyptians and the English, who merged the northern, brown-skinned Hamito-Semite peoples, who are Arabs, with the Negroid tribes of the south. It was a merger between different economies as well as races: The northern tribes' traditional economies were based on Nile River Valley trading routes, using camel caravans, while the southern peoples were rainforest dwellers or, in the case of the Dinkas, nomadic cattle herders.

As usual, it was the colonists' greed for raw materials that set the north-south conflict into motion. The "raw material" in this case was people—black slaves. In the 1800s, the Egyptians urged the Arabic peoples of the north to kidnap dark-skinned southerners for the slave trade, creating enmities that have never subsided. Matters were made more complex by the Christian missionaries from England, who divided up the southern regions among Roman Catholics, Anglicans, and Presbyterians, creating new polarities. When Egypt granted independence in 1957, and a new, fictional Sudanese "nation" was created that attempted to amalgamate all this diversity, northern military generals staged a coup to establish the north's rule. More coups have followed, though the rulership of the north has been maintained, along with the bloody war.

Ethiopia

When the Italian colonists withdrew in 1941, after fifty years of occupation, they handed rule to the minority Amharic people, led first by Menelik II and then Hailie Selassie. Though the Amharic account for only 15 percent of the population of the amalgamated state of Ethiopia, they have forcibly dominated government posts and ruling committees. The Oromo people, more than 50 percent of the population, are not permitted to speak their language in schools or in public, and are forced to serve in the army against their will. Other tribes include the nomadic pastoralist Somalis, who rightfully should be part of Somalia to the east, as well as the Eritreans and Tigrayans. All of these groups have, separately and together, waged war against the Amharic rulers, with the Eritreans gaining apparent independence in 1991.

The Sahel

Unlike the old forms of colonialism, which exercised military power, neo-colonialism is the process by which economic domination achieves comparable results. The consequences of this are evident in the Sahel.

Until recently the Sahel, a thin strip of semi-desert in north-central Africa, stretching from Senegal through Mali, Upper Volta, Niger, and Nigeria, was under French domination. In many ways it still is. The Sahel is home to about 14 million nomadic pastoralist peoples, mostly Berber. They constantly move according to season, rainfall, and desert growth. Having survived for millennia in this manner, in recent decades their existence has been threatened by drought and by short-sighted development strategies pushed upon the former colonies by the International Monetary Fund and the World Bank.

Julian Burger, in *Report from the Frontier,* praises the nomads of the Sahel for their "highly flexible way of life suited to fragile marginal scrublands. . . . By their adaptation to the conditions of the semi-desert regions and their reciprocity with local settled farming communities, pastoralists were able in the past to survive long periods of drought and withstand famine. The pastoralist way of life, far from being an inefficient and primitive mode of production [as Western bankers claim], has proved to be a most effective system for survival and even prosperity."

The Minority Rights Group report *Nomads of the Sahel*, by Patrick Marnham, describes the intricacies of the cooperation among the nomadic tribes, who permit each other to move freely across the vast desert terrain they share. Similar cooperation with farmers living at the fringes of the desert enables nomads to leave animals to breed on farmers' lands, in exchange for food. But this delicate pattern of reciprocity is now being threatened by new agricultural models introduced by Western interests: large-scale irrigation, massive farming of export crops, and pesticide use, all of which create pressures on grazing lands and water resources. (Interestingly, water-resource management has been a high art among wandering tribes, who would plant their wells at intervals across the desert, conserving the resource while providing flexibility to the herders.)

The Minority Rights Group report gives one particularly telling example of Western development attitudes, describing a 1976 visit by Dr. Henry Kissinger: "Kissinger wound up his African shuttle with a visit to Dakar where he announced a $10 billion development program to 'roll back the desert.' US AID [Agency for International Development] has run bigger development programmes than this, but few which have had an equivalent capacity to destroy the society which is on the receiving end."

Kissinger's plan envisioned a 5 percent annual growth rate in the GNP by bringing 2.1 million new acres under irrigated cultivation, increasing agricultural output fourfold and doubling the per capita income of the Sahelian population.

According to the Minority Rights Group, "the plan makes no distinction between the objectives to be achieved for nomads and those for settled people, and apparently regards every Sahelian as a potentially well-settled citizen of the future. . . . [The plan foresaw] increased industrialization and urbanization where there is not even enough firewood to provide domestic fuel for the local needs of the relatively small urban settlements that have recently been established . . . terrible odds for the pastoralists to face."

Southern Africa

The San, who include the Bushmen and the Pygmies, were among the original inhabitants of what is now Botswana and South Africa. They fled northward when white settlers forcibly encroached upon their lands in the seventeenth century. Some 62,000 San now live in the Kalahari desert region of Botswana, Namibia, and Angola; few are left in South Africa.

The subject of several famous books praising their unique culture, notably *The Lost World of the Kalahari* by Laurens van der Post, the San speak a distinctive language featuring extraordinary clicking sounds. They live in small roaming bands moving through as much as 4,000 square miles, in a very egalitarian society with no notions of private property.

Recently, San tribes have suffered increased competition for their lands from cattle-raisers, and many of the San have had to give up their traditions and work as laborers in the villages. One country, Botswana, has shown unusual official dedication to preserving the San culture and autonomy. Botswana has encouraged the San to maintain their traditional egalitarian structure while also inviting them to participate in the central government. The San, however, have resisted this invitation, fearing that it will disrupt their own traditions.

For the 200,000 Pygmy people who inhabit the dense rainforests of western and central Africa, survival is threatened by the rate at which the forests are cut down for lumber and coffee plantations. In Zaire, transmigration policies have brought thousands of workers to the forests, where they clear their own plots and/or become workers on the plantations. This policy has already impacted one of the most wonderful examples of intertribal cooperation, between Pygmy nomads and Bantu villagers. For 2,000 years, the Pygmies have been bringing forest products to the Bantu villages in exchange for food, while the Bantu also represent the Pygmy interests to governmental authorities and the outside world. But as the forests disappear, the Pygmies are being forced to retreat further into isolated regions, or to give up nomadism and become agriculturalists or plantation workers, thus destroying their own culture.

LATIN AMERICA

There are about 13 million Indians in Central America (including Mexico), and about 10 million in South America. Here are the country-by-country population estimates of the Minority Rights Group of London:

Country	Indian Population	Percent of Total
CENTRAL AMERICA AND MEXICO		
Belize	15,000	10
Costa Rica	20,000	0.1
El Salvador	960,000	20
Guatemala	3,600,000	50
Honduras	250,000	7
Mexico	8,000,000	11
Nicaragua	135,000	5
Panama	200,000	5
SOUTH AMERICA		
Argentina	350,000	0.1
Bolivia	4,000,000	66
Brazil	200,000	0.1
Chile	1,000,000	9
Colombia	300,000	1
Ecuador	2,070,000	10
French Guiana	84,000	4
Guyana	30,000	4
Paraguay	100,000	3
Peru	242,000	39
Surinam	7,000	1
Venezuela	150,000	1

The situation for native peoples varies greatly from place to place in Latin America. The spectrum ranges from sport-hunting of Indians in Colombia (only recently banned); to full-scale wars pitting Indians against non-Indian domination, as in Peru, Guatemala, and, until recently, Nicaragua; to economic development schemes that directly impact tribal peoples, as in Amazonia; to a fair degree of integration, as in parts of Central and South America.

Unfortunately, the United States has usually played a major role in conflicts and development projects detrimental to Indians. Throughout the region we have been the primary supporter of minority governments who have been hostile to social justice for any segment of society, but especially for the native population.

Central America and Mexico

In most of Central America, including Mexico, Costa Rica, Honduras, and El Salvador, Indians have been somewhat assimilated into the general population, so land reform programs and other civil rights activities tend to have less of an *Indian* label than they do a *class* or a *peasant* label. Indian communities have often been able to maintain many of their traditional cultural characteristics, albeit watered down and altered by hundreds of years of imposed Catholicism. Economically and politically, however, their participation in government policy and their general economic welfare are markedly inferior to that of non-Indians.

In Panama, there are now significant struggles between Indian tribes and mining interests (especially copper mines) on traditional Indian lands. And in Nicaragua and Guatemala (as in Peru) extensive warfare between Indians and non-Indians over questions of cultural and political autonomy has been the norm for decades, though the media reduces this to "ethnic rebellions" or "terrorism" or "insurgencies," depending on the political bias of the participants and of the media.

In Nicaragua, the military resistance of the Miskito, Sumo, and Rama nations to the Sandinista government—a resistance movement that joined with the U.S.-funded Contras, though it had very different goals—finally succeeded in gaining substantial concessions of regional and cultural autonomy for the Indians. Now it remains to be seen if the new Chamorro government will honor those Sandinista agreements and permit the Indian tribes along the Atlantic Coast to rule themselves.

Guatemala

In Guatemala, however, the story is not so hopeful. The descendants of the great Mayan nation form the majority of Guatemala's population, but the Spanish descendants are still the rulers. The Mayans suffer one of the worst cases in the world of substandard living and government-sanctioned violence. Beginning in the sixteenth century, the Spanish brutally attacked and destroyed the leadership of what had been one of the world's most culturally, spiritually, and scientifically advanced civilizations, and then stole the fertile Mayan farmlands. Except for the least-accessible mountain regions, where some Mayan communities were able to retain their traditional self-sufficient economies, most Mayans had no choice but to become plantation laborers on the lands they formerly owned.

This pattern continued until the 1940s and 1950s, when there were some improvements for the Indians. A National Indian Institute was established to preserve Indian culture and rights, and some land reforms made headway, despite the opposition of the few large landowners. But most important was the surprising election in 1954 of President Jacobo Arbenz, promising a new day of justice and reform. It turned out that Arbenz was a bit too progressive for the large landowners and for the CIA, which supported their interests. A CIA coup overthrew the president and led to thirty-five years of uninterrupted dictatorship. Rural unions, made up of mostly Mayan members, became illegal. Poverty became endemic. Death squads were invented and roamed the landscape, accounting for thousands of murders. Massacres of whole Indian villages were not uncommon, until finally, a small guerrilla movement emerged: the Guerrilla Army of the Poor, which is still operating today.

The series of military dictators who ran Guatemala after Arbenz's overthrow only differed in degree of harshness, but all took aim at the Indians. The worst period was 1975 to 1987. First, President Romeo García Lucas, with American backing, engineered murders of labor leaders, village leaders, and Catholic priests sympathetic to the peasantry and the Indians. Then, Lucas was succeeded in 1982 by an American-trained, born-again Christian, General Ephraím Rios-Montt, who announced that "all Indians are subversives" and undertook Vietnam-style village-pacification programs that systematically destroyed all aspects of Indian culture. According to Julian Burger, "Soldiers were instructed to destroy traditional clothing. . . . Religious festivals were forbidden; the use of the various Indian languages was aggressively discouraged. Most importantly, the army killed domestic animals and burned fields of maize, a crop that is not merely the staple food but also the basis of Mayan traditional religious life."

The United States' role in all this was to supply the dictatorships with military aid. Ostensibly, this aid was to thwart the guerrillas, but in fact it was used directly against villagers, which effectively drove the Indians right into the arms of the guerrillas, who offered protection.

In the early 1980s, however, a quirk in U.S. policy required that Guatemala become a "democracy" and end all death-squad activities. This came about because of our massive funding of the Contras in Nicaragua and of the government in El Salvador, which we claimed was in support of democracy. It was awkward for the U.S. to make such claims while continuing economic support for the insane slaughters that Guatemala's military leadership was committing against the majority population. In 1984, Guatemala finally elected its first non-military president in thirty years, Venicio Cerezo. Though he campaigned as a reformist, once in office Cerezo understood that his power was only nominal. The military still decided what happened. Cerezo's attempted reforms were blocked at every turn and then, after a few years of quiet, death squads again began roaming the countryside, slaughtering village leaders, labor-union activists, and anyone who was suspected of any contact with even moderately liberal reform ideas.

As I complete this book, a new president, Jorge Serrano Elias, has been elected. A right-wing evangelical Christian, Elias was a strong backer of former dictator Ephraím Rios-Montt. This is an ominous development for Guatemala's Indians.

South America

South America has seen some positive recent developments. In Paraguay and Colombia, where Indian slaughters were very nearly official policy until quite recently, there have been major changes. In Paraguay, the death of dictator Alfredo Stroessner has led to a more liberal attitude toward Indian interests. And in Colombia, new laws now forbid molestation of Indians; Colombia has also guaranteed a reservation-type status for Indian rainforest dwellers in the southwestern highlands.

Similar guarantees were also recently extended in Bolivia, where Indians are actually a majority population. Until recently Bolivian Indians were never able to realize their political clout, but lately have been insisting on certain reforms. Finally, in mid-1990, the Indians were given control of about two million acres of tropical forests. Certain logging and mining schemes will continue to be permitted by the government, however, and it remains to be seen if the Indians are successful in keeping development within bounds.

In Peru, on the other hand, a major war enters its second decade, pitting the government against the highland guerrillas who call themselves the "Shining Path." The group is usually decribed as Maoist by the media; it is rarely noted that much of the organization is made up of Indians who have grievances about the theft of Indian lands. Lately the guerrillas have joined an alliance with coca growers to resist the U.S.-created crop-eradication program, which is intended to impact both the coca crop and the Shining Path's rural support. The effect of the crop eradication has been to destroy farmers' one last cash crop and turn them into the arms of the Shining Path.

In Chile, the Mapuche people of the Andean highlands, who always considered themselves to be a separate nation—not part of Chile—expected to have their wishes for autonomy honored by the election of Salvador Allende in 1972. Instead, the Mapuche were met with Marxist preconceptions that insisted on a class interpretation of the Indian struggle. The government sought the Indians' re-education and integration into the revolution as part of the peasant class, rather than as Indians seeking and deserving autonomy. When the CIA overthrew Allende, the whole issue became moot. Under General Pinochet, the Indians were left in a kind of limbo. But now, with Pinochet gone, the Indians are again optimistic that they will achieve meaningful negotiations toward the sovereign status they have sought for centuries.

Amazonia

The Amazon Basin of Brazil, Peru, and Ecuador is one of the places on the planet where the drama of Indian resistance to Western technology is being played out with the greatest ferocity. In this vast region of three million square miles, hundreds of thousands of Indians, among several dozen Indian nations, have had little contact with outsiders. Some had no contact at all until as recently as a decade ago. And yet they now find themselves in a life-or-death struggle against the Western onslaught.

The Amazon has been identified as one of the most promising economic development arenas on Earth. The World Bank and other major development banks have given multinational corporations sanction to pave thousands of miles of road into the forest, to build new cities, to flood hundreds of miles of valley with huge dams, and to clear thousands of miles of rainforest.

These development schemes, however, often prove to be as disastrous economically as they are environmentally. For example, the thousands of acres of cleared rainforest land that were devoted to raising beef cattle have proven unproductive for that purpose. And the policy of transmigration has been a terrible failure. Though tens of thousands of poor urban dwellers made the trek to Amazonia, after the government promised them free land for farms, the settlers discovered that the rainforest lands could not sustain agriculture. Now they are stranded, while the forest has been ravaged.

One positive result of all the activity has been to create worldwide alarm at the rate at which the rainforest and its wildlife are disappearing, along with native plant species that might form the basis of a new pharmacology. Despite all the attention to rainforest issues, however, only recently did the media notice that, in addition to plants and animals, hundreds of thousands of Indians live in the rainforest as well.

In Brazil alone, more than 180 tribes, including 200,000 Indians, are spread through the Amazon Basin. No regard was given to them in the economic planning for the region. And media attention only emerged when the first construction crews were met with military resistance—bows and arrows—as they pushed into Indian areas. (When first reported, these events were described with tongue-in-cheek sarcasm by most Western media, or else with the standard cliché of "Indians versus Development.")

As we enter the last decade of the twentieth century, the Indians of the Amazon Basin have begun to show an astounding ability to quickly grasp what is happening to them, and to effectively organize their resistance. With some help from rainforest activist groups, an extraordinary convention of 700 Amazon tribal leaders representing a dozen tribes was convened in 1989 at Altamira, in the heart of the Amazon region, joined by non-Indian environmentalists, biologists, a few progressive political leaders, and some celebrities, including rock star Sting. This was the first time many of the tribes had ever met each other. It was also the first time certain tribes that traditionally are at war with each other gathered for the common good.

At the meeting, the tribes shared their experiences, attempted to create common strategies, and offered themselves as photo opportunities for the small army of media people who had also come along. The media went for the chance to report on the oddness of the situation. For example, the *San Francisco Examiner* reported: "The conference opened with a peace ceremony staged by members of the Xavante tribe from the southern Amazon, an austere group with bowl-shaped hairdos dyed red at the fringes. The Kaiapo [of the Xingu River Valley] dressed much more lavishly, sporting rainbow headresses, feathered armbands and full coats of body paint. Several carried marmosets, small monkey-like creatures, on their arms."

The media could not have *all* its reporting confined to decribing exotic clothing, and so it also offered a fair amount of detail about the Indians' struggles. In some quarters these stories were the first that ever emerged about the rainforest Indians' situation. Combined with the fact that this was the largest gathering on any environmental issue in the history of Brazil (which is alarming in itself), the event generated considerable local and worldwide attention.

Soon after the Altamira gathering, the Brazilian government, which had previously been intransigent on rainforest issues, announced it would destroy all illegal landing strips that had been built on Indian land, and prosecute anyone who attempted to enter rainforest lands without government permits. It also began the first tentative negotiations with some of the tribal leaders, in what may simply prove to be a ploy to calm world reaction. For amidst this apparent support, the government also continues to arrest and prosecute "outsiders"—biologists, botanists, and environmentalists who, in the government's eyes, come to Brazil to "stir up the Indians."

At present the largest issue concerning rainforest Indians is Brazil's "Plan 2010." Backed by the World Bank and many international aid organizations, Plan 2010 calls for development of virtually all the Amazon's water resources, a vast supply that represents one-fifth of the whole world's developable water. Plan 2010 envisions 136 high dams in Brazil alone, 22 of which will flood a rainforest area the size of the United Kingdom and home to several nations of Indians.

To try to block this project, and in a further demonstration of sophistication, many of the Amazon's tribal leaders have begun traveling to world capitals to persuade government and banking leaders of their position: 1) they have a right to live in their ancestral homelands without outside intrusion, 2) they desperately want to do this, as they prefer no other existence, and 3) there is absolute value, even to Westerners, in the Indians maintaining their way of life.

Meanwhile, on the Ecuadorian side of the Amazon Basin, an extraordinary coalition of ten Indian tribes has threatened to take up arms against the government if their demands for local autonomy and land reform are not met. In a report in the *San Francisco Chronicle,* Luis Macas of the Indian umbrella group called the Federation of Indigenous Nationalities of Ecuador (CONAIE), was quoted as saying, "We are committed to peace, but if our needs are not met, we will have no option but armed struggle."

CONAIE is demanding that most of eastern Ecuador's jungles be converted into "territory of the indigenous nation." They also want Ecuador officially declared a "multinational" country. And they seek the break-up of the large haciendas, dating back to the Spanish conquest, that occupy the country's best farmland and were stolen from the Indians.

A liberal president, Rodrigo Borja, has opened negotiations with the Indian coalition and seems willing to satisfy some of their demands.

But the Indians are not patient. They have set a deadline for their interests to be satisfied: the 500th anniversary of Columbus setting foot in the New World. CONAIE's slogan is "Not one plantation in Ecuador by 1992."

EPILOGUE

THE NEW ORDER AND THE
NEW RESISTANCE

I. MARKET ECONOMY

The U.S.-Iraq war of 1991 shed a harsh, clarifying light on certain trends discussed in the preceding pages.

In explaining why it was necessary to send half a million troops and to mobilize the entire industrial world against Saddam Hussein, George Bush initially suggested that the interruption of the flow of oil, or the rise in its price, "threatens our way of life" and "the new world order." This latter phrase was at first greeted with puzzlement, so Bush changed the emphasis to "naked aggression," "stopping another Hitler," and "restoring the legitimate government of Kuwait."

But President Bush had already demonstrated in Panama that he is comfortable with aggression. Comparing Saddam to Hitler obviously trivialized Hitler (which angered many Jews). And calling the Kuwaiti royal family "legitimate" rulers, when they were arbitrarily installed by British colonialists only a few decades earlier, was simply farcical. No, George Bush had it right in the first place. He *was* fighting for a new world economic order.

The Persian Gulf war revealed as nothing before the shape of modern techno-economics, and the deals that have been made among its major players, all made possible and inevitable by the evolution and interweaving of new technologies. Satellite resource mapping from space, centralized global financial management via satellite-computer-banking transfers, the homogenization and massification of cultures resulting fom the nearly universal reach of TV and advertising, and the enforcement capabilities of high-technology warfare have conspired to give the largest economic powers an ability to operate more efficiently than ever before on a global scale, and to interlock their economies. The corporate economies of North America, Western Europe, Japan, and more recently the Soviet Union and the Eastern Bloc countries, are becoming so merged and interdependent that it is almost meaningless to speak of each economy as separate from the others. This is why so many quickly joined, or at least acquiesced to, Mr. Bush's military coalition.

Only a few years ago, when the Soviet Union was our archenemy, the world was divided into three distinct camps: pro-American, pro-Soviet, and non-aligned. But as "market economics" broke out in Eastern Europe, the World Bank, the International Monetary Fund (IMF), and the Japanese Overseas Development Bank, among others, began pressuring Third World countries to mold their economies to Western development models. Worldwide homogenization was thereby accelerated. The old Trilateral Commission model of a *one world planned economy* (mentioned briefly in Chapter 7, and more thoroughly in Holly Sklar's *Trilateralism: The Trilateral Commission and Elite Planning for World Management*) was finally achievable. Based on unlimited industrial production, the free flow of resources and labor, unlimited commodity consumption, and continuous ever-increasing exploitation of nature, it posited that all countries would arrive at a conceptual agreement on what the world economy should be and collaborate on attaining that common aim.

George Bush is the perfect world leader to stimulate this process. A member of the Trilateral Commission himself, born into the economic elite, a multinational oil company president, a former head of the Central Intelligence Agency, and a former international diplomat, Bush came to power just at the moment of Soviet decline. He knew how to seize the moment, and what to do if things went awry.

Right now it is still true that one country can gain an individual trade advantage over others in food, or computers or other technologies, or in control of some resource. But such advantages are short-lived nowadays. Trade among the industrial countries is so interwoven, and goals so unified, that all countries have begun to move in unison, as if they were one creature. As the Geneva-based negotiations toward a General Agreement on Tariffs and Trade (GATT) continue to progress, with the U.S. exerting tremendous pressure, the present minor discrepancies in policy and economic advantage will soon be sacrificed on behalf of the unified world development scheme. The European Economic Community, which merges the economies (and inevitably, the cultures) of its members, will soon be matched by a North American Economic Community (already proposed by Mr. Bush), and then a Western Hemisphere economic community, and an Asian community, and others around the world. As all these economies interlock, any economic threat to one is perceived as a direct threat to all, as was already the case when Iraq invaded Kuwait.

The term "market economics" is the catchall pop phrase that is commonly used to decribe the present economic trend, but the term is wildly imprecise. The only places on the planet where a market economy truly functions now are places such as Flint, Michigan, or Houston, Texas, where thousands of workers have lost their jobs because free-enterprise capital has moved to Korea, or Thailand, or Poland; or else where a small manufacturer is crushed by a multinational's larger resources; or else where an energy conglomerate invades some great wilderness to seek oil or gas; or else where the last great rainforests, protected only by ancient forest tribes, are assaulted by Western-style development.

"Market economy" is really only a public-relations term to conceal the larger global picture: the forced abandonment of local controls on development, trade, prices, or lifestyle in favor of the new *centrally planned economy,* supervised by banks and corporations and enforced by the U.S. military. "New world order" is a much more precise term than market economy to suggest that international bankers and developers can now literally map the world's resources and plot the flow of development according to a larger plan for an ultimate techno-paradise of the kind I have described in this book.

In the new world order, the large economic powers do not seek to exclude smaller countries from the development process; on the contrary, they urge the smaller countries to participate. Many economic development projects are created by bankers to help the poorest countries, but are implemented only on the condition that those countries agree *a priori* to play by certain rules, which is to say, they must effectively give up their national sovereignty.

The first set of rules has to do with poor countries restructuring their own economies to conform with the centralized development model. The specific structural changes are usually dictated by the International Monetary Fund, and include 1) opening all markets to outside investment and trade, 2) eliminating all tariff barriers, 3) severely reducing government spending, especially in areas of services to the poor, 4) converting small-scale, self-sufficient food farming to high-tech agribusiness, in order to produce export commodities such as coffee and cattle, and 5) demonstrating an unwavering dedication to clearing the last forests, mining the last minerals, diverting and damming the last rivers, and getting native peoples off their lands by any means necessary. All of these adjustments are intended to conform indigenous economies to the multinational corporate drives of the new world economic order.

The second set of rules concerns the participant countries' commitment to be team players. If any one country steps out of line, all others must join forces to bang the offender back into place. Countries that do not agree with the dominant policy face sharp cuts in United States, British, Japanese, and international bank aid, which further threatens their survival. An example of this was the way the U.S. and its allies responded to Jordan, Cuba, Yemen, Malaysia, Brazil, and other countries that opposed the Iraq war.

I doubt that Saddam Hussein knew he was offending such an elaborate scheme when he undertook his invasion of Kuwait, a country that, along with Saudi Arabia, is an eager participant in the new world order. Hussein was angry that the price of oil was being kept low by Kuwaiti overdrilling—low energy prices serve the interests of the larger industrial countries—and he was fearful of the effects on his own economic plans. Saddam thought he might do something about it, but he failed to grasp that individualism of that sort just doesn't fly anymore.

Saddam Hussein was caught in a kind of time warp. Perhaps he felt he was just being a typical, individualistic, nationalistic, corporate-raider type—a Michael Milken with nerve gas and missiles—following the old logic of the Reagan years: "Look out for number one." He didn't understand that in the new megatechnological age, on a tiny planet, *all* countries with resources have to be on the same team. There's no room for upstarts or freelancers, and now that the Soviet Union has defected to the West, no protection either.

Finally, the Persian Gulf crisis revealed one more critical, hidden truth about the new economic order: *It is extremely vulnerable.* The mere threat to slow the flow of just one key resource, such as oil, sets the entire technological system reeling like a creature whose air supply is choked off. In its present structure, our society is utterly dependent on this one natural resource. We will do anything for it, including killing hundreds of thousands of people and irreparably ravaging the landscape. And yet, did we not criticize and scorn stone-age peoples and their economies—those poor hunter-gatherers who did not create surplus or storage—for being so vulnerable to disaster? Wasn't this whole technological pathway created to *resolve* that ancient vulnerability to nature? Wasn't that the fundamental rationale, the essential promise of the machine?

2. "WE CAN'T GO BACK"

In *The Dream of the Earth,* Thomas Berry describes the entire industrial age as a "period of technological entrancement, an altered state of consciousness, a mental fixation that alone can explain how we came to ruin our air and water and soil and to severely damage all our basic life systems." Berry goes on: "During this period the human mind has been placed within the narrowest confines it has experienced since consciousness emerged from its Paleolithic phase. Even the most primitive tribes have a larger vision of the universe, of our place and functioning within it, a vision that extends to celestial regions of space and to interior depths of the human in a manner far exceeding the parameters of our world of technological confinement."

Because our vision became so confined, says Berry, we got caught in what he calls "species isolation" that led to "a savage assault upon the Earth such as was inconceivable in prior times. The experience of a sacred communion with the Earth disappeared. . . . Such intimacy [with the planet] was considered a poetic conceit by a people who prided themselves on their realism, their aversion to all forms of myth, magic, mysticism, and superstition. Little did these people know that their very realism was as pure a superstition as was ever professed by humans, their devotion to science a new mysticism, their technology a magical way to Paradise."

Berry believes that our society does not grasp the nature of our fixation. "That is what needs to be explained," he says, "our entrancement with an industrially driven society. Until we have explained this situation to ourselves, we will never break the spell that has seized us. We will continue to be subject to this fatal attraction."

In Chapter 3 I discussed some ingredients of the pro-technology paradigm, in order to try to explain what Berry calls our "entrancement" with technology. Included among those ingredients were the domination of information by corporations, which present only *best-case scenarios* for their schemes; our envelopment in *artificial environments,* particularly the media, that shield us from an alternative reality; and our tendency to view technology strictly in *personal rather than holistic terms,* which misleads us as to its ultimate effects. I also discussed technology's *inherent appeal,* how it always presents itself in a seemingly beneficent light. If it did not seem to benefit us, of course, we would not have gone for it at all. The bad news came later.

But while working on the last stages of this book, I became aware of yet another ingredient of the paradigm, another ingrained attitude that keeps us caught in our spell: It is summarized in the often-heard assertion

"We can't go back." I usually hear it in social situations. Typically, someone would ask me about the book I was completing. Then after I describe the book's main ideas, the person might say, "Sounds interesting, Jerry, but you know, we can't really go back to the way the Indians lived. You're being romantic to think we can."

This comment always startles me. It seems such an extrapolation from what I was intending to communicate that I begin to wonder if I'd been woefully imprecise. But now I've come to see it as merely an expression of discomfort. It's difficult for us to consider living our lives without the excess of commodities that, in today's world, seem to give life its primary meaning. It's one of those "unthinkable thoughts" mentioned earlier. It stimulates gloomy fantasies of what would happen to our lives that are far more extreme than anything I have suggested.

In fact, we *don't* have to live as the Indians did, and in many places still do. But we *do* need to recognize a few simple points:

• Living as we do now, using the resources we do, following the inherent drives of a commodity-oriented technological society, we are doomed to fail.

• The signs of failure are already vivid and rampant in the environment, within our social systems, and in our desperate international behavior.

• Still worse than the failure of this society would be its success, which would bring on something infinitely more awful: that space-bubble EPCOT-type existence and beyond that, a postbiological "utopia." The intrinsic logic of technological society is leading in that direction; we are already well down the road.

• In pursuit of this terrible technotopian dream, we inevitably chew up the societies that have always warned that this path could not work, and that want to be left out of our mad fantasies. Worst of all, these are the very people who are best equipped to help us out of our fix, if only we'd let them be and listen to what they say.

Let's suppose we did decide to change course. Would that constitute "going back"? Surely we in the Western world could learn and apply some principles that might help us live more peacefully on the earth. We do not have to assume that giving up car culture, or computer culture, or commodity culture, or using energy in a controlled and sustainable manner, or educating ourselves to the true limits of technology, or reacquainting ourselves with an age-old appreciation of the natural world, would necessarily mean having to dig for grubs every night or to hunt for beavers in the Hudson Valley.

Fortunately, there are now dozens of people and groups who have put countless suggestions on the table. In addition to Indian organizations (see Appendix) they include the bioregionalists, the Greens, and many environmental groups. Authors such as Ernest Callenbach, Lester Brown, Wendell Berry, Thomas Berry, Wes Jackson, Ann Ehrlich, Paul Ehrlich, David Brower, Hazel Henderson, Gary Coates, Erik Dammann, Leopold Kohr, Kirkpatrick Sale, Joanna Macy, Carolyn Merchant, Dolores La-Chapelle, Riane Eisler, Ivan Illich, Peter Berg, Richard Register, Hunter Lovins, Amory Lovins, Gary Snyder, Langdon Winner, Frances Moore Lappé, Fritjof Capra, Stephanie Mills, Vandana Shiva, Elizabeth Dodson Grey, Charlene Spretnak, Arne Naess, Susan Griffin, Starhawk, Bill Devall, George Sessions, E. F. Schumacher, Malcolm Margolin, and Chellis Glendinning have all helped create a collective vision of a sustainable society that could accommodate the demands of native and other alternative societies to exist on their own terms. And of course there are also the oral teachings and writings of Indians themselves: people such as the late Phillip Lame Deer, Black Elk, Louis Bad Wound, Bill Wahpepah, and Dan Bomberry; among today's leaders and philosophers there are Jeannette Armstrong, John Mohawk, Winona La Duke, Dagmar Thorpe, Chris Peters, Oren Lyons, Leslie Silko, Vine Deloria, George Erasmus, N. Scott Momaday, Leonard Peltier, Leon Shenandoah, Alfonso Ortiz, Thomas Banyacya, Marie-Helene Laraque, Wilma Mankiller, and Paula Gunn Allen, to name a small number from this continent alone.

I will not try to rearticulate proposals that can be found in the works of others. But I will indicate a few changes that many of these people agree with and, in any case, seem to me to be basic necessities for the survival of a healthy planet:

- We surely need to abandon all values that place emphasis on commodity accumulation as something desirable in life.

- Growth economics, the profit motive, and the market economy, all counterproductive to a sustainable future, must be regarded as short experiments that have failed miserably, and must be abandoned as such; there is no more room for them on Earth. (Simultaneously, world population needs drastic steady reduction, even among Western industrial nations, where each individual consumes twenty to thirty times the resources of a person in a nonindustrial nation. A more equitable allocation of the already available resources is also an obvious necessity.)

- A long list of technologies and technical systems must be re-examined from a holistic, systemic perspective. The many that have been named in this book are just the beginning. Those technologies found incompatible with sustainability and diversity on the planet must be abandoned.

• Finally, we need to rethink our relationship with nature and with native peoples. This includes relearning history, and grappling with the forces that caused this history to occur. And we need to directly support the struggles of native people to recover and maintain their land base and sovereignty, wherever this battle occurs.

There is no denying that all of this amounts to considerable adjustment, but it's not as if there were much choice. Truly, such change is inevitable if sanity and sustainability are to prevail. To call this adjustment "going back" is to conceive of it in fearful, negative terms, when the changes are actually desirable and good. In fact, it is not really going back; it is merely getting back on track, as it were, after a short unhappy diversion into fantasy. It is going *forward* to a renewed relationship with timeless values and principles that have been kept alive for Western society by the very people we have tried to destroy.

As for whether it is "romantic" to make such a case, I can only say that the charge is putting the case backwards. What is romantic is to believe that technological evolution will ever live up to its own advertising, or that technology itself can liberate us from the problems it has created. So far, the only people who, as a group, are clear-minded on this point are the native peoples, simply because they have kept alive their roots in an older, alternative, nature-based philosophy that has proven effective for tens of thousands of years, and that has nurtured dimensions of knowledge and perception that have become opaque to us. It is the native societies, not our own, that hold the key to future survival.

3. SIGNS OF LIFE

In the first pages of this book, I quoted a conversation I'd had with a friend who works as a book editor in New York. He had reacted cynically to my plan for a book that included reports on present-day Indian issues. "Indians are finished in New York," he told me. "Indians shmindians."

But by the time I was finishing this book, he told me that to his surprise, he was editing three new books, all by Indians. "Jerry, Indians are hot now," he said. "I think people are ready to hear what they say."

A few days after that conversation, I took my mother to see Kevin Costner's *Dances with Wolves*. While watching the movie I was thinking how different it is from most films about Indians. It is one of the few films that attempts to present history from the Indians' point of view, and the first spoken in a native tongue with English subtitles, itself a statement of respect. Set among the Lakota (Sioux) in the 1860s, the film takes us inside Indian villages and family life, and explores the Indian decision-making process. Unfortunately, Costner does not adequately include the women's role in the decision making, and he makes the film's hero a white soldier, played by himself. But on the whole this is a sincere effort to bring an American audience closer to Indian ways and Indian philosophy, within a commercial Hollywood format. I even like when Costner shows moments of extreme brutality by Indian warriors, which I take to be the filmmaker's attempt to be even-handed and not too romantic, though the rationale for the Indians' behavior is always clear. Most of all, the film delivers a pretty good sense of Indian life on the plains in a preindustrial world.

When we left the theatre, my mother said, "It's so sad. They had such a beautiful life. What a shame it's all gone."

No, Mom, it's not all gone. Even the Sioux are not all gone. Even now they're struggling to stay on their land, just like millions of other natives around the world.

I wish Costner had found a way to make that film without leaving everyone with the feeling that Indian culture is a part of the past. But credit goes to him for a great effort.

Then, a month later, I tuned into the ABC-TV adaptation of Evan Connell's *Son of the Morning Star*. Though it was an inferior production of that excellent book, it was clear that the producers tried hard to step out of old clichés about Indian savagery, presenting Custer as the savage and the U.S. as invaders.

Is something shifting here?

• • •

Claus Biegert is a German writer who has reported brilliantly on Indian struggles throughout the world. He has a new project now which he calls the World Uranium Hearing, scheduled for 1992, the 500th anniversary of Columbus's setting foot in the Western Hemisphere.

Biegert's idea is different from most international gatherings concerning Indians in that he wants to establish a "Board of Listeners," composed of non-Indians. He wants Nobel Laureates, politicians, scientists, artists, writers, and businesspeople to sit in a hall for three days, *silently,* to listen to what the Indians are saying.

"We are always giving our advice to the Indians, telling them what they should do, and how to react to things," Biegert says. "The scientists study them, the businessmen plan their economies, the politicians push them around, and everyone tries to change them. We do not hear what they say."

The booklet promoting the event articulates that uranium is a worldwide problem, not only because of its end result in bombs and nuclear power plants, but at every stage of its cycle, beginning at the mines and ending with the dumping of the wastes, usually on native lands:

> Death is everywhere that uranium touches. But what we perhaps don't realize is that the destructive properties of uranium are unleashed the moment it's mined from the ground. The victims are usually indigenous peoples of the earth . . . it contaminates their food, their drinking water, and it turns their sacred places into restricted dumpsites. . . . Over 70 percent of the world's uranium resources lie buried in lands inhabited by indigenous peoples. . . . [Yet] the dumpsites go unprotected. Wind and rain spread the deadly, carcinogenic dust from the tailings, contaminating the surrounding countryside. . . . Still, we speak of nuclear technology's "peaceful" use.
>
> Native peoples tell us that uranium should stay in the ground— but their voices are lost in the wind. Tribal peoples possess the knowledge of the past that could help heal and restore the earth— but their views are in conflict with the nuclearized, neo-colonial mindset of the multinational energy corporations. We in the West are in possession of the most advanced strain of ignorance the world has ever developed. . . . Native peoples don't think [this] way. By resisting the repeated incursions of industrial society into their lands, their cultures and their religions, they have heroically preserved a worldview which carries the concept of sacred earth. . . . It's time we listened.

• • •

It is relevant to ask, *can* we listen? This is the question now being asked among certain Indian groups that have decided to take on the task of attempting to introduce native spiritual values to American activist communities. Among the leaders of this project is Christopher Peters, a Poliklah Indian who lives on the Hoopa Reservation in northern California, and who is the new executive director of the Seventh Generation Fund.

In 1991, Peters designed a symposium for the Elmwood Institute, located in Berkeley, California, on "Native Thinking and Social Transformation." In the planning memorandum for the event, Peters wrote: "As we approach the end of the twentieth century, we witness a world society that is rapidly approaching a 'must change society.' The earth's ecosystem can no longer tolerate the devastating demands of this society's narcissistic definition of prosperity. Much of contemporary literature suggests that a cultural revolution is needed . . . but unlike other revolutions that perpetrate doom and destruction, this pending rebellion shall be positive, reinstating optimism and renewed favorable expectations for a better society. It will be a revolution for something, rather than against something. Embodied within this pending revolution will be a consciousness-raising, new paradigm intellectualism, and perhaps, greater cosmic awareness."

Peters raises some important questions as he introduces his concepts to Western activism, among them, What role, if any, can native spiritualism play in the new paradigm shift? Can the values, mood, tempo, and/or perceptions embraced in native spiritualism be transferred to non-native people? Can spiritualism be learned or is it instinctual to the nature of native people? Can non-native people participate in native spiritual ritual? Can ritual produce a change in the value systems of non-native people or would a values change be necessary before a spiritual ritual could be created? Can non-native people be trained in the use of sacred sites? Could the use of sacred sites be made a part of the lost religiousness of the new society?

• • •

I have noticed a change in attitude recently among some of this country's major environmental groups, leading them to become far more cognizant of current Indian issues and to take seriously the Indian viewpoint. Even organizations such as Greenpeace, which at one time led the battles against native subsistence hunting practices such as whaling and sealing, seem now to have understood that something greater is lost by failing to support traditional practices. The survival of Indian cultures is beginning to be understood as critically important to the survival of our own society. The Sierra Club, Friends of the Earth, Earth Island Institute, and others have allied themselves with Indian causes in recent months. (Bioregional and Greens organizations have always been supportive of Indian rights.)

In 1990 a new organization was founded, Unrepresented Nations and Peoples' Organization (UNPO), which is attempting to join the struggles of the Indian nations with those of other officially unrecognized nations, such as those found in the Baltic republics, Georgia, Tibet, Kurdistan, the Pacific island nations, and East Timor, among other places. The goal is for these nations to find common ground and to form a sort of alternative

United Nations that can speak on behalf of their concerns. If successful, this organization may contribute greatly to the international impact of Indian movements, which have been mainly supported until now by such groups as Cultural Survival.

But among the leading non-Indian environmental organizations, Rainforest Action Network (RAN) in San Francisco has demonstrated clear leadership. In Chapter 18, I mentioned that this group was first to support the Native Hawaiian struggle to block geothermal drilling on the Big Island, an issue that the natives say is as much a religious issue as an environmental one. RAN has been an active supporter of native peoples all over the planet, especially those who are trying to survive within their traditional rainforest homelands, now under such fierce attack. RAN expresses its activism through direct action, public education, lobbying, and most recently and most originally, using advertising in the *Wall Street Journal* to directly attack the belly of the beast: the World Bank and the International Monetary Fund.

The RAN ad called the two agents of the new world order "the world's leading architects of environmental destruction," which encourage poor countries to rape their own natural environments and drive away their native populations. "The fault lies with the operating attitudes of the bankers," the ad said. "They follow models of western development that have nothing to do with local realities or the wishes of the people on the land. Sitting in their air-conditioned offices in Washington or Tokyo or Paris, the bankers are sure they know what is best for the natives of Irian Jaya or the Amazon forests. They have an image of what the world should look like—something like a suburban mall—and they are devoted to making that happen. That millions of lives are affected, or that whole communities are destroyed, or that entire forests disappear does not loom large in the bankers' minds. The arrogance is appalling."

The ad caused enormous reactions from both international banks, causing them to issue detailed denials, to hold press conferences, to run ads of their own, and to stimulate their client states to do the same. The government of Indonesia, for example, which was named in the ad as among the worst offenders of native rights for its behavior in New Guinea, issued an official statement that the goal of Indonesia "has always been to strike a balance between development and the need to preserve the environment . . . [though] the need for development is paramount." The size of the reaction to this one advertisement is yet another indication of how vulnerable development agencies really are to outsiders discovering the truth of their activities.

• • •

I have mentioned that continental Europeans, particularly the Dutch and the Germans, are among the most aware of the non-Indian populations about Indian issues. A case in point is the current campaign of the Working Group on Indigenous Peoples (WIP) in Amsterdam to focus public anger at the NATO low-altitude bomber training flights over the traditional Innu Indian lands in Labrador, Newfoundland, Canada. More than 10,000 times each year, airplanes scream overhead at 700 miles per hour, just 50 feet above the trees, causing animals to scatter in shock and panic, and utterly disrupting the millennia-old Innu hunting-and-gathering practices, not to mention the peace and quiet of their still-beautiful world.

"The thirty-ton planes fly so low the pilots' faces are visible," according to one Innu hunter. "The planes' passing shakes trees, ripples canvas tents, leaves oil slicks on the water. We have seen the effects on wildlife such as caribou, beaver, fish, minks, ducks, and geese . . . low-level flying causes cattle to stampede, waterfowl to leave their habitat, and mink and foxes to eat their young."

The Working Group on Indigenous People has asked Public Media Center to create an advertising campaign to publicize the issue, with ads to be run in Holland, Germany, Canada, and if funds are raised, in the United States. The campaign is coordinated by two young Dutch anthropologists, Jan Van Boeckel and Govert De Groot, who have worked on North American Indian issues for many years. In addition, Van Boeckel and his colleagues Frits Steinmann, Ceciel Verhey, and Pat Van Boeckel produced an excellent film, *The Earth Is Crying,* documenting a tour of Europe by American Indian activists, including Bill Wahpepah, Floyd Westerman, and Leslie Silko. The group is also completing a film about aboriginal attitudes on the sacredness of land. The group's interest in the Innu issue stems especially from the fact that the Dutch air force is involved, along with the Germans and Canadians.

"The flights used to take place here in Holland and in Germany," said Jan Van Boeckel, "but the populations here couldn't stand the noise and rose up in opposition. So now they do it over the Indians." The biggest problem stems from the fact that "every spring and autumn the Innu move out to the woods to hunt and to fish. This is where the traditional knowledge of gathering, cooking, and living in the woods is passed on to the kids. Without this seasonal migration of about eight months, the Innu culture would not exist."

Van Boeckel continues: "The Canadian government says it has rules that forbid such low-level flights in places where there are Innu camps, but it's not true. The Innu have now stopped even notifying Canada about their camp sites. They say that it's their land anyway and they shouldn't have to tell anybody where they go. In fact, like most Indians, they don't acknowledge that Canada has any rights over their land, which they call Nitassinan. Anyway, they don't live in fixed camps but move around within a radius of about 100 kilometers where they are hunting, fishing, and gathering, just as they have done for 9,000 years. Along the riverbanks is where they find the fish and game, but it's also the riverbanks that are most suitable for the bomber runs. We think that when the populations here in Holland, Germany, and Canada find out what's going on, there will be plenty of outrage. It can be stopped."

•   •   •

Just after we begin to work on the campaign against the overflights of the Innu, Marie-Helene Laraque telephones from the Northwest Territories, Canada. (I described Laraque earlier in Chapter 6, concerning the Dene Indians.) She tells me that low-level bomber training flights are now also planned for the Dene lands in the NWT. In this case, it's the United States military who's conducting them. We had already been flying cruise-missile test-flights along a path from the Arctic Sea down the Mackenzie Valley into Alberta, but those were relatively quiet. Now, says Laraque, "they want to start with American B-52s, F-111s, and F-15s, joined by Canadian CF-18s. They'll begin with four days per year. They will take off near Snowdrift at the eastern end of Great Slave Lake, playing war games as they head south. That's the way they began in Labrador, with just a few flights. We expect things to develop the same way here. A new Cross Canada Alliance has been formed to work together with the Innu and other native groups to oppose it. But since this is an American proposal, supported by the Canadian government, it probably has to be blocked in the States."

Marie-Helene then goes on to tell me about another alliance. She has just returned from a unique conference in Quito, Ecuador. Five hundred representatives from 120 Indian nations gathered there to unify their efforts, with particular focus on the 500th anniversary of Columbus's landing. Marie-Helene, who has always been a passionate advocate of a pan-Indian movement, is happy that it seems to have begun.

"Spain, the Vatican, the United States, and other governments are planning a lot of pompous celebrations of the so-called conquest of America," Laraque says. "From the native point of view there is nothing to celebrate.

There is, however, a lot to commemorate: a whole history of struggle and survival, and a heritage to share with the world."

Laraque also tells me about the workshops that took place at the meeting, on networking, culture, religion, education, self-determination, land and natural resources, native philosophy, and dealings with colonial governments.

The conference issued two official documents, Laraque says. The Women's Commission document includes these words: "As women, we are particularly identified with our Mother Earth . . . we must respect her, care for her, love her. We [are here] to defend the Earth. . . . The churches must respect our religions as we respect theirs. We have the right to practice our native beliefs, to have our sacred sites and our sacred objects. Instead of celebrating the 500 years in 1992, the churches should ask our forgiveness."

The general declaration of the conference says, in part: "The Indians of America have never abandoned our struggle against the oppression, discrimination and exploitation which were imposed upon us as a result of the European invasion of our ancestral territories. . . . From this point we consider it a priority [that there be] complete structural change; change which recognizes the inherent right to self-determination through the Indian peoples' own governments and through control of our territories."

• • •

The quincentennial of Columbus's landing is also providing a focus for Indian activism in this country. In early 1991, the Traditional Circle of Elders, an organization of traditional American Indian leaders, issued their 1992 Alliance Planning Document, which said, in part:

"It is fitting at this time to remind the children of the human race that we Native people were placed in this part of the world by the Creator, and that no person 'discovered' us. . . . We declare 1992 as the Year of the Indigenous People."

The document calls for activities throughout the United States to memorialize the indigenous peoples and nations that did not survive the invasion or the ensuing wars; to acknowledge the "genocidal practices that have claimed millions of Native people from 1492 to the present"; and also to give "thanksgiving for those indigenous people and nations who have survived the excesses of 'civilization.'

"We call upon teachers, historians, and scientists to tell the truth about our past and current situations, and to allow the truth to guide their future actions."

The Circle of Elders plans to seek a memorial for the Indian nations that were destroyed or enslaved, as well as a "Day of Atonement." It seeks a formal apology from the King of Spain and from the U.S. government. Among its other plans are a mock trial of Christopher Columbus, community forums throughout the country, a traveling photography show by native artists, an American Indian Festival in Paris, and "a major gathering of traditional Indian Elders of North America" at Stanford University. "The Elders will discuss spiritual prophecies that relate to the present and future state of the world. This will be followed by a conference between the Elders and scientists to discover parallel thinking on prophecy and environmental conditions and trends. The Elders seek scientific corroboration of the environmental trends predicted by their forebears."

4. AGAINST PESSIMISM

I will conclude with some comments about despair. I have begun to hear from people, even some who have been active campaigners for years in the resistance to the technological juggernaut, that it may now be too late to turn things around, to save the last wildernesses, to protect the oceans, to ensure the survival of native cultures, to make the lifestyle changes that are required to recover a sense of the sacred. Worst of all, I have begun to hear such talk from young people. The situation was worsened, of course, by the U.S.-Iraq war, which dealt a metal-fisted blow to everyone's psyche, revealing as it did such a deadly, out-of-date paradigm for human behavior.

I am personally sensitive to this issue, since I am sometimes accused of encouraging despair. Some people say my television book created such a negative picture that they felt depressed and disempowered after reading it. They believed what I wrote, but were disappointed that I offered no plan for action. Since this book also discusses what's gone wrong, I have been concerned about reactions.

My rationale for ending the TV book as I did was simple. It is not easy to bring down such a technology. But if ever we do, the first change must be in our own minds. We need to make a mental "click," of sorts, about our culture's passivity to the onrush of technology altogether. I did not want the power of the *idea* that TV should be eliminated to be measured against what would surely be a less-than-perfect plan for achieving that goal.

Secondly, as indicated earlier, television is no modular unit that can be lifted out of the technological system, with everything else left in place. It is an integral part of the megatechnological web, and the web itself is what we must learn to deal with. So the task is even more daunting than it first seems.

Nonetheless, I was surprised that some people reacted as they did, since I am personally not pessimistic. My feeling has always been that describing the reality of a problem will encourage activism, not withdrawal. In any case, that is my wish. If I didn't believe that the present negative trends could be reversed, I probably would not have put so much effort into writing about them.

But as my late partner in the advertising business, Howard Gossage, used to say, "It's not enough to make people feel bad; you've also got to offer something they can do." This was why, in the mid-1960s, working with David Brower of the Sierra Club on the ads against Grand Canyon dams, Gossage invented the multiple-response coupon, so readers would have a means of direct expression. It allowed people to make a simple first act of commitment and involvement. Clipping and mailing that coupon changed people internally; it politicized them.

As for being faced with overwhelming odds, Gossage also said, "It may be that everything we do will be futile, but we will do everything anyway."

I think a similar attitude drives the people at Public Media Center, the nonprofit public-interest ad agency, where I spend many of my days. It especially seems to characterize our brilliant and invariably optimistic executive director, Herb Chao Gunther. He maintains a relaxed, calm, and cheerful attitude in the face of every adversity, and by that attitude has inspired all of us to see that the obstacles are not nearly as great as they first seem. As a result, Public Media Center clients have prevailed on many issues against great odds.

But surely the best examples, yet again, are the native peoples. Here we are speaking of tens of millions of people around the world who, within only the last few centuries—and in some cases only the last few years— have seen their successful societies brutally assaulted by ugly destructive forces. Some native societies have been obliterated. Some peoples have suffered separation from the source of their survival, wisdom, power, and identity: their lands. Some have fallen from the pressure, compromised, moved to urban landscapes, and disappeared. But millions of natives, including tens of thousands here in the United States, have gained strength in the face of all that. Their strength is fed by the knowledge that what they are doing is rooted in the earth and deserves to succeed. But aside from that, they fight their battles without real thought of failure. They do it on behalf of their values, as well as their children and grandchildren. They also do it—though I've perhaps not given it sufficient emphasis in this book—with a humor and kindliness that is itself inspiring.

So in that context, I feel that talk of failure is very short-sighted, unwise (since it is debilitating), indulgent, inaccurate, but most of all useless.

So then. At the conclusion of these comments you will find an Appendix with a list of organizations, some of which have already been discussed, all of which are engaged in some element of the struggle described in these pages. They don't necessarily agree with my views, nor do I always agree with theirs. But we are all moving in a similar direction, and they each have a piece of the picture. Contact one or more of them. They need your help. Get involved. Send money. Bring friends.

When you do, I think you will find yourself enveloped by an enthusiasm and optimism that ought to give courage to the faint of heart. None of the groups I have named suffers from a failure of realism about the present state of the world. In fact, it is precisely *because* of their realism that they are so alive and energetic.

On a personal level you can also do a great deal. Aside from the issue of your own lifestyle—and we each need to arrive at a standard and live by it—there is surely something happening near where you live that could use your direct participation. Perhaps it's a condo development planned for the last open space in your neighborhood. Perhaps it's the home-porting of a nuclear vessel. Perhaps it's a threat to some Indian fishing rights. Perhaps it's an assault on a regional habitat. Take time to learn what's happening, and *make yourself felt*.

I admire the bioregionalist idea of finding a place on the planet, on your street, in your city, in your region, and deciding that that place is one you will protect. Learn its natural history and its cultural history. Visit the place regularly. Watch it carefully. If it's threatened, *do something*.

Of course I hope you will also keep challenging yourself about technology, and begin to think about each glitzy new machine in other than its advertised terms. I also hope you will read everything you can by and about Indians and their struggles, and that you find a way to become engaged. The quincentennial of Columbus's landing will offer numerous opportunities.

Most important, keep in mind that the big issues are far from settled. Don't despair. All is not lost. There is a growing awareness of what needs to change. We are making progress. We have seen that the bigger the machine, the more vulnerable it is. With the changes in Eastern Europe, we can also see how rapidly the world can be altered, and how quickly paradigms can change. There's plenty of room for maneuvering. And do not be too self-conscious to speak, from time to time, the words "Mother Earth."

Thank you.

April 26, 1991
San Francisco

APPENDIX: ORGANIZATIONS AND PERIODICALS

The following is a list of organizations and periodicals that are good sources of information in areas related to the preceding text. The list is by no means exhaustive, since it would be impossible to list local groups throughout the country. It is offered as a resource for further investigation and involvement.

Adbusters Quarterly, The Media Foundation, 1243 West Seventh Ave., Vancouver, BC V6H 1B7, Canada.

Unique new publication that combines blistering critique of commodity society with detailed coverage of environmental destruction; to this organization, the connection between the two is clear.

Akwesasne Notes: A Journal for Natural and Native People, Mohawk Nation, P.O. Box 196, Rooseveltown, NY 13683.

Best (and oldest) source of news from Indian country. Covers native sovereignty rights and struggles, as well as the philosophical underpinnings of the native movement.

AMERICAN AGRICULTURAL MOVEMENT, 100 Maryland Ave. NE, Washington, DC 20002.

Strongest single voice for family farmers; grew out of huge tractor demonstrations of 1970s.

Buzzworm: The Environmental Journal, 2305 Canyon Blvd., Ste. 206, Boulder, CO 80302.

Slick but comprehensive. Provides news, features, and useful directories.

CENTER FOR INVESTIGATIVE REPORTING, 530 Howard St., San Francisco, CA 94105.

An affiliation of news reporters devoted to ferreting out the stories that corporations and governments seek to bury and that other news organizations do not pursue.

CITIZENS' CLEARINGHOUSE FOR HAZARDOUS WASTES, P.O. Box 926, Arlington, VA 22216.

The first national grass-roots organization focused specifically on toxic waste problems; was formed as a result of the Love Canal tragedy.

COMMITTEE FOR RESPONSIBLE GENETICS, 186 South St., Boston, MA 02111.

Conferences, research, and activism on the full range of biotechnology issues.

COMPUTER PROFESSIONALS FOR SOCIAL RESPONSIBILITY, P.O. Box 717, Palo Alto, CA 94301.

First group specifically focused on how computerized society affects civil rights, the military, and life in the workplace, among other issues.

THE COUSTEAU SOCIETY, *Calypso* and *Dolphin Log,* 930 West 21st St., Norfolk, VA 23517.

Education and activism around issues of ocean and marine life preservation.

CULTURAL SURVIVAL, *Cultural Survival Quarterly,* 11 Divinity Ave., Cambridge, MA 12038.

This quarterly publication, along with CS's other books and occasional papers, provides an enormous quantity of information on native peoples around the world under siege from Western development. CS also takes direct action on certain important issues and strategizes on long-term solutions.

DATA CENTER, *Corporate Responsibility Monitor,* 464 19th St., Oakland, CA 94612.

Extensive library and research facility that investigates corporate and governmental activity throughout the Third and Fourth worlds.

Daybreak: American Indian World Views, P.O. Box 98, Highland, MD 20777-9989.

Edited by John Mohawk and Oren Lyons, two of the world's leading native thinkers. Presents current views on major native and planetary issues.

EARTH FIRST!, *Earth First! The Radical Environmental Journal,* P.O. Box 2358, Lewiston, ME 04241.

Loose affiliation of local direct-action groups creating their own projects under the common banner "No compromise in defense of Mother Earth." Direct-action tactics include roadblocks, "monkey wrenching," etc.

EARTH ISLAND INSTITUTE, *Earth Island Journal,* 300 Broadway, San Francisco, CA 94133.

Founded by David Brower, this extensive domestic and international program focuses on protection and restoration. Present emphases are marine mammal protection, global warming, international trade agreements, and relationships between politics, economics, justice, and ecology. *Earth Island Journal* is by far the most interesting and comprehensive news publication in the ecology movement.

ELMWOOD INSTITUTE, *Elmwood Newsletter* and *Global File,* P.O. Box 5765, Berkeley, CA 94705.

Conferences, publications, studies, and think tanks attempting to refine and articulate a new paradigm of systemic solutions to environmental problems.

FAIRNESS AND ACCURACY IN MEDIA (FAIR), 130 W. 25th St., New York, NY 10001.

One of the few organizations working to offset the pro-government, pro-industry bias of U.S. mass media.

FAIR TRADE CAMPAIGN, Box 80066, Minneapolis, MN 55408.

Coalition of over one hundred grass-roots organizations (environmentalists, farmers, and consumer, labor, and church groups) working against the GATT agreement and other free trade proposals.

Fifth Estate, 4632 Second Ave., Detroit, MI 48201.

Very radical, in-depth criticism of technology and technological society.

FOOD FIRST/INSTITUTE FOR FOOD AND DEVELOPMENT POLICY, 145 Ninth St., San Francisco, CA 94103.

Research and publishing about how corporate and government elites control agriculture, food supplies, and other resources, this being a major cause of world hunger and oppression. Many publications. Founded by Frances Moore Lappé and Joseph Collins.

FOUNDATION ON ECONOMIC TRENDS, 1130 17th St. NW, Washington, DC 20036.

Jeremy Rifkin and Andy Kimbrell have been the leading battlers in virtually every fight against the excesses of the biotechnology industry.

FRIENDS OF THE EARTH, 218 D St. SE, Washington, DC 20003.

Worldwide advocacy on issues across the spectrum of environmental concerns, such as ozone depletion, biotechnology, toxics, and groundwater pollution.

FRIENDS OF THE RIVER, Fort Mason Center, San Francisco, CA 94123.

Grass-roots organization fighting dams and river diversion projects; also active in water issues.

GATT-FLY, 11 Madison Ave., Toronto, Ont. M5R 2S2, Canada.

Good source of information and programs on the economic and environmental implications of the debt crisis and international trade agreements. GATT-FLY's position: "The debt has already been paid."

GREEN COMMITTEES OF CORRESPONDENCE, P.O. Box 30208, Kansas City, MO 64112.

Network of two hundred local Green organizing groups; organizing vehicle for the international Green movement in the U.S.

Green Letter, P.O. Box 14141, San Francisco, CA 94114.

News and articles about Green political activity here and abroad.

GREENPEACE, *Greenpeace,* 1436 U St. NW, Washington, DC 20009.

Direct action in local and international campaigns to protect wildlife and to oppose nuclear arms and power and toxic waste dumping. Latest emphasis is on war as an environmental issue.

HUMANITAS, P.O. Box 818, Menlo Park, CA 94206.

International human-rights organization with major emphases on nonviolence and on regional struggles such as in Tibet, Kurdistan, and Eastern Europe. Founded by Joan Baez.

INDIAN LAW RESOURCE CENTER, 601 E St. SE, Washington, DC 20003.

Nonprofit law firm devoted to native sovereignty rights: land, water, civil rights, human rights, and resistance to land grabs of Indian Claims Commission.

INSTITUTE FOR LOCAL SELF-RELIANCE, 2425 18th St. NW, Washington, DC 20009.

Promotes locally controlled, democratically managed small-scale economic development. Good resource on issues of solid waste management, recycling, and green city programs.

INSTITUTE FOR POLICY STUDIES, 1601 Connecticut Ave. NW, Washington, DC 20009.

Progressive think tank and publisher that deals with social, political, and environmental problems of the new world order. Focus on trade agreements, militarism, debt crisis.

INSTITUTE OF NATIVE KNOWLEDGE, 1767 Iverson Ave., Arcata, CA 95521.

New organization dedicated to publishing and otherwise disseminating Native American philosophical thought.

INTERNATIONAL INDIAN TREATY COUNCIL, *Treaty Council News,* 710 Clayton St., San Francisco, CA 94117.

Outgrowth of the American Indian Movement; has NGO status at United Nations and advocates within international bodies for native rights. Many local support groups.

INTERNATIONAL RIVERS NETWORK, *World Rivers,* 301 Broadway, San Francisco, CA 94133.

Research, publishing, and activism concerning threats to rivers, watersheds, and indigenous populations caused by dams and other development schemes.

THE LAND INSTITUTE, 2440 East Water Well Rd., Salina, KS 67401.

Founded by Wes Jackson, the leading organization attempting to retain biodiversity within agriculture, to save the Midwest prairies, and to promote the family farm.

LEONARD PELTIER DEFENSE COMMITTEE, P.O. Box 583, Lawrence, KS 66044.

Fighting for freedom of Native American spiritual and political leader falsely accused by FBI of murdering two agents.

Minority Rights Group Reports, 36 Craven St., London WC2N 5NG, England.

Outstanding source of information concerning native peoples, nationhood movements, and ethnic struggles.

Mother Jones, 1663 Mission St., San Francisco, CA 94103.

News, features, and analysis from left-progressive perspective. Heavy concentration on U.S. government and corporate excesses and invasions.

The Nation, 72 Fifth Ave., New York, NY 10011.

This venerable left-wing magazine is still the best source of news and reports of government and corporate behavior on all major current issues.

NATIONAL ABORTION RIGHTS ACTION LEAGUE, 1101 14th St. NW, Washington, DC 20005.

Leading advocate for women's choice on reproductive issues.

NATIONAL AUDUBON SOCIETY, *Audubon,* 950 Third Ave., New York, NY 10022.

Effective grass-roots organization dedicated to protecting wildlife, habitats, and forests. Many local chapters.

NATIONAL COALITION AGAINST MISUSE OF PESTICIDES, 530 Seventh St. SE, Washington, DC 20003.

Clearinghouse for information on pesticides and alternatives to their use.

NATIONAL FAMILY FARM COALITION, 80 F St. NW, Washington, DC 20001.

Coalition of state-level progressive family farm groups.

NATIONAL TOXICS CAMPAIGN, 37 Temple Place, Boston, MA 02111.

Very active grass-roots organization. Nine regional offices provide information and assistance in local fights against toxic pollution.

NATURAL RESOURCES DEFENSE COUNCIL, 40 W. 20th St., New York, NY 10011.

International campaigns against toxics at home, in food, and in the workplace. Broad range of involvement in environmental campaigns.

NEW ALCHEMY INSTITUTE, 235 Hatchville Rd., East Falmouth, MA 02436.

Highly innovative research group focusing on small-scale agriculture.

News from Native California, P.O. Box 9145, Berkeley, CA 94709.

Outstanding publication on culture, history, and activities among native communities in California.

The New Yorker, 25 W. 43rd St., New York, NY 10036.

If you can somehow avoid all the ads, this is still a great source for lengthy, comprehensive special reports on major issues of our time.

NORTH AMERICAN CONGRESS ON LATIN AMERICA (NACLA), 151 W. 19th St., New York, NY 10011.

Country's leading researcher on social, political, environmental, and indigenous issues in Latin America and the Caribbean.

OCEANIC SOCIETY, 1536 16th St. NW, Washington, DC 20036.

Protection of marine biological diversity against such hazards as ocean dumping, dredging, and pollution.

PELE DEFENSE FUND, P.O. Box 404, Volcano, HI 96785.

Native Hawaiian activist organization working to halt new energy developments leading to environmental destruction; also active in rainforest issues and against militarization of Hawaiian Islands.

PLANET DRUM FOUNDATION, *Raise the Stakes,* Box 31251, San Francisco, CA 94131.

Research, publishing, and programs promoting indigenous nationhood movements, bioregionalism, and green cities.

PLANNED PARENTHOOD FEDERATION OF AMERICA, 810 Seventh Ave., New York, NY 10019.

Leading worldwide advocate for women's reproductive rights, international family planning, health programs, birth control, sex education, and population control. Programs and clinics now under furious assault from American right-wing groups. Hundreds of local and international affiliates.

Privacy Journal, P.O. Box 28577, Providence, RI, 02908.

Newsletter concentrating on civil liberties implications of the computer age.

Processed World, 1095 Market St., San Francisco, CA 94103.

Extraordinary journal dealing with implications of high technology. Emphasis on its effects in the workplace.

PUBLIC CITIZEN, *Multi-National Monitor,* 215 Pennsylvania Ave. SE, Washington, DC 20003.

Ralph Nader's organization, coordinates coalition of Washington-based groups working against GATT and free trade agreements. Also sponsors a broad range of legal, lobbying, and publishing efforts on consumer, environmental, corporate responsibility, and indigenous peoples' issues.

PUBLIC MEDIA CENTER, 466 Green St., San Francisco, CA 94133.

Nation's only nonprofit ad agency, serving environmental, Indian, civil rights, women's, and peace organizations.

RAINFOREST ACTION NETWORK, 300 Broadway, San Francisco, CA 94133.

Direct action, lobbying, education, and organizing to protect the world's rainforests and the rights of their indigenous forest dwellers. Major emphasis against World Bank, IMF, GATT.

ROCKY MOUNTAIN INSTITUTE, 1739 Snowmass Creek Rd., Old Snowmass, CO 81654.

The country's outstanding think tank and educational organization fostering new thinking about energy use and global security. Founded by Hunter Lovins and Amory Lovins.

SEA SHEPHERD CONSERVATION SOCIETY, P.O. Box 7000S, Redondo Beach, CA 90277.

Nonviolent confrontation and ecotage to protect oceans and marine life.

SEVENTH GENERATION FUND, P.O. Box 536, Hoopa, CA 95546.

Native-run foundation providing technical assistance and grants to native communities working toward self-sufficiency and sovereignty. Also involved in many native rights campaigns.

SIERRA CLUB, *Sierra,* 730 Polk St., San Francisco, CA 94109.

Country's oldest and best-known major environmental group. Offers lobbying, publishing, legal action, education, activism, and wilderness outings. Local chapters throughout the country.

SOUTH AND MESO-AMERICAN INDIAN INFORMATION CENTER, P.O. Box 7550, Berkeley, CA 94707.

Education for human rights community and the public, both in the U.S. and abroad, concerning self-determination struggles of native peoples of South and Meso-America.

The Trumpeter: Journal of Ecosophy, Lightstar Press, P.O. Box 5853, Stn. B, Victoria, BC V8R 6S8, Canada.

Philosophical explorations toward a new ecological consciousness, from scholarly and nonscholarly sources.

UNION OF CONCERNED SCIENTISTS, 26 Church St., Cambridge, MA 02238.

Scientific and technical research and advocacy on problems of advanced technologies, with particular emphasis on nuclear and military technology.

UNREPRESENTED NATIONS AND PEOPLES ORGANIZATION, 347 Dolores St., San Francisco, CA 94110.

A kind of alternative United Nations for the thousands of nations and peoples presently under colonial control; attempting to create unified international lobbying force.

Utne Reader, 1624 Harmon Place #330, Minneapolis, MN 55403.

Outstanding source of digested and summarized articles on full spectrum of environmental, social, and philosophical concerns. "The *Reader's Digest* of the progressive community."

Whole Earth Review, 27 Gate Five Road, Sausalito, CA 94965.

Formerly *Co-Evolution Quarterly,* this publication has recently turned celebratory of some doubtful new technologies, but retains its place as the single best source of debate and discussion of a full range of issues about technology, lifestyle, environment, and consciousness.

Wild Earth, P.O. Box 492, Canton, NY 13617.

Philosophy and news on the thinking and actions of the deep ecology movement. Editors include Dave Foreman, founder of Earth First! Emphasizes inherent value of wilderness.

WORLDWATCH INSTITUTE, 1776 Massachusetts Ave. NW, Washington, DC 20036.

Research and publications that report on the state of the world's resource supplies and distribution and the ecological consequences of government and corporate policies and practices.

Wrenching Debate Gazette, 1801 Connecticut Ave. NW, Washington, DC 20009.

Unusual, radical debates and essays on environmental, political, and social issues, edited (and much of it written) by organizer and iconoclast Richard Grossman.

ZERO POPULATION GROWTH, *ZPG Reporter,* 1440 16th St. NW, Washington, DC 20036.

Long-time advocacy group for no-growth population in U.S. and abroad.

ACKNOWLEDGMENTS

In a project that took more than a decade, I am indebted to so many dozens of people that I can only name a small percentage of them here. My deep apologies to anyone who may be left out.

In particular, there are three people who especially deserve my gratitude.

Back in the early 1960s, it was Marie-Helene Laraque who first exposed me to the unique character and importance of the Indian struggle and the failure of our society to understand or come to grips with it. She helped me see that all native nations are engaged in the same battle against the presumed superiority, the technical imperatives, and the expansionism of the Western technological-industrial countries. It was during my conversations with her that I decided I would someday attempt a book on these themes, and she has remained a constant advisor, ally, and friend.

I met and began working with David Brower at about the same time. Surely the most visionary, effective, and inspiring environmentalist of our age, it was his brand of no-compromise activism and thinking that essentially vaulted the ecology movement into becoming a major international force. I am only one of hundreds, perhaps thousands, of people whose lives were irrevocably changed by this man.

Dan Bomberry—brilliant, joyful, mellow, and fierce—was my close friend, advisor, and teacher for most of the years I worked on this book. Some of my happiest days were spent with him, on long slow drives through the southwest deserts, visiting small Indian communities, camping in the Grand Canyon, talking, hanging out. His untimely death while still in his thirties deprived the native sovereignty movement of one of its most articulate and inspired leaders and was a terrible personal blow to his family and to hundreds of us who had come to depend on his ideas, his humor, and his creativity. His spirit remains tangible to us all.

● ● ●

When a manuscript evolves as slowly as this one did, publishers are known to get testy. Not so with the folks at Sierra Club Books. I am forever indebted to them for their patience, confidence, guidance, and wisdom. Special thanks are due Jon Beckmann, who was supportive from beginning to end; to Diana Landau, who worked with me as editor in the early days; and then to Danny Moses for his steady hand, his intimate knowledge of the issues, his good advice, and his Buddha-like calm. The copyeditor was Marcella Friel, who gave an unkempt manuscript whatever bits of grace it achieved. Thanks also to Peter Beren and Erik Migdail, to Shana Penn for her manuscript rescue service, and to Meredith Maran for undertaking the huge midterm edit. No less important for hanging in there during these years were my friends and agents John Brockman and Katinka Matson.

Lots of people read the manuscript (or parts of it) in various stages, offering advice and feedback. Ernest Callenbach did so twice, with his usual brilliance and candor. Thanks also to Rita Aero, Susan Benson, Alison Denham, Jack Edelson, Elizabeth Garsonnin, Chellis Glendinning, Jean Krois, Peggy Lauer, Ani Mander, Margo Nelson, Marybeth Riggs, Rob Waring, Albert Wells, and R. L. Wing.

Albert Wells was important in other ways. Early in the project he introduced me to Oren Lyons of Onondaga, Steve Tullberg and Tim Coulter of the Indian Law Resource Center, and to Dan Bomberry, all of whom became critically important from that point on. Wells also introduced me to Lee Swensen, who proved to be a great source of ideas and information, and then became a collaborator on the 1982 conference in San Francisco, *Technology: Over the Invisible Line,* together with Stephanie Mills, Toby McLoud, Diana Dillaway, and Carole Levine. That was a landmark event in my own thinking and apparently for many others who participated.

My education on Indian matters came from so many sources, Indian and non-Indian, that I can scarcely begin to recite them all. I must give particular mention, however, to Dagmar Thorpe for her constant encouragement, feedback, and information, and to John Mohawk, who may be the preeminent philosopher today among young Indians (or anyone else for that matter), and whose (unsigned) critique of modern society is at the heart of the brilliant *Hau de no sau nee Address to the Western World.* Special thanks also to Emmett Aluli, not only for the time he spent with me on the Hawaiian issues, but also for proving that these difficult battles can be won.

Thanks to Bob Antone, Thomas Banyacya, Jose Barreiro, Danny Blackgoat, Victoria Bomberry, Carrie Dann, Mary Dann, Shelton Davis, Palikapu Dedman, Cindy Gilday, Richard Grow, Corbin Harney, Ilka Hartmann, Randy Hayes, Glenn Holley, Winona La Duke, Jack Loeffler, Lehua Lopez, Tom Luebben, Colette Machado, Malcolm Margolin, Steve

Most, Mike Myers, John O'Conner, Joe Sanchez, Kee Shay, Floyd Westerman, Raymond Yowell, and to the late Louis Bad Wound, Philip Deer, and
Bill Wahpepah.

Susanne Swibold and Helen Corbett of Flying Tomato Productions in
Alberta offered their incredible wealth of personal knowledge about the
major issues of the north, as well as a fabulous library. Art Davidson and
the Association of Village Council Presidents of the Yupik Nation made
available their magnificent work *Does One Way of Life Have to Die So Another Can Live?* For their help on northern issues, thanks to Joan Ryan,
Susan Alexander, Bob Childers, and Sarah James of the Gwich'in Steering
Committee.

Howard Levine was the first person to walk me through the full range
of important issues surrounding genetic engineering, and Jeremy Rifkin
deserves thanks for being such a fountain of ideas and strategies about
almost everything. Gary Coates educated me on the full implications and
utter weirdness of lifestyle-theme communities, bubble domes in space,
and megamalls—we eagerly await his book on the subject. For their en-
cyclopedic knowledge of the nationhood movements of the world and the
bioregionalist response, thanks to Peter Berg, Judy Berg, and the people at
Planet Drum Foundation.

Invaluable research help was provided at several critical stages by Sara
Rahe. Other important research, ideas, and suggestions were provided by
Diana Adler, Constance Casey, Pamela Chess, Howard Dugoff, Jennifer
Elias, Ed La France, Dotty Lemieux, Anne Karpf, Terri McCullough-
Klene, Kai Mander, Yari Mander, Lisa Moran, Alexandra Paul, Karen
Payne, Mark Ritchie, Marc Roudebush, Michael Singsen, Gar Smith,
Randy Tinkerman, and Tom Turner.

Herb Chao Gunther of Public Media Center not only contributed his
unique brand of creative thinking, wisdom, good cheer, and strategy, but
also a continuing fellowship and Fellowship, a desk, an office, and a whole
staff of brilliant, talented people to work with every day. Thanks to him
and to all my colleagues at PMC.

And in the important category of inspiration by example, dedication,
and new thinking, thanks to my friends Fritjof Capra, Mark Dowie, Chellis Glendinning, Susan Griffin, Frances Moore Lappé, Charlene Spretnak,
Godfrey Reggio, Doug Tompkins, Langdon Winner, and the council and
staff of the Elmwood Institute.

• • •

Financial survival while working for years on a book is not easy, but I had
help. My thanks for their confidence and faith goes to David Hunter and

Barbara Hunter, Carole Bernstein, Leah Brummer, Helen Doroshow, W. H. Ferry, Wade Green, Adam Hochschild, Tom Layton, Laura Lederer, Carl Levinson, Sid Shapiro, Marion Weber, the Abelard Foundation, Commonweal, the Laras Fund, the Gerbode Foundation, the Levinson Foundation, the Skaggs Foundation, and the Seventh Generation Fund.

Finally, and most importantly, for their love, friendship, support, and encouragement when even I was not sure this book would ever get done, my appreciation, gratitude, and love to my wife and partner, Elizabeth Garsonnin; my sons, Yari and Kai Mander; my mother, Eva Oken; and to Cecelia Brunazzi, Ernest Callenbach, Henrietta DiSuvero, Alvin Duskin, Sara Duskin, Jack Edelson, Veva Edelson, Elaine Frederick, Perry Garfinkle, Linden Glickman, Rubin Glickman, Claire Greensfelder, Catherine Ingram, Mark Kasky, Paul Krassner, Catherine Laroche, Michael Lerner, Carole Levine, Christine Leefeldt, Ani Mander, Wes Nisker, Sharyl Patton, Andy Rader, Shanna Rader, Marc Roudebush, Terry Vandiver, Toni Varner, and my friends at Rerun Video, on Camperstraat in Amsterdam, and Zubu.

BIBLIOGRAPHY AND SOURCES

The following includes books, articles, and source materials that were quoted or referred to in the preceding pages, as well as other books and articles that are of special relevance.

"A Basic Call to Consciousness: The Hau de no sau nee Address to the Western World." In *Akwesasne Notes*. Rooseveltown, NY: Mohawk Nation, 1978.

Adamson, Fiona. "Focus on the Kurds: A Divided and Endangered People." *Humanitas* no. 1 (1990), pp. 4–5.

Allen, Paula Gunn. *The Sacred Hoop: Recovering the Feminine in the American Indian Tradition*. Boston: Beacon Press, 1986.

Anderson, Walter Truett. *To Govern Evolution: Further Adventures of the Political Animal*. Boston: Harcourt Brace Jovanovich, 1987.

Appelbaum, Stanley. *The New York World's Fair 1939–1940*. New York: Dover, 1977.

Arena-DeRosa, James. "Indigenous Leaders Host U.S. Environmentalists in the Amazon." *Oxfam America News,* Summer/Fall 1990, p. 1.

Arens, Richard, ed. *Genocide in Paraguay*. Philadelphia: Temple University Press, 1976.

Armstrong, Jeanette. *The Native Creative Process*. Penticton, B.C.: Theytus Books, 1991.

———. *Slash*. Penticton, B.C.: Theytus Books, 1985.

Avedon, John F. "Tibet Today." *Utne Reader,* March/April 1989, pp. 34–41.

Barnet, Richard J. *The Economy of Death*. New York: Atheneum, 1969.

Barreiro, Jose. *Indian Roots of American Democracy*. Ithaca, NY: Northeast Indian Quarterly, 1988.

Berg, Peter. "Devolving Beyond Global Monoculture." *CoEvolution Quarterly,* Winter 1981, p. 24.

Berg, Peter, ed. *Reinhabiting a Separate Country: A Bioregional Anthology of Northern California*. San Francisco: Planet Drum Foundation, 1978.

Berger, Thomas R. *Northern Frontier, Northern Homeland: The Report of the Mackenzie Valley Pipeline Inquiry, Volume Two*. Ottawa, Ontario, Canada: Minister of Supply and Services, 1977.

————. *Village Journey: The Report of the Alaska Native Review Commission.* New York: Hill and Wang, 1985.

Berkhofer, Robert F., Jr. *The White Man's Indian.* New York: Random House, 1978.

Berry, Thomas. *The Dream of the Earth.* San Francisco: Sierra Club Books, 1990.

"Bolivian Indians Regain Control of Rain Forest." *San Francisco Chronicle,* September 26, 1990, p. A11.

Booth, William H. "Ironing Out Greenhouse Effect: Fertilizing Oceans Is Proposed to Spur Algae." *Washington Post,* May 20, 1990, p. A1.

Bradbury, Ray. *Fahrenheit 451.* New York: Ballantine Books, 1953.

Brand, Stewart, ed. "The Gaia Hypothesis." *CoEvolution Quarterly,* Summer 1975.

Broad, William J. "Scientists Dream Up Bold Remedies for Ailing Atmosphere." *New York Times,* August 16, 1988, p. B5.

Brodeur, Paul. *Currents of Death: Power Lines, Computer Terminals, and the Attempt to Cover Up Their Threat to Your Health.* New York: Simon and Schuster, 1989.

————. *The Zapping of America: Microwaves, Their Deadly Risk, and Their Cover Up.* New York: Norton, 1977.

Brower, David R. *For Earth's Sake.* Salt Lake City, UT: Gibbs Smith, 1990.

Brown, Dee. *Bury My Heart at Wounded Knee.* New York: Henry Holt, 1970.

Brown, Lester. *State of the World, 1991.* New York: W. W. Norton, 1991.

Buraku Liberation Research Institute, ed. *Human Rights of Minorities in Asia-Pacific.* Tokyo: The International Movement Against All Forms of Discrimination and Racism, 1990.

Burger, Julian. *Report from the Frontier: The State of the World's Indigenous Peoples.* London: Zed Books, 1987.

Burnham, David. *The Rise of the Computer State.* New York: Vintage Books, 1980.

Burton, Bruce. "Iroquois Confederate Law and the Origins of the U.S. Constitution." *Northeast Indian Quarterly,* Fall 1986, p. 4.

Caillé, Alain. "The Two Myths: Scarcity and Rationality." *Development: Seeds of Change* (3) 1986: 198–204.

Callenbach, Ernest. *Ecotopia: The Notebooks and Reports of William Weston.* Berkeley, CA: Banyan Tree Books, 1975.

Capra, Fritjof. *The Tao of Physics: An Exploration of the Parallels Between Modern Physics and Eastern Mysticism.* New York: Bantam Books, 1984.

————. *The Turning Point: Science, Society, and the Rising Culture.* New York: Simon and Schuster, 1982.

Capra, Fritjof, and Charlene Spretnak. *Green Politics: The Global Promise.* New York: E. P. Dutton, 1984.

Carson, Rachel. *Silent Spring.* Boston: Houghton Mifflin, 1982.

Castaneda, Carlos. *A Separate Reality: Further Conversations with Don Juan.* New York: Simon and Schuster, 1971.

————. *The Teachings of Don Juan; A Yaqui Way of Knowledge.* New York: Simon and Schuster, 1968.

Catton, William R., Jr. *Overshoot: The Ecological Basis of Revolutionary Change.* Urbana: Illini Books/University of Illinois Press, 1982.

Cernetig, Miro. "Arctic Pact Completes Largest Land Claim." *The Toronto Globe and Mail,* May 1, 1990, p. A3.

Chagnon, Napolean A. *Yanomamo: The Fierce People.* New York: Holt, Rinehart and Winston, 1977.

Chargoff, Edwin. "Engineering a Molecular Nightmare." *Nature,* May 21, 1987, p. 199.

Chatwin, Bruce. *The Songlines.* New York: Penguin Books, 1987.

Clastres, Pierre. *Society Against the State.* New York: Urizen Books, 1977.

Clay, Jason, ed. *Indigenous Peoples and Tropical Forests: Models of Land Use and Management from Latin America.* Cultural Survival, Report no. 27, 1988.

————. "Militarization and Indigenous Peoples: Part I—The Americas and the Pacific." *Cultural Survival Quarterly,* Report no. 3, 1987.

Coates, Gary J., ed. *Resettling America.* Andover, MA: Brick House, 1981.

Collier, Robert. "Ecuadoran Indian 'Uprising.'" *San Francisco Chronicle,* September 26, 1990.

"Congress and Company: An Alliance Fed by Money." *Washington Post,* June 13, 1988.

Connell, Evan S. *Son of the Morning Star: Custer and the Little Bighorn.* San Francisco: North Point Press, 1984.

Connor, Michael. "Biotech Ready to Boom." *San Francisco Examiner,* February 9, 1990, p. B1.

Coombs, H. C. *Australia's Policy Toward Aborigines: 1967–1977.* Minority Rights Group, Report no. 35, March 1978.

Coulton, G. G. *The Medieval Village.* New York: Dover Publications, 1925.

Crichton, Michael. *The Andromeda Strain.* New York: Alfred A. Knopf, 1969.

Crowe, Keith J. "Claims on the Land." *Arctic Circle,* November/December 1990, pp. 14–23.

Dammann, Erik. *The Future in Our Hands*. New York: Pergamon Press, 1979.

Darrow, Ken, and Michael Saxenian. "Worshipping a False God." *Development Forum,* October 1984.

Dassman, Raymond. *California's Changing Environment*. San Francisco: Boyd and Fraser, 1981.

———. *The Destruction of California*. New York: Macmillan, 1965.

———. *No Further Retreat*. New York: Macmillan, 1971.

Davidson, Art, ed., and the Association of Village Council Presidents. *Does One Way of Life Have to Die So Another Can Live?* Bethel, AL: Yupik Nation, 1974.

Davis, Shelton H. *Victims of the Miracle: Development and the Indians of Brazil*. Cambridge, MA: Cambridge University Press, 1977.

Debord, Guy. *Society of the Spectacle*. Revised ed. Detroit: Black and Red, 1977.

Denendeh: A Dene Celebration. Yellowknife, Northwest Territories, Canada: Dene Nation, 1984.

Devall, Bill, and George Sessions. *Deep Ecology*. Salt Lake City, UT: Gibbs Smith, 1985.

Diamond, Irene, and Gloria Orenstein, eds. *Reweaving the World: The Emergence of Ecofeminism*. San Francisco: Sierra Club Books, 1990.

Diamond, Stanley. *In Search of the Primitive*. New Brunswick, NJ: Transaction, 1974.

Dodson-Gray, Elizabeth. *Green Paradise Lost*. Wellesley, MA: Roundtable Press, 1979.

Domhoff, G. William. *Who Rules America Now?* New York: Simon and Schuster, 1983.

Dowie, Mark. "Brave New Tiny World." *California Magazine,* November 1988, p. 90.

———. *"We Have a Donor": The Bold New World of Organ Transplanting*. New York: St. Martin's Press, 1988.

Drexler, K. Eric. *Engines of Creation: The Coming Era of Nanotechnology*. New York: Anchor Press/Doubleday, 1987.

Dreyfus, Hubert L. *What Computers Can't Do*. New York: Harper Colophon Books, 1979.

Eco, Umberto. *Travels in HyperReality*. San Diego: Harcourt Brace Jovanovich, 1986.

Egan, Timothy. "Hawaii Debates Peril to Rain Forest as an Energy Project Taps a Volcano." *New York Times,* January 26, 1990, p. A13.

Ehrlich, Paul R., and Anne H. Ehrlich. *Population/Resources/Environment.* San Francisco: W. H. Freeman, 1970.

————. *The Population Explosion.* New York: Simon and Schuster, 1990.

Eisler, Riane. *The Chalice and the Blade.* San Francisco: Harper and Row, 1987.

Ellul, Jacques. *Propaganda: The Formation of Men's Attitudes.* Translated by Konrad Kellen and Jean Lerner. New York: Vintage/Random House, 1973.

————. *The Technological Society.* New York: Alfred A. Knopf, 1964.

Emery, Fred, and Merrelyn Emery. *A Choice of Futures: To Enlighten or Inform?* Canberra: Centre for Continuing Education, Australian National University, 1975.

Engels, Frederick. *The Origin of the Family, Private Property and the State.* New York: International Publishers, 1972.

Epstein, Edward J. *News From Nowhere.* New York: Random House, 1973.

Erickson, Brad, ed. *Call to Action: Handbook for Ecology, Peace and Justice.* San Francisco: Sierra Club Books, 1990.

"Expert on U.S. Poverty Says It Got Worse in the 1980's." *Washington Post,* July 5, 1989, p. B7.

Federal Trade Commission Staff Report on Television Advertising to Children. Washington, DC: U.S. Government Printing Office, February 1978.

Feit, Dr. H. A. "James Bay Cree Indian Management and Moral Consideration of Fur-Bearers." In *Native People and Renewable Resource Management,* the 1986 Symposium of the Alberta Society of Professional Biologists, pp. 49–62.

Fenton, William N., ed. *Parker on the Iroquois.* Syracuse, NY: Syracuse University Press, 1968.

Fiske, Edward B. "Computers in the Classroom." *New York Times,* December 9–11, 1984.

Fjermedal, Grant. *The Tomorrow Makers.* New York: Macmillan, 1986.

Forbes, Jack D. *Tribes and Masses: Explorations in Red, White and Black.* Davis, CA: D-Q University Press, 1978.

Frankel, Charles. "The Specter of Eugenics." *Commentary,* March 1974.

Freedman, Dan. "Indian Rite Denied Use of Drug Peyote." *San Francisco Examiner,* April 17, 1990, p. A15.

Freeman, Milton M. R. "New/Old Approaches to Renewable Resources Management in the North." In *Northern Frontier Development—Alaska/Canada Perspectives,* the Twenty-Third Annual Meeting of the Western Regional Science Association, Monterey, CA, February 1984.

————. "Renewable Resources, Economics and Native Communities." In *Native People and Renewable Resource Management,* the 1986 Symposium of the Alberta Society of Professional Biologists.

Fumoleau, Rene. *As Long as This Land Shall Last.* Toronto: McClelland and Stewart, 1973.

Funding Ecological and Social Destruction: The World Bank and International Monetary Fund. Washington, DC: The Bank Information Center, 1990.

Gerbner, George, and Larry Gross. "The Scary World of TV's Heavy Viewer." *Psychology Today,* April 1976, pp. 41–89.

Gitlin, Todd. *The Whole World Is Watching: Mass Media in the Making and Unmaking of the New Left.* Berkeley, CA: University of California Press, 1980.

Glendinning, Chellis. "Apollo's Eye View." *Woman of Power,* Fall 1988, pp. 45–52.

————. "Notes Toward a Neo-Luddite Manifesto." *Utne Reader,* March/April 1990.

————. *Waking Up in the Nuclear Age.* New York: William Morrow, 1987.

————. *When Technology Wounds.* New York: William Morrow, 1990.

Glover, J. Denis. "Forebears of the Founding Fathers: Spirit of the U.S. Constitution Rests with Iroquois League." *Los Angeles Times,* December 11, 1987.

Goldsen, Rose Kohn. *The Show and Tell Machine: How Television Works and Works You Over.* New York: Dial Press, 1977.

Griffin, Susan. *Woman and Nature: The Roaring Inside Her.* New York: Harper and Row, 1978.

Grinde, Donald A., Jr. *The Iroquois and the Founding of the American Nation.* San Francisco: The Indian Historian Press, 1977.

————. Personal interview by Catherine Stifter, October 15, 1989.

Hamilton, Andrew. "Dinners Without Drudgery." *Popular Mechanics,* April 1947, pp. 174–177.

Hancock, Graham. *Lords of Poverty.* New York: Atlantic Monthly Press, 1989.

Hanke, Lewis. *Aristotle and the American Indians.* Chicago: Henry Regnery Company, 1959.

Hatfield, Larry D. "Prosperity Slipping, Study Says." *San Francisco Examiner,* September 3, 1990, p. 1.

Hart, Alexandra. *North American Bioregional Congress II Proceedings: August 25–29, 1986.* Forestville, CA: Hart Publishing, 1987.

Horn, Kahn-Tineta. "The Akwesasne War: Why Can't the Mohawks Settle It Themselves?" *The Toronto Globe and Mail,* May 3, 1990, p. A7.

Howard, Ted, and Jeremy Rifkin. *Who Should Play God?* New York: Dell, 1977.

"Human Gene Therapy Gets Support of Medical Experts." *San Francisco Chronicle,* August 1, 1990, p. A6.

Huxley, Aldous. *Brave New World.* New York: Harper and Brothers, 1932.

Illich, Ivan. *Energy and Equity.* London: Calden and Bryars, 1974.

————. *Medical Nemesis: The Expropriation of Health.* New York: Pantheon Books, 1976.

Ingram, Catherine. *In the Footsteps of Gandhi: Conversations with Spiritual Social Activists.* Berkeley, CA: Parallax Press, 1990.

International Union for the Conservation of Nature. "Ensuring a Future for Traditional Knowledge." *Tradition, Conservation and Development* no. 2 (September 1984), p. 1.

————. "Women and Tradition." Op. cit., p. 1.

Iyer, Pico. "Tibetan Spirit." *Utne Reader,* March/April 1989, pp. 44–46.

Jackson, Wes. *New Roots for Agriculture.* San Francisco: Friends of the Earth, 1980.

Johansen, Bruce. "Indian Thought Was Often in Their Minds." In *Indian Roots of American Democracy.* Ithaca, NY: Northeast Indian Quarterly, Cornell University, 1988.

Johnson, Cliff. "Launch on Warning Is Unconstitutional." *The Computer Professionals for Social Responsibility Newsletter,* Fall 1984, p. 1.

Johnston, Tracy. "Culture Shlock: Can TV Be Saved?" *New West Magazine,* April 10, 1978, p. 34.

Jorgensen, Joseph G., et al. *Native Americans and Energy Development.* Washington, DC: Anthropology Resource Center, 1978.

Josephy, Alvin M., Jr. *Now That the Buffalo's Gone: A Study of Today's American Indians.* New York: Alfred A. Knopf, 1982.

Jung, C. G. *Memories, Dreams, Reflections.* New York: Vintage Books, 1965.

Kahn, Herman. *World Economic Development.* New York: Morrow Quill Paperbacks, 1979.

Kahn, Herman, William Brown, and Leon Martel. *The Next 200 Years.* New York: Morrow Quill Paperbacks, 1976.

Kammer, Jerry. *The Second Long Walk: The Navajo-Hopi Land Dispute.* Albuquerque: University of New Mexico Press, 1980.

Kanehele, Pualani. Court testimony from Contested Case Hearing, Conservation Use Application, Volume 1. Hawaii County, Hawaii. February 18, 1986.

Kelly, Lawrence. *The Navajo Indians and Federal Indian Policy.* Tucson: University of Arizona Press, 1976.

Kennedy, Joseph, ed. "Kalo, Ho'okupu," *Native Planters,* Spring 1982.

Khan, Sadruddin Aga, and Hussan bin Talal. *Indigenous Peoples: A Global Quest for Justice—A Report for the Independent Commission on International Humanitarian Issues.* London: Zed Books, 1987.

Kilborn, Peter T. "Workers Using Computers Find a Supervisor Inside." *New York Times,* December 23, 1990, p. 1.

Kleiner, Art. "The Ambivalent Miseries of Personal Computing." *Whole Earth Review,* December 1984/January 1985, pp. 6–9.

Kleiner, Art, ed. "The Health Hazards of Computers." *Whole Earth Review,* Fall 1985, pp. 80–93.

Knox, Paul. "Tribes Hold Conference in Brazil." *San Francisco Examiner,* February 22, 1989, p. A14.

Kohr, Leopold. *The Breakdown of Nations.* New York: E. P. Dutton, 1957.

———. *The Overdeveloped Nations: The Diseconomies of Scale.* New York: Schocken Books, 1978.

Krugman, Herbert E. "Brain Wave Measures of Media Involvement." *Journal of Advertising Research,* February 1971, pp. 3–9.

LaChapelle, Dolores. *Earth Wisdom.* Boulder, CO: Guild of Tutors Press, 1978.

LaFarge, Oliver. "Notes for Hopi Administrators." Washington, DC: Library of the Department of the Interior, 1937.

———. "Running Narratives of the Organization of the Hopi Tribe of Indians." Austin, TX: From the LaFarge Collection of the University of Texas, 1936.

Lamb, David. "Aleutian War's Forgotten Victims." *San Francisco Chronicle,* September 13, 1987, p. 3.

Lame Deer, John (Fire), and Richard Erdoes. *Lame Deer: Seeker of Visions.* New York: Simon and Schuster, 1972.

Land Rights Now: The Aboriginal Fight for Land in Australia. Copenhagen, Denmark: International Work Group for Indigenous Affairs, Document no. 54, October 1985.

Lappé, Frances Moore, and Joseph Collins. *Food First: Beyond the Myth of Scarcity.* New York: Ballantine Books, 1978.

Laraque, M. Helene. "Toward the Next 500 Years." *Native Press,* October 12, 1990, p. 9.

———. "Unity Grows After 500 Years." *Native Press,* September 28, 1990, p. 12.

Laughlin, William S. *Aleuts: Survivors of the Bering Land Bridge.* New York: Holt, Rinehart and Winston, 1980.

Lawless, Edward. *Technology and Social Shock.* New Brunswick, NJ: Rutgers University Press, 1977.

Leary, Joanna, and Timothy Leary. *Terra II: The Starseed Transmission.* San Francisco: Imprinting Press, 1974.

Lee, Dorothy. *Freedom and Culture.* New York: Prentice-Hall, 1959.

Lee, Richard. "Kung Bushman Subsistence: An Input-Output Analysis." In *Environment and Cultural Behavior.* Garden City, NY: Natural History Press, 1969.

———. "What Hunters Do for a Living, or How to Make Out on Scarce Resources." In *Man and the Hunter.* Chicago: Aldine Publishing, 1968.

Le Guin, Ursula K. *Always Coming Home.* New York: Bantam Books, 1987.

Levin, Henry M., and Russell W. Rumberger. "Debunking High Tech Mythology: Industry Will Not Be Jobs Mecca." *Sacramento Bee,* February 3, 1983.

Lewis, Paul. "Land Deal for Eskimos: Canadian Pact Imminent for Eastern Arctic." *San Francisco Chronicle,* September 6, 1989.

Lifton, Robert Jay. *The Genocidal Mentality.* New York: Basic Books, 1990.

———. *Thought Reform and the Psychology of Totalism.* Chapel Hill: University of North Carolina Press, 1989.

Lings, Kjeld K., trans. *The Mapuche Tragedy.* Copenhagen, Denmark: International Work Group for Indigenous Affairs, Document no. 38, 1979.

Liversidge, Douglas. *The Luddites: Machine Breakers of the Early Nineteenth Century.* London: Franklin Watts, 1972.

"A Look at 2049." *Time,* August 22, 1949, pp. 16–17.

Lovins, Amory. *Soft Energy Paths: Toward a Durable Peace.* San Francisco: Friends of the Earth, 1977.

MacDougall, A. Kent. "Americans: Life in the Fast Lane." *Los Angeles Times,* April 17–19, 1983.

Macy, Joanna. *Despair and Personal Power in the Nuclear Age.* Philadelphia: New Society, 1983.

Macy, Joanna, Arne Naess, Pat Fleming, and John Seed. *Thinking Like a Mountain: Towards a Council of All Beings.* Philadelphia: New Society, 1988.

Mander, Jerry. *Four Arguments for the Elimination of Television.* New York: William Morrow/Quill, 1977.

———. "Four Arguments for the Elimination of Advertising." In *Advertising and the Public,* Kim B. Rotzoll, ed. Urbana: University of Illinois Press, 1980.

————. "Kit Carson in a Three-Piece Suit: Forced Relocation of 9634 Indians—Happening Now." *CoEvolution Quarterly,* Winter 1981, pp. 52–63.

————. "Six Grave Doubts About Computers." *Whole Earth Review,* December 1984/January 1985, pp. 10–20.

————. "This Land Is Whose Land?" *The Village Voice,* December 10, 1979, p. 25.

Mander, Yari Vesel. "Brothers Behind Bars: Nelson Mandela and Leonard Peltier." *City on a Hill,* October 30, 1986, p. 21.

Margolin, Malcolm. *The Ohlone Way.* Berkeley, CA: Heyday Books, 1978.

Margolin, Malcolm, ed. *The Way We Lived.* Berkeley, CA: Heyday Books, 1981.

Margulis, Lynn, and James E. Lovelock. "The Atmosphere as Circulatory System of the Biosphere—The Gaia Hypothesis." *CoEvolution Quarterly,* Summer 1975, pp. 30–40.

Marnham, Patrick. *Nomads of the Sahel.* Minority Rights Group, Report no. 33, April 1979.

Matthiessen, Peter. *Indian Country.* New York: Penguin Books, 1990.

————. *In the Spirit of Crazy Horse.* New York: Viking/Penguin, 1991.

Maxwell, Neville. *India and the Nagas.* Minority Rights Group, Report no. 17, November 1973.

Maybury-Lewis, David Howe, and James Howe. *The Indian Peoples of Paraguay.* Cultural Survival, Report no. 2, October 1980.

McCarthy, Frederick D., and Margaret McArthur. "The Food Quest and the Time Factor in Aboriginal Economic Life." *Anthropology and Nutrition.* Volume 2 of *Records of the Australian American Scientific Expedition to Arnhem Land.* Melbourne: Melbourne University Press, 1960.

McDonald, Robert. *The Maori of New Zealand.* Minority Rights Group, Report no. 70, December 1985.

McKibben, Bill. *The End of Nature.* New York: Doubleday, 1990.

McLuhan, Marshall. *Understanding Media.* New York: McGraw-Hill, 1964.

Medhurst, Kenneth. *The Basques and Catalans.* Minority Rights Group, Report no. 9, September 1977.

Meller, Norman. *The Congress of Micronesia: Development of the Legislative Process in the Trust Territory of the Pacific Islands.* Honolulu: University of Hawaii Press, 1969.

Menosky, Joseph A. "Computer Worship." *Science '84,* May 1984, p. 40.

Merchant, Carolyn. *The Death of Nature: Women, Ecology, and the Scientific Revolution.* San Francisco: Harper and Row, 1980.

Micronesia Support Committee, Palau: Self-Discrimination vs. U.S. Military Plans. Honolulu: Micronesia Support Committee, 1983.

Mills, Stephanie. *Whatever Happened to Ecology?* San Francisco: Sierra Club Books, 1989.

Mills, Stephanie, and Peter Berg, eds. Special section on Bioregions. *CoEvolution Quarterly,* Winter 1981, pp. 1–99.

Mitchell, John G., and Constance Stallings, eds. *Ecotactics: The Sierra Club Handbook for Environmental Activists.* New York: Pocket Books, 1970.

Momaday, N. Scott. *House Made of Dawn.* New York: Harper and Row, 1985.

The Montagnards of South Vietnam. Minority Rights Group, Report no. 18, March 1974.

Moravec, Hans. *Mind Children: The Future of Robot and Human Intelligence.* Cambridge, MA: Harvard University Press, 1988.

Morey, Sylvester M., ed. *Can the Red Man Help the White Man? A Denver Conference with the Indian Elders.* New York: Myrin Institute Books, 1970.

Morrison, Godfrey. *Eritrea and the Southern Sudan: Aspects of Some Wider African Problems.* Minority Rights Group, Report no. 5, May 1976.

Moulton, Harold G. *Controlling Factors in Economic Development.* Washington, DC: Brookings Institution, 1949.

Mumford, Lewis. *The Pentagon of Power.* Volume 2 of *The Myth of the Machine.* New York: Harcourt Brace Jovanovich, 1970.

———. *Technics and Civilization.* New York: Harcourt Brace Jovanovich, 1934.

———. *Technics and Human Development.* Volume 1 of *The Myth of the Machine.* New York: Harcourt, Brace and World, 1967.

———. *The Transformation of Man.* New York: Harper and Row, 1956.

Naess, Arne. *The Deep Ecological Movement.* Philosophical Inquiry no. 8 (1986), pp. 10–13.

Navajo and Hopi Indian Relocation Commission, U.S. Government: Report and Plan. Flagstaff, AZ, April 1981.

Neihardt, John G. *Black Elk Speaks.* Lincoln: University of Nebraska Press, 1961.

Nietschmann, Bernard. "The Third World War." *Cultural Survival Quarterly* (11) no. 3, 1987.

1991: Making It Work—A Guide to Public Law 100–241, 1987, Amendments to the Alaska Native Claims Settlement Act. Anchorage: Alaska Federation of Natives, 1988.

Oberg, James. *New Earths: Transforming Other Planets for Humanity.* Harrisburg, PA: Stackpole Books, 1981.

"One Hundred Leading Advertisers." *Advertising Age,* September 27, 1989.

O'Neill, Gerard K. *The High Frontier.* New York: Bantam, 1976.

Onosko, Tim. *Wasn't the Future Wonderful? A View of Trends and Technology from the 1930s.* New York: E. P. Dutton, 1979.

Ortiz, Roxanne Dunbar. *Roots of Resistance: Land Tenure in New Mexico, 1680– 1980.* Los Angeles: University of California Chicano Studies Research Center Publications and American Indian Studies Center, 1980.

Orwell, George. *1984.* New York: New American Library, 1949.

O'Shaughnessy, Hugh. *What Future for the Amerindians of South America?* Minority Rights Group, Report no. 15, May 1973.

Papert, Seymour. *Mindstorms.* New York: Basic Books, 1980.

Parlow, Anita. *Cry, Sacred Ground: Big Mountain U.S.A.* Washington, DC: Christic Institute, 1988.

———. "Peabody Would Send Hopiland Coal to Japan." *Gallup Independent,* April 27, 1989.

Peper, Erik, and Thomas Mulholland. "Occipital Alpha and Accommodative Vergence, Pursuit Tracking and Fast Eye Movements." *Psychophysiology* no. 5 (1971), pp. 556–575.

Peters, Christopher. *Native Thinking and Social Transformation.* Memorandum prepared for the Elmwood Institute, Berkeley, CA, January 11, 1991.

Petit, Charles. "Test of Deadly Bacteria Fails to Stir Opposition." *San Francisco Chronicle,* September 13, 1990, p. A8.

Pillar, Charles, and Keith R. Yamamoto. *Gene Wars: Military Control Over the New Genetic Technologies.* New York: Beech Tree Books, 1988.

Pittock, A. Barrie. *Australian Aborigines: The Common Struggle for Humanity.* Copenhagen, Denmark: International Work Group for Indigenous Affairs, Document no. 39, 1979.

Pool, Ithiel de Sola. *Forecasting the Telephone: A Retrospective Technology Assessment.* Norwood, NJ: Ablex, 1983.

Price, Monroe. "ANCSA in Perspective." In Haines, John, et al. *Minus 31 and the Wind Blowing.* Anchorage: Alaska Pacific University Press, 1980.

Ramos, Alcida R., and Kenneth I. Taylor. *The Yanomamo in Brazil, 1979.* Copenhagen, Denmark: International Work Group for Indigenous Affairs, Document no. 37, 1979.

Register, Richard. *Ecocity Berkeley: Building Cities for a Healthy Future.* Berkeley, CA: North Atlantic Books, 1987.

Reisner, Marc. *Cadillac Desert.* New York: Viking/Penguin, 1986.

Report to the Kikmongwis. Washington, DC: Indian Law Resource Center, 1979.

Retbøll, Torben. *East Timor, Indonesia and the Western Democracies.* Copenhagen, Denmark: International Work Group for Indigenous Affairs, Document no. 40, 1980.

Rifkin, Jeremy. *Algeny.* New York: Viking Press, 1983.

———. *Biosphere Politics.* New York: Crown, 1991.

———. *Declaration of a Heretic.* Boston: Routledge and Kegan Paul, 1985.

———. *Entropy.* New York: Viking, 1980.

———. *Time Wars.* New York: Henry Holt, 1987.

Ring, R. H. "The Computerized Forest." *New Age Journal,* July 1984, p. 51.

Rosenheim, Daniel, and Elliot Diringer. "Biotechnology—The Ethics, Safety and Riches." *San Francisco Chronicle,* September 28–30, 1987, p. A1; October 2, 1987, p. A1.

Roszak, Theodore. *The Cult of Information.* New York: Pantheon/Random House, 1986.

Ryan, Joan. *Wall of Words: The Betrayal of the Urban Indian.* Toronto: Peter Martin Associates, 1978.

Sahlins, Marshall. *Stone Age Economics.* Chicago: Aldine Publishing, 1972.

Said, Edward W. *Orientalism.* New York: Random House, 1978.

Sale, Kirkpatrick. *The Conquest of Paradise.* New York: Alfred A. Knopf, 1990.

———. *Human Scale.* New York: Coward, McCann and Geoghegan, 1980.

Schiller, Herbert I. *The Mind Managers.* Boston: Beacon Press, 1973.

———. *Who Knows: Information in the Age of the Fortune 500.* Norwood, NJ: Ablex, 1981.

Schneider, Keith. "Betting the Farm on Biotech." *New York Times Magazine,* June 10, 1990, p. 26.

———. "Cloning Offers Factory Precision to the Farm." *New York Times,* February 17, 1988, p. A1.

———. "Science Debates Using Tools to Redesign Life." *New York Times,* June 8, 1987, p. A1.

———. "U.S. Ends Curb on a Vaccine Using Altered Virus." *New York Times,* April 23, 1986, p. A1.

"Scholars Examine Indian Origins of U.S. Constitution." *Daybreak.* Charlottesville, VA.

Schumacher, E. F. *Small Is Beautiful.* New York: Harper and Row, 1973.

Schwarz, Walter. *The Tamils of Sri Lanka.* Minority Rights Group, Report no. 25, September 1985.

Scudder, Thayer. *No Place to Go: Effects of Compulsory Relocation of Navajos.* Philadelphia: Institute for the Study of Human Issues, 1982.

Shiva, Vandana. *Staying Alive: Women, Ecology and Development.* London: Zed Books, 1988.

Singh, Indu B., ed. *Telecommunications in the Year 2000: National and International Perspectives.* Norwood, NJ: Ablex, 1983.

Sklar, Holly, ed. *Trilateralism: The Trilateral Commission and Elite Planning for World Management.* Boston: South End Press, 1980.

Smith, Gar. "Space as a Wilderness." *Earth Island Journal,* Winter 1987, p. 24.

Snyder, Gary. *Axe Handles: Poems.* Berkeley: North Point Press, 1983.

————. *Passage Through India.* San Francisco: Grey Fox Press, 1983.

————. *The Real Work: Interviews and Talks, 1964–1979.* New York: New Directions, 1980.

Soifer, Bill. "EPA Adds 21 Bay Area Cleanup Sites." *San Francisco Chronicle,* October 3, 1984, p. 2.

Southeast Asian Tribal Groups and Ethnic Minorities. Proceedings of a conference co-sponsored by Cultural Survival and the Department of Anthropology, Harvard University. Cultural Survival, Report no. 22, 1987.

Spretnak, Charlene. *The Spiritual Dimension of Green Politics.* Santa Fe, NM: Bear, 1986.

Steiner, Stan. *The Vanishing White Man.* New York: Harper and Row, 1976.

Stephen, David, and Phillip Wearne. *Central America's Indians.* Minority Rights Group, Report no. 62, April 1984.

Stevens, William K. "Scientists Debate Health Hazards of Electromagnetic Fields." *New York Times,* July 11, 1989, pp. B7–8.

Stewart, Jon. "Folkelig; Nation Building in Northern Europe." *CoEvolution Quarterly,* Winter 1981, pp. 32–33.

Stone, Christopher D. *Should Trees Have Standing? Toward Legal Rights for Natural Objects.* Los Altos, CA: William Kaufmann, 1972.

————. *Where the Law Ends: The Social Control of Corporate Behavior.* New York: Harper Torchbooks, 1975.

Strategic Computing: An Assessment. Palo Alto, CA: Computer Professionals for Social Responsibility, 1984.

Sullivan, Kathleen. "True Believer: Group Fights Silicon Valley's Hidden Danger—Toxic Chemicals." *San Francisco Examiner,* April 29, 1990, p. D1.

Tarr, Joel A., ed. *Retrospective Technology Assessment—1976.* San Francisco: San Francisco Press, 1977.

Taylor, Stuart, Jr. "Court Allows Road Through Sacred Indian Land." *New York Times,* April 20, 1988, p. 1.

Tedlock, Dennis, and Barbara Tedlock, eds. *Teachings from the American Earth: Indian Religion and Philosophy.* New York: Liveright, 1975.

Thompson, E. P. *The Making of the English Working Class.* New York: Pelican Books, 1968.

Thorpe, Dagmar. *Newe Sogobia: The Western Shoshone People and Land.* Lee, NV: Western Shoshone Sacred Lands Association, 1982.

Tinkerman, Randall M. "The Iroquois League and the Covenant Chain: A Lost Legacy of Native America." Unpublished paper.

Todd, John, with George Tukel. *Reinhabiting Cities and Towns: Designing for Sustainability.* San Francisco: Planet Drum Foundation, 1981.

Tradition, Conservation and Development. Newsletter of the Commission on Ecology's Working Group on Traditional Ecological Knowledge, no. 1 (January 1984), no. 3 (August 1985).

Turner, Frederick. *Beyond Geography: The Western Spirit Against the Wilderness.* New Brunswick, NJ: Rutgers University Press, 1983.

Van der Post, Laurens. *The Lost World of the Kalahari.* New York: William Morrow, 1958.

Volkman, Toby Alice. *A Guide to N!ai, the Story of A !Kung Woman.* Volume 1 of *The San in Transition.* Cultural Survival, Report no. 9, November 1982.

Walt Disney World. Anaheim, CA: The Walt Disney Company, 1986.

Watkins, Mel, ed. *Dene Nation—The Colony Within.* Toronto: University of Toronto Press, 1977.

Weatherford, Jack. *Indian Givers.* New York: Crown, 1988.

Weyler, Rex. *Blood of the Land.* New York: Everest House, 1982.

Whorf, Benjamin Lee. *Language, Thought and Reality.* Cambridge, MA: MIT Press, 1956.

Williams, Nick B., Jr. "Indonesia Economy Is Coming of Age." *San Francisco Chronicle,* February 1, 1989, p. Z-1.

Wilson, Alexander. "The Betrayal of the Future." *Socialist Review,* November/December 1985, pp. 41–54.

Wilson, Edmund. *Apologies to the Iroquois.* New York: Random House, 1959.

Wilson, James. *Canada's Indians.* Minority Rights Group, Report no. 21, 1977.

Winn, Marie. *The Plug-In Drug.* New York: Viking, 1977.

———. *Unplugging the Plug-In Drug.* New York: Viking/Penguin, 1987.

Winner, Langdon. *Autonomous Technology: Technics-out-of-Control as a Theme in Political Thought.* Cambridge, MA: MIT Press, 1977.

————. "Mythinformation." *Whole Earth Review,* December 1984/January 1985, pp. 22–29.

————. *The Whale and the Reactor.* Chicago: University of Chicago Press, 1986.

Wittenborn, R., and C. Biegert. *James Bay Project—A River Drowned by Water.* Montreal: The Montreal Museum of Fine Art, 1981.

World Uranium Hearing. Revised ed. Munich: World Uranium Hearing Society, 1990.

Zwerin, Michael. *Devolutionary Notes.* San Francisco: Planet Drum Foundation, 1980.

INDEX

ABC, 89, 385
"Aboriginal rights," 288, 289, 290, 296, 312, 317
Aborigines, Australian, 212, 215, 248–50, 262, 348, 349
Acid rain, 47, 180
Adam-and-Eve story, 148–50
Adams, John, 233, 234
Addiction, TV, 84, 109
Advertising: American Dream, 21–22, 187; on bombers over Innu, 389; for computers, 53–54; corporation, 122, 124–25; Dene and, 106; "Earth National Park," 159; gene-line therapy, 170; Indian imagery in, 204–5; against international banks, 388; Public Media Center, 139–40, 332–34, 337, 389, 393; about sacred place desecrations, 222, 332–34, 337; technology of, 85; on television, 78, 79, 85, 95, 122, 135
Advertising Age, 78
Afghanistan, native peoples in, 354
Africa: geographical boundaries, 365–66; native nations, 227, 249, 250, 251–52, 365–69, 368
Age: native vs. technological view of, 217. *See also* Elders

Aggression: corporate, 129–30. *See also* Warfare
AID (Agency for International Development), U.S., 135, 368
AIDS, 168, 177
Ainu, in Japan, 350–51
Air Force, U.S., 313–14
Akaka, Daniel, 340
Akwesasne Notes, 113, 191–93
Akwesasne reservation, 241, 363
Alaska: native peoples in, 5, 246–47, 252–54, 287–302; State of, 289–90, 291, 296, 297
Alaska Federation of Natives, 290
Alaska Native Claims Settlement Act (ANCSA), 206, 275, 277, 287–302, 325, 361; details of, 290–92; results of, 294
Alaska Native Review Commission, 290, 295
Albany, 231
Albany Plan of Union (1754), 230, 233
Albert, Mike, 301
Alberta Society of Professional Biologists, 59
Aleutian Islands, 288, 289
Aleuts, 289
Allen, Paula Gunn, 383
Allende, Salvador, 373
Allotment (Dawes) Act (1887), 201, 275–77, 287, 325

Aloha aina, 320
Aloha Aina Action Congress, 340
"Alpha" brain waves, 80, 82, 86
Alta-Kautokeino Dam, 365
Altruism, 202; corporations and, 130–31; and expansionism, 140–41, 146; of genetic screening, 168
Aluli, Emmett, 321–23, 327–36 passim, 340
Aluli v. Brown, 328–29
Amazon, native nations of, 6, 225, 262, 370, 373–76
American Dream, 21–24
American Indian Religious Freedom Act (1978), 339
Amharic people, 366–67
Amorality, of corporations, 125–26, 130–31, 136
Anasazi, 269
Anderson, Walter Truett, 176–77
Anderson, Warren M., 126
"Andromeda Strain," 166–68
Andrus, Cecil, 304, 311, 313–15
Angola, 368
Animal-rights groups, 168, 289, 296, 387
Animals: encountering technologies, 33–34; genetically engineered, 162–63, 168–70; Hopi, 269; hunting, 101, 256–59, 289, 290, 296–97, 387